IN THE PIPELINE

IN THE PIPELINE

Memoirs of an International
Concert Organist

Carlo Curley

HarperCollins*Publishers*

HarperCollins*Publishers*
77–85 Fulham Palace Road,
Hammersmith, London W6 8JB

First published in Great Britain in 1998
by HarperCollins*Publishers*
1 3 5 7 9 10 8 6 4 2

A catalogue record for this book
is available from the British Library

ISBN 0 00 627990 2

Printed in Great Britain by
Mackays of Chatham plc

CONTENTS

PREFACE

It had never occurred to me that I might one day write my autobiography. I suppose, in the back of my mind, I thought it was a task to be tackled, at the very earliest, in the late afternoon of one's years or, better still, to be undertaken by someone else long after one was well and truly six feet under.

However, my manager Paul Vaughan subtly floated the notion past my eyes one day and, once I had agreed to open a notebook of reminiscences and recollections – aided by an alarming number of diaries and datebooks – he was not slow to come up with several interested publishers of whom we soon chose HarperCollins, largely I have to say, on account of the enthusiasm of their then senior editor, Giles Semper, since succeeded by the patiently determined Kathy Dyke. Their patience, regular encouragement and gentle goading are mainly responsible for what follows.

While Giles knew of me, he had never heard me play live. So I immediately invited him to a concert and kept my fingers crossed (trying not to do so during the performance). Meeting him was a bit of an audition since I'd never even written him a letter let alone a book. Nevertheless, I needn't have fretted, for he rapidly invited me to lunch and over the subsequent and memorable Dover sole (*off* the bone) asked me to submit an outline as soon as possible.

I readily admit that I am equally an optimist as well as a skeptic but I suspect that, at that stage, Giles wasn't aware that I'm a bit of a procrastinator as well. Once I took it on board that he really was serious, I'm embarrassed to confess that it took me two years to absorb the idea and yet another one to complete the outline! As I now realize, outlines usually take the form of a few short lines on each chapter. Blissfully unaware of this, I eventually delivered to him a somewhat bulky parcel containing no fewer than thirty-seven pages, 14,000 words, my video, a dozen CDs and press clippings dating back to the Stone Age. The courier nearly toppled off his motor bike! Originally, I really hadn't thought that there was going to be much to tell but, as Giles later remarked dryly, the outline for the Bible must have been shorter.

As I set about my task, it gradually dawned on me that maybe there was a tale to tell after all. I've been truly blessed with friends and fortune, and that rarest of God-given gifts, the opportunity to do what I want in life. If all of this was going to provide the bones of a good story, then so much the better.

Since I am primarily a musician and not an author, I knew that I needed help. Jonathan Ambrosino is a writer who has worked closely with organs and the people who build them. Together, we have spent many joyful months poring over dusty scrapbooks, talking to colleagues and acquaintances around the globe, excavating facts, listening intently to old recordings and reminiscing happily. While it has all been far more work than I could have ever imagined, hopefully it will prove to have been worth the effort. It has also brought back, in the clearest focus, many wonderful and moving memories. Better yet, it has motivated me to contact a number of valued friends with whom, I'm ashamed to say, I had lost touch over the years.

Throughout the narrative, I have endeavored to keep the technical aspects of organs and organ playing to a minimum. However, the glossary of terms at the back of the book offers simple explanations.

In conclusion, I am both grateful and relieved to report that mine continues to be a rich and varied life; intense and colorful – just like good music, fine wines and the best organs.

Carlo Curley
London
March, 1998

CHAPTER ONE

BLOOD AND THUNDER

It was only after I had pressed the forbidden button that the prehistoric monster in the sub-basement groaned as if roused from centuries of slumber. The earth shook as the arthritic bellows creaked and hissed into life and it filled its wheezing lungs. But there was blood everywhere – still flowing from this eight-year-old's arm – over the keyboards and back in an incriminating trail across the sanctuary, down the steep stairway, across the kitchens where I'd stopped off for an ineffectual bandaging with paper towels, through the musty church basement and up to the ledge and broken window which had been my entrance.

The blood was now soaking my clothes and I hoped it would hurry up and drain away completely so that I could get on with things. I had been denied so much as a peep at the organ console long enough and here I was and here it all was before me: two ivory keyboards, stepped one on top of the other with lots of small white buttons below each (now what were they for?), a single long tier of ivory stop tabs with unfamiliar yet fascinatingly unpronounceable names carefully engraved upon them. Jutting out towards me they just begged to be grasped (surely the final resting place of a herd of elephants was just under my nose). Then there was the giant pedal-board – I could just about reach that – and glinting metal toe studs on both sides of the expression and crescendo pedals, which looked like larger versions of automobile accelerators. I wondered then if they served a similar purpose, and sometimes still do.

High on adrenaline, I began to play, filled with the certainty that, for me, this was what life was about. It was nothing short of glorious. There could and would be no debate.

I don't know how long I sat and played but I do know that I tested every single stop and nearly every possible combination. What a sonic panoply – the colors and shades were seemingly endless and, especially for an eight-year-old, the power truly awesome. Even though the experience was making me dizzy (or was it loss of blood?), my natural high left me feeling like the Boy Who Would be King. Only the crown was missing.

Having satisfied my initial curiosity, I am embarrassed and alarmed – even to this day – to recall what I did next. Finding a small door at the back of the loft, I clambered into the very depths of a dark and secret place where it was obvious that I had no business. I will never forget the scent of aged leather, dustiness and mustiness that embraced me. Then, as my eyes grew accustomed to the gloom, I realized that I was surrounded by masses of complex machinery – action, wind-chests, trunking and so on – and the literally thousands of pipes, metal ones, wooden ones, round ones, square ones, triangular-shaped ones, tiny ones, huge ones, all of which go together to make an organ the maddening conundrum it is. Removing a selection, I blew into them (particularly damaging for reeds) won-dering at the varying sounds I was producing. Finally, I disconnected every part of the mechanism I could reach and generally tinkered about, prying into every-thing I could see or touch. It was a magical playtime.

I can't begin to estimate the damage I did but the blood-spattered evidence was there for all to behold. The services of Mr. Sherlock Holmes were not going to be necessary to identify me as the culprit and while I was to pay dearly for my vandalism, at that moment I regretted nothing. It had been something of a religious initiation. Like a Red Indian brave, my blood was now well and truly mingled – I still bear the scars and, for a small consideration, am always willing to reveal them to the ghoulish or merely curious!

So that's how I got into the pipeline. I had rudely introduced myself at the age of eight to the instrument which has occupied the best part of my life, not with a handshake but with a gory orgy. And I can only be amazed that I was ever allowed within a hundred yards of the King of Instruments again.

But perhaps we should begin at the beginning ...

Yes, Carlo Curley is my real name. You can't imagine how often I am quizzed about this. And what's more, to the best of my knowledge and belief, I have neither Italian nor Sicilian forbears. Rather – and the reason is this simple – as my grandfather was named Carl, my grandmother decided that 'Carlo' would be sufficiently different to avoid confusion within our four-member household – grandfather Carl, grandmother Ella, mother Gladys and me. And so Carlo Curley it is.

Admittedly a publicist's dream, my only occasional small grumble is that I'm sometimes called 'Carlos,' 'Carley' or 'Curlo,' with every conceivable combination of those three and the genuine two. But nothing will ever surpass my amazement at once being welcomed to the platform for a major Virginia recital by a myopic or uninterested sponsor (I couldn't tell which) with the enduring line: 'Ladies and gentlemen, please give a big hand to our distinguished performer this evening ... Mr. *Cudlo Cudley*.' Still I suppose it could have been worse.

I was born in the early hours of August 24, 1952, in the Ellen Fitzgerald Hospital, Monroe, a small town (population 12,000) which lies in the Central Piedmont region of North Carolina, USA. I'm an only child and Virgoan to the core. Those falling under this sign of the zodiac usually lead busy lives, are versatile, extremely critical (both of themselves and others), nit-picking in details, cloyingly scrupulous, obsessive, and prone to excess in all forms – including long sentences! In my case, the Virgo sign manifests itself by making me alternately compulsive and reckless. On the one hand, I make lists and check them off studiously as I go. My homes have always been fastidiously tidy and I am compulsively organized; every scrap of paper in its place, every picture frame perfectly level. On the other hand, I confess to a certain degree of devil-may-care fancy. When I see something that strikes me – be it a fine antique or even a bauble on a junk-shop shelf, an enormous pile of warm nachos or a lavishly described item on the menu of a fine eatery – I plunge for it with great gusto. Plunging comes naturally; so does consternation. When I see one dirty dish on my kitchen counter or a stack of papers strewn about the study, I sulk and fume until all is set right. You might be thinking that obsessiveness and recklessness would be incompatible goals. They are! Trying to achieve balance within that disparity constantly colors an already lively existence.

At the time I was born, we lived in a white frame house at 305 East Windsor Street. Although a typical Southern single storied affair, in common with most of the others in the district, it was large by any standards, with wooden gables and a big back yard where my grandfather held sway as the unchallenged gardener of the family. There was a wide front porch, framed by rhododendrons and complete with a swing, where I would often sit well into the evening listening to the chirping of the crickets and watching the fireflies come out to play as the sun sank low. No wonder there were so many UFO sightings in the South. Massing and swarming as fireflies do, anyone could have been forgiven for believing that they were witnessing the arrival of aliens from the planet Zarg! It was all quite mystical.

What wasn't in the least bit mystical was when, on sweltering summer evenings, noisy trucks would tour every street in town, spewing forth not only diesel fumes but also dirty-white clouds of pesticide, in an effort to annihilate any mosquito in sight. It certainly looked like the kind of cure that is worse than the affliction, and it's a wonder that the citizens didn't start growing sixth fingers. Happily, the fireflies seemed to survive.

The primary influence on my young life was my grandmother, Ella Wilson Maynard, a widely respected and often revered piano teacher who, throughout a long and distinguished career, taught hundreds of pupils. She also served as pianist to the local lodge of the Order of the Eastern Star, the women's branch of Freemasonry. A reserved china doll of a woman, only some five foot five in height, Ella attired herself expensively yet conservatively; her dresses always of a proper length and color. There was nothing outwardly showy about her and I well recall gloves of varying lengths being an essential part of every outfit. While make-up never featured at her dressing table, she seemed to be powdering her face incessantly, although the majority of the clouds she sent up never seemed to settle on her cheeks but hung, briefly suspended like a hazy halo, in the atmosphere around her. She was clearly the head of our household – at least there wasn't any doubt in her mind on this matter, and I was extremely fond of her.

Playing a vitally important role, inevitably, was my mother, Gladys Maynard Curley. She was a proficient musician who had studied piano with my grandmother from age five and had taken up the violin in the seventh grade. She was later to play professionally both as a soloist and in various orchestras and ensembles. Sadly, she had to set much of her music aside when she went out to work in 1954, no doubt to provide for her rapidly growing son. She was and still is a strikingly attractive woman, full of energy and determination but with a single-mindedness and a fresh temper. She had a very clear sense of what was right and wrong and, let me tell you, as I have good cause to remember, believed firmly in the values of discipline.

My grandfather Carl Newton Maynard, in common with his wife and daughter, was well educated and widely read. He always seemed to have his head in a book, magazine or newspaper. A big man, impressive both in stature and personality, he wore gold-rimmed spectacles and was fine-featured with silver hair and big, fleshy hands. In his latter years, he suffered badly with arthritis and diabetes but, despite all of this, or perhaps on account of it, could be as stubborn as a mule.

Conspicuously absent from our little household was my father, James Dennis Curley. According to my mother who spoke little of him, he was 'a liquor-loving Catholic from Boston.' Faint praise indeed! The only item I had to remind me of his existence was an old telephone directory from the Boston suburb where he lived. Thumbing idly through its pages one day, I discovered, among many other hitherto inconceivable delights, that New Englanders could call up a liquor store and have a bottle of whatever delivered to their door, even to a hotel room – quite unlike North Carolina, where the sale of alcohol was so tightly controlled that it was only available through ABC (Alcohol Beverage Control) Stores. Even twenty-odd miles up the road in Charlotte, a veritable flesh-pot of a sin city according to the bible-bashing burghers of Monroe, liquor-by-the-drink was not on the cards until I was well into my teens. My father's family were, so I was later advised, on the periphery of the New England Curleys, the leading light of whom was Boston Mayor James Michael Curley. He served no fewer than four three-year terms between 1914 and 1949, and was rightly dubbed by his supporters 'The Mayor of the Poor.'

To the best of my knowledge, my mother Gladys met my father while she was a student at the Jacksonville School of Music in Florida. While he was not a practical or performing musician, he loved to listen to music and was much moved by its power. After they fell 'head over heels' (Gladys' definition) and married, it was, alas, only a matter of months before cracks and even chasms began to appear in their relationship. Gladys was and still is a strict Methodist of the southern school – and they don't come much stricter than that – while my father was a Roman Catholic of Irish descent. Isn't it just a fact that religion has always played a central role in warfare and strife. In my parents' case, despite the fact that, to put it politely, I was already 'on the way,' they were soon parted and divorced. My mother erased him from her memory and got on with life. In answer to my occasional questioning, she would make it quite clear that he did not exist while at the same time forbidding me to make any attempts to seek him out. Her annoyance when I eventually did so does not bear description.

Being a practical chap, and having decided that age twenty was about the right time to meet one's father, I rang the telephone enquiry service in Boston and to my surprise was given his number. It was that easy and having waited so long to commence my little investigation, I greatly regretted the delay. After a few unsuccessful calls – he was always out – I eventually spoke with him, and although it was only over the telephone, found it quite a traumatic experience. Clearly, he did not relish the notion of my turning up at his home – he had remarried and had children – so, in response to my announcement that I was going to pay him a visit, come what may, he invited me to his place of work the very next day.

He turned out to be a stocky yet handsome man, blessed with gleaming teeth, twinkling eyes and a head of the thickest, most luxuriant, dark hair imaginable. Aside from having inherited certain of his physical features, and most definitely the hair, I am saddened to say that he played no role in my upbringing, or indeed my later life. Our encounter was brief, to say the least. Had I had a stop-watch, it could not have recorded more than five minutes. He just did not want to know. In his strident New England accent, I recall but two sentences. Firstly, *'Yourah biggun!!'* – I was after all, a strapping lad, fully 6ft 3½in by then – and later, almost by way of polite conversation, he asked, *'Howz ya Muddah?'* So that was that, and still is.

Unfortunately, my hometown didn't offer much drama or art, and the highlights were barely perceptible. For personalities, Monroe had but one celebrity native son: the ultra-conservative Senator Jesse Helms. Oh boy! For entertainment, there would be the occasional parade down Main Street (marching bands, floats, football teams, southern belles). More impressive, and often quite terrifying, were the thunderstorms that blanketed the region in sheets of rain and lightning.

Aside from these moments, about the most exciting event was clambering into the family Chevrolet and cruising slowly – my grandfather always studiously ignoring the impatient honkings of those stuck behind – towards our weekly outing at the local Winn-Dixie, our regional grocery store. These were the days when a chilled Coca-Cola (pronounced 'Ko-Kola') was five cents and long before anything non-Southern was so much as contemplated in our supermarkets. Chardonnay, Perrier and hand-rolled Belgian chocolates had not even been heard of in that part of the world.

Although I didn't realize it at the time, there were a few small aspects of our family life which could be considered a tad unusual. To begin with, I never addressed my mother or my grandparents by anything other than their first name. So mum, mom, mummy and even mother have never formed any part of my vocabulary and likewise grandad, grandpa, gramps or granny, grandma and grandmother. But while it was always Gladys, Ella and Carl, this should not be taken to imply an absence of affection between us. That's just the way it was and I was perfectly comfortable with it.

Ella and Gladys were religious to the point of zealotry (Gladys remains steadfastly so), both being imbued with the stereotypical brandmarks of the passionately and unquestioningly faithful. It seemed to me that the Southern bible belt surely had its regional head office at 305 East Windsor. Carl, while still devout, was happily less vociferous, preferring to take his religion in smaller and calmer doses.

Perhaps it was this, coupled with his arthritis and diabetes, which led to another slightly unusual aspect of our family existence. Our house was conveniently bisected by a central corridor which ran from the front door to the back. In retrospect this was tantamount to a demilitarized zone and with a strictness of demarcation worthy of the palace of some eastern potentate, the two ladies confined themselves to the eastern half, while the men, Carl and I, took the west. While he clearly loved his wife and daughter dearly, I suspect that he could endure only so much of their incessant harping on the wrath of *Gawd* and *eeevil* and had long since felt compelled to seek refuge and solace in a large room, sparsely but comfortably furnished as a combined bedroom and den.

Steeped in devout and formal Methodism – a day never passed without hymns, prayers and Bible reading – at twilight, all attention turned to the radio which relayed all that I considered bizarre and unctuous in the religious spectrum. This was abuse of the indubitable power of the media at its most blatant. There were more religious stations on our dial than there are rose-petals at an Indonesian wedding and my kinsfolk would invariably select a nightly program which plucked the fiercest fire and brimstone, hell and damnation preaching from the ether.

A regular radio visitor was Herbert W. Armstrong with his program *The World Tomorrow* from Ambassador College in Pasadena, California, throughout which he relentlessly thundered forth what were certainly articulate but, to me, fatuous contemporary political predictions which he somehow wrung, chapter by chapter and verse by verse, out of the Bible. I suspect that Herbert could, had he so wished, have found a series of biblical references to convince vegetarians to eat sirloin steaks.

By the time I had been packed off to bed, the religious temperature coming from Carl's radio in the room next to mine was approaching white heat and it was while lying abed, the interconnecting door always slightly ajar, that I came to recognize the mellifluous tones of Oklahoma-based Oral Roberts. Before imploring his listeners to send oodles of money – as most of the radio evangelists did – he always closed his extraordinary show by inviting us to lay hands upon our radio sets 'to receive Gawd's *tree-menders, dee-vine healin' pah.*' Occasionally, Carl would quietly call me through and get me to lay my hands on top of the red Zenith bakelite radio. Feeling the warmth of the tubes – which surely owed more to the local power company than any divinity – was at least a little luxury on a cold winter's night. I just hoped that some of Oral's faithful flock, while taking their evening bath, exercised great care when the instruction came through to receive the *'dee-vine pah.'*

But best of all came a clarion call to my ears, even if only once or twice a week (depending on weather and corresponding signal strength). 'From the Crossroads of the West' in Salt Lake City (the words spoken by the unforgettable voice of Richard Evans) came a thirty-minute program of such quality that it was almost worth enduring all the other guff just to hear it. Offered by the Mormon Tabernacle Choir and Mormon church speakers, the program entitled 'Music and the Spoken Word,' was just that; a beautifully produced half-hour based upon the timeless truths of religious belief. It was never patronizing and always inspiring. Viewed against the calm dignity and low-key elegance of the Tabernacle broadcast, the other religious radio rantings looked increasingly ridiculous by comparison.

I suppose all of this may well give the impression that I was intolerant and to an extent I was and still am. But, unwittingly I admit, I had been well and truly inoculated against religion in a big way and can only be grateful that the Tabernacle Choir and organ inspired me so deeply. So each to their own. If hell-fire radio and television evangelism lifts you, so be it, but for me, at its very mention, I am out of the house and up the street like a scalded cat. And small wonder.

I have never worn my religious beliefs, such as they are, upon my sleeve, firmly believing that these are intensely personal and private matters between man and his Maker. But having been less than polite about one end of the religious scale, I am perhaps duty bound to add a little that is subjective.

I believe that I have a very deep spiritual sense. Ever since childhood, I have been moved by dramatic and artistic events. Much that I consider religious I have gleaned through my eyes and ears. I can be moved to tears by a work of art or architecture, a landscape or a piece of music. It is when we come to organized religions, especially those that seek to exercise power and control by instilling fear, that I begin to feel uncomfortable.

All religions interest me, but my interest is primarily artistic and historical. Several evangelicals have told me bluntly, as if I need their permission, that I cannot possibly perform religious music – and the majority of organ music is religiously inspired – unless I am a 'born again, washed-in-the-blood-of-the-Lamb' Christian. To that I say 'nonsense'. In these things I am not naturally gregarious and prefer to stand at a dignified distance. And from what I see and know of some breast-beating Christians I say *Good Lord, preserve us.*

As a little boy, there were few means at my disposal to douse the hell-fire, brimstone, blood and thunder which literally terrified my childhood, but I certainly sought earnestly for relief. Gladys' cats helped; she was an inveterate cat lover and at one point had no fewer than seven, mostly strays she had lovingly adopted. Still more solace came from Carl. He liked to work with his hands and, like many of his age and station, loved to fish. I would be allowed and often encouraged to tag along and played the role of Huck Finn, dutifully baiting hooks with worms and crickets. While I have to confess that I never inherited his passion for this pastime, it sure was a happy way to spend a Saturday afternoon. I'm sure my present-day affection for bow-ties stems from Carl's fondness of them, nor did I fail to be fascinated by his swinging gold watch chain, attached to a weighty railroad time-piece.

Dear Carl was also a keen gardener. Apart from the flowers he tended so lovingly, his green-fingered talents extended to the substantial vegetable patch. I can still almost taste the superb tomatoes, okra, collard greens, runner beans and all of the other fresh vegetables he grew and harvested each year. A summer lunch treat was tomato sandwiches; not the daintily polite English teatime variety, but made with two generous pieces of fresh white bread, lathered in cold mayonnaise, surrounding a well salted and peppered thick fillet of blood-red, ripe beefsteak tomato; and if that doesn't make your mouth water, read on.

He was also a fine cook, albeit in common with many master chefs, an untidy one. He really needed a brigade of assistants and washers-up to follow in his wake. Nevertheless, from the chaos of his kitchen came forth some of the finest food I've ever tasted: delicious cornbread, grits, black-eyed peas, oyster stew, buttermilk biscuits and fried chicken – made all the more delectable by butter and salt in quantities sufficient to create aortal gridlocks. Mind you, this was the South.

My grandmother had an ultra-conservative mind set, especially when it came to 'those *Communists*.' (Do remember this was directly in the aftermath of the McCarthy era, and temperatures were still running high.) During the Cuban missile crisis, convinced that our house could be annihilated at any moment, she instructed Carl to buy a dozen brooms, saw off the bristle ends, and wedge the handles into every window frame (and there were many). Presumably this would not only prevent the intrusion of any Communist/Atheist, it would also protect us against nuclear blast, for she was convinced that the first strike would pinpoint Monroe, North Carolina while ignoring such targets as Washington, New York City or even such plums as Edwards Air Force Base. Carl, with a gentle sigh born of long experience, picked up his saw and got started.

Perhaps the most refreshing thing about Carl was that, totally unlike Gladys and Ella, he actually had two or three vices. He was not averse to the occasional tot of his own home-made wine, fermented in a remarkable apparatus secreted in the garage; stronger stuff, I suspect, being occasionally obtained from the State Store. Let me not give the impression that he was a drinker. In fact, I rarely saw him drink but sometimes his breath would speak a brief chapter if not a volume.

However, another indulgence – you could hardly call it a vice – was chewing tobacco, and this was all too obvious. Spittoons were placed strategically for the disposal of the 'pleasure,' and from an impressive distance, he would expectorate with laser-like accuracy. Actually, to tell the truth, it was quite disgusting, but one had to admire his skill.

Carl's musical leanings really didn't lean that far. He adored the hymn 'Abide with Me,' and was forever humming it as he pottered about the house. He also loved tight-knit gospel harmony, and would tune it in when – alas all too rarely – 'serious' religious programming was not available. In general, though, he preferred to read or watch television: *Amos 'n' Andy, Perry Mason, George Burns* or *I Love Lucy* were high on the list. He also enjoyed conversation and I was not slow to notice that his colorful language grew more vivid when the ladies were away. Indeed the temperature of his voice was somewhat related to the 'mercury' in his blood. When sober, he would speak as well as any educated gentleman but, when the spirit moved him, he could turn the air blue with a variety of ripe expletives which were uniquely his.

Both Gladys and Carl worked as telegraph operators and ticket agents for the Seaboard Air Line Railroad which ran through the heart of the town. Not surprisingly, therefore, railways and everything connected with them have always loomed large in my life. The rail yards were only a few minutes from home and I was inexorably drawn to them for much of my childhood recreation. While Gladys and Ella hated the thought that I might be out 'stirring up sin,' the yards were at least nearby and since the engineers, brakemen and conductors worked alongside my mother and grandfather, I was to some extent considered family. While the individual freight cars were being assembled into long trains, the local crews might occasionally allow me to ride along on the shunting engines. And if there were a short run to a nearby factory or town, these guys would take me with them. I was in heaven.

As a contrast to the regular freights, I might sometimes catch a fleeting glimpse of the few luxury passenger trains, such as the appropriately named Silver Meteor, Silver Comet and Silver Star. It was like another world and I figured that if trains could be this grand, their destinations, spanning the gamut from New York to Florida, must be pretty special too. I pined to know more.

I was not the only person to seek diversion in the rail yards. The majority of Monroe's indigents were usually out in force too, squatting on or nearby discarded cross-ties and rails. While they were certainly malodorous, they were a lively and motley bunch, each one with a story to tell. Given their lot in life, they could be enormously funny, a fact that possibly had much to do with their addiction to alcohol. Not having access even to the likes of my grandfather's home-brewed inebriant, this remarkable band of hobos had opted for a more readily available source of quaffable pleasure: Polly Peachtree Aftershave Lotion! Its pungent fragrance permeated every nook and cranny. Even the shimmering rails seemed to reek.

Sober or not, these fellows appeared to have a life and sparkle that was markedly absent from my own home life and it was refreshing for me to meet people who couldn't afford piety. The rail yards and their rich variety of denizens instilled within me a deep affection for trains and train travel which has endured to this day. And, as the ensuing pages will surely testify, I suppose I have become something of an itinerant myself.

Given my mother's and grandmother's abilities, a musical direction seemed predetermined. On my third Christmas, Carl gave me a baby piano – from Schirmer's in New York City. Although miniature, it was a real piano, with hammers striking strings (and quite costly, Gladys reminds me!). It was carefully placed in the living room alongside Ella's pride and joy, her highly polished Honduras mahogany Steinway Model M (five-foot-seven baby grand) which she had purchased from the Steinway dealer in Charlotte in 1929. (Gladys remembers what a big event this was; she was seven years old.)

A few months later, I toddled in to find my grandmother practicing a piece of Bach on the big piano. Gladys recounts how I went to my instrument and began to follow, verbatim, the melody line of what she was playing. Ella was drunk with emotion (it certainly wasn't Polly Peachtree) to think that such a promising student was not only so near to hand but was her only grandson to boot. That very day, a strict regime of piano practice began, about as monotonous as anyone could possibly imagine. She ordained that I would play no proper pieces, not even elementary Clementi, but only exercises by Czerny and Hanon, as well as scales, scales and more confounded scales. It was to be two interminable years before I was allowed to graduate to melody and compositions of any real stature.

To make matters worse there was no way in which Ella would allow me to look at, let alone touch, her cherished Steinway. Instead I was banished to a ghastly old Gulbransen upright player piano which was tucked away with her other secrets – if she had any – in her boudoir. Having probably declared the player mechanism sinful, she had long since had it removed, unwittingly creating a concealed space in which I would occasionally hide to avoid punishment. I don't know what other mechanism was contained within the forbidding black case but the touch was akin to wading in tapioca and the tone so disagreeable that no one could have possibly cared about its pitiful state of regulation.

Being simultaneously force-fed religion and technical piano exercises by a strict, puritanical grandmother – especially when I was intent on getting out of the house and horsing around with other lads, to say nothing of the hobos down at the rail yard – ensured that I had no taste whatever for church or concert-hall. Not only was I virtually chained to the piano, I was forbidden to watch television – extremely sepia, in those days – which, in Ella's opinion (and there was no other) ran liquor a close second in the sinfulness stakes. It's hardly surprising therefore that even though I held her in high esteem, I later nurtured a deep resentment towards my grandmother. Worse still, to my school-mates, my involvement with classical music was considered sissy and little short of dressing up in lacy petticoats and high-heeled shoes! Nevertheless, as I would come to appreciate greatly later in life, Ella was right on target. Her many students – me included perhaps – were the proof. Over the years, in countless radio and television interviews, I have often joked that I worshipped the ground she was going to be buried under! However, I must record that I worshipped her too and will forever be grateful for her influence on my formative years. She had clearly identified my abilities and by applying a relentless program of old-school discipline provided me with the foundations upon which I have built my professional career and much of my life.

However, the fates were not altogether deaf or unsympathetic to the plight of a small child. In the living room, alongside the Steinway sat a Hammond electric organ. Originally developed in the mid-thirties as a substitute for genuine pipe organs, it eventually won wide acceptance in the world both of jazz and gospel. Spinning tone-wheels produced the sounds and although the effect was totally unsuited to classic organ repertoire, it had, for me, the great advantage of responding instantaneously to a player's touch; this in marked contrast to the sluggishness of the practice piano in the room next door.

I will always give thanks for the presence of this little instrument in our household. It gave me the opportunity to begin the rudimentary study of organ music at the startlingly young age of seven, and as soon as I'd learned a series of pieces on the piano, I would hurry to the Hammond and experiment, creating as many contrasting colors as I could devise via the drawbars. Ella – from whom no secrets were hid – immediately assigned me Bach's *Eight Little Preludes and Fugues* along with the sure-fire Marcello *Psalm XIX* (a favorite selection from the E. Power Biggs *Treasury*). Since I was a tall lad, I could just reach that twenty-five-note pedal-board, an achievement usually denied organ students until they are somewhat older.

During my childhood practice on the Hammond in summertime, we would combat the debilitating heat with a powerful green Vornado fan. Although touted as 'quiet-running' it nonetheless produced gale-like winds that invariably found any open music scores in the room and sent them scattering. But to this day, I can't get to sleep unless a fan is running in the room. The security and constancy of both noise and breeze perhaps harks back to some of the simple early comforts.

It is amazing how elements of childhood resurface later in life. For example, Ella was absolutely right where television is concerned. It does corrupt the attention span, not much of it is worth watching, and it wastes time. To this day, I barely watch any.

It of course goes without saying that our family was regular in church attendance; the radio preaching merely a devotional bridge between Sundays. We belonged to the local Methodist preaching palace, an all-American Main Street church. It was typical of mainline Protestant church buildings in its acoustical deadness, a result of thick velvety pew cushions, wall-to-wall carpeting and absorptive tiled ceiling. Based on the Akron plan – a three-sided sanctuary facing a semi-circular auditorium – choir and clergy shared a platform front-and-centre, organ chamber behind. With its elegant, dark woodwork and fine stained glass, the building certainly made a firm impression on a youngster. Most importantly, it was clearly imbued with some sense of sanctity, even if I would come to realize, in liturgical terms at least, the Methodist way left much wanting as I became increasingly fond of such heady trappings as richly embroidered altar-frontals, candles and incense. Perhaps it was all down to my father's Roman Catholicism?

Although the front of the organ – the part that faced the congregation – probably contained no pipe taller than twelve feet, this was still tall for a kid and I was entranced by their opulent stencilling and faded gilt finish. If the mysteriously elegant appearance caught my attention early on, so did the fact that the organ was probably reaching the end of a long life. Whenever it wheezed into operation, the numerous leaks caused every possible aroma of antiquity to waft forth – dried-out wood and decades of dust with an occasional dash of damp conspiring together to create a unique bouquet which will forever remain in my consciousness.

The organist who ruled over this rapidly failing instrument was – to say the least – an objectionable piece of work. With the best will in the world, I can describe him in no other manner. He refused to show the organ to visitors or even to congregants and when asked by my grandmother, a veritable pillar of the church, if he might possibly be kind enough to show her young grandson the console, responded in no uncertain terms. After all, the organ bench was his fiefdom and his alone. I was bitterly disappointed and not a little frustrated, a state of mind which I subsequently came to recognize as dangerous. Determined to defeat his intransigence, I resolved not merely to take a peep at the console but also to sit down and play the darned thing. In the manner of naughty boys from time immemorial, I hatched a plot, and one Saturday afternoon I headed confidently for the church and a date with destiny.

But the best laid plans of naughty boys rarely run smoothly and, having discovered every door and window tightly bolted against me, I decided that crime was the only way forward. At first, heaven smiled upon me for underneath a scruffy yet convenient bush I found an empty Coke bottle and employing a vigor which surprised even me, I bashed out a basement window. This, as they say in the movies, is where we came in. However, it is not the very end of the story for even now I can feel the merciless sting of my grandfather's belt and sense the shame which I had brought upon my hearth and home.

When I entered the third grade, I joined the Methodist church primary choir. Luckily, the unfriendly organist had gone on to pastures new and the new incumbent musician was a lovely lady who not only encouraged us, but also gave us the training of an adult choir. As my treble voice developed, I was given several solos to sing (I particularly remember Franck's *Panis Angelicus*). At the same time, Ella was providing me with the basics of music theory at home: harmony, solfège and counterpoint. The choral experience gave me a chance to put theory into practice.

My solo career as a keyboard artist began at age ten, in the form of a piano recital at the local recreation centre. I was familiar with the place, because I had developed a reputation for shooting pool (American-style billiards), particularly eight-ball – how Ella had sanctioned this was beyond me, it being one of the few glitches in her piety software. Seated at the keyboard, I was a nervous wreck. Unlike the solos at church, this recital had no director, no choir, no organ – in other words, no competition but more importantly perhaps, no safety net. The program included Beethoven's 'Moonlight' Sonata and *Für Elise*, a selection from Bach's *Well-Tempered Clavier* and a group of toe-tapping Joplin rags.

Conspicuously and thankfully absent were hymns or gospel tunes: at last, a musical offering without religious overtones. Better still was the applause, a tonic that thrilled me to the core and, to be honest, still does.

At about this time, the local Baptist church was getting ready to receive a new pipe organ. In 1956, the congregation had commissioned a new building, neo-colonial in design, and seating about 650. The large windows happily flooded the space in light. The organ, built by M. P. Möller of Hagerstown, Maryland, was not installed for a further six years. A three-manual instrument of twenty-nine ranks (voices), it had an Antiphonal division in the rear balcony which was blessed with the inclusion of a set of chimes. I was fascinated by this effect and dreamt of all kinds of uses for them. No organ should be without them.

Clearly, I was becoming organ mad and since the Baptists now had the best organ in town, it made perfect sense to me to become a Baptist! Subsequently, I was received into the Baptist faith in the traditional manner: total immersion. To my surprise my family didn't seem to mind this leap-frogging of denominations, perhaps because they thought I was showing religious enthusiasm for the first time. Neither were they to flinch when some years later I switched again, this time to Monroe's beautiful Episcopal church. Here, I was often asked to stand in for their own organist on Sundays, playing their ancient Hammond – an instrument I knew all too well from home. Although the building was tiny by comparison, seating only about 100, I felt immediately as if I belonged with these people. At specified times they sat, stood or knelt, always moving together in unity. Their services had a formal and dignified air without being stuffy. I never felt the momentum lapse.

But back to the new organ in the Baptist church. Before I became a member, and as such was *encouraged* to play the new instrument and to use it for practice, I would often sit inside the Antiphonal organ chamber during services, mesmerized by the movements of the bellows, the swell shutters and all the other fascinating mechanisms. Here too was a new set of bells 'n' smells for me to savor and much fresher than those emanating from the old Methodist organ.

In common with most Americans, I remember vividly the day President John F. Kennedy was assassinated. I was eleven at the time and recall hearing the news while we were on the playing fields. School was closed immediately, and all the churches opened for prayer and reflection. I went immediately to the Baptist Church, and all afternoon played and improvised on the hymn Melita ('Eternal Father, Strong to Save') as JFK's love of the nautical was well-known.

Eternal Father, strong to save, whose arm doth bind the restless wave.
Who bidd'st the mighty ocean deep its own appointed limits keep,
O hear us when we cry to thee, for those in peril on the sea.

All day long people streamed through the church in mass mourning. The nation was united in grief.

CHAPTER TWO

ON AND OFF THE RAILS

In many ways it was clear to me, if not to others, that I was growing up. The horizons offered by a small town in North Carolina were becoming confining. I yearned for new experiences and vistas but, in order to pursue my burgeoning ambitions, I knew that I had to hatch yet another plot. The door was now definitely ajar, and no longer just to the radio preachers.

Even a new organ, and ultimately a new church, could not satisfy my curiosity or longing for the enticing destinations of the silver railway cars. While I was not unhappy at home, I was not necessarily totally content either. So I used the most efficient means of exploration. Firmly believing that the grass must surely be greener on the other side of the county line, I decided to run away.

Actually, I ran away twice, since I failed to make a proper job of it the first time round. The first attempt came at age eleven. Through my railway connections, it was no problem to hop an east-bound freight heading for Hamlet, the hub of the Seaboard Railroad in that part of the world. I felt like a king for a day or two, hobnobbing with journeymen on the box-cars. Perhaps the strongest recollection was experimenting with my first cigarette, or rather, the disgusting taste. My return to home a few days later was met inevitably by the now familiar sting of grandfather's belt. There may have been many varieties of misdemeanors ... but there was only one form of punishment.

But memories are short and my second unauthorized vacation came about a year later when I hitch-hiked to Charlotte. This little trip was slightly longer but hardly better planned. I managed to steal some small wherewithal from Ella's purse but, typically for a youngster, forgot to take enough clothes. So, when I got to Charlotte, I had to 'rough it'. Boy Scout training had prepared me for sleeping outdoors, and I existed exclusively on fast food. So I resolved to stay for a week, and therefore experienced what would set the stage for my life's preoccupation.

My first triumph was inveigling my way into Covenant Presbyterian Church, home to a glorious four-manual Æolian-Skinner organ installed curiously enough in 1952, the year of my birth. The instrument was crowned with fanfare trumpets and a pedal department the like of which I had only dreamed about; my introduction to real 32' sound, which produces 16 cycles per second on the lowest note. Dr. Richard Peek, Covenant's Director of Music and a highly respected figure in American Presbyterian music circles, generously allowed me to play to my heart's content. Having satisfied myself there, I then conned my way into no fewer than six other churches, claiming – so I seem to remember – to be the organist of the Pillar of Fire Baptist Tabernacle in East Cupcake, Nowhere. Through three or four days I sampled both sanctuary and chapel organs by such diverse builders as Möller, Pilcher, Kilgen, Austin, Schlicker, together with a most impressive, brand-new Casavant (designed by Lawrence Phelps). Having experienced several examples of the efforts of seven organ-builders in seven days, I was finally in seventh heaven.

It struck me, even at that early age, that the organ was not blessed with the 88-note discipline of the piano, and therein lay its immense challenge. Every diapason, while similar in character, sounded different; some flute stops gurgled while others made a percussive sound in their attack, called *chiff*; some string stops chiffed while others sounded smooth and elegant; and some of the reed stops – the ones that work with a beating tongue inside them, much like an oboe, clarinet or saxophone – had sonority and roundness, while others sounded awful, like swarms of mosquitoes incarcerated in a toaster. Not all the sounds that necessarily appealed to me were musical. I was again entranced by the whooshing of the electro-pneumatic swell shutter mechanism on the Æolian-Skinner; the unmistakable pneumatic *ka-chunk* of the Möller console; the *clickety-click* of the keyboard on the Schlicker's all-mechanical action; the cash-register-like metallic shiver of the Austin console and the chrome-plated, rubber-tipped swell shutter-control-shoes of the Casavant. The variety was staggering – and to a twelve-year-old, pure paradise.

At each instrument, I ran through my extensive repertory of the Bach *Eight Little Preludes and Fugues*, a few pages of the Franck *Chorale in A minor*, together with my old trump-card, the Marcello *Psalm XIX*. No one laughed, at least in my presence. Everywhere I was received generously and not without a little humor, due perhaps to my seemingly unquenchable enthusiasm and tender age. At my final destination, a friendly yet curious choir director finally got the truth out of me – that I really belonged twenty-five miles down Highway 74 – subsequently making sure that I returned safely to my nest.

Once more, I had to suffer the inevitable punishment, if only because my efforts had this time proven so fruitful. Although my loving family must have been extremely worried, they became convinced that I was nothing less than determined in my ambition to pursue a musical career. After eight years of piano and organ study with my dear grandmother, she and my mother decided I should apply for admission to the North Carolina School of the Arts (NCSA), a new performing arts school in Winston-Salem and about a two and a half hour drive north of Monroe. For me it was a heaven-sent opportunity, not only to flee the nest, but also to see what life was really about beyond the confines of small town America.

Opened in 1965, NCSA was the first publicly funded institution in the United States to offer both high-school and university-level instruction exclusively for young students of dance, drama and music. Those who came from outside the state paid their own way, but North Carolina residents attended *gratis*. All a parent had to provide was transportation and spending money. We set about filling in the application, and an audition was scheduled to take place at Centenary Methodist Church, Winston-Salem, on its practically new 1963 four-manual Austin organ (a rebuild of a 1931 instrument by the same builder).

The church's organist, Margaret Sandresky, was a member of the NCSA organ faculty, and it was she who was to hear my audition. It was a fine and comfortable instrument in a beautiful church, but these facts combined with my nervousness failed to insure against a rotten performance. To the best of my recollection, I attempted a few of the simpler works by Bach and Langlais, but my closing rendition of the Alain *Litanies* was truly memorable because it was so thoroughly excruciating. I played quickly, loudly and terribly inaccurately and was mortified afterward, thinking I had blown my big chance. Jehan Alain could have composed an entire *fantaisie* with the wrong notes I had bashed out. A few months later, as I was unpacking in my dormitory room at NCSA, I recall thinking that Mrs. Sandresky must have been blind, deaf, or *phenomenally* Christian to have accepted my application. Enrolling in September of 1967, I was just fifteen years old.

NCSA was a brave new world, and a beautiful one. For starters, Winston-Salem, unlike Monroe, was a major city. Though not as large as Charlotte, it still offered basic urban amenities which I had never known. Then there was the school itself, teeming with budding musicians, actors and dancers, all of us delighted to be surrounded at last by kindred spirits. To be sure, there was a certain concentration of North Carolinians, due no doubt to the generous financial incentive, but students flocked from all over the USA, Canada, Europe and Asia. Regardless of origin, I suspect many of them came from backgrounds in which their interests had marked them out as exceptional. At NCSA, I found it refreshing that one would have been mocked for *not* being artistic. It was a rare place where idealism was fostered; that it was fostered virtually for free seemed almost fantastic.

The organ remained the heart and soul of my studies, and soon enough I was substituting in local churches. To be honest, for me, this was not so much a desire for experience as for pocket money. It was, nonetheless, a great grounding in all of the various denominational liturgies, ranging from bible-thumping fundamentalism at one extreme to high Catholicism at the other. I had to be ready to change gear at a moment's notice. A further welcome source of income came from the local funeral parlor where I was required to play yet another Hammond. It was the third such instrument in my life and I was determined that it should be my last.

NCSA's teaching staff was undoubtedly first-rate and augmenting them were top-flight stars from august conservatories such as Juilliard, Peabody and Curtis. Rose Bampton, a famous New York vocal coach and ex-Metropolitan Opera soprano, would fly down regularly for an intensive day or two. Piano being my second subject, I was privileged to accompany some of her pupils, and to see her in action was in itself a salutary lesson. Without any question, singers have always seemed to me to be the ultimate musicians, since they must produce everything from within. How many instrumental teachers say to their students, 'Make that line *sing*'? Imagine a singing teacher saying 'Make that line *saxophone*'! Vocalists cannot rely on the inherent beauty of a good instrument, but must stand entirely responsible for the effect. By comparison, all instrumentalists have to filter their music through an intermediary device. To create vocal line and inflection, even on the violin, is still a detached function from vocal production. How would this translate to the organ, obviously the most mechanically complex of all instruments? Rose Bampton had a wonderful ability to articulate these thoughts, and I relished the exposure to them and to her.

One of my favourite teachers was Arthur J. 'Pete' Ballard, who taught English. He brought to his lectures the rich background of a colorful life. He had worked in Saudi Arabia for ARAMCO, the prominent Middle East oil consortium, and was the first great raconteur I knew, imparting zest and humor to all that he did. His pupils cherished him and, more than anything else, he greatly inspired them to read, learn, mark and inwardly digest.

Shortly after arriving at NCSA, it rapidly became apparent to me that my organ technique was badly in need of honing and direction. While I could not fail to be grateful to my dear grandmother for having provided me with an enviable piano technique, she had, alas, only been able to suggest rudimentary elements of a proper approach to the organ. Furthermore, I had always been a quick study – too quick if the truth be known. My new teachers made it clear that things came too easily for me and that I needed to buckle down to some serious practice. And were they ever right. After all, I was now lucky enough to be under the tutelage of seasoned organists for the first time, a fact that my apology for an audition had driven home firmly. Consequently, I tried my utmost to respond to their advice and began work in earnest.

My organ professor, John Mueller, proved to be a superb teacher in many ways – all the more so in hindsight, since our artistic goals on the pipe organ could not be more dissimilar. Then and now, his interests centered around mechanical-action organs, early music scholarship, and authentic performance practice: rendering music as closely as possible to the composer's style and intentions. This was the mid-1960s, when the anti-romantic movement in organ-playing and building was at fever pitch. John Mueller stood at the forefront of this movement not only by virtue of his position at NCSA, but also his church appointments throughout the region. He was also instrumental in bringing several modern mechanical-action organs to North Carolina. Margaret Sandresky thought along similar lines. In correspondence relating to a chapel organ built by Austin for her church, their representative wrote:

> The organ does not have enough chiff to satisfy fully the desires of the presiding organist, Mrs. Sandresky, who is all Holtkamp, Schlicker and Flentrop and who also teaches organ at the School of the Arts here in town.[1]

Stops that chiffed were particularly fashionable with the neo-classical builders listed – even though chiff is rarely found in the old classical organs – whereas Austin was more middle-of-the-road. Nevertheless, I continued to admire Mrs. Sandresky greatly, even if she was 'all Holtkamp, Schlicker and Flentrop'!

While Professor Mueller's theories only interested me for a while, I have to confess that some of his enthusiasms stuck: in particular, his love of early French organ music, with its complex conventions of ornamentation. I doubt I would have explored this repertoire without him. Overall, however, I remained curious to learn more about other organists, primarily Virgil Fox, whose recordings had

---

1 Three of the most widely respected, while strictly classically inclined, organ builders of this century.

already enthralled me by their vivacity, bravura, drama and unbridled confidence. But an organist like Dr. Fox was anathema to Prof. Mueller, who instead promoted what I considered to be a detached and even aloof style of playing. I determinedly resisted any stifling of my style, and my relationship with my teacher seemed headed for the rocks. However, what I needed at this stage was not style so much as substance and John Mueller was masterful in providing precisely that. He pursued the same disciplined approach on the organ as my grandmother had applied with the piano, incisively identifying every aspect of my technique that needed strengthening, before assigning pieces to meet the task.

But there was an interesting subtext to the whole scene. Prof. Mueller's wife, Margaret, was also an organist, and a really fine one at that. They were co-professors of organ at Salem College in Winston-Salem, but Margaret did not teach at NCSA. Husband and wife were a study in contrasts. While John was serious, Margaret sparkled; where John was well-groomed, Margaret was attractively disheveled; where John could be reserved, Margaret was ebullient, spontaneous and full of pluck. She played at St. Paul's, the local Episcopal church, which I attended occasionally, primarily to hear her play.[2]

Considered small by some standards, St. Paul's Episcopal Church is an elegant Ralph Adams Cram building, with an especially beautiful 1929 Skinner organ.[3] In the 1950s, Margaret, encouraged by her husband, was eager to alter the instrument in order to bring it in line with neo-classical ideals. Happily, it was to be saved from this fate by, of all people, Dirk Flentrop and Charles Fisk, two of the most prominent neo-classical builders in the world, both of whom worked in a style diametrically opposed to that represented by this lush, romantic Skinner.

Sometime later, John Mueller commissioned a sizeable Flentrop for Reynolda Presbyterian Church in Winston-Salem, where he served as organist. Dirk Flentrop himself came over from Holland to oversee the finishing touches. It was during that visit that the Muellers consulted him about their scheme to rebuild the St. Paul's Skinner. Clearly expecting him to be enthusiastic at the prospect of converting a romantic masterpiece into something it was never intended to become, his answer must have surprised them. 'Leave it exactly as it

---

2 Taxi-tickets were offered to organ students for rides to many area churches for rehearsals, a privilege that was dreadfully abused.

3 On paper, the Skinner stop list seemed curious: of its 51 ranks, 27 were in the Swell alone, the remaining 24 distributed among Great, Choir, Solo and Pedal divisions. However, it had a complete ensemble and a terrific 32' Bombarde (Skinner's first such stop with metal resonators, I am told, and far better than any I'd heard in Charlotte).

is. Do not alter a pipe,' he told them firmly. Subsequently, they put their ideas to Charles Fisk who declared the instrument to be far superior to any Skinner he had ever heard and, that if it needed restoration, they should do precisely that and no more. To their eternal credit, John and Margaret Mueller heeded the unequivocal advice of both builders and have jealously guarded this treasure ever since.[4]

Upon this regal instrument, Margaret played service after terrific service, not quite High Anglican, not quite Protestant, but always utterly Margaret. She utilized all the organ's strengths, and through her skilled improvisation created a unique atmosphere. Her variation in color choices was made all the more remarkable since she had to change most of the stops by hand, owing to a sadly limited provision of console playing aids – there were but two general pistons.

To be honest, Margaret's particular performance style impressed me far more than her husband's. It was colorful, lyrical and utterly personal. In common with her personality, Margaret's music was spontaneous and, secretly, in many ways, I wished I could study with her instead. Upon reflection, I'm not sure what difference it might have made. I was a rotten student and must have been horrible to teach. Part of it was the 'things-came-too-easily' aspect; I did not practice enough, and the embarrassing outcome was often poorly prepared performances. Another aspect was my desire to rebel against what I saw as John Mueller's rigidly literal, impersonal approach, which no doubt led me to further lack of taste in my youthful determination to 'be myself.' On the other side of the coin however, I was struck by the peculiar contrast between my work and that of my fellow non-organist students. All around me, dance and drama pupils were happily learning to imbue their work with personality and feeling while I was being strictly taught to fashion my playing after a rigid and sterile ideal. While other students could boast about their recent dramatic or musical performances – all distinctive and individual – I felt as if I was in a straitjacket.

To make matters worse, my fellow organ students eagerly devoured the worst extremes of anti-romanticism, parroting the notion that just one kind of organ music and manner of playing was inherently superior to every other. Their attitude was snooty – to the same degree, to be sure, that mine was rebellious. One overtly hostile pupil who loathed romanticism in any form went to the school record library and inflicted deep scratches on all of Virgil Fox's LP recordings. I had listened to these discs many times, and was horrified when I discovered this mindless vandalism. In a potentially spiteful moment, I almost

---

4 Having given some seventy years of relatively trouble-free service, the organ has since been restored by the A. Thompson-Allen Company, Curators of Organs at Yale University.

did the same to all Marie-Claire Alain's Bach recordings – but I decided I liked them too much. The incident merely served to strengthen my resolve further.

In the end, and luckily for me, John Mueller remained resolute in the face of my stubborn tenacity. He was careful to ensure that my organ technique matched my piano technique. Additionally, he gave me an appreciation for certain aspects of touch and control. Thus, after my initial petulance, I finally settled down to regular and intensive practice. And even if I didn't get to study with his wife, I was to be profoundly influenced by other teachers during this period. Perhaps the most important of these was Arthur Poister, organ professor at Syracuse University in New York State and a pupil of Karl Straube – who had not only been a personal friend and champion of Max Reger but also Organist and Kantor at the Thomaskirche, Leipzig. Poister had also studied with Dupré and was rumored to have played for Widor.

Dr. Poister had been prominent in the organ world since the 1940s, a generation before John Mueller, and although he was also interested in early music and the baroque movement, he had a broad regard for all that was best in every school of organ literature, particularly Reger and the French romantics. By way of illustration, he had had one of Walter Holtkamp's finest instruments installed at Syracuse, one more suited to romantic music than most of Holtkamp's organs, with its inclusion of older pipework by Roosevelt and Æolian.

I first met Poister at a masterclass he gave at Duke University Chapel in Durham, North Carolina. At first I was awe-struck by the Chapel itself, a sizeable neo-Gothic building, the tower of which dominated the surrounding skyline. The 1932 Æolian organ was of epic late-romantic proportions with stunning reeds and a pedal department of earth-shattering power. It literally moved the very foundations.

The man cast a striking figure: tall with well-chiselled, craggy features, topped with the most lustrous white hair I'd ever seen. His likeness could have easily appeared on any denomination of United States currency. Curiously though, he had unusually large and clumsy-looking hands, like those of a manual laborer. He did not waste time with superfluous commentary and thus every instruction produced results – surely he was an organists' organist. Since we were there to play for *him* – and not the other way around – all I ever heard him perform were small sections in illustration of various points. Alas, I can't recall what I played for him at our first meeting but I clearly remember the way he took it to pieces – albeit constructively and in a gentlemanly manner such as to build my confidence. He would often say that organists should love a phrase instead of just playing it because it was printed on the score. He was clearly a devoted servant of the music. Voice-leading and the controlled use of non-legato playing were very important techniques which he championed in particular.

Occasionally, he'd become swept up in the rhythmic drive of a piece he was adjudicating and grab hold of the console jamb with both hands, swaying to and fro while attempting what appeared to be a mini fandango! It was all most enlightening. Although initially I found him terrifying, he soon put me at my ease. He was an exciting, vibrant teacher and I am greatly enriched by having known him. Some years later, I was to study with him in Atlanta under similar circumstances, where the local chapter of the American Guild of Organists (AGO) engaged him for a masterclass and private instruction. I had several lessons from him at this time, and once again, he was superb.

It was also in Duke Chapel that I was privileged to meet the world-famous organist E. Power Biggs, who was inaugurating a new Holtkamp organ in the Memorial Chapel, which forms part of the main building. Of course, I had become aware of this great man some years before, both through his many recordings and his legendary CBS radio broadcasts from Harvard University's Busch-Reisinger Museum.[5]

At that time, Biggs and Fox were the two names most immediately recognizable by the general public as concert organists. Alexander Schreiner was certainly popular through the weekly broadcasts from the Mormon Tabernacle and his own exacting recital schedule. There was, however, a renowned rivalry between Biggs and Fox. While I loved Fox's recordings, I derived great pleasure from Biggs' too. He just *had* to have a sense of humor to play Scott Joplin rags so joyously on the pedal harpsichord, and humor in music has always been something I regard highly. My favorite Biggs recording, and in my opinion the best he ever made, included a stellar performance of Dupré's *Variations sur un Noël* at St. George's Church, New York City. It thrilled me through and through.

When I met Biggs at Duke, I was delighted to find him warm, kind and somewhat reserved, with an ever-present sense of humor. Furthermore, he somehow looked like his music sounded: distinguished, trim and fit. He was soon chatting to me intermittently while he practiced, talking candidly about his debilitating arthritis and telling me about the many exercises and treatments he had to perform daily to keep his fingers agile. He approached these hardships as a matter of course and without complaint. He was English to the core, even after decades in the States.

He was delighted to learn – and boy was I eager to tell him – that I was an admirer of his, and a pupil of John Mueller. When he kindly asked me about my

---

5 The Duke Chapel Holtkamp has been replaced with a new, mechanical-action instrument by Brombaugh.

aspirations, I replied at once, 'Why, to study with Virgil Fox!' I couldn't have been more gauche if I'd tried. What an effort it must have been for him to smile in response. 'Oh, wonderful.' What a perfect gentleman he was.

In retrospect, I am especially grateful for that afternoon spent with him, for if I had merely turned up for the recital, I might have come away bitterly disappointed. In contrast to the sparkle and accuracy of his recordings, this particular performance lacked lustre and was, alas, littered with wrong notes. Realizing how physically difficult performance had become for him, I could readily accept all of this and sympathize with him; but I shuddered to think what the audience thought.

All in all, exposure to these great men finally inspired me to a Battle-Hymn-of-Practice regime. Clearly, they had not achieved their success by great talent alone, and if I wanted a career remotely like theirs, I would have to buckle down. Fortunately, I had access to a good Holtkamp practice organ, one of the company's 'Martini' models (so nicknamed because Walter Holtkamp had conceived the instrument's design with friends on cocktail napkins over drinks). The organ's tones were delicate on the ears over several hours of practice, and in all it was a superb note-learning medium.[6]

Though barely a year old, the Holtkamp was considered something of a compromise because it did not adhere to anti-romantic precepts (in essence, because it had electric key action, not mechanical which was the preferred mode of transmission for the classical school). However, I cherished it for exactly that reason. Unlike mechanical-action organs, the Holtkamp's touch was uniform throughout, bass to treble, manual to manual, and it meant I didn't have to fight the keys which, with mechanical action, can be difficult to depress, especially in the lower octaves or when the keyboards are coupled together. On occasion, I practiced on one of the small mechanical-action instruments in the city, but I soon grew to dislike it. It was austere and harsh, without a single inspiring sound. And, given its size, the touch was preposterous. What should have handled like a well-oiled racing bike felt instead like an old pick-up truck with a dodgy transmission.

I was warned when embarking on this autobiography that I might have

6 The five-stop unit organ contained a 16' Quintadena, 8' Gedackt, 4' Principal, III Mixture and 8' Schalmey. Except for the Mixture, the stops were unified across two manuals and pedals, but very cleverly, so that you could obtain relatively 'straight' effects from manual to manual. There was a footrest where a swell pedal might have been, and a small glass partition around the pipes. This prevented the mixture from screeching in your face ... as well as protecting the pipework from spilt Martinis!

to reveal an occasional secret. Well – with name removed to protect identity – I should tell you that I also have good reason to remember the organ practice room at NCSA, for there it was, while rehearsing Bach's *Prelude and Fugue in C* (9/8), no less, that I conducted my first foray into the hitherto murky world of physical passion. My partner was a delightfully pretty violinist and it is with some embarrassment that I recall my clumsy explorations, cuddling up to her in the distinguished vicinity of a pipe organ. We nestled affectionately on a patchwork quilt alongside the largest pipes, the tiny blower (a Spencer Orgoblo 'Junior') whirring away comfortingly in its sound-attenuating box. Goodness knows what Freud would have made of that!

That such a liaison could take place will surprise no honest school or college graduate. With liberty comes the need to explore, and there were few cups or indeed tankards from which I did not drink with some relish. For example, with all my new-found freedom, it was small surprise that I was not slow to discover the merits of alcohol – not, it should be added, that this was readily available to most budding teenagers. Apart from the communion wine at the Episcopal Church in Monroe – and I suspect that that had been well watered down – I had never tasted anything stronger than iced tea or 'Ko-Kola.'

The only controlled beverage a teenager like me could purchase legitimately was cooking sherry. In my first serious sherry session I consumed more than one large bottle in the space of an hour and a half. Small surprise then that I was violently ill for the rest of the weekend. Since my head felt like it had been trapped in a vice and my mouth as if it were lined with a skunk-pelt, I figured my system must have been trying to tell me something. But all teenagers tend to be forgetful, especially when it comes to such matters, and the following weekend I'm ashamed to admit that I repeated the exercise, gulp by sickly gulp. But I'd learned a thing or two in the interim, including how food should accompany all such activities. Perhaps I got the finer points of the instructions wrong, for after bingeing three cans of Vienna Sausages on top of the sherry, I soon sensed an impending, involuntary and not altogether surprising upsurge. Having blocked my sink with an initial colorful expression, I rushed to the window and delivered the rest of the sermon all over my housemaster's motor bike, parked three stories below. I was growing up.

Much of the impetus for this brash fanfare of adolescence came from my roommate, Neil Brawley, a 'good ole Southern boy' and a string bass player from

Salisbury, North Carolina.[7] In fact, all the Brawleys were Southern through and through. Neil's daddy, Boots, was the wire editor of the *Salisbury Post* and the local historian. Boots' brother, Bone (no, I'm not making this up!) lived in a large, sprawling 1890s Tudor-style house in the center of Salisbury. Bone always called me 'Carley,' either because he had deliberately merged my two names or he was lazy; it didn't seem polite to ask! Both Boots and Bone were scions of the Confederacy and were delighted to assert their allegiance to Robert E. Lee. Bone was often proclaiming, and not in jest, 'Carley! The South will *riiiiiiiese* agin!' Another favourite quip which tended to amuse was when he referred to the war between the States as 'The War of Northern Aggression.'

It was at Uncle Bone's house that I graduated from cooking sherry to hard liquor. Bone's kitchen was novel in that it contained virtually nothing edible. Every cabinet above arm's level was filled with empty Ancient Age Bourbon bottles (a bargain-basement American brand), while the full bottles were secreted below the sink. He taught me his swigging technique. His 'sink drink' consisted of a generous jigger of bourbon served up in a jigger-glass. The instant you gulped back the booze, you filled a second tall glass with cold water from the gushing tap and immediately downed it in one to chase the hard stuff. A serious session entailed at least three or four 'sink drinks.' Bone was amazed by my capacity, and after my first visit suggested I bring my own bottle next time.

Many of my fondest memories from these days came from time spent at the Brawleys'. Two of Neil's best friends were Bob and Tommy Isenhour. While they were brothers, Bob and Tommy didn't resemble each other in the least. Tommy was average in height and stature, while Bob was 6ft 4¾in and almost 300 pounds. Bob never exercised (but he did drink a lot), yet he was extremely fit and strong with an enormous appetite. If we went to a buffet lunch, the rest of us would merely troupe up for seconds while Bob would go round the circuit at least five times. At one restaurant, the kitchen staff would super-salt the fish at the all-you-can-eat fish fry to get Bob to stop. He didn't.

Their family owned the Isenhour Brick and Tile Company in Salisbury, a premier brick-yard. The Isenhour mansion on Mocksville Avenue had many bedrooms and the singular luxury of an enormous swimming pool, something I'd never ever seen at a residence. And did the Isenhours know how to have a party! Their 1969 New Year's Eve bash was a deafening extravaganza, with two rock bands and a bluegrass group. Beer, sloe gin and broken glass was everywhere underfoot, and maybe two hundred revellers all over the property. On account of my imposing stature, I was asked to double up as a bouncer. Just after midnight,

7 Neil later become principal bassist for the Sydney Symphony in Australia.

one befuddled party-goer decided he'd had enough and it was time to leave. Instead of using the imposing driveway, he drove his car down the wooded footpath which led to the swimming pool. A crowd of us hoofed it down in a valiant attempt to save him. Remarkably, the car tottered on the brink, half in half out of the pool. In a daring move, Mr. Isenhour Senior clambered gingerly behind the wheel while we bounced the car up and down until the back wheels made contact. Moments later, car and party-goer were thankfully out on the street.

In the Isenhour house there was something anachronistic in the furnishing of Bob and Tommy's quarters. There were Victrolas with horns and other windup gramophones. Bowlers and top hats hung on the walls, giant leopardskin rugs and wonderful threadbare Persian carpets were strewn about and ship models stood imposingly on sideboards. The effect resembled nothing so much as a 1920s gentlemen's club. I was much impressed by it all and still am; and my own home could today be said to fit this same description, even though my clutter is a tad more Dickensian. The boys had acquired their collection through sharpwitted auction attendance and many Saturday afternoons whiled away in 'junque' shops. I would join them for some of these expeditions and admired the rapport they had developed with many of the shop proprietors. One dealer, who always saw us coming, took to hanging signs on delicate items, which read:

> Beautiful to look at, delightful to hold,
> If you break it, we mark it sold!

The best thing about visiting the Isenhours was the exposure to the authentic, acoustic bluegrass music they so dearly loved. While there may have been no physical resemblance, both brothers were intensely musical – Bobby played the banjo up a storm as did Tommy, the latter also being a first-rate exponent of the mandolin. On the weekends, Bobby, Tommy, Neil Brawley and others in their circle would assemble for a 'jam' session. I had always liked jazz and country music, and my piano technique easily allowed me to join them. Soon, I developed the same passion for this infectious music, absorbing a sense of rhythmic nuance within a strict meter, as well as a keen grasp of ensemble playing.

With this group, I attended my first fiddlers' convention in a small smudge on the rural map called Union Grove, North Carolina. Thousands of bluegrass aficionados were there, as it was a big annual event. Imagine my surprise when the opening parade was led by the local Ku Klux Klan motorcycle brigade, executing perfect figure-eights and other formations. Why in heavens were that lot decked out in white bed sheets, hats and hoods in the heat of mid-summer?

A great friend of the Isenhours, particularly of Bob, was Terence Mulligan, a native of Montclair, New Jersey, and a French major at Clemson University in

South Carolina. Bob and Terence were classmates. It was only natural that they should meet, because Terence's affection for 1920s paraphernalia was possibly even stronger than that of the Isenhour boys. In addition to deerstalkers and walking sticks, Terence was obsessed with trains, and on this topic, we had a lot in common. His knowledge on such matters as private railroad cars (like Paderewski's) and the history of the Pullman company was encyclopaedic. Another of his great loves was for 78 rpm records, which he owned by the thousand, and while, like many 78 rpm fanatics, 'Ter' was primarily devoted to the vocal art (the one facet of musical expression 78s captured with surprising fidelity), his collection encompassed piano, violin, orchestral, and even organ music. Therefore, he was readily familiar with such organists as Louis Vierne, Marcel Dupré, Charles Tournemire, and some nearly forgotten names such as Alfred Sittard in Germany and Eduard Commette, once wildly popular as Columbia's principal organ recording artist in France. Through these recordings I was exposed to a style of playing much different than what I was being taught, and yet a different kind of romanticism than that of Virgil Fox, for example.

Ter came from an interesting family. His mother was a newspaper writer, and his father, Denis, had been a pioneer aviator who had flown a fighter plane in the silent movie *Wings*, the first film ever to win an Academy Award. Later, he was director of US Civil Aviation under Franklin Roosevelt. But most thrilling of all to me, Denis had travelled majestically on the airship Hindenburg from Germany to the US shortly before it exploded in Lakehurst, New Jersey in 1937. He knew everybody in aviation history and had even taken his wife to dine with Orville Wright. When I met Denis in 1970, he was retired and wore an odd collection of mixed gear. Boisterous tales, mainly of heavy industry, flowed from him freely. The Army's Gamma Goat personnel carrier – the longest story of all – was quite a two-pipe problem, I remember.

Terence shared his father's past-think. But unlike his father's reminiscences, the past Ter worshipped was rich with opera singers, trains, pith helmets, the 78 rpm 'brick records,' old men's clubs, books and politics – all thoroughly researched or hundreds of examples collected, all Very Serious. Although only a few years older than me, Ter as a twenty-year-old Clemson undergraduate was more like a polished fifty-year-old eccentric, the oldest person I had ever met, but certainly the kind of person I was drawn to. Furthermore, he bore a startling resemblance to Louis Vierne, the great blind organist of Notre-Dame in Paris.

Because of the distance from NCSA to Clemson, I got to know Terence slowly. The first excursion I made to Clemson was at Bob Isenhour's invitation to attend a New Year's Eve Beaux-Arts Ball on campus. What an eye-opener! NCSA was lively enough, but here was a *real* university, with all the seemingly limitless freedoms which accompany such an institute of higher learning.

It was quite possible to dance on the tables until dawn without fear of reprimand. I remember learning the Lambada (the strongly suggestive South American dance) by rehearsing it endlessly on many Clemson table tops. Those
attending the Ball had worked especially hard to create distinctive costumes. For
example, the professor in charge set the tone by arriving in nothing but a garden
hose. (It was novel but not entirely flattering.) From that point on, my memory
of the event is vague, although I remember waking up the next morning in a
daze, profoundly exhausted and lying in a patch of kudzu outside.[8]

In course of time, my bonds with the Brawley and Isenhour clans strengthened still further. The following summer, Bob Isenhour hatched a plan whereby
all of the most eccentric people he knew would spend the summer in the beautiful North Georgia hills, ninety miles north of Atlanta, at Vogel State Park in
Blairsville. Vogel was designed for masses of visiting families with house-trailers
and caravans. There was an exhibition pavilion seating many hundreds, placed on
a pier extending into the lake. Bob was assigned to Vogel to fulfil a requirement
of his Recreation and Parks Administration major at Clemson. His interpretation
of this assignment was to hire all of us to work at Vogel for a summer-long bluegrass party. Eventually the whole Salisbury scene was re-enacted in Blairsville,
amidst the pines and for a real audience. I would take tickets, dispense conces-
sions (finally! a retailer), and of course join in the band. I occasionally made a
few attempts on the double bass, but otherwise stuck to the piano and contributed a vocal solo from time to time. Some of the most popular pieces that
summer were taken directly from Bob's 78s: 'Lindbergh the Eagle of the USA'
and '(I Love My) Chili Bom Bom,' among others.

> I just got a line, from a friend of mine, living in Chili Land; living a life so
> grand.
>> He said: Tell the world, I'm down here to stay, neve' come back no more,
> never will leave this shore.
>> 'Cause I got a gal named Bom Bom, believe me when I say; she did a cute
> little dance with the Tom Tom and stole my heart away. Say!
>> (Refrain)
>> I love my Chili Bom Bom, my Chili Bom Bom, and Chili Bom Bom loves
> me.

---

8 Kudzu was imported from Japan in the 1890s by the Southern Railway as an erosion preventive.
  Comprised of large ivy/spinach leaves, the vine grew at an alarming rate, and kept the earth near
  rail lines from wearing away.

We get so chummy chum chum, so chummy chum chum, as silly as we can be.

I tell you, she's got a little grass hut, where both of us strut, it's nuthin' but har-mo-ny.

You've heard about the kind of girls that men forget, well here's a baby you'll remember all your life I bet.

Believe me, I have a lot of fun fun with Chili Bom Bom, 'cause Chili Bom Bom loves me.[9]

My most vivid memory is of our final summer concert, given before a capacity audience of several hundred. After all of our musical offerings, we gave the crowd a grand finale by lifting the $25 (but still extremely heavy and unwieldy) upright piano to the edge of the stage, and heaving it ceremoniously overboard into the lake. It sank instantly, amidst the wild cheering of the assemblage. What can I say? That was the 1960s for you.

While the lively intervention of bluegrass music certainly augmented my wider education, I was never diverted from my primary interest in the classical organ. Although most of the substituting venues didn't offer much inspiration, there was one notable exception: the magical sound of the residence pipe organ at 'Reynolda,' the home of the R. J. Reynolds tobacco family, producers of the Winston and Salem brands of cigarettes.

While the Æolian organ in Duke Chapel was very much a cathedral organ in every sense of the word, this firm built almost exclusively for the homes of the wealthy, and were in a class by themselves. The residence consoles were elegant pieces of furniture, blending seamlessly with their surroundings. All were equipped with roll-playing devices – similar to those on player pianos – which enabled the organ to become something of an early form of home music center, albeit with uncanny fidelity. As the roll moved along, the player mechanism read the stops, notes and expression. If you could load the roll and switch on, you were instantly an organ virtuoso. What's more, these units were equipped with a speed control, allowing the 'performer' to achieve wildly varying tempi. You could take

9 Published 1923 by Irving Berlin Inc., '(I Love my) Chili Bom Bom,' words by Cliff Friend, music by Walter Donaldson.

the *William Tell Overture* from zero to sixty faster than a Ferrari 'Testarossa.'

It was the weird stop names, however, which really set the Æolian apart. The builders knew all too well that normal organ nomenclature would simply confuse their well-to-do clients, so they resorted to a Dick-and-Jane simplicity. What might be called 'Viola da Gamba' to denote a string stop on any other organ was simply called 'String' on the Æolian, accompanied by a designation of volume, and if necessary, pitch (since all stops were assumed to be unison unless otherwise indicated). To any organist, this was sheer hilarity; to Mr. and Mrs. Stocks-and-Bonds, however, it had its merits. However, I well remember my glee upon first seeing the label 'Flute High' (a 2' piccolo), 'String MF Vibrato' (Viola Celeste), and 'Deep Diapason' (32' Pedal Bass). Furthermore, the stop tablets moved left to right, arranged in stop jambs on either side of the keydesk. Since organ stop knobs move in and out and conventional stop tablets up and down, the unique left-to-right business meant that, at a quick glance, it was near impossible to figure out what was on or off.

The tone was certainly beautiful, albeit distant, since the organ had to bellow through heavy tapestries into the spacious living room in order to have any effect. The house was open to the public and I occasionally substituted for the regular organist and enjoyed it immensely – especially, I must admit, for the prank potential. First, I would put on some impossibly difficult roll, such as *Ride of the Valkyries* or the overture to *Mignon*, a rendition that could never have been easily hand-played in the first place, but instead expertly and convincingly arranged by roll 'editors' to produce the effect of several organists performing at once. Then, as I pretended to play, my right hand would never be far from my favorite control – the tempo lever – while my shoulders made my hands look busy. If a crowd gathered, I would fully throw myself into this charade, making passionate facial expressions and closing my eyes at the end of a sensuous phrase. Then, just before the piece came crashing to an end with all the stops deployed, the tapestries flapping in the gale of this musical din, I would throw both arms high, wave madly to the audience and announce, 'Greetings, folks!' as the organ relentlessly powered on into the final chords, clearly without my assistance. One poor man, jaw agape, turned an alarming shade of gray before collapsing onto a sofa!

Clowning aside, it was at Reynolda more than anywhere else that I discovered the organ's ability to provide *mystery*, something I hadn't fully experienced before. It was an opulent and expressive American 'effect' organ in the best sense – yet another beneficial influence on my formative years.

CHAPTER THREE

DREAMS DO COME TRUE

Reflecting on my various experiences both at home and school, two contrasting aspects come into focus: spontaneity and a lack of planning. For me, everything seems to have unfolded with its own logic. Only now do I realize the magnitude of what has happened, and how fortunate I am that so many dreams have become reality.

Take Virgil Fox. After seeing all his records scratched in the NCSA library, I went out and acquired my own. The man and his playing fascinated me, but even then, I sensed that recordings were at best a substitute for what I imagined to be the Total Fox Experience. As my interest in him developed, it was banjo-pickin' Bob Isenhour who struck gold. Thanks to his always being abreast of the Atlanta music scene, he discovered that Virgil would be performing with the Atlanta Symphony. As the concert date luckily fell during a school break, Bob and I determined to get to Atlanta to hear Virgil play.

The concert was so overwhelming that I do not hesitate to say – cliché or not – that my life was changed instantly. And it was all the more amazing, since the event contained the seeds of anti-climax. Among other selections, Virgil played the Handel *Organ Concerto No. 4* and Joseph Jongen's *Symphonie Concertante* – pieces I already knew well from his recordings. Then there was his touring organ, the Rodgers electronic 'Black Beauty.' While this packed a punch with very solid 32' tone, it was bound by the limitations of its early technology. And the acoustics were far from spectacular.

However, Virgil rose above all this and dazzled me. With due respect to every previous influence, I can still remember how that initial contact with his music-making caused me to understand, for the first time, why I was so driven to play the organ. Everything before, good or bad, had always fallen within clearly confined boundaries, elegant at best, but all too often dryly academic and generally uninspiring. But here was Virgil, a no-holds-barred musician who played with razor-sharp technique, creating an edge-of-the-seat electricity in the listener. Furthermore, the man exuded emotion, with clarity, rhythmic drive and imaginative registration. Yet he made it all look like fun and magic, driving the audience wild in the process. I was elated like never before.

At once, I began wondering how I could possibly meet my newfound idol and play for him. Bob Isenhour and Terence Mulligan paved the way without even realizing it. Ter was moving from Clemson to Atlanta and needed a roommate. Bob convinced me that it was right for me to leave school, room with Ter, try to find a church job, and in general step up a notch in life. Atlanta was the New York of the South, and nowhere else I had known, even Charlotte, could match the splendor of this newfound Eden. On consideration, I knew that my friend was right. I had gone as far as I could at NCSA. A whole new world lay before me. Surely it was mine for the taking.

In the summer of 1969, Ter and I found a hideous modern shoebox of an apartment in Atlanta opposite Piedmont Park on Tenth Street. This was on the edge of the big Atlanta hippie district, which at least provided us with local color. Having found our lodgings, Ter proceeded to spend virtually all his time elsewhere. Perhaps he was trying to tell me something! He would regularly get into his mechanic's garb and head down to the train yards to work on a sixty-year-old steam engine and train that his railroad club wheeled out for smoke-belching excursions all over the rural South. He would return around three in the morning, from places like Albany, Rome or Warm Springs, Georgia, dizzy with nostalgia, mostly deaf, definitely red-eyed, and covered with oil, soot and coal dust. He looked like Satan's hired man.

Meanwhile, since I lacked money, I got on the phone and started job-hunting. After several discouraging calls, I was pointed in the direction of Druid Hills Baptist Church, situated on glamorous-sounding Ponce de Leon Avenue. The church's associate pastor, Rev. Bob Maddox, took my call, and confirmed that the church was indeed looking for an organist. Perhaps, and understandably, he was defenseless in the face of my relentless enthusiasm, so he invited me round for an audition. Imagine the look on his face when a sixteen-year-old boy showed up on a particularly cold Saturday morning at the door of this socially prominent church, determined to compete against a number of established adult organists. Curiosity, together with a lot of quick lip on my part, got the better of him and having convinced him that I knew the intricacies of the Baptist liturgy, he invited me to have a short play. Heavens be praised. That was all that I needed.

Ironically, my audition was on another Austin, not quite so comprehensive as the one in Winston-Salem. My major problem lay mainly in the truly arid acoustics, which cruelly drew attention to every wrong note and rhythmic infelicity. I played hymns, accompaniments, repertoire, the Doxology in every possible key, even a snatch or two from Ives' *Variations on 'America.'*

Rev. Maddox reacted frantically, and called every important member of the church to come hear me play. Having arrived at 8.30 am, I did not leave until 6.00 pm that evening – with the promise that if I could get through the next day's services without mishap, the job would be mine.

That first Sunday was beyond anything I could have anticipated. The congregation went wild. They were practically shouting out the hymns, and the postlude created such a stir that a large group of people stayed behind and insisted that I carry on playing for them. Ever the showman, I happily obliged, and it won me the job.

At last! A real position in a real church with a real organ and a real office with my very own real telephone! A few months later, after I had settled in, a distinguished-sounding lady rang up. In a pronounced Southern accent, she announced herself as Mrs. Candler, a member of the church who, because she had just returned from a round-the-world trip, hadn't been able to make the 'pleasure of my acquaintance.' Hesitant to refute her assumption that making my acquaintance would bring her any pleasure whatsoever, I wisely allowed her to continue unabated. She went on to tell me that in her previous home, the Æolian Company (builders of the 'Reynolda' organ) had installed a large four-manual instrument (Opus No. 1542, built in 1925), to which she had invited world-famous organists including Marcel Dupré, Joseph Bonnet, Marco Enrico Bossi and many others. The organ had been regularly broadcast by WSB Radio, a popular Atlanta station, most of the programs being performed by the Candlers' private organist Dr. Charles Sheldon, who was also the Atlanta Municipal organist.[1] And by the way, she wanted to know, what was I playing for next Sunday's closing postlude? *She* adored Bach, Franck and Widor. And when might I 'come 'round' to her present house in Buckhead for luncheon? She would, of course, send her car and driver to fetch me.

---

1 I later learned quite a bit about Dr. Sheldon, who, in addition to his artistic duties, also sold organs for the Pilcher Organ Company. It was rumored that one of his best sales tactics was to take a committee into the forests outside Atlanta, point to the most towering, stately pines and proclaim, 'If you purchase an organ from us, ladies and gentlemen, these very trees will be used in the production of your instrument.' Talk about a tall tale!

Car ... *and* driver? I wanted to make the pleasure of her acquaintance immediately.

Of course, she never mentioned that she was *the* Mrs. Asa Griggs Candler Jr., widow of the son of Coca-Cola's founder. Furthermore, I subsequently learned that she was a pillar of our church, a great supporter of music and the arts, and a delightfully eccentric and refreshingly down-to-earth heiress. And although I was impressed that *any* individual had ever owned a four-manual organ in any home, I would soon come to know that she was referring to an instrument of no fewer than eighty-seven stops – larger than that of most cathedrals. There was a comprehensive Main organ with Echo and Antiphonal divisions forming a second section. The third department, named 'Solarium' on account of its exotic location, was sited so far away from the console as to be virtually inaudible. Happily, the majority of this instrument survives to this day at Weslyan College in Macon, Georgia.

Having filled in the details, Rev. Maddox left me in no doubt that I should accept her invitation without delay. So I put on my best suit, polished my shoes and got on over there to Buckhead.

As it turned out, I found Florence Candler's wealth neither intimidating nor ostentatious. From that first luncheon, we were fast friends; two Southern jabber-mouths who loved each other's company and had the whole world of music in common. She unofficially adopted me and, after a few weeks, generously suggested I live in her house. Please recall that at this point, I was a sixteen-year-old Southern boy, whose life had been saved not by religion, but by music. Curiosity and optimism had gotten me this far, and I had never craved money or 'fine living.' But after experiencing a single afternoon of Mrs. Candler's style, who was to refuse it? She was not about to lower her standard of living just to teach me a thing or two about the humility of wealth. Her lessons were to prove far more subtle and effective.

This happy and crucial development in my life fortuitously dovetailed with Terence's ever-increasing ambition to move to New York to begin what was to be a distinguished career as an advertising copywriter. Without a second thought, we cleared out of the Tenth Street shoebox, Ter packed off to the Big Apple, and I transferred my meager effects to Buckhead.

Without delay, I was introduced to a lifestyle of the famously rich. Mrs. Candler, having outfitted me in fine clothes, put her servants at my disposal and amazingly gave me free reign at her clubs. The one I recall most fondly is The Capitol City Club, an institution chartered in May of 1883 'to promote the pleasure, kind feeling and general culture of its members' (how *naaaice*! and utterly Southern).[2] Built in 1911 in Georgian Revival style, it was one of Atlanta's social

2 'Atlanta Club May Bow To Tradition of Newness,' Dudley Clendinen, *The New York Times*, March 4, 1986, p. 10.

landmarks and my favorite place within it was the Art Deco Mirador Room. The decor was rather anti-geometric, not a pointed tip on any surface in the place; even the tines on the forks had rounded ends. An instrumental ensemble played there nightly, and my many friends and I were not slow to nickname it the Zu-Zu Orchestra, on account of a suave musical style and the undeniable fact that one could (and did!) mumble 'Zu Zu' to almost every familiar tune they played (such as 'Strangers in the Night'). The lead saxophonist was extremely gifted; we liked to think that the gleaming bell of his instrument was filled with sour mash whiskey. The pianist, the spitting image of Alfred Hitchcock, slumped over his keyboard while producing the most magical harmonies.

Did I love this? I *did* love this! But Florence had better lessons in mind than those to be learnt in the deeply luxurious sofas and *chaises longues* of the Capitol City Club. Sure, her position in life could provide all that a sybarite could possibly desire, but just by being around her and her carefully selected set insured that I began to learn the larger lessons of life. She taught me quietly the very best of good manners, consideration for others and style. She was no pedant, but it was impossible for me not to absorb elements of her stateliness, as well as her determination and pluck. Rather than money, it was pride that Mrs. Candler had to burn.

Born in 1895 in the small farm town of Lithonia, Georgia, she had attended Tift College, a distinguished school for women in Forsyth where she studied secretarial skills, piano and clarinet. Later, she moved to Atlanta where she was employed in the Candler Building, then the tallest skyscraper in Atlanta. Eventually, Florence was to become private secretary to Asa G. Candler Jr. himself.

Some years later, after the first Mrs. Candler had sadly died, Mr. Candler asked Florence to marry him. Florence always intimated that she had played hard-to-get, which, in light of my experience with her, is entirely believable. While wealth for wealth's sake interested her not in the slightest, Mr. Candler's humor and sense of adventure eventually won her over.

Certainly from her account as told to me, the two of them enjoyed a wonderful marriage. Florence often recounted fond tales about him, his life and his business triumphs and failures. Candler was one of the best-known family names in modern Atlanta, and going through the city you couldn't help stumbling over some testament of their largesse: the zoo, the churches, the hotels, the musical establishment – all in addition to Coca-Cola and real estate, the keystones of the Candler empire. For example, the Plaza, Georgia's first shopping center, was a Candler development and was just across the street from Druid Hills Baptist. The Atlanta airport began life as Candler Speedway (where Asa Jr. had been photographed with Caruso). Then there was Candler Field, from which the family operated its fleet of planes. Florence would proudly show me photos, with her decked out in tailored leather flying-suit with cap, goggles and scarf all from Abercrombie & Fitch, posing beside their 1931 Lockheed 9 Orion 'Executive Transport.' In those early days of aviation, she would say, 'the railroad was your compass – none of this *radar* nonsense.'

Nicknamed 'Bud' by his closest acquaintances, Asa Jr. became involved in any new business in which he sensed rewards. His instincts rarely failed him, and seemingly simple projects reaped huge profits. One of Florence's favorite lines was, 'My husband *always* dealt in superlatives.' For example, just outside the music salon doors of Briarcliff, the Candler mansion, was an enormous swimming pool with a powerful fountain in the middle. With his Midas touch, Mr Candler opened it to the public and made a fortune.

Then there were the animals. According to Florence, Asa, during one of his well-publicized trips to Africa, met up with a local notable with whom he went safari hunting. One night they settled down to a game of poker, with Asa obliterating his opponent, winning virtually the shirt off his back. In settlement, he accepted a Noah's Ark of exotic animals: leopards, giraffes, elephants and so on, all in pairs. Having been transported across the Atlantic they were settled on several acres at Briarcliff, subsequently made over into a zoo – yet another Candler money-spinner. A final flight of fancy came in his naming of the elephants. Unlike the single pairs which comprised the rest of the collection, there were two pairs of elephants. For Asa, the choice of names was obvious: Coca, Cola, Delicious, and Refreshing. Only in America can a Methodist win a zoo in a poker game and name the animals after his own commercial product. But Asa's Briarcliff neighbors weren't too keen on having so many beasts of the wild nearby, especially whenever they escaped. To their great relief, the poker game collection was later transferred to the Atlanta Zoo.

Florence herself was a shrewd businesswoman, as she demonstrated when Asa put her in charge of Westview Cemetery. She marketed it into the most exclusive and profitable burial ground in Atlanta. 'Carlo,' she chuckled, 'people were just dying to get in there!' Consisting of some 600 acres, Westview was the largest cemetery in the South. Knowing this would be their final resting place, Asa and Florence took great pains to make the grounds as beautiful as possible. They oversaw the construction of Westview Mausoleum, a huge and stately edifice of stone, marble and stained glass begun in the mid-1930s and completed in 1946. Cathedral-like in its dimensions, the crowning glory was the Florence Candler Chapel, an architectural accomplishment that few Atlantans know about, even today. Here, the decorative program reached a crescendo of adornment, with richly carved furniture, paintings by Athos Menniboni (who had also created similar artworks for the Mirador Room at the Capitol City Club), and of course, Florence's initials emblazoned over every door.[3] But the Chapel was not so much about Florence as Asa's love for her. Visiting the Chapel, which she did on a regular basis after Asa's death, brought him back to her for a few precious moments, and she derived solace from it.

Like all great characters, Florence was not above a few contradictions and as she gleefully recounted the past, it was sometimes hard to interpret the twinkle in her eye. By the time I moved into her house, she had sold the cemetery. 'Carlo,' she said, 'we made a *killing*!'

Florence and Asa were soul mates. Since Asa did not immediately remarry after the death of his first wife, Florence was not branded with the stigma Southerners sometimes attach to a rich man's second wife. Indeed, the family loved her and accepted her as their own. Asa was a devout Methodist, Florence a devoted Baptist. With Asa, she would attend services at First Methodist on Sunday morning but she would come alone to Druid Hills Baptist in the evening. She played a full role in society while he was alive, but after his death she was altogether more private. Perennially youthful herself, she sought out the company of young people, and was happy to revert to a calmer life-style.

When someone at the Church dared to raise a judgmental eyebrow regarding my residency, she clarified the situation crisply and with characteristic candor. 'Carlo doesn't live *with* me; he lives *in my house*' – always one for the neat quip, dear Florence. In her bedroom hung a small framed motto: 'Never explain: your friends don't need it, and your enemies wouldn't believe you anyway.'

She was always active in the church. Entertaining her Bible class to luncheon one day, it became obvious that her guests' interests lay primarily in the house's elegant trappings, as they kept commenting about this *beautiful* marble statue, that *elegant* music box, that *gorgeous* oriental carpet, that *divine* oil paintin'. Florence held her peace for a while but finally could stand no more. Ushering them out of the front door after the coffee cups had been collected, she declared, 'Ladies, while I appreciate your comments about my *things*, just remember that the most beautiful thing in my house is *me*!' In most other women, such a quip would have had the sure-fire ring of conceit. In Florence's case, it exemplified a disdain for those who judged others solely on the strength of their possessions.

Florence was the greatest fun. Mornings began with the sharp knock of her cane on my door. She was enjoying the new day, and she damn well wanted

---

3 Many consider Menniboni the greatest painter of birds since Audubon. In the Mirador Room, his glass panels feature birds and flowers indigenous to Georgia.

company – now. 'Kid, get outta that bed!' This was never easy, since the Candler beds were all custom-made, the mattresses stuffed with horsehair. They were supremely comfortable and difficult to vacate. As I dragged myself up and pulled on a robe, Florence would bid me to the grand dining room, furnished with all the best pieces from the old mansion: antique sideboards, a heavy clock of solid silver (bolted into the wall to prevent disaster), épergne, sparkling crystal, crisp linens and highly polished silver flatware. Breakfast was mandatory, the portions gargantuan. Louise, the cook and housekeeper, whipped up the food, which was presented by 'Slim,' the chauffeur-handyman-butler. The menu customarily included freshly-squeezed orange juice, grits, Jimmie Dean sausage patties, thick back-bacon slices, salt-rising bread from the Rhodes Bakery (a discontinued line, but still made specially for Florence), buttermilk biscuits, eggs to order – and these just the standard items that came unbidden. Louise would make anything else on demand. When supplies became diminished or Florence had some other desire, she would step on a floor buzzer – surely her own personal 'Great to Pedal' toe-piston – plainly audible above the hubbub of the kitchen. Louise or Slim would come flying through the swing-door and snap to attention: 'Yes, Miz Canle?'

These were old and trusted servants. Slim had been hired in 1929 as a gardener and was eventually brought 'into the house.' Presumably, if he didn't wander off with the pruning shears, he wasn't going to pinch the silver. By the time I arrived on the scene, Slim had seen so much grandeur that he was unfazable: witnessing everything while saying nothing. And he was still slim. Pete Rich, a friend from Druid Hills who spent a lot of time with Florence, remarked that it was like being waited on by Methuselah himself.

The servants' relationship to Mrs. Candler was strictly old-fashioned. The kitchen was equipped like a first-class hotel. Every appliance was of commercial catering standard and size. The large central marble preparation table had come from Briarcliff, but had been cut in half in order to fit into Buckhead. Ironically, Florence forbade her staff to use most of the labor-saving devices, denouncing them as wasteful. She insisted that Louise chop all the food and wash glasswear, plates and cutlery by hand. Clearly the kitchen was a foreign land to Florence. 'I'm a short order cook,' she would tell me, 'the shorter the order, the better the cooking.'

As with most things, Florence had strong views on food. 'Take the grease out of Southern cookin', Carlo,' she proclaimed, 'and you take away all the taste.' She was quite right, of course, but when she wasn't looking, in a valiant attempt to achieve a healthier diet, I would wrap the sausage patties in my thick linen napkin, position the parcel on the floor and, using the balls of my feet, squeeze out as much grease as possible. Alas, this was only to partial avail. A healthy cuisine was not for Florence, and she was scornful of anything like muesli or bran. 'I don't serve that *leftist* food in this house. Roughage is for cattle, and I'm *not* a cow.'

Equally resolute on breakfast table decorum, she deplored my arrival in anything less than a suit and tie, even though I shuffled in most mornings in a bathrobe and slippers. 'Oh, Carlo,' she would sigh, 'my husband *always* dressed for breakfast in a three-piece suit, necktie and diamond stick-pin. *He* knew that breakfast was the most *impo'tant* meal of the day.' Lunchtime was never a simple sandwich, always a proper meal. I well remember Louise's outstanding crabcakes and special Southern ham. Here, Florence's one cooking tip came into play, that Louise should 'pour a warm Ko-Kola over that ham when it comes out of the oven, 'cause it brings out the flavour *so naaaiiiccce.*'

Paradoxically, Coca-Cola was a rarity in the household. I once offered Florence a glass, and she snapped, 'Kid, don't you know that stuff's *bad* for you? Why, if you put a rusty nail in a glass of Ko-Kola overnight, it'll come out shinin' like a brand new penny come morning! Hooo-ee! Just think what that stuff does to a person's *insides*!' Although Florence was a member of the Baptist faith, the consumption of alcohol for her must have been strictly medicinal for, when it came to the cocktail hour, she preferred what I suspected was a time-honored Southern concoction: Jack Daniel's, grapefruit juice and shaved ice. 'Never trust someone who doesn't know how to savor a liquor cocktail. And let me remind you Carlo, I've *never* spent a night in a hospital.' I can certainly vouch for this as indeed the only night dear Florence ever spent in a hospital was the night she died.

If Florence had one failing, it was unquestionably driving. She always had a new Cadillac, the largest one available that was not actually a limousine (which, heaven forbid, would have been ostentatious). They invariably came from Capitol Automobile Company of Atlanta, whose president and founder had ostensibly taught Florence to drive. While he was probably a very nice man, he can't have been much of a driving instructor for, behind the wheel, Florence was a one-woman assault weapon. On occasions, she did allow Slim (or me, once I had obtained my license) to drive her around, but otherwise she cherished this palpable means of asserting her independence. At least in that aspect, she succeeded wildly, utilizing a combination of lumbering gas barge and unique driving style to intimidate everything in her path.

Florence was not a tall woman, and she could barely peer over the steering wheel. Understandably perhaps, she was afraid of turning left – or, come to think of it, right. Nevertheless, she overcame her fear by pointing the wheel, shutting her eyes tight and flooring it. '*Surely* those *naaiice* people will get out of the way if they see I'm coming,' she said, and let me assure you from bitter personal experience, she was not joking. Her method of parking wasn't much different. She just stepped on the accelerator until the car hit something. The Helen Keller school of parallel parking.

Of course, being a 'character' is a Southern specialty, and Florence certainly knew the routine. In this role she was more elegant, effective and successful than any other character I'd met. Widely read and travelled, Florence rarely discussed anything unless she knew about it firsthand. Accordingly her words assumed an unmistakable authority. She was a talented communicator who knew how to express her ideas and her emotions. She also knew how to convey excitement, not only by her choice of words and inflection, but through her eyes and facial expressions. Even in the simplest conversation, she could turn my views around and make me want to explore things more deeply. Most importantly, she insisted on living by her own rules, not just because she could afford to, but because her personality demanded it.

Communication, expressing emotions, conveying excitement, and the responsible assertion of individuality: are these not the first tasks of the musician? Florence helped me to learn these skills first in words. By her daily existence she further proved that a born 'character' could make that fact work to one's advantage. And in her approach to me lay perhaps the most important lesson. Florence cared for me not as a mother would, but on equal terms, as one adult to another. I had spent a childhood feeling, to some extent, that adults were there to cut me down and curb my natural tendencies. Florence took the opposite view, building me up and spurring me on to new heights. Furthermore, she placed few restrictions on her affection for me. Perhaps her only condition was that I should prove my worth. Florence knew better than anyone that I yearned for inspiration far more than money. And she always had another trick up her perfectly tailored sleeve.

Florence was an ace at producing surprises, made all the better because she knew how to keep a secret. One morning, while seated at the typical oleaginous breakfast, she brought up the subject of future visitors. Oh and by the way, one of her dearest friends had just called out of the blue and would be visiting in a few days' time. By any chance, had I ever heard of the brilliant virtuoso organist Virgil Fox? Godfathers! By any chance had Mrs. Candler ever heard of Coca-Cola? Florence delighted in my excitement.

Soon enough, the house was bustling with preparations for the great man's arrival. Florence had invited several other guests, so I was moved out of my room and onto one of the living room sofas. Who could have cared? From the moment Virgil set foot on the premises, the house was transformed into magic territory; me an instant convert to his enchanting personality. The man radiated inspiration and kindness, both of which were underscored with charm and an outrageous sense of humor. At last, Florence finally had some real competition and she reveled in it.

Virgil and I spent the better part of two days together, talking non-stop organ and music. After dinner, we would play duets on the Mason & Hamlin piano while the others chattered away with gossip and clever tales, coaxed along by the general *bonhomie*. It is amazing that anyone ever got to bed. However, as I drifted off to sleep, Virgil draped his famous cape over me, before insisting that Slim set every repeater and case clock in the house to the *off* position. It was a small but indicative foretaste of the consideration he would later show me.

Virgil's skills as a raconteur were greatly enhanced by an unmistakable vocal tone and inflection, rich with character and Midwestern twang. Those lucky enough to have attended his recitals will recall it well and fortunately, it is captured clearly on some of his recordings. He could put the most hilarious but effective spin on dramatic words, like 'hairrrrraising' and 'suuu*preme*,' not to mention the ways in which he strung words together.[4]

The next day, Virgil and I drove up Ponce de Leon Avenue to Druid Hills Baptist so that I could play for him. I went through about forty-five minutes of music, mostly Franck, Bach and Buxtehude. Looking back on that experience, I feel much the same about it as I do my NCSA audition: too fast, too furious, too precocious, too much. Virgil paid me a kind but not unqualified compliment. '*Chicken*,' he said (his moniker for any youngster under 100), 'in the tip of the little finger of your right hand, you possess more talent than any fifty organists strung together.' (Wow! I thought, not bad.) '*However*,' he continued (my heart began to sink), 'as I give with one hand, I am obliged to take with the other. You have the work of *one hundred* organists remaining to do. Only then, will you get it right.' He was entirely correct.

Later, I would realize that Virgil's technique had come only with tremendous

---

4 Two instances are the *Bach Live at Fillmore East* LP recording on Decca (re-released under the same title on CD by MCA Classics, No. MCAD2-9827A) which captures the premiere of this show at New York's Fillmore East, and *Soli Deo Gloria* on Bainbridge (No. BCD 8005), the two-CD recording of Virgil's 1979 recital at the Riverside Church. On this last disc, Virgil's loquacious addresses are entirely typical. Who else would take five entire minutes lecturing an audience on how to sing one hymn?

discipline. Even late in life, he continued rigorous daily practice, and before every concert he chained himself to the console. One perfect example was the 1966 national convention of the American Guild of Organists, held in Atlanta. Virgil, remarkably, had been excluded from the main body of the program. Not to be outmaneuvered, he arranged to give a pre-convention recital at the city's most prominent reformed synagogue. Typically, he was practicing down to the last moment, while the audience lined up outside. Because he didn't want them to hear a single note beforehand, he insisted on keeping every window closed, even though it was a sweltering, Southern July and the building lacked air-conditioning. When the capacity audience was finally admitted, a sauna was transformed into a steambath and Virgil had little option other than to remove his trousers and perform in his underwear while seated on a bath towel. Fortunately, the console was situated in a gallery so that when he took his bows over the rail, no one could see his state of undress – except for those in the gallery with him!

The man possessed boundless, magnetic energy. Who else, during a busy visit to Atlanta, would have found the time to teach me to swim, and do it with such conviction? Virgil was constantly singing the praises of swimming, and decreed that I should '*par-take!*' We used the pool at the home of Florence's step-grandson, John Candler, whereupon with loud instructions and dramatic gestures, Virgil demonstrated correct breathing and the basic strokes. He did it all so seriously that it was hard to keep from giggling.

Looking back on all of this, it is amazing that I actually spent any time away from Florence's elegantly appointed house. But I was young, enjoying my friends at the Capitol City Club and elsewhere, busy playing in church and developing a life of my own. Likewise, although Florence had found a new chum, she certainly continued with her round of activities. And there was much to do in Atlanta and beyond.

Many fortunate people fell within the sphere of Florence's generosity. She loved Virgil dearly and helped him in numerous ways. The most visible gesture had been the gift of a Cadillac (another gas-guzzler from the Capitol Automobile Company). True, it was not quite as enormous as Florence's, but it was every bit as unwieldy. Riding with Virgil was both hilarious and frightening, since he was a good driver but didn't mind taking risks – in fact, the same could be said of his console technique!

In earlier years, Florence had also been a quietly strong supporter of Virgil's activities as organist at the fashionable Riverside Church in New York City. For instance, in 1955, she underwrote a goodly portion of the inaugural concert on the new Æolian-Skinner – no simple recital this, since it also involved Dimitri Mitropoulos and the New York Philharmonic Orchestra. While Florence professed herself pleased with the outcome, she did admit that it was 'a mighty loud concert. I could just as well as have stayed in Atlanta, left the windows open, and avoided all those damned Yankees.'

She rarely made reference to these acts of philanthropy. When I later learned about her many kindnesses from Virgil and asked her directly about them, she would quietly pass the matter off, saying such things as 'Oh, you have to help these poor starving artists out.' Her circle of musical friends was certainly wide and, at the other end of the spectrum, she was a good friend to Liberace. Although his outrageous stage attire did not meet with her approval, his programs certainly appealed to her, and she attended them from time to time.

At Druid Hills Baptist, Florence generously financed a thorough rebuilding and revoicing of the organ, and the complete remodeling of the front of the church to provide a larger choir loft and direct sight line to the console. What's more, she then underwrote Virgil's fee for the inaugural recital. Through another friend in Atlanta, Charles Walker, we devised a *son et lumière* presentation for this performance. Charles set up not only lights, lights and more lights of varying shades, but also every kind of theatrical effect machine including cloud projectors for the ceiling and a mirror-ball which cast a particular magic. Attending every practice session to ensure a unified result, Charles then orchestrated the effects as Virgil played. The result was dignified and certainly enhanced the music. Virgil was delighted and was later to employ such devices in many of his later concerts, kindly crediting me, Charles and Florence's checkbook with planting the seed for his subsequent sound-and-light concerts, including that at Bill Graham's Fillmore East rock-palace in New York City. Back in Atlanta, Charles and I did several similar recitals at Druid Hills Baptist; the church soon being nicknamed *Loews Ponce de Leon*. Had it been in Britain, it would probably have been called *Palladium Ponce de Leon*.

Although she gave quietly, Florence loved seeing her money work. She gave to the symphony, theater and opera with dependable regularity but without fanfare. But she never gave blindly. I remember her being approached to help save the Atlanta Fox Theater, a most amazing example of neo-Moorish/Aztec/Art Deco completed in 1928–29 and seating 5,000. The Fox is what is known as an 'Atmospheric Theater.' The auditorium interior is decorated in *trompe-l'oeil* to resemble an exotic exterior, the ceiling a most convincing sky. Cloud machines (called Brenographs) projected onto the ceiling for daytime effects, while twinkling lights created the night sky. The Fox also boasted the largest Möller organ ever built for a theater. It was a dazzling, brilliant and unquestionably successful instrument. At the time it was installed, it was the largest theater organ in the United States, and was only surpassed in 1932 by the Wurlitzer in New York's Radio City Music Hall.

While Florence liked certain things about the Fox, especially the atmospheric effects, she was not entirely impressed and, since the theater had been built during her lifetime, the historical aspect meant little to her. At the time of their appeal for her help, it could no longer support itself as a movie house. However, and as all the commercial developers could not fail to realize, it sat on highly desirable prime downtown real estate on Peachtree Street. Fully aware of this, Florence declined to contribute. 'It's too darned big for the lot,' she said and, what's more, she had a point, since the theater came right out to the sidewalks and had no grounds or elegant approaches. But the final straw was that there was no proper drive to allow patrons to alight from their cars. 'A lady shouldn't have to step in the gutter before going into a performance.' Case closed! Fortunately, other means of support were secured, and this unique theater has continued to this day as a successful performing arts center.

My good friend Charles Walker, the lighting genius behind Virgil's Druid Hills concert, played an active role in the initial stages of the effort to save the Fox. Born in Griffin, Georgia, Charles had a passion for the conservation and preservation of fair-ground carousels – he now owns no fewer than four – which he has lovingly restored. Through him I came to know others in his circle, most notably Luis Maza and Dick Munroe, leading lights in Atlanta's dramatic community. Originally from Cuba, Luis was a set and costume designer; Dick was an enterprising arts administrator and treasurer of the national Fédération des Alliances Françaises aux États-Unis.[5] Both spoke several languages and were recognized as cultured members of the Atlanta arts scene. Where Florence appreciated the arts from the standpoint of a benefactor and audience member, these fellows were on the front lines. Together they owned the Pocket Theater on Courtland Street, something like Atlanta's off-Broadway. To pay the bills, they staged light operettas, musicals and some of the more standard theatrical repertoire; to gain a reputation, they put on risqué shows such as *The Glad Girls* and even *The Boys in the Band*.

Since Luis could create anything on the set, he did the same for the house he shared with Dick, filling the place with unique furnishings. And just as they were fluent in languages, so too they were proficient in many national styles of

5 Dick was an ardent Francophile who remained active in the local Alliance Française d'Atlanta until his untimely death. In January 1989 the French government presented him with the Palmes Académiques. In addition, he was a sculptor and a fine theatrical director.

cuisine; Cuban, French, Italian, Spanish, all created with typical Mediterranean flair. These feasts were marvelous, and brought together our many friends. A favorite after-dinner entertainment was playing the piano in turn. Luis introduced me to the works of Cuban pianist-composer Ignacio Cervantes, this elegant music blending mid-19th century European ideas with a distinctive flavor. Florence would come over on occasion and when my mother and grandmother visited, the guys hosted a big soirée in their honor. Years later, when Jean Guillou, the celebrated French organist, played a recital on the Casavant at nearby Emory University, they again responded rapidly to my tentative request that they give a party for Jean and his wife Suzanne. And what a swell evening it was.

During my time in Atlanta, Luis and Dick decided to close the Pocket Theater. There was so much work involved in its running and they wanted to move on to other challenges. The Pocket became Luis' design studio, and he continued to work for private clients, mostly for exhibitions, museum shows, or freelance work for other theater companies. In fall 1991, Dick died in a tragic accident while bicycling in Nova Scotia. It was a terrible blow to Luis, his many friends and the entire Atlanta arts community. Luis carried on, although now, semi-retired, he lives quietly in Miami Beach, while still maintaining the Atlanta residence which holds so many happy memories. I stay with him when I visit, taking real pleasure in Rudi, to whom Luis refers as a seeing-eye cat and watchdog rolled into one. Perhaps the most butch feline I've met, his food bowl is labelled DOG. Their other cat, Hysterica, has since gone on to Pussy Heaven.

Another wonderful friend from my formative years was Tommy Teaver who played at the Metropolitan Community Church. The church was actually the old Highland Theater on Highland Avenue (within two blocks of Druid Hills Baptist), and was home to a recycled Skinner organ which Tommy had obtained from a church in Savannah and Charles Walker had helped to install. Charles introduced me to Tommy, who already knew of me (I had become something of a local celebrity since getting the Druid Hills job at such a young age) and we fast became pals.

I had forgotten, until recently reminded by Charles, of my insatiable desire to visit new organs. He pointedly describes it as an addiction – I simply *had* to play a new organ every other day. Soon enough we had exhausted all the local venues, then everything of interest in Georgia, and eventually a large portion of the Southeast. North of the Mason-Dixon line seemed the next logical goal, New York the obvious ultimate destination. This desire culminated in two road trips in Florence's golden Cadillac, with me, Charles Walker, Tommy Teaver and Charles Poole, who acted as the local representative for Casavant organ sales. The first trip was extensive; we stopped in North Carolina to see my folks, and also at Duke Chapel to play the large Æolian. We then went on to Richmond, and played several Æolian-Skinners as well as an exceedingly fine Möller. From there we cruised up the freeway to Washington D.C., visiting such famous churches as the National Cathedral and the Basilica of the National Shrine of the Immaculate Conception.

Finally we reached New York and set up base at the Gotham Hotel on Fifth Avenue, directly opposite Fifth Avenue Presbyterian and just blocks from St. Thomas's Church, St. Patrick's Cathedral and the Rockefeller Center. Our first stop was the Austin across the street, followed by the revised Æolian-Skinner at St. Thomas's, and then the large old Kilgen at St. Patrick's Cathedral. Here we were beguiled by the magnificent acoustics into which wafted oceans of tone, including the most enchanting string and celeste choruses imaginable – nor could we fail to be moved by the stunning organ case and the building which housed it. Perhaps less romantic, but equally unforgettable, was the massive 40 horsepower DC motor which brought the giant blower to life. It was only accessible via a winding, narrow staircase in the dusty southwest tower and although I had to blink twice, I'm sure I spotted Quasimodo glaring down on us from the belfry above!

Most memorable of all, however, was the Cathedral of St. John the Divine, the largest Gothic cathedral in the world. It is not merely that this vast building made an unforgettable impression on me; it is that in the South, we simply didn't have anything remotely like it. The organist, Dr. Alec Wyton, could not have been more hospitable. He had us sit in the crossing so we could hear the Æolian-Skinner properly. After building up the organ to its full resources, he then introduced the incomparable State Trumpet, sited at the west end (500 feet from the console) and speaking on an exorbitant fifty inches of wind pressure. Liquid fire, that sound; its report transcendent. Afterward, Dr. Wyton kindly let me play, so that I could for myself release chords into that immense acoustic (in excess of twelve seconds' reverberation). He also took pains to show us the two charming chapel organs – a first-rate visit all around. It was nearly all too much, but not quite.

True Southerners that we were, we made new friends everywhere. Not far from St. John the Divine we discovered St. Michael's Church on Amsterdam Avenue, home to a newly imported von Beckerath organ from Germany. As we entered we were overwhelmed: the windows and much of the interior decoration was all priceless vintage Tiffany. We heard someone practicing a clearly difficult but intriguing modern piece (it turned out to be Guillou's *Saga No. 6*). At the conclusion, I started applauding and cheering 'Bravo.' The organist came to the gallery rail, revealing both her beauty and her surprise. Her name was Cherry Rhodes, and I was surprised to learn that even with a name like that, she was a Yankee. Cherry was at once informal; she was (and remains) a gorgeous gal, with a knock-'em-dead smile that has lost nothing of its force over time. She beckoned us all upstairs, and we took turns in playing the organ, which had many attractive qualities.

Once we had finished, we were standing in the doorway about to come down the loft stairs. Without a nanosecond of warning, Cherry reached over, grabbed a handful of my hair and tugged hard. I shrieked; she shrieked; we all shrieked together into the glorious reverberation. 'What gives, woman?' I gasped. Not only were her actions inexplicable, it darned well *hurt!* Then, the story came pouring out. For as long as she could remember, she had fantasized about ripping the hairpiece from a toupée-wearing man. My hair was so thick, she reckoned it *had* to be ersatz, and besides which, she instinctively felt I wouldn't mind being the target of her long-standing prankish desire. Even though her explanation compensated a little for my pain, I think Cherry was so embarrassed that she invited us to her home nearby for a most memorable chicken dinner. I'm delighted to say that I've remained good friends with this fine organist who has also become one of America's most respected teachers. And in the competition for the world's loudest laugh, Cherry and I are still neck and neck.

At long last, we had to face the long trek home. We called in along the way first at colonial Williamsburg in Virginia, and then further south in Salisbury, North Carolina (home of the Brawleys and the Isenhours) before at last reaching Atlanta. If we had learnt nothing else, we had certainly learnt how to persuade our way craftily into a wide variety of organ lofts. By no means was every church organist or secretary as kind as Alec Wyton or Cherry Rhodes, and some of them were, quite justifiably, cautious of strangers dropping in to play instruments without prior appointment. A couple of them were just bloody minded. But Southern charm can thaw the most icy reserve (especially when it's surrounded not just by one but by four Southerners). In the end we nearly always managed to waltz our way to every console.

Tommy Teaver has the distinction of being my first ever agent. He began booking recitals in the local vicinity, some of which Florence kindly underwrote. Through it all, we got to know each other better as we traveled back and forth to performance venues. One of my recitals was to be played on an old Möller at a downtown church in a small town near Atlanta. We arrived early in the afternoon, only to discover that what had been sold to us as a comprehensive and up-to-date instrument turned out to be a ghastly old thing that hadn't been touched since its installation in the 1920s, entirely unsuited to the big program I had prepared.

Luckily, Tommy knew that just down the street was a new church with an equally new organ, far more appropriate to my needs. 'You know the manual keys on these Möller consoles?' he asked pointedly. 'I wonder if we couldn't make one of them fail, say, middle F, and then the concert would be *quite* unplayable.' Brilliant! He pulled a small screwdriver from his briefcase, opened the keydesk, tinkered with a tiny spring and soon enough middle F fell down, slain and temporarily dead.

Now we had to carry the drama through to the final curtain. First, we called the Möller service man, who, conveniently, lived a hundred miles away. Next, I ex-plained to the pastor that a great many of my pieces were in the key of F. 'I'm playing the Bach Toccata in *F*, and then there's the Handel Concerto in *F*, and the Widor Toccata, I guess that's in *F* too ...' He agreed (did he have any choice, the poor man?), so we telephoned the pastor of our alternative venue and he readily welcomed me to give the recital there. I practiced, set up my pistons, and went to change.

Deception always comes with a price tag. The organist at the first church lived in Atlanta, but kept a motel room to obviate the need for constant commuting. He had arranged for me to use the room as changing quarters before my recital. It was decidedly seedy, and after discovering a drawer filled with 'French letters' and suggestive reading materials, it dawned on Tommy and me that perhaps he used the room for passing encounters of a questionable kind. I took a shower and shaved, but had forgotten to bring along any after-shave lotion. Looking over the lengthy row of toiletries on the bathroom shelf, I came across a bottle labeled A-200, which sounded like a fancy new brand of cologne. I slapped it onto my face and neck profusely. Within seconds, my skin was burning up. I yelled at Tommy, who grabbed the bottle, glanced at it and yelled back, 'You great fool!' As I now know, A-200 kills body lice and, in the process, gives off a foul stench. I doused my face in water but the clock was against us and we had to rush to the venue to start the performance on time. But the burning continued and throughout the recital, tears of pain streamed down my cheeks. Addressing the audience through swollen eyes, I must have appeared quite emotional, and although this incident would have come to pass no matter which of the two churches I had played in, I nonetheless ascribed it to our tinkering with the Möller. I know divine retribution when I see it.

CHAPTER FOUR

THE GREAT BATH

My late-teen years saw an increase in both organ study and recitals, which gained me a wider recognition in the greater Atlanta community. I welcomed the exposure, the experience and of course the applause, all of which provided a greater incentive to learn new music. In addition to recital and concert work, I continued to be busy with the organ and choirs at Druid Hills Baptist Church, as well as in my rich social life with Florence and friends. I also tried to attend as many other musical events as possible, most notably concerts of the Robert Shaw Chorale and the Atlanta Symphony, to which Florence subscribed. Even the High Museum of Art featured regular programs of chamber music in addition to its fine exhibitions.

Nevertheless, while other events were to take me away increasingly, if only temporarily, Atlanta would remain my primary residence. In a very real sense, Virgil's visit had changed everything. It had converted my dream into reality and transformed an unapproachable star into a role-model and mentor. While I doubt that Florence had engineered his visit solely for my benefit, I think she knew perfectly well how it would alter the direction of my life. She actively encouraged my friendship with Virgil and not only suggested that I take lessons from him but also generously pledged to provide whatever financial support was necessary. I can just see the ghost of E. Power Biggs smirking to himself that the wish I had uttered in Duke Chapel should come true.

Even though he was widely considered the organ's *enfant terrible*, Virgil Fox had been a wonder from the start. Born in 1912 in Princeton,

Illinois,[1] and after childhood piano study with Hugh Price, he took a year's organ instruction from Wilhelm Middelschulte, Chicago's most prominent organist in the late 1920s and a native of Leipzig. From there, he won a scholarship to the oldest music conservatory in America, the Peabody in Baltimore, where he studied with Louis Robert. At Peabody, Virgil became the first one-year student in the school's history to graduate with the conservatory's highest honor – the Artist's Diploma. After Peabody, he went to France to study with Marcel Dupré, and made his European debut in London's Kingsway Hall. Returning to New York, he then made his American debut at the Wanamaker Auditorium at age twenty-one. From then on, it was one success after another; recordings for Victor, prominent recitals and rave reviews; being named head of the Peabody organ department in 1938 and subsequently, in 1946, organist of New York's fashionable Riverside Church, in which post he was to remain until 1957, continuing on through 1963 as artist-in-residence.

At that time, no organist could hope for a more prestigious position than Riverside. John D. Rockefeller Jr. had established this famous New York City church as a non-sectarian Protestant parish almost specifically to provide a magnificent backdrop for the preaching of Harry Emerson Fosdick. Completed in 1930, the towering neo-Gothic building rises high above the banks of the Hudson on Riverside Drive. In 1948, two years after Virgil arrived, Æolian-Skinner installed an imposing five-manual console, and between 1952 and 1955 they built a new organ to go with it. Indeed, it was the dedication concert for this very instrument with the New York Philharmonic to which Florence Candler had subscribed.

Virgil treasured this position in such an influential church. It offered not only a lofty pedestal from which to launch an international career, but a new organ and console (both to his design) that acted as a laboratory in which to refine and record his organ art. From the Riverside console, he undertook a series of superb LPs for RCA, Columbia and Capitol in the 1950s and early 1960s. When I came to know him, he had already left Riverside to devote his time exclusively to recordings, recitals and concerts. His situation bore clear evidence of his success, since only a handful of organists have ever been able to support themselves without a teaching or church position.

1 Princeton, Illinois (not to be confused with the university town of Princeton, New Jersey) lies approximately 100 miles west of Chicago on Interstate 80. Virgil is buried there in the Prairie Repose Cemetery.

Of all the characters I have encountered, Virgil Fox was undeniably the most colorful. Intensity was his byword and he wanted nothing less than to heighten all five senses for those around him. The company or circumstances didn't matter. He was the same person whether he was amongst his intimates or before an audience of thousands.

Color was incredibly important to Virgil. As a youth, he had learned to paint surprisingly well, and some of his early canvasses hung in his home, displaying a penchant for light and color very early on. The same ethos spilled over into his music, as well as into the rest of his life. Few people could get away with wearing a full-length black cape lined in red satin, but somehow Virgil pulled it off. Musically, his playing drew its greatest subtleties from his relentless search for color.

The sense of smell also figured high on Virgil's list. At home, he was adamant about having fresh flowers, not merely for the visual delight but the variety of fragrance they afforded. The house itself had an additional aroma due to an air-perfuming system. Small vases hidden in each room were filled with scent, dispensing a woodsy whiff throughout the house.[2] If beautiful aroma was important, then rank smells were a capital offense. When Virgil later visited me at Girard College during my tenure as college organist, I had worked feverishly on a hot summer day in an uncooled building in preparation for his visit. But Virgil arrived early before I had had a chance to shower. We embraced nonetheless, and he quickly pulled me aside, whispering, '*Chicken*, I'm the *only* person who can say this to you: soap and water are *practically free*.'

Virgil lived in Englewood, New Jersey, just across the Hudson River from Manhattan. Studying with him thus entailed a few logistical hurdles: the distance from Atlanta was one, and I was still a full-time church organist who had begun to settle into the musical and artistic life of Atlanta. But to work with Virgil? This was no time for excuses! Besides, Florence was pushing me to do so. When she destined that I should come to know Virgil better, she knew that the sheer act of keeping company with him would turn out to be an education all itself.

As it happened, commuting to Englewood became second nature. I would fly or take the train, each trip lasting several weekdays, during which Virgil would give me lessons. I also took part in the organ masterclasses he began holding at his house around that time. From the train station or airport, I would hail a cab to Virgil's, and be received by Merle Webster, the caretaker and cook, whose

---

2 I can still smell the home-perfuming system, since I use it in my own home. The vases and fragrance are still manufactured by Edco Fragrance, Inc. of Whitestone, New York. The fragrance is called 'Trefle.'

efficient and orderly manner kept the house spotless and running smoothly – certainly as smoothly as anything could run where Virgil was involved. And Merle had a lot to look after: a 27-room gray stone, ivyclad English-style residence, a big garden, a full-length swimming pool, and a carriage house out back where Virgil's manager, Richard Torrence, lived with his associate Marshall Yeager. Virgil shared the main house with his companion, David Snyder.[3]

Virgil's convictions, religious faith, abhorrence of tobacco and alcohol, mania for cleanliness and zaniness, set the general pattern for home life. These tenets manifested themselves in his three daily devotions: tireless organ practice sessions, swimming and the ritual meal time socializing – each taking their priority in that order. His practice was its own religion, a ceaseless attempt to attain perfection. Others recall his late-night sessions at Riverside, partly hard work, partly social in nature. Sometimes he would spend an evening gathering chums around the console to play for them and at other times he would work diligently by himself or with a few devoted friends. Sometimes he would hold court early in the evening, later asking to be left alone for serious practice.

I regret having arrived too late on the scene to join fully in these events, tales of which have become part of Virgil lore. The late Jean-Jacques Courtemanche (a French-Canadian whom I knew in Atlanta through Dick Munroe and Luis Maza)[4] told of having arranged to spend an evening at Riverside with Virgil. Jean-Jacques arrived early and, not wishing to disturb him before the appointed hour, seated himself quietly in the rear gallery. Unfortunately, he got locked in but, still not wishing to interrupt the master, sat patiently and listened. The uncensored Virgil practicing by himself was by no means light-hearted and certainly incredibly intense.

High on Virgil's practice list that night was Max Reger's Choral Fantasy on *How Brightly Shines the Morning Star*, a work which, in time, I was to study with him in depth. Of this monumentally difficult composition, Virgil used to

---

3 It was rumored one of Joseph P. Kennedy's mistresses was the actress Gloria Swanson, and furthermore that he had built her a mansion down the street from Virgil's. Years later, Marshall Yeager had the chance to meet Miss Swanson and asked if she lived on Palisades Avenue. She denied it vociferously.

4 It was for Jean-Jacques, Dick and the Alliance Française d'Atlanta that I performed perhaps the most ambitious concert of my early career. *L'évolution de la musique d'orgue en France* was given at Druid Hills Baptist Church and consisted of works of twelve composers, from Clérambault to Widor, Vierne and Langlais. With Jean-Jacques' in-depth commentary before each selection, plus the actual playing of the music, the program lasted almost four hours – without an intermission! The experience elicited the priceless comment from Don Westfield a few years later that, in his experience, 'There's never been an organ recital that's been too *short*.'

say, 'it is the mathematics and complexity of Sebastian Bach *times five!*' Jean-Jacques related how Virgil repeated certain measures and sections over and over, getting it right not just once or twice but twenty or thirty times in succession. In due course, he arrived at a particularly demanding passage not even he could master, every attempt failing in some respect. As the frustration mounted to a frenzy, Virgil stormed off the bench. He got down on his knees and pounded his fists on the chancel floor, screaming at his Maker for not granting him the gift of being able to play things perfectly. Gradually, the tempest subsided, and Virgil sat down in a choir stall to cool off. At last, he climbed back on the bench. This time, he played the passage perfectly, sighed, and continued his rehearsal.

There was no less fervor in Virgil's daily swimming ritual. The mansion had not originally possessed a pool, so he had had a large solarium and heated pool built on one side. It must have cost a fortune both to build and maintain, but no matter – it remained an object of tremendous pride, and he kept up the daily regimen I had first witnessed in Atlanta. Although I would sometimes join in, Virgil did not require company for encouragement. Nor did he neglect exercise or practice if company were present. Henry Hunt, one of Virgil's longtime friends, recalls that even at holidays with a full house, Virgil would retire to the console for at least two hours, often three or four.

After practice and swimming, food, or more accurately dinner followed naturally. This essentially meant the bantering company of friends. Where others relax over a meal, Virgil transformed it into a high ceremonial event. Although he had several favourite eateries in Englewood and New York, what I remember most is his loyalty to the Stouffer's chain of restaurants, which he sought out everywhere. At the Fifth Avenue Stouffer's, near Rockefeller Center and St. Patrick's Cathedral, he enjoyed a first-name relationship with the wait-staff. He kept up with these people, knowing their backgrounds and even the churches they attended. They, in turn, greeted and treated him like family.

Stouffer's was not gourmet food, but solid and well-prepared home-style American fare. By no means a vegetarian, Virgil was nonetheless keen on vegetables and salad; '*Forget* about the meat,' he would say, 'tell me about the *vegetables.*' He was mad for beets, and always ordered them, regardless of how they would be prepared. He insisted on a proper three-course supper: appetizer or soup, meat, potatoes, vegetables and – that great anticipated climax – the hot fudge sundae. Double portions were mandatory. 'Honey,' he would say to the waitress, 'I want *twice* as much of that *gorgeous hot chocolate sauce.*' In fact, it didn't have to be mealtime to have ice cream, and we were regularly heading down to Baumgart's ice cream parlour in central Englewood.

Exceedingly particular about the preparation of his food, he would elaborate his likes and dislikes to the waitress. Once in Michigan, he was so demanding about how he wanted his steak prepared that he actually went into the kitchen, cooked it himself, and brought it back to the booth. Another typical incident I recall was at the Philadelphia Penn Center Stouffer's, just round the corner from the Wanamaker Store. On this particular evening, our waitress was a new employee, probably a college student working her way through school. When she came to take our order, Virgil began reciting in friendly but precise terms *exactly* how he wanted everything prepared. I can't duplicate it word-for-word, but it went something like this:

> ... and now listen then, I want the lettuce to be *fresh*, nothing that has been out for several days, and none of that stuff that you've sprayed *chemicals* on to keep it *stiff* for a week, I want *fresh lettuce*! And I want tomatoes that are not rock hard, just a little firm but a touch of age on them, and on this garden salad there will be *fifteen* croutons, no fewer and no more, because I *will* count them, and now about those potatoes *au gratin*, I *don't* want the cheese on top to be a *burnt offering* to the *gods*, I want it cooked *properly*, that means the cheese sauce must be *perfectly* smooth, not lumpy – and as far as my beverage goes, I will make my *own* lemonade, you will bring me two lemons sliced into quarters, not thirds and not halves, and bring me those and a bowl of white sugar and water and ice, and I will create my *own* beverage ...

It was like watching General Custer deploy his troops before the Battle of Little Big Horn. After this poor gal had filled up several pages of her order pad, Virgil closed by saying, 'And honey – could you bring it *now*?'

But Stouffer's was not home, and in the privacy of his own dining room, Virgil did not always practice what he preached with such fire and brimstone when dining out. In fact, one staple 'house' food was Cheeze-Whiz, which he would smear over the special salt-rising bread from Atlanta (which I brought up for him) or, defeated and desperate, Ritz crackers. I remember him picking up the Cheese-Whiz bottle and saying, 'Why, it has *plenty* of vitamins and minerals, it says so *right here* on the label.' If prompted, Virgil could rationalize the nutritional value of a paper bag. For formal occasions, however, Virgil, David and Merle would stir up a tasty fuss in the kitchen.

All of this fervor personified Virgil's drive. He did nothing halfway, and was determined to surmount any obstacle. I see now that merely taking lessons with

Virgil would have been an activity out of context. The energy he brought to music-making would have been difficult to comprehend, and thus hard to take seriously, without spending time in his company.

Our sessions were more intense than the teacher-student relationships of my previous experience. Virgil was determined to instill in me something of his own diligence, and guided me to strive for mastery in all aspects of performance, far beyond the mere playing of the notes. After all, the organ involves much more than just manipulating a keyboard. There are multiple claviers, usually two or three, often four, sometimes even five, six or seven. Then come the stop controls, couplers, swell pedals, combination pistons, and toe studs: all have to be handled with confidence and facility.

With Virgil the notes came first, and they *had* to be right. In those formative days, I was still in fast-and-furious mode, where I could devour large and difficult passages with relative ease, but at the expense of accuracy. Considering how diligently Virgil strove to play note-perfectly, he wasn't about to tolerate my careless attitude. Before now, I had been too concerned with dazzle to care much about accuracy or musicianship. But Virgil's exacting standards were not to be ignored, and I worked harder than ever before. If I played a passage or note incorrectly, Virgil would cock his head to one side and intone, 'Carlo, it *could* have been written that way.'

Virgil maintained non-traditional views about pedaling. Most organists use the terms *heel* and *toe* when discussing pedal technique to denote which part of the foot (front or back) is used to strike certain notes. But Virgil insisted on using *heel* and *point* instead.[5] He continually stressed the difference, because to him, the term *toe* was inadequate to describe what could be any part of the foot forward of the arch. To stress this point, he would tell me, 'Carlo, you should pedal *precisely* as you walk.' Because of my proportions, I couldn't always follow this decree, so he advised me to do what was most comfortable.

In order to achieve and maintain his breathtaking pedal technique, Virgil had developed his own pedal scales for practice. They went through the circle of fifths, starting up the pedal-board in C major, coming down in G major, starting up in D and so forth, beginning again in C minor. He had me study them exhaustively, and often out of nowhere, he would demand that I play them at a tempo of

---

5 Virgil's attitudes toward pedaling largely derived from his work with Louis Robert (of Haarlem, Holland), his teacher at the Peabody Conservatory in Baltimore before Virgil succeeded him in 1938. Also during this period, Virgil was organist at Brown Memorial Church in Baltimore, which contains a fine 1930 Skinner organ; and at St. Mark's Church in Hanover, Pennsylvania, home to an enormous Austin of more than 200 ranks.

his choosing, beginning the scales at a note chosen randomly. Since I dared not disappoint him, I practiced these scales incessantly and my pedal technique improved dramatically as a result.[6] He encapsulated some of his pedal rules in the following handout, given to his masterclass students:

- Right foot a bit ahead of left foot
- Right foot crosses ahead of left foot
- Ankle Action: Treat ankle as the wrist is treated in piano technique when octaves are played. The knee does not move up and down. Knee travels freely to the right and left ...
- Employ toe to toe wherever possible, as one achieves the greatest clarity between toes.
- Play as you should walk.
- Whenever three whites [successive naturals] are played with one foot, play on the inside of the foot.[7]

Virgil's theories on wasted motion also extended to the hands. He lambasted other organists for wasting motion and energy trying to adapt piano techniques to the organ. He advocated moving the hands only from the wrist forward and the feet from the ankle down. If you confined your movement to this range, Virgil argued, then you would be able to master speed and attack with newfound ease.[8] Furthermore, the thumbs were never to touch the black keys, since such action forced the remaining fingers into a potentially compromising position.

In a given lesson, we would examine several pieces from technical and musical standpoints. Virgil excelled at details such as fingering, ornamentation, refining swell pedal control while suggesting how best to shape registrations. More substantial questions centered on voice leading and dynamic phrasing. He was particularly strict about the shaping of melodic lines. By carefully weighting and connecting each note, he demonstrated how convincingly a theme could be ultimately expressed. He also applied his own technique to the playing of big, loud chords, which might otherwise sound fragmented in dead rooms. By scrupulously

---

6 Fortunately, I was not put to the rigors of what Dupré put Virgil through. Dupré not only had Virgil learn all six Bach trio sonatas (a movement a week), but on occasion would ask Virgil on the spot to transpose them into some other key – often without the music!

7 While Virgil insisted on the term *point*, he did not want to confuse the issue with new masterclass pupils, and therefore did employ the term *toe* in this introductory document.

8 Later in life, a journalist would describe my technique as 'prestidigitation on parade.'

connecting both the melody and bass lines in an ultra-legato fashion, while play-ing the inner voices in a slightly detached manner, he emphasized the melody while simultaneously heightening the effect.

But it all began with voice leading. Since the organ was not touch sensitive like the piano, Virgil argued, the voice leading would not happen automatically. Only with close attention would themes sing out. In fact, he regularly turned to singing in order to illustrate how the organ should be played, often invoking the name of the great Wagnerian soprano Kirsten Flagstad. 'Think how she would *sing* this, connecting one note to the next, emphasizing *this* note at the expense of *that* one,' he would say. And if you play it *just so*' – a vocal and console demonstration would then follow – 'think how it will *soar*.'

After note accuracy, pedal technique and voice leading, we probably spent more time on registration than anything else. Virgil was first and last a colorist, and searched endlessly for special timbres. If a melody called for a solo flute, he would try every one of them until he achieved the desired quality. Since *he* made the effort, nothing less would do for me. 'Now then,' he would say during a lesson, 'can't it be *prettier*' or 'can't you *feel it more?*' – always an indication that I hadn't sufficiently searched the scores for hidden mysteries.

Virgil also had certain trademark effects, or 'de-*vices*,' which he strove to impart. One of the most frequently invoked was the 'acoustic release' for use in non-reverberant buildings. On the last chord of a big piece, Virgil would let his fingers roll off in a downward arpeggiated release, letting go of the pedal note last of all. When carefully handled, the acoustic release created a warmer effect than an otherwise sudden cut-off. In later years, it became so much of a trade-mark with Virgil that he would use it everywhere, from the deadest parish church to the largest cathedral. Play any of Virgil's recordings and you're bound to collide with an acoustic release before long.

Another device – and one I considered quite far-fetched until I appreciated its usefulness – was his energy-conserving trill. In a building with plentiful reverberation, he would often start a long trill properly, only to depress both keys simultaneously for the remainder of its duration. If the music's texture were sufficiently complex, Virgil believed the listener's ear would be deceived into hearing the trill continue, while the player would be spared the energy and concentration of its execution. When he first demonstrated this for me in Englewood, it seemed like utter nonsense, but when I heard it in context, I couldn't believe my ears. Under the right circumstances, I use Virgil's trill to this day. (Of course, his genuine ornamentation was exhilarating.)

One device about which I remain doubtful however is 'the snowball.' Undeniably effective when well done, it is just as maddening when abused. Both cadenzas at the close of the Bach Toccata and Fugue in D Minor are perfect examples of where Virgil would 'snowball': starting at a snail's pace, gradually gaining momentum and accelerating inexorably into a whirling vortex of sound. The music became a freight train, sluggish and lumbering to start, but soon rolling downhill without brakes. If this analogy sounds melodramatic, Virgil's was downright theatrical: 'It's like a tiny drop of hail landing on the pinnacle of a great mountain, rolling down, getting larger and larger, growing faster and faster, until it is nothing less than a veritable AVALANCHE!' To my ears, the most densely packed snowball can be found on the recording Virgil made for the Command label on the Æolian-Skinner originally installed in Philharmonic Hall, New York City and now incorporated into the organ at the Crystal Cathedral, Garden Grove, California. Certain moments in the concluding toccata section of Messiaen's *Dieu parmi nous* are, for me, the musical equivalent of cardiac arrest!

Lessons always began with scales on the piano. He would take his pedal scales and have me play them for hands only. Then, just like my grandmother, he would expect me to have learned one of the preludes and fugues from Bach's *Well-Tempered Clavier*. His use of the piano as the foundation for good organ playing was a sentiment quite distinct from his theories that some motions necessary to good piano playing were wasted in organ technique, especially in the use of the feet. Here, the technical was separated from the musical; he believed that piano playing always helped an organist to make better music.

Before approaching either the piano or the organ it was necessary, both literally and figuratively, to 'walk the plank'! The pipework of Virgil's organ was distributed carefully around the house. There were divisions in the sun-porch, the attic and also the basement. In order that the sound of the basement pipes could be properly heard, a large lattice grille had been installed in the living room floor. Homes with pipe organs often had similar arrangements and one could walk over the grilles without comment. To do so at Englewood was to court disaster, since the apertures were large enough for toes, heels, pieces of china and small children to fall directly through. For safety's sake, a narrow wooden plank was placed across, so that one could walk from entrance hall to living room without incident.

Once I had 'walked the plank,' I entered the sumptuously furnished living room, the focus-point of which was an elegant four-manual French-terraced console, finished in a honey-colored oak. It had begun life in 1917 as the three-manual Æolian Opus 1377, of 25 ranks, installed in the E. E. Allyne residence in Cleveland, Ohio. When Virgil acquired it, four new keyboards were supplied by Æolian-Skinner while the Æolian rocker-tablets were replaced by new stop jambs and knobs, most of whose faces were covered by white stick-on labels, as the instrument was in a seemingly on-going state of flux.

The tonal core of the organ included not only Æolian pipework but numerous ranks from the 1915 E. M. Skinner, Opus 231, installed in the New Old South Church, Boston and sold to Virgil when a new Reuter instrument was installed. It had a responsive action, perfectly suited to Virgil's rapid-fire requirements. Over the years, several builders had been involved with this instrument in a number of ways. Still, the sound could indeed be moving and very exciting. The timbres I particularly recall were the sensuous Flute and Spitzflöte Celestes, perhaps the most pure and moving tones I have ever heard come from pipes. The *tutti* was enormous. Thank heavens that Virgil's was a detached house or the police would have been hammering constantly on the door!

Although I had my lessons on this instrument, I practiced on a Baldwin Model 5 electronic which Virgil had placed in the morning room next to the pool. It was akin to studying with my grandmother all over again. Unlike the confounded upright piano of my youth, the Baldwin was in reasonable condition.[9] Virgil also arranged practice privileges for me at St. Cecilia's Church in the center of Englewood. This not only had glorious acoustics but a brand new organ. It was also close to Baumgart's Ice Cream Parlour.

Looking back, I now believe that I learned the most by watching Virgil practice. Often while working out a piece on an unfamiliar instrument, he would talk through his interpretations, pointing out melodies, harmonies and special effects that merited emphasis. Witty commentary aside, he would always articulate his musical views elegantly. Often, when I thought he was producing an effect for its own sake, and had the nerve to say so, he would respond with a logical rationale. Such mild rebukes were invaluable. What had originally drawn me to his playing was the spectacular overall effect, and I had assumed that many of his trademark characteristics were little more than bewitching whims. One of my best lessons from Virgil came from the dawning realization that I had assumed incorrectly.

As I reflect back on my time in Englewood, I regret that, even though I was motivated to more regular practice than before, I still did not work hard enough, especially in the light of Virgil's exacting discipline. On this score he would at times grow exceedingly impatient with me. Alas, it was still too easy for me to digest a big piece in a few days and then to rattle it off half-baked. Short-sightedly, I continued to view this as an asset.

9 In 1967, Virgil made an LP for Baldwin entitled *Virgil Fox plays the Baldwin Organ*. This may explain the presence of the Model 5. Occasionally, I would practice in the library on the disconnected four-manual Skinner console, formerly installed at the New Old South Church in Boston. While practice on dead keyboards may seem odd, it was in fact beneficial. Virgil encouraged it.

Virgil was in such demand for concerts that it became increasingly difficult to find him in Englewood. Determined that this should not be an obstacle to my growing relationship with him, Florence asked Virgil if I could occasionally accompany him on tour so that our sessions could continue.[10] Druid Hills Baptist graciously accommodated these new vagaries in my schedule.

On tour as well as at home, Virgil was always accompanied by his companion and multi-talented personal assistant David Snyder. Canadian by birth, David was unswervingly loyal to Virgil, and was especially adroit at helping to navigate through the rigors of a hectic concert schedule. Upon arriving at a performance location, he would immediately take charge of organizing lighting, public address system, record sales tables, organ tuning and maintenance, and hotel arrangements. At home, he handled most of the day-to-day details, organizing recording projects, establishing a mail-order recording business, and later on developing 'Revelation Lights', the *lumière* show for Virgil's 'Heavy Organ' Bach concerts.

Backing up David's skills was the brilliant management team of Richard Torrence and Marshall Yeager. Their artistic direction shaped and marketed the entire package of Virgil's public image. Richard was an aggressive manager and a keen organizer. As bookings were secured, he would map out Virgil's touring itinerary in the most logical fashion possible. Marshall, a trained writer and successful playwright, had a flair for advertising, a great gift of language – he wrote many of the sleeve notes for Virgil's records – and a clear vision of how to market a classical musician in a rock age. Each of them highly talented in their own right, as a combination they were unbeatable.[11]

A typical tour which I would be allowed to join might begin in Atlanta, before heading to Tuskegee, Alabama. Then into Tennessee, on to North Carolina, from there to Richmond, Virginia, and so forth. Every concert required preliminary communication, contractual negotiation, sending out of publicity materials, hotel and travel arrangements for Virgil and David (and the touring organ and its driver, if needed). This would be considered an east coast tour, from which Virgil would then head home to Englewood for rest.

All this would have taxed a lesser man. But on the road, Virgil was ever charming and gracious, always knowing when to draw the line between sentiment and saccharine. The smoothest talk flowed effortlessly from his voice. He was also generous with his retinue. While practicing, he would invariably ask for

10 Florence's continued generous financial support luckily went without saying.

11 I was also managed by Torrence Associates from 1977 to 1980 until I signed on with Columbia Artists Management, Inc. (CAMI).

an opinion on registration, especially if he was at a stationary console in poor proximity to the pipework. 'Now then, Carlo, is that Krummhorn *too* weak on its own or does it need the Koppelflöte added for a bit of *backbone*?' or 'Do these nasty reeds come on and *grab* your trouser leg *too* strongly here?' After careful listening and registering an opinion, he would make the change, thank us and continue his work. But in performance, more often than not he would use the original, supposedly flawed registration, seemingly ignoring the much-sought opinions. I've always felt he did this to make me listen more intently, and also to make all of us feel included in the preparation for his recitals.

People have occasionally criticized Virgil for being self-centered. From my point of view, they overlook the fact that Virgil could not have been any *less* self-centered and still remain Virgil Fox. And while he could occasionally lack diplomacy, this side of his personality was usually reserved for the inner circle. So was his penchant for lusty off-color jokes and bawdy limericks, which he would seek out and recite gleefully to his minions. One example will suffice. Virgil had never cared for a certain midwestern spinster organ teacher, whose artistic bent was far from his own. Undoubtedly the feeling was mutual! As Virgil passed through her state concertizing, he chanced to meet a student of hers and expressed genuine surprise to hear that the pedagogue was finally marrying. He told the student through clenched teeth: 'That old maid's only getting married *so she won't die wonderin'*! Her man had better be prepared to take a *good book* to bed!'

In performance, Virgil was never less than the superb showman and a master at handling crowds. A favorite quip was, 'If *you'll* come across, *I'll* come across.' A Fox recital was always far more than just the playing. In a church, he would insist that any candles remain unlit, since he wanted to present his concert as a secular offering, not a liturgical one. Then there was his inimitable commentary to the audience, which could range from profundity to hilarity, politics to religion, seriousness to downright camp. Virgil's playing also had a visual element, since he maintained that wherever possible, the audience should be able to see the console.[12] Where they couldn't, he would employ dramatic gestures, throwing his hands high above his head (particularly after big chords) to remind people he was there. If concert sponsors ever complained about his insistence on being seen, his stock reply was, 'Heifetz would *never* fiddle from behind a potted

---

12 At many venues, most notably the Riverside Church, he used an enormous mirror behind the console – effective, of course, but with the peculiarity that scales and fast-running passages always appeared to be going in the wrong direction. To Virgil, this would have been a minor compromise.

palm!' His persistence in this matter has made it much easier for organists of my generation to insist that consoles be visible.[13]

Once underway, Virgil knew precisely how to steer the mood of an audience. He could fire them up with one piece only to hush them with the next. He enjoyed substantial programs, and would sometimes include two intermissions to allow the audience to catch its breath. He had a sensational memory for names and faces and after concerts, would greet his fans as friends and loyal subjects, making them feel like the most important people in the world. He also signed records and programs until the entire queue had disappeared happily.

After the evening had wound down, Virgil would return to his hotel and take what I dubbed The Great Bath, an all-important ritual in his post-recital routine. Not surprisingly, he perspired heavily when he played, and The Great Bath was a time-proven method of thorough cleansing. First, the tub would be filled with scalding hot water. Then, after divesting himself of his perspiration-drenched clothes, he would gingerly lower himself into the tub, and thus, 'Open the pores! Get those toxins out!'

As soon as the first part of The Great Bath was done, we were all instructed to locate every available receptacle and fill them with ice cubes from every machine in the hotel. When the tub had been drained, it was re-filled anew, this time with cold water into which the gathered ice would be poured. There then followed his descent into the glacier-like cold, and the 'closing of the pores.' Eventually he would emerge a new man, refreshed and revitalized from the rigors of the performance.[14] Quite why he never succumbed to pneumonia, I will never know.

It is hardly surprising that meals on the road were less predictable than in Englewood, and sometimes – horror of horrors – a Stouffer's could not be found. Indeed on one occasion I remember when nothing else was available, we often dined at a truck stop. Amidst the male-dominated, cigarette-smoking clientele, Virgil swept in, beret atilt, paisley jacket lightly draped over his shoulders, entourage in tow. Joe's Diner had never seen the like before. After the stares of curiosity and the occasional stifled commentary had subsided, we settled down

13 On modern electric-action organs with movable consoles, the console can be brought to a point of audience visibility. Where the console is stationary, I like to use closed-circuit television with monitors throughout the building. From my standpoint, this is critical to audience enjoyment.
14 I remember the first time I saw the film *Mommie Dearest* which portrays the life of Joan Crawford. The opening scene is of Mrs. Crawford doing much the same thing as in Virgil's bath, but to her face, first by washing it in boiling water, then by sealing the pores in an iced mixture of water and rubbing alcohol. Perhaps all great characters cleanse alike?

into our booth to contemplate the menus. Rather than order at once, Virgil went off to the lavatory, where he found the doors to both men's and ladies' directly adjacent. Virgil peeped into the men's briefly, then knocked delicately on the door of the ladies', and, getting no response, darted in. When he returned to the table, I could not refrain from asking the inevitable question. 'Don't you know,' he responded confidentially, 'the ladies' are *always* cleaner, and the *mirrors are larger!*'

But Virgil did not always get the last laugh. One night the party arrived late at a diner that did not serve food after midnight. As the waitress indicated a table, she emphasized the time and the consequences of a delayed order. Fresh from The Great Bath, Virgil was determined to avoid drafts, and thus perturbed when he found himself directly underneath an air-conditioning vent. Having moved to another table, he found this too was drafty and so, the group moved yet again. Satisfied at last, Virgil took up his menu and began preparing to recite his litany of requirements. In response to his gesturing, the waitress returned only to inform him – with not a little pleasure – that the kitchen had closed. At once, panic set in and Virgil's undiplomatic side made a rare appearance, pleading hunger, insisting on service, and eventually becoming extremely cross and on the verge of apoplexy. But the waitress stood her ground, and closed the matter with a put-down which many of us will long remember: 'While you was busy *feathering* yo' nest, the food went *off*!'

It would have been difficult to spend any span of time with such a man and not absorb some element of his larger-than-life personality. Of course the mirrors were larger – Virgil was too. How right Florence had been. Her plan had not only worked, but once again she had presented it to me on a silver platter. The events of those years have stayed with me powerfully and positively. I cannot imagine where my life would be now without the benign influence of Virgil Fox. The combination of this all-giving man and generous woman would indeed anchor my life.

CHAPTER FIVE

SILVER LININGS

When Virgil, his entourage and I arrived in Grand Rapids, Michigan in March 1970, my only knowledge of the city was as an American furniture-building hub.

We had already dined en route, so Virgil immediately began practicing for his concert to inaugurate the newly rebuilt organ at Fountain Street Church. The instrument was thrilling, powerful and flexible with some ravishing solo stops. Unfortunately, a small family of gremlins had settled into the console's inner workings, creating complications which were to prove devastating.

During the early 1970s, organ-builders began using electronics to memorize the combination pistons (the buttons between the keyboards which instantly move the knobs and recall pre-set stop combinations). Solid-state was a much-needed advance: it was less expensive, contained no moving parts and required a fraction of the space of conventional machinery. The Fountain Street organ was one of the very first to adopt this new technology.[1]

---

1 The organ began life as a 1924 Skinner of four manuals, and although it had been much changed by the time I arrived in Grand Rapids, the old Skinner and its console were still affectionately referred to as 'Catherine the Great.' Quite what it had to do with a Russian queen, I'm not totally certain, but in late 1959, Casavant rebuilt the organ, adding much new pipework. Tellers rebuilt it again in 1970, and their most notable contributions were the Bombarde division and the new four-manual console with the fated combination action.

But with anything brand-new, teething problems are inevitable. At first everything worked fine but once the organ had been running for an extended period – during a Virgil practice session, for example – the solid state equipment overheated causing the piston-system to develop amnesia. The fault had been intermittent up to now but shortly before Virgil's recital, the system became unusable. *'Chicken,'* he declared, 'there is something *oh-so-wrong* with this *equipment!'* Pushing a button not only failed to recall what he had carefully selected and pre-set, but often drew some hilariously implausible stop combinations. As the condition deteriorated, it became clear that the recital would have to be canceled. Virgil agreed to return when the system was fixed.

Clouds, however, do sometimes have silver linings. During Virgil's practice sessions, I became friendly with the Director of Music and Organist, Mr. Beverly Howerton. Bev was another North Carolinian, hailing from Durham, the home of Duke University, where I had met Arthur Poister and E. Power Biggs. He had studied at Duke with Mildred Hendrix, the chapel organist and something of a legend. Subsequently, he attended Westminster Choir College in Princeton, New Jersey, a well-known American institution of sacred musical education. Here he studied with Alexander McCurdy, one of the leading professors of the day. Having graduated in 1951, he was immediately appointed to Fountain Street Church where he remained until 1990.[2]

When this imposing edifice was built in the early 1920s, Grand Rapids had no municipal auditorium or other public concert space. With selfless magnanimity the church fathers generously determined that their new building should address both sacred and secular needs. Thus, the new Fountain Street Baptist Church was constructed with a raked floor and plush theatre-style seating for 1,800.

With the arrival of the Rev. Duncan E. Littlefair in 1944, Fountain Street embarked upon a new and exciting era. Duncan Littlefair was a brilliant liberal philosopher and a compelling preacher and, under his leadership, the church's fame spread far and wide. Increasingly at odds with Baptist theology, his church was stripped of its affiliation in the mid-sixties. But the congregation didn't much care. Fountain Street excised the word 'Baptist' from its notice-boards and stationery and never looked back. Duncan, the church and Bev formed a trio that was hard to beat.

Following the gremlin debacle, Bev kindly invited me to stay on in Grand Rapids for a few weeks. I reported back to Florence who, having ensured that

---

2 Later in the 1950s, Bev also took a post-graduate summer session at the University of Michigan with Dr. Robert Noehren, completing a cycle of sorts, since Dr. Noehren had held the Fountain Street job from 1941 to 1943.

Virgil was in support, gave me her blessing and pledged to continue to provide. I had nothing to lose and everything to gain and, having checked into the grand old Pantlind Hotel, now the Amway Grand Plaza, I proceeded to spend all my time at Fountain Street. What an education. Bev was not only a sensitive organist but also a skilled choirmaster. We got on so well that by the time Virgil returned to dedicate the rebuilt organ, he had invited me to stay on in Grand Rapids as artist-in-residence. I eagerly accepted, and thus began a busy period of commuting from Atlanta where I continued to discharge my responsibilities as organist at Druid Hills Baptist.[3]

My tenure as artist-in-residence at Fountain Street Church came at a particularly opportune point in my development. For me, the principal issue still remained one of discipline, something Virgil had earnestly attempted to instill. Of course, had I been older and wiser, I would have simply buckled down to hard practice. And to be fair, my practice habits had improved noticeably. From necessity, my lessons with Virgil had been somewhat erratic, either as a result of my commuting or our road trips together. Consequently, there was no regular pattern of tutorials to ensure a proper practice regime. So, never having been naturally imbued with discipline in the first place, it was unlikely that I would develop it fully without a more settled existence. Grand Rapids and Bev Howerton were to provide that settled existence and thus began yet another important chapter in my musical education.

While I was not a staff member at Fountain Street, and therefore had no formally assigned duties, I gladly played whatever accompaniments, preludes or postludes Bev requested of me and, to my delight, was paid for my efforts. But the real incentive to learn new repertoire came from my weekly coaching session with Bev himself. In this role he was superb, bringing a seasoned and reasoned ear to my performance, and a kindly discipline to my practice habits, expecting at least one new piece from me every fortnight. Having listened carefully, he would criticize me if I had failed to prepare thoroughly. He was also a practical technician who kept a sense of humor throughout. Despite his repeated attempts to slow down my playing, I continued to forge through things at breakneck

3 In the interim, I used an apartment in the Pantlind, where Don Westfield, the local Allen representative, furnished me with one of the earliest computer organs for practice.

speeds. He turned it into a joke by giving me a bulletin board depicting an old roadster with the slogan 'SPEED KILLS' printed across the bottom. I took it as a compliment, not advice. I must admit that I still love playing fast and enjoy the favourable reaction it often has on audiences.

One immediate benefit of all this was a distinct improvement in my sight-reading, a skill in which I had never been fully proficient. During my tenure at Druid Hills Baptist, I had improved but much work was still needed in order to achieve the fluency I envied in other musicians. In the midst of learning, week by week, complicated anthem accompaniments and two or three organ pieces, I finally got it right.

Three other elements of the Grand Rapids scene proved immensely beneficial. Firstly, I had a comprehensive four-manual organ at my disposal, certainly far more exciting than those at NCSA or Druid Hills Baptist. Secondly, I learned a great deal from Bev's choir rehearsals which I attended faithfully, even if I wasn't always needed to accompany. Although he occasionally 'blew his top,' Bev approached conducting as a diplomat, not as a taskmaster, providing directions and encouragement with good humor. He also enunciated clearly, a model of how singers could improve their diction.

The third benefit of the Fountain Street set-up was the visiting musicians, all of whom were of the highest caliber. The annual organ series brought such luminaries as Simon Preston, Gillian Weir and Cherry Rhodes to Grand Rapids. I distinctly remember the visit of the great organist-composer Maurice Duruflé and his virtuoso organist wife, Marie-Madeleine, always respectfully referred to as 'Madame.' After opening the concert with two or three well-chosen works, Duruflé conducted the choir in his famous *Réquiem*. This was followed by Madame who contributed the *Prelude and Fugue in D Major* of Bach, her husband's *Prélude et fugue sur le nom d'ALAIN* and Tournemire's famous organ improvisation on *Victimæ paschali*, which Duruflé had transcribed from one of Tournemire's 78 rpm recordings.[4] Always the consummate organist, Madame played brilliantly, but the performance that really moved me was Maurice Duruflé's exquisitely lyrical playing of the Franck *Fantaisie in A*.

The after-concert dinner was held at the Cypress Cellar in the Pantlind Hotel. Duruflé remained quiet throughout, always responding politely when addressed, but otherwise keeping to himself. While I had expected serious talk, quiet wit and recollections of other great musicians, I did not expect him to pinch the rolls for it soon became obvious that his attention was not on dinner chat, but

---

4 My first exposure to this work had come years earlier from the original Tournemire 78 rpm disc, thanks to Terence Mulligan. Tournemire recorded the improvisation at Ste.- Clotilde on April 30, 1930; Duruflé reconstructed the work and published it in 1958.

on the bread basket! I soon realized that, whenever he thought no one was looking, he would fill his copious pockets with rolls. Only when they were crammed to capacity, like the cheeks of a hamster, did he rejoin the conversation. Having worked up the nerve to ask, he smiled at me sheepishly: 'Because the breakfasts in America are so *terrible*!'

It was not just classical music which filled Fountain Street. Opera, jazz and popular music came too; Ella Fitzgerald, Stan Kenton, the Modern Jazz Quartet, George Shearing – the cream of the crop came right through the door. One especially high point for me was the appearance of Dave Brubeck, who premiered three of his choral pieces with Bev's choir. The reception was so great that Brubeck was later to use these as the basis for his oratorio *Light in the Wilderness*, a series of choral versets interspersed with his own piano improvisations, which received one of its earliest performances again at Fountain Street with Bev conducting. In all, Brubeck appeared there six times. At another concert, Duke Ellington brought his orchestra to perform his *Sacred Service*. I remember Bev recounting how self-conscious he had felt conducting the orchestra and choir with Ellington seated at the piano!

Rock music concerts came under the aegis of the Fountain Club, the church's youth group. As is typical in a rock program, a support act would precede the main attraction. Johnny Winter's brother, Edgar, had a rock group called White Trash and, unusually, the Fountain Club asked me to open the show. At the time, Virgil was just beginning his 'Heavy Organ' concerts at Fillmore East, the rock bastion in New York City. 'Heavy Organ' consisted of Virgil playing Bach on his touring organ, Black Beauty, and Joe's Lights, a rear-projection light show. Using this as an initial point of inspiration, I planned a short program, mostly of Bach, with a Frankenstein-like rendition of the Boëllmann *Toccata* tossed in for good measure. Aware that the Fountain Street organ could be *very* loud upon demand (thank you, Bombarde Organ), the capacity crowd heard volume as powerful as all the wattage that White Trash was soon to inflict upon them. They went wild with cheering, stomping, yelling and whistling. For a brief instant, I felt like Freddie Mercury.

Unlike other churches that embrace liberal philosophies, Fountain Street never permitted its ideology to collapse into the unfocused informality inherent in much modern worship. Newcomers, while always being welcomed, would find themselves in the midst of all the refined trappings of a traditional church: ushers with carnations, elegantly printed bulletins, first-class music and dignified rubric. We had our own, regularly updated loose-leaf hymnal and a weekly radio broadcast entitled 'The Voice of the Liberal.'

Architectural lighting enhanced the service, thanks to a system Bev designed and ran from a swing-out control panel attached to the console. Two of the most sensational effects were a powerful pin spot on the pulpit and dramatic backlighting of the choir. As Duncan ascended the pulpit stairs, Bev would slowly dim the main lights while raising the pulpit spot and choir backlighting, thus focusing attention on Duncan and forming a radiance around him. It may sound theatrical, but Bev exercised great restraint and the results were most effective.

Preaching remained the focus of every Sunday service and the cornerstone of the entire church. A man of moderate height and build, with a great shock of silver hair, Duncan eschewed robes, enhancing his Sunday appearance with a full-dress morning suit, like the best man at a royal wedding. His resonant voice and stately deportment served to reinforce his innate ability as an orator, and he kept the congregation hanging on his every word. On the surface, his sermons may have seemed purely political, since he often used current affairs to illustrate his topic. His wasn't 'feel-good' talk or California 'mellow-speak.' He consistently encouraged his parishioners to search inside themselves to find God, and in that way to derive the strength to confront sin, learn forgiveness, combat hypocrisy and spread good. And while he would draw important lessons from both New and Old Testaments, using Jesus as an example of integrity and religious piety, he never failed to denounce biblical literalism while also suggesting much of the Bible to be a great fairy tale. Only a master could express such iconoclastic beliefs without alienating the old guard. A few parishioners did leave, but many fresh faces replaced them.

Weekly church life followed Duncan's Sunday morning canons. Two tenets – breadth of scope and pursuit of excellence – guided everything we did. While the music program was one tangible example, it was only one of many forms of outreach. In place of Bible study, there were discussion sessions. Talk groups catered for the more conventional members, while those in search of something else occupied the bean-bag furnished Gestalt rooms, where the feel-good factor was very much at work. There was something for everybody.

Duncan's support of fine music was absolute. Together with Bev, he played a major role in the fundraising for a ring of bells and, in 1976, the first six were cast and hung in the imposing tower together with an automated pealing system. Bev's wife Barbara Jane – affectionately known to all and sundry as BJ – helped to program this for automatic change-ringing. In 1978, two additional bells were added to complete an E major scale, and there was a gala inaugural July 4th concert to which I, as artist-in-residence, contributed an organ recital.

It is interesting to note that Duncan Littlefair and Virgil Fox were the same age – both had been born in 1912 – and had enjoyed a roughly parallel development in their respective careers. Beginning in the thirties and forties, they both came to national attention in the sixties before enjoying a crest of prominence in the seventies.

One on one, Duncan was as expansive, welcoming and spiritually invigorating as he was in a service or at parties. While I practiced, he would drop by the console for brief but pointed conversations about music, art, people and my future. He was blessed with great intelligence, honesty and humility and had a certain aura about him. No problem was insignificant to Duncan. He unhesitatingly tackled it head-on. 'Are you *making* it?' he asked me. 'Carlo, are you getting what you want? Are you aiming *high* enough?' If I said something he considered foolish, he would come right out and say, 'Oh Carlo, that's so much *crap*,' before proceeding to refute my statements – not tearing them to ribbons so much as elevating my perspective. I treasure the memory of those short encounters. As with his preaching, it was hard to leave Duncan's presence without feeling somehow reinvigorated. Even now, when I get into a jam, I often think of what words of wisdom he might have bestowed. While Florence taught me a certain sensitivity in my dealings with others, Duncan instilled the value of turning my attentions inward, and then thinking *beyond*.

By this time, I had acquired a certain 'look.' I was now at my full height of 6ft 4in, and broadening of beam. In the spirit of the times, I sported shoulder-length hair and an arresting wardrobe. My armoire celebrated polyester as if it were the Second Coming. Colors were seemingly chosen for their ability to clash with each other and blind anything else; for example, a violently orange jacket, a selection of ghastly, though beautifully tailored lace shirts, Nehru jackets, kaleidoscopic bow ties and leather boots laced to the knee. I could easily have been mistaken for a ringmaster at a psychedelic circus or a bingo-caller at the local Catholic church. A gentleman would have cut a swathe through local society, but I excavated a trench. No one could say I was forgettable.

My new sartorial appearance and mien were certainly positive aspects of my new life in the North. Alongside the daily bustle of life at the church, Grand Rapids almost represented a return to the disciplined ways of my childhood. I moved into my own apartment, kept house, practiced daily, preparing for my lesson with Bev and in general, settled into a weekly routine. It worked surprisingly well, stabilizing and motivating me in equal proportions.

The Thursday evening get-together after choir rehearsal was another highlight of the week. Some of us would head over to the Cottage Bar for a beer. The bar served food too and, after a bowl of their superb, rich bean soup – especially welcome on a winter's night – I would proceed to demolish one of the kitchen's large cheese-molten, onion-laden hamburgers (100 percent beef, 200 percent grease). Beans, beef and beer, to say nothing of onions, proved to be a worrying combination. Let me say no more.

After a few weeks, I got to know the friendly bartender, Don Faasen. At first, he was horrified to realize that he had been serving his famous 'Bacardi Cocktails' to an underage patron – I was seventeen and the drinking age in Michigan was twenty-one. Nevertheless, we soon became firm friends and I was to discover that there was much more to him than had initially met the eye. Skilled with his hands, Don could paint both portraits and houses with equal facility. He had been a professional football player before training as a physiotherapist and, in addition to his interests and abilities in holistic healing and massage, he was a follower of macrobiotic teaching. He made every attempt to follow a healthy diet and kept himself in great shape all along.

To say the least, I had never exercised much, and in several ways, Don got me focused toward a better respect for my body. He encouraged me to join him in his daily run and taught me to appreciate the value of vitamins. In fact, my favorite activity with Don was to run two or three miles around the track and follow that with enough calisthenics and other exercises to ensure complete exhaustion. Then we would restore ourselves in the sauna, steam room and whirlpool, purging our pores of what Virgil called 'the dreaded toxins.'[5]

I can truthfully say that I have never been in such good health since that time in Grand Rapids.[6] But to be totally honest, I mustn't give the impression that all we did was exercise. Don and I also spent much of our time eating and drinking. This proved something of a challenge for Don, since his self-imposed dietary strictures rarely suppressed his craving for tasty food. But by the time I met him, he could concoct delectable dishes which, while honoring his macrobiotic code, bore little resemblance to stereotypically tasteless vegetarian fare. Did I learn to cook a single thing during this period? Did I, heck! Did I eat everything put in front of me? What do you think? Fortunately, fine wine fell entirely

---

5 Don continued to be a good friend for more than twenty years. For a time in the mid-1970s, he drove me and my touring organ all over the United States for my Community Concerts. Later, he moved to Denmark and became naturalized there.

6 Cherry Rhodes remembers me during this period. She once said, 'Oh Carlo! *You just don't look right!*'

within his personal macrobiotic beliefs, and we spent many evenings toasting that fact.

During my time in Grand Rapids, I did my best to keep up with my two mentors in Englewood and Atlanta. Eager to share news of my reformation, I called Virgil to tell him about my fitness program, the healthy eating and the new friend who had made it all happen. He was not slow to express delight, although inwardly he must have harbored a few doubts. He did know me quite well, after all.

It was important for me to keep in touch with Virgil because I also wanted him to know that I was at last locked into a proper practice regime. He would ask about every piece and anthem I had learned, and while always encouraging and enthusiastic, he never failed to warn me of the dangers of paying too much attention to the plaudits of my audiences. I recall one telephone conversation in particular. 'Honey, if you bask too much in applause, it'll go straight to your head and then you'll stop practicing! But,' he continued, 'if you keep working hard, it'll *pay off.'*

An interesting reminder of Virgil was his favorite Grand Rapids restaurant, the Schnitzelbank, which served such traditional German cuisine as bratwurst, mettwurst, German potato salad, sauerkraut, lamb shanks, black bread and lentil soup. Virgil developed an obsession for the place, and if he was anywhere within reasonable proximity of Grand Rapids, he would insist on driving to the Schnitzelbank for dinner. Virgil was confounded by their policy of seating no patron after 8.00 pm, especially since he preferred to eat after a performance, not before. But where his schedule allowed, he would get to the Schnitzelbank one way or the other.

I got to know the Schnitzelbank during my first week in Grand Rapids, and in particular a senior waitress named Eileen Schooley, who also happened to be a member of Fountain Street Church. While it would be impossible to portray her Western-Michigan nasal Dutch twang via the written word, suffice it to say that in her hands no vowel ever survived intact. Eileen was the one person I can forgive for relentlessly calling me 'Carlos' over the last twenty-five years. She remains unfailingly cordial and a superb waitress. The food arrives as if by magic – and who couldn't forgive a woman who comes bearing such delicious fare?

During my time in Grand Rapids, I returned regularly to Atlanta to visit with Florence and on one occasion to introduce her to Bev Howerton, my latest mentor and colleague. But it was not all one-way traffic for Florence once honored me with a visit. She put up in a suite at the Pantlind, and we had a fine meal at the Cypress Cellar. I realized just what a dear friend she was, and how much I relished her convivial company. Where other women were merely stylish, Florence exuded style itself, charming everyone with her down-to-earth nature and good humor. Whenever we weren't together, I would telephone her regularly in order to keep her abreast of developments and to reassure her of my gratitude for her continued generosity.

Just as momentous as Florence's visit to Grand Rapids was our joint trip to New York to attend Virgil's premiere of 'Heavy Organ' at the Fillmore East on December 1, 1970. I doubt if Florence would have gone on her own, but as Virgil had invited her specially, I encouraged her to make the effort. We flew up to New York and checked in at The Gotham, her favorite Manhattan hotel. Virgil had reserved seats for us in the middle of the stalls from where we could not fail to appreciate the music, the lights, his mellifluous voice and inimitable presence.[7]

Who but Virgil could sell an all-Bach program to a cheering, whistling rock crowd on an electronic organ? While Black Beauty was no more appealing to my ears than when I first heard it in Atlanta two years before, its undeniable attributes were its overall power in general and earth-shaking bass in particular. In the same way that he had transcended the medium at the Atlanta Symphony concert, he did it again at the Fillmore East. His playing was extraordinary. For the most part, he adhered to strict rhythms, with almost inhumanely perfect attention to articulation. Should you be able to get hold of the recording, listen to the *vivace* from Bach's Trio Sonata VI. It says it all.

There was much more to the Fillmore East than music, and no sound recording can convey all the effects. Virgil's attire had never been more exuberant. He looked like the Elton John of the organ with an outlandish bow tie, paisley jacket accented in shimmering silks and rhinestones on the heels of his organ shoes. Behind the console came the light show, the different hues swirling in all directions and even Bach's stern features popping up occasionally. The final *coup de théâtre* was achieved by clouds of artificial smoke which billowed forth most noticeably from beneath the pedal-board, all over the stage. At the end of the final encore, the console was again engulfed in smoke, completely obscuring Virgil. As the music concluded, the crowd went wild, but when the smoke cleared, he had vanished. Had Virgil become the Invisible Fox?

After the program, Virgil confided to Florence and me that he had never been more nervous in his life. One wouldn't have guessed this from out in the stalls, but I felt he was not quite his usual self. The commentary was slightly less rhapsodic and far more pointed; the playing more direct and with fewer

---

7 The seating was not happenstance. Virgil believed that acquaintances, especially close friends, should not be seated where he could have eye contact with them from the platform. Otherwise, he felt that he would communicate with his friends instead of the audience as a whole. The premier event was released on an LP albeit with some dreadful cuts in the music.

snowballs and other 'de*vices*.' It was all quite understandable however, for this new style of presentation was, after all, untested and he had had no idea how the crowd would react to his marriage of music and theatre. After all, he was offering the most unlikely instrument to a traditionally uninterested audience.

In the final analysis, the cheering was as much for Virgil as it was for Bach. All dolled up and sporting that telltale voice, he undoubtedly possessed mountains of charismatic appeal. 'Heavy Organ' played throughout the United States and was phenomenally successful.

Florence however, greeted 'Heavy Organ' with undeniable reserve. She thought the lights were pretty, but asked 'What are they supposed to contribute?' When the smoke effects started, she genuinely believed that the console was on fire. 'Holy Smoke!' she whispered urgently in my ear. 'No, dear,' I replied. 'Dry ice.'

There were two particular milestones during my residency in Grand Rapids. One was my LP recording *Principals Unshackled* on the Fountain Street organ. This was not my first recording – that dubious honor goes to a disc I made at age sixteen on the rebuilt Austin at Druid Hills Baptist which, to my ears now, is embarrassing to listen to. While every recording artist has to start somewhere, the tempi sound as if the phonograph was erroneously set to 45 rpm! *Principals Unshackled* however belies a certain, if slight, maturity over that first recording. Goodness only knows what the local police thought when I asked to borrow a set of hand-cuffs. The full-color sleeve featured a startling photograph of yours truly standing amidst organ pipes directly below the vast rose window. In my right hand was a Principal organ pipe and from the other dangled the borrowed manacles. Even when I remember the period, the atmosphere and my youth, I still cringe. Of the Bach, Franck, Pierné and other works represented on this disc, the playing is somewhat more responsible, but certainly no *molto moderato*. 'With youthful gusto' is how any charitable colleague or friend would sum it up.

Perhaps my most enduring friendship was born out of my time in Grand Rapids. Don Westfield was the sales agent for the rebuilding work and new console installation at Fountain Street Church, and we met up almost immediately upon my arrival. Don had been affiliated with Allen, builders of electronic organs, for several years and was soon appointed their area dealer. Multi-talented, he had studied organ with Bev Howerton, becoming proficient in both classical and theater performance. For several years, he played a Barton theater organ at the Majestic Theater, and was also the sub-organist at Fountain Street during the time I was artist-in-residence. Previously, he had served as an organist in Cleveland, Ohio, on the five-manual, 10,042-pipe E. M. Skinner *magnum opus* at the enormous Cleveland Municipal Auditorium.

It was inevitable that Don and I became fast friends. We worked side by side, supped together at the Schnitzelbank and thought alike on many issues. Don knew Virgil and loved his playing but had also been enamored with popular organ music from very early on, adoring the stylings of such theater organ legends as Jesse Crawford and George Wright. He was also devoted to the great American oratorio choral tradition.

During my time in Grand Rapids, Allen introduced their first generation of computer organs, a radically different line of instruments which grew out of joint research and development with Rockwell International. Don took delivery of one of the first digital instruments in mid-spring 1971. To my ears the computer organ still had a long way to go but, nevertheless, it represented a distinct advance over anything else electronic I had heard. The difference between even the small Allen computer organ and Virgil's Black Beauty, for example, was unquestionable.

Don arranged for me to be invited to the Allen headquarters in Macungie, Pennsylvania to attend 'Seminar,' the annual sales meeting for their principal North American dealers, who tended to be the most influential music merchandisers in the country. For example, an Allen dealer might also have represented an illustrious piano maker such as Steinway, Bösendorfer or Yamaha, while also retailing fine wind and brass instruments, and sheet music of all kinds.

By this time it should be noted that I had placed advertisements in some of the national organ magazines, bravely announcing my services as a recitalist. My announcement was a model of cheeky behavior. Beneath a cameo photograph of myself (I looked like Shirley Temple's brother) I listed most of the major organ works. The headline declared, 'If you are interested in a concert by Carlo James Curley, please select the pieces you would like from the repertoire below.' Alarmingly, I did not even play the majority of the works listed at that time, but was certainly prepared to learn anything that was requested. Virgil expressed a certain amused dismay over this advertisement. 'This isn't false advertising, chicken, it's *utterly bogus*. Why didn't you let me see this *first*?' Oh well ... I learned my lesson when a recital booking came in from that first Allen Seminar. I received word on a Monday that one dealer had requested Saint-Saëns' *Fantaisie* in E Flat. Seminar was that weekend! Bev quickly found the music, and I had it memorized by the time I left – thank heavens.

I have Don to thank for many things including the launch of my concert career at the Allen Seminar. He was fully aware that dealers were seeking a good 'inaugural' player, someone who could provide a fun, colorful and engaging opening recital and get an instrument off to a good start. However, while Allen welcomed testimonials and the support of organists, they did not want to be put in the position of recommending any one artist exclusively over another.

Accordingly, Don suggested how I might polish my act in order to create the maximum impact. I practiced hard and played everything from memory, which made a favorable impression. Being of Dutch extraction, Don taught me a code-phrase in his family's native language that he would utter when he thought my conversation was becoming excessive: '*Beetje fatsoen*' translates into 'A bit of manners, please!' He seemed to hiss these two words constantly during our time in Macungie. Whenever I teased Don about his Dutch background, he fired back, 'If you're not Dutch, you're not much!' But his mother-hen attitude really kicked in where my dress-sense was concerned. I wasn't about to leave my orange jacket, yellow bow tie and knee-high boots at home, but somehow he managed to convince me that a slightly more reserved image might yield greater success.

As always, his instinct proved uncannily accurate. We left the Allen Seminar with the promise of many concert bookings and since Don had managed my other appearances up to this point, he took these on as well, and has continued to organize my bookings on Allen organs in the United States ever since. To date, I have proudly inaugurated more than a thousand of these instruments throughout the world.

While summer proceeded at a slower pace, Don and I busy-beavered a season's worth of concerts. Sadly, my work-load deemed that I could no longer maintain my church position in Atlanta as I had adopted Grand Rapids as my home. Still, I realized that it would be unfair to commit to a weekly affiliation with Fountain Street Church. Once again Bev Howerton exhibited his generosity, allowing me to return and play whenever our mutual schedules permitted. The year that followed turned out to be the most hectic ever. While I was expecting most of my bookings to come from Allen dealers, word had begun to spread, and I secured a fair number of prestigious pipe organ dates as well. Once the 1971–72 season had begun, my life reached a feverish pace I could never have anticipated.

At the conclusion of that busy season, Don and I went again to the Allen Seminar, but this time I was determined to take a little holiday. From Macungie, my first stop naturally was Englewood. Luckily Virgil was home, and we talked through the Grand Rapids experience and the recent developments with Allen. He pondered my future, saying that if I went to every major city to open an Allen and made good inroads with local organists, I should secure the following season's worth of bookings. In other words, I could use the Allen connections to build a solid footing on the pipe organ concert circuit.

As soon as I told Virgil that I was taking the Southern Crescent train down to Atlanta to see Florence, he immediately suggested that I stop over in Philadelphia to experience the many fine organs in that great city, chief among which were his two all-time favorite American romantic instruments; the largest playing pipe organ in the world, in the Grand Court of the Wanamaker Store, and the magnificent Skinner in the Chapel of Girard College. Virgil got on the telephone and arranged things for me. The next morning I boarded my train to the City of Brotherly Love.

CHAPTER SIX

GOLDEN OPPORTUNITIES

Having already travelled so widely, it is surprising that I hadn't hit Philadelphia before this visit in June of 1972. The three very busy days I spent there were to provide an introduction on a grand scale. Virgil's telephone calls had not merely opened but had flung wide the doors to some of the most prominent organs in an impressively handsome city.

My arrival at Philadelphia's lavishly conceived 30th Street station set the tone. Riding the escalator up from track level, I found myself in a vast reverberant space, richly ornamented throughout and with a grand coffered ceiling. All it lacked, in my opinion, was an organ of significant proportions. The whole place cried out for a stirring performance of the Berlioz *Grande messe des morts*.

I hopped a taxi to the Barclay Hotel on Rittenhouse Square. Situated in the heart of Center City – as downtown Philadelphia is called – the stately Barclay was a smart address. Indeed, Eugene Ormandy had been a long-term resident. City Hall, the John Wanamaker Store and the Academy of Music were merely a few blocks away and the Curtis Institute of Music was right next door.

As soon as I'd checked in, I made my way to Tenth Presbyterian Church, where the distinguished organist Robert Elmore was Director of Music. It being a Sunday, I heard him play for evening service. His choral accompaniments were the height of elegance and his hymn-playing nothing short of magnificent. At the end of the postlude, I made my way to the console to pay my respects. Elmore was fully as tall as myself but, in contrast, lanky and trim. He exuded dignity and received me warmly, mentioning that he had already heard of me through friends. I was somewhat taken aback. It was the first time that my name had preceded me, and I must confess that I glowed a little.

The next morning, eager to make the best use of my time, I walked over to the John Wanamaker Store, a unique cathedral of commerce. Wanamaker's is famous to organ buffs because it contains the Wanamaker Organ, the largest functioning pipe organ on earth, with six keyboards and 28,579 pipes. To put this in context, imagine an organ some three times the size of the enormous instruments in Westminster Abbey or Notre-Dame, and then house it in – of all places – a department store. It goes without saying that Wanamaker's is hardly your average neighbourhood five-and-dime. At the heart of the building is a vast atrium known as the Grand Court, rising seven stories or 150 feet in height. The instrument occupies the second, third and fourth floors on the south side, with additional sections on both north and south sides of the seventh floor. Since the shopping floors are open to this vast atrium, a husband being fitted for a suit on floor five could theoretically peer over the balustrade and see his wife selecting shoes on floor two.

Why so mammoth an instrument in such an unlikely setting? After all, nothing similar is to be found in Macy's, Sak's or Harrods. John Wanamaker was a religious man who greatly appreciated the uplifting power of the organ and his son, Rodman, while also devoted to the Almighty, kept a special place in his heart for all things bright and beautiful. He was well known for his several acts of generosity to the arts, the most tangible of which was this organ. From another perspective, the Wanamakers considered that their investment was good for business and something of a status symbol, well before the tedious times of omnipresent pre-recorded music. Furthermore, especially in Rodman's day, the Wanamaker concerts elevated their image far above that of a mere retailer. They were, after all, purveyors of all things fine and artistic.

The nucleus of the instrument came from the festival organ built for the 1904 St. Louis Exposition. Having served its purpose there, it was purchased by the Wanamakers in 1909, being inaugurated upon the completion of the store in 1911. Even though the St. Louis organ had been the world's largest when built, that fact didn't satisfy the Wanamakers for long. Expansion soon began, intensifying in the mid-twenties under the regime of Rodman, who was determined to create nothing less than the most extraordinary musical instrument in the world. In order to achieve his ambitions, he set up his own in-house organ factory with a crew of some twenty specialists. The outcome of all this is the ultimate romantic-symphonic organ. Myriad stops portray orchestral sonorities, and almost one third of its pipes are devoted to simulating the sweep and sheen of a gigantic string orchestra.

Throughout the first quarter of the 20th century, the instrument and Grand

Court were put to excellent use. In addition to mini-recitals every business day, grand evening galas were held, many of them involving the Philadelphia Orchestra. An army of workers would clear away the merchandise and displays, not only on the main floor, but also throughout all six galleries, before positioning well over 10,000 chairs. Thus the talents of great performers such as Marcel Dupré, Marco Enrico Bossi and Charles M. Courboin would share the stage, and sometimes unite with, the conducting prowess of the legendary Stokowski. Tickets were free.

After the death of Rodman Wanamaker in 1928, although the daily recitals continued, the Store's musical activities were, alas, curtailed. In the late 1930s, the young Virgil Fox came to know the instrument intimately while preparing his recital for a Philadelphia convention of the American Guild of Organists. At that time, in conjunction with his work at the Peabody Conservatory, he lived in Baltimore. Consequently, to practice for his programme, he took the train to Philadelphia for eight concentrated evening sessions after store hours. The extensive practice, while typically Virgil, was also a penalty of the unique situation at Wanamaker's. Not only was the organ immense, but there was almost no method for conveniently controlling the stops. The console had been equipped with plentiful playing aids, but they had given trouble early in life, and were unreliable.[1] Therefore, the entire organ had to be registered by hand – a Herculean feat considering the 729 tilting stop controls. The only assistance came from the cancel piston, which retired all of the stops instantly. The hallmark work to emerge from all this effort was Virgil's soul-stirring rendition of Bach's *Come, Sweet Death*, patterned after Stokowski's moving orchestral setting of that chorale. The recital was a great success; the Bach an unequivocal triumph and although Virgil had already gained a reputation, it propelled him to stardom. He was to return to Wanamaker's a quarter of a century later to make a superb LP for the Command label.

Virgil often reminisced about Wanamaker's, making special reference to Mary E. Vogt, titular organist between 1917 and 1966. Barely five feet tall – hardly a helpful size when tackling such an enormous console – Miss Vogt nevertheless handled the instrument with style. A rolled-up newspaper always near to hand, she would run it along the tilting tablets to achieve massive registration changes, like a boy running a stick along a picket fence. I wish I could have seen her in full flight.

---

1 The combination action and pistons were ultimately disconnected by the 1950s. When I came to the organ, there was only a General Cancel (called General Release) and five preset combinations for solo effects. A new electronic combination action has since been installed which makes the player's job far less frustrating.

Maintaining such an instrument required the full-time attention of two salaried curators. During my initial visit, these posts were filled by John McCormack and Nelson E. Buechner. Although I never met McCormack, Nelson Buechner was unforgettable. On my arrival on that memorable June day, a security guard showed me to their office – right inside the organ itself – and there sat Nelson: smiling, rotund and as bald as the huge bronze eagle perched plum in the center of the Grand Court. Always glad to receive visitors, he pumped my hand and pointed out a few of the notable ranks and mechanisms around us before whisking me away to the console gallery. In order to get there it was necessary to promenade through what seemed like the largest selection of ladies' shoes in the northern hemisphere. Imelda Marcos would have had a field day! Although I'd been warned what to expect and had seen many photographs, the console was impressive indeed, its six keyboards and hundreds of multi-colored stop controls being crowned by a gleaming chandelier. Over the balcony rail, the panorama of the busy Grand Court lay before us: shoppers chattering, cash registers ringing, perfumed scents wafting. The impressive case rose almost incongruously above the scene.

Since the resident organist Keith Chapman was away, Nelson played the morning recital himself. At that time, the three Monday through Saturday offerings were 10.00 to 10.15, noon to 12.30 and 5.30 to 6.00. My first reaction was something of a disappointment. While the tones were lush indeed, they were also disturbingly distant, especially against the background noise and bustle of shoppers and sales staff. But Nelson explained that the management exercised a strict policy, forbidding the organ to be played at anywhere near its full volume during business hours. Indeed, as soon as he attempted to demonstrate certain powerful reed and percussion stops, the console telephone began to ring in protest.[2] Nelson picked it up and having placated the salesperson, said wearily, 'To be expected.' As the recital came to a close, he invited me to take his place on the bench. Talk about the space shuttle of organs! I nervously launched into Schubert's *Marche Militaire in D* while Nelson kindly assumed the mantle of registrant, darting between the two jambs. After all these years, I still remember that I had stepped into a legend. It was yet another dream come true.[3]

---

2 Installed on the seventh floor, the Major Chimes stops are Deagan Tower Chimes, meant for outdoor use. The largest, Note C, is 12 feet long, 5 inches in diameter and weighs 600 lbs. It is struck by a leather-topped hammer 4 inches in diameter, the stroke of which is 9 inches. The hammer weighs 18 lbs. and is pneumatically activated with an impact force of 72 lbs.

3 For interest, there is a society devoted to this great instrument. Friends of the Wanamaker Organ, Inc. is an international organization approaching 1,000 members in virtually 50 states and more than a dozen foreign countries. They work extremely hard to raise public awareness and to

After the recital, Nelson led me on a tour of the entire instrument, from second floor to seventh. I saw pipes in sizes and shapes I had never imagined, perched upon massively over-built mechanisms. Surely this was the Industrial Revolution in full swing. The immense wind capacity demanded by such a giant was generated by no fewer than seven blowers, requiring 168 horsepower to operate them.[4] Our excursion culminated with a journey up two sets of escalators to the String section, home to more than 7,000 pipes devoted exclusively to string tone. From a keyboard in the chamber – a convenience for the tuners – I was able to play the entire division, and was enraptured by the effect. In no other organ could one hear such an ensemble. It is an ethereal, almost luminous sound. This was truly the 'big strings' tradition.

We later adjourned to the Great Crystal Tea Room, a commodiously luxuriant restaurant on the ninth floor.[5] Here, at least, the old Wanamaker elegance still reigned supreme. The majority of the dowager-like patrons wore hats and spoke in the hushed tones of a previous generation. Over delicious fresh chicken salad and iced tea – a lunch right out of a Hardy Boys mystery story – Nelson and I caught up on many of the friends and organs we had in common. The food, the service, the ladies and their hats – it was the essence of Wanamaker's in a nutshell. Here was a building – admittedly not quite pristine – conceived with a degree of elegance unmatched anywhere in the Delaware Valley. Perhaps much of that former era was long gone from the fabric of Philadelphia, but Wanamaker's standards had, in the main, stood the test of time well. The Crystal Tea Room, the Grand Court organ and Nelson Buechner's hospitality were to serve for me as poignant reminders of past glories and hopes for the future. I would not have missed the experience for the world.

Returning to my hotel in exhilarated mood, I next rang Bob Morrison, the head of the music department at Girard College. Virgil had called him specially, since this was the organ Virgil was most keen for me to see. After a short chat, Bob asked that I meet him at the Chapel the following morning. I told him that,

ensure the preservation of this inimitable treasure. Information is available by writing to the Friends at 224 Lee Circle, Bryn Mawr, Pennsylvania 19010-3726 (USA). I am pleased to serve on the International Advisory Board of the Friends and do not hesitate to commend their untiring and professional efforts in heightening the awareness of this monumental instrument.

4 In fact, the seven blowers required a total of 190 horsepower when I first visited but this figure was reduced to 168 hp. when the String and Ethereal blowers were subsequently replaced with new and more efficient models.

5 When I say 'commodious' I do not jest; the Crystal Tea Room could accommodate as many as 1,400 patrons in its dark-paneled Edwardian elegance.

in all honesty, I didn't expect to be more than an hour with the instrument. At this point, I was still reeling a bit from the Wanamaker encounter and believing that nothing could match it, intended going to Girard mostly on Virgil's insistence.

Nor was I much encouraged the next morning as the taxi took me through some of the poorest sections of the city. Urban blight was clearly in evidence. What *was* this place after all? The first thing I saw was a high stone wall surrounding the campus. But as we drove through the college gates, I perked up immediately. Directly ahead stood a monumental Greek Revival building of granite and marble, the 'Founder's Hall.' The guard directed me down the road to the Chapel, another imposing structure, less of a Greek temple and more a great mausoleum. While it certainly adhered to certain orders of classical architecture, it clearly wasn't your everyday house of God.

On this bright June morning, it was typically hot and humid. Every door to the Chapel being open wide, I sauntered into the marble and stone lobby which bore no relation to the outside world. It remained cool, calm and still – almost timeless. Phrases from the quill-pen of Stephen Girard, the founder, were engraved in the stone walls, highlighted in gold leaf. I paused to read:

> ALL THE INSTRUCTORS AND TEACHERS
> IN THE COLLEGE SHALL TAKE PAINS TO INSTIL
> INTO THE MINDS OF THE SCHOLARS THE PUREST
> PRINCIPLES OF MORALITY SO THAT ON THEIR
> ENTRANCE INTO ACTIVE LIFE THEY MAY FROM
> INCLINATION AND HABIT EVINCE BENEVOLENCE
> TOWARDS THEIR FELLOW CITIZENS AND A LOVE
> OF TRUTH, SOBRIETY AND INDUSTRY

Gosh! Pondering this maxim, I slowly opened the doors to the auditorium itself. Here was yet another unforgettable moment. There are certain buildings that never fail to take my breath away: Liverpool Anglican Cathedral, St. Peter's, Rome, the Abbey of St.-Ouen in Rouen, Ulm Munster, St. Paul's Cathedral in London and the Cathedral of St. John the Divine in New York City. No matter how many times I enter these sacred spaces, my senses stop in their tracks. Although Girard Chapel does not compete in dimensions with these other edifices, the moment I stepped within its walls, I felt an uncommon sense of awe.

Part of the Girard effect comes from sheer mass and volume, achieved through the use of substantial elements such as stone walls, soaring scagliola colonnades and black marble floors inlaid with flashes of red and green, giving the appearance of a Persian carpet. Another part undoubtedly derives from the cavernous acoustics; one can hardly take a step or utter a whisper without stirring the sound in the building. The light too is extraordinary. Gold-leafed medallions affixed to the twenty-six amber windows which girdle the auditorium, color and diffuse the sunlight so that it streams down in honeyed rays. The effect is at once both surreal and calming. At night, the light from recessed fixtures reflects off the gold-leaf ceiling, flooding the room in a similarly mystical radiance. As I advanced slowly down the main aisle, the wedge-shaped, descending raked floor and converging walls intensified the sense of space. I quietly took a pew and drank in the atmosphere.[6] And when it seemed that my host would be a few minutes late, I enjoyed a walkabout round the outer corridor, admiring both the cast aluminum and carved mahogany doors.

As soon as Bob Morrison arrived, we fell to discussing Virgil, organs and music in general. He reminded me that it was on the Girard organ that Virgil had made his first-ever recordings in the 1930s, for the Victor label. At last, we climbed the platform steps toward the choir loft, and arrived at the Skinner console. Even its wooden case had been architect-designed. Everything about the place was unusual. However, I must admit that I had taken Virgil's forewarning at face value. He had dozens of 'favorite' organs, and while he was rarely wrong about an instrument's merits, he was constantly proclaiming this or that particular instrument as 'hands-down, the *finest* thing on *this great earth*.' It takes one exaggerator to recognize another and I simply took Virgil's endorsement in my stride.[7]

Being installed above the gilded ceiling, the pipework was completely hidden away some ninety feet above the chapel floor. Perhaps it was on account of this fact that my immediate impressions did not shout 'masterpiece.' Bob engaged the blower, and the big thump of the starter emitted the first sound I heard. As the instrument slowly groaned into life, the hissing of leaking air was plainly audible.

Having paused for a moment, I drew what I knew would be the organ's quietest stop, the Choir Dulciana. The result was so soft that I couldn't hear it at all. I

---

6 The Chapel seats 2,400.

7 The instrument is Æolian-Skinner Opus 872, contracted in 1931 and completed in May of 1933. The organist at that time was Harry Banks, who remained at the College through the 1950s. At the time, Ernest Skinner was in conflict with the management and ownership of the Æolian-Skinner Organ Company, with an increasing number of clients choosing the work of Skinner's successor, G. Donald Harrison. However, Harry Banks was not impressed with Harrison's work, stipulating instead that Skinner take control of the job. Skinner personally saw to the finishing touches during May of 1933.

cocked an ear and opened the swell box to increase the volume but still I couldn't detect any sound. Clearly, I thought, Virgil could not have been kidding when he told me how mysterious this instrument was. Perhaps the softest sounds were only audible in the main body of the building. But Bob tapped me on the shoulder. 'That stop's not working, son. Try another.' Relieved, I drew the Swell Flauto Dolce and Flute Celeste. At last, ravishing tones floated forth. Here was Virgil's magic and mystery.

After a while, Bob left me to it and at that point I still didn't think I would stay much more than an hour. Continuing my explorations, I drew the soft stops one by one. Together they formed an ethereal choir of transcendent beauty. Then, in turn, I checked out the flute stops, the various diapasons, and the orchestral colors such as the French and English horns before gradually building up to full organ. I could scarcely believe my ears. Almost every stop was exquisite, and the bass registers shook the building to its core. Different stops combined to form surprising and beautiful new sounds. The lofty location made the tone sound as if it had no specific source, yet the organ was clear and un-muffled. Not only was this organ the finest I had ever heard, but it made me realize how undiscriminating my ears had been up to this point.

By the time Bob returned several hours later, I was so transfixed that it seemed only a few minutes since he had left. I told him I'd never heard anything like it, and would give anything in the world to play such an organ on a regular basis. Bob chuckled in response, and proceeded to describe the function of the Chapel organist, and the general musical life of the College. Bearing in mind that I had to catch Southern Crescent the following afternoon, I asked if I might return the next day to play some more. Arrangements made, I left the college in a daze. For the first time in my experience, Virgil had not overstated his case.

When I returned the next morning, Bob met me once again, but this time brought along the College president, Dr. Gayle Lawrence. We had a pleasant chat, during which Bob confided that he was due to retire shortly and there were certain openings on the music staff. Afterwards, I played while they walked around the building. Knowing the organ quite well by now, I proceeded to trot out many of the showpieces I had studied with Virgil and Bev. Dr. Lawrence was a genuine music enthusiast and he was not slow in expressing his delight in hearing such robust playing. Before I finally prized myself away, Bob asked how he could reach me. Meanwhile, I continued to marvel at the organ. If anything, it was even more beautiful on this second hearing. Perhaps some of the initial shock had worn off, enabling me to relish the sounds more rationally.

Back in Atlanta, I made the usual round of visits, including a stopover at Druid Hills Baptist. But as I sat down to play, I realized that I was no longer the same person trying out a familiar organ. It quickly became obvious that something had taken hold of my ear on those Philadelphia mornings – and to a far greater extent than I had realized.

I was now fast approaching my twentieth birthday and my long-term plans were somewhat nebulous, displaced by more immediate pressures, such as my work at Fountain Street, learning more music and fulfilling my concert engagements.

A few weeks later, and completely unexpectedly, I received a friendly letter from Bob Morrison, saying how much he had enjoyed my visit. And, by the way, had I realized that the College had been interviewing for an organist and choir-master? *Hello?* How dense could I have been? Suddenly, like the emergence of the sun from behind a cloud, I realized all the hints he had dropped during my visit. Without delay, I immediately rang Don Westfield, Bev Howerton and Florence. They were all enthusiastic, and Don made me promise him not to let this opportunity slip through my fingers.

My interview for the posts of College Organist, Choirmaster and Teacher of Music at Girard was wide-ranging. Since Bob had already heard me play a sub-stantial amount of organ literature, he asked me to play hymns and discuss choral music. I met Dr. Lawrence, the President, again, and my interview with him proceeded smoothly. In short, I landed the job, and I was not yet twenty years old. On this second visit, the campus, chapel and organ hadn't lost an iota of their hold over me. Another golden opportunity had landed in my lap.

Born and raised in Bordeaux, Stephen Girard, the founder of the College, was a fatherless boy, a merchant, mariner and an extraordinarily successful financier. Generally considered to have been one of the two or three richest men in America during the first part of the 19th century, he is best known for his mag-nanimous granting of an $8 million loan to the United States treasury, enabling the country to continue to fight the war of 1812.

Upon his death in 1831, Girard left an estate worth $7 million, an astronom-ical sum of money in those days. Five million was allotted toward the founding of Girard College, the purpose of which was to provide formative education for fatherless boys.

His will is clear evidence of his life-long attention to detail – perhaps he was another Virgo? It not only prescribes the layout and architecture of the main college building, but clearly defines such matters as the siting of doors – north and south only – the detail of the cellar windows which match those in Girard's farmhouse and even the geometry of the steps – nine inches in the rise, ten inches in the tread – a demand worthy of Virgil Fox. But the most revelatory clauses in his will refer to religion. The words of the Chapel architects, Walter Thomas and Sydney Martin, clarify an essential element of the institution:

> [a dominant consideration in the Chapel architecture] was the creation of a place for daily worship that would convey, as it was believed Stephen Girard desired, a distinct religious and moral impress and yet avoid identification with any existing sect.
>
> ... Many of Girard's ideas concerning religion have been misunderstood and carried to extremes. He was a man of unusually strong Christian character but he carefully decreed in his will that all sectarian influences should forever be barred from the College. This viewpoint was contested by his heirs as being 'derogatory and hostile to the Christian religion' and therefore contrary to the Common Law of Pennsylvania, but although their counsel was Daniel Webster, the Supreme Court of the United States in an unanimous opinion supported the will.
>
> The problem, therefore, as stated in the program of the competition [for the design], was to erect a Chapel which should conform in style with the other buildings on the Campus, which are chiefly of the Greek Revival, and yet be in no sense reminiscent of an architectural style associated with any existing religious faith – a Chapel nonsectarian throughout, welcoming all creeds and giving offense to none, a Chapel that without benefit of reredos, baldachin, altar, pulpit or other outstanding expression of any sect should devise its own dramatic climax.[8]

A dramatic climax indeed. Entirely by architecture in place of architectural adornment, Thomas and Martin's chapel masterfully fulfilled the intent of Stephen Girard. But since architecture alone could not enforce the exclusion of ordained clergy or those of religious sects, all subsequent administrations have had to police the campus for this kind of intruder. Printed on the reverse of all tickets for Chapel concerts is the following excerpt from Girard's will:

8 'The Girard College Chapel, Philadelphia,' Walter Thomas and Sydney Martin, *The Architectural Record*, Vol. 73, No. 6 p. 381 (June 1933).

'... no ecclesiastic, missionary or minister of any sect whatsoever, shall ... be admitted for any purpose, or as a visitor, within the premises of [Girard] College ...'

No exceptions were made in this regard; if a Girard alumnus becomes ordained, he will never be allowed to set foot on the campus again.

In 1848, only white orphaned boys of mariner fathers qualified for admission. In the subsequent century and a half, the parameters have had to be broadened to include all children from grades 1 through 12, regardless of gender, race, class or the gender of the deceased breadwinner. Children from single-parent families are also admitted. However, during my tenure, which was to last from 1972 to 1974, Girard College was still exclusively a boys' school.

I moved to Philadelphia in August 1972 and settled in an apartment on South 13th Street, about three blocks south of the Wanamaker Store. To celebrate my birthday and the opening of this new chapter in my life, Florence had given me a bright yellow Plymouth sedan. I recall that when she originally asked what sort of car I would like, I replied, unhesitatingly, 'A bright gold Cadillac!' She threw me a priceless look. 'You can't afford to run it, kid. Let's go choose something sensible.' Well, it had been worth a try.

Enjoyable though it was to live in Center City, the journey to and fro soon prompted me to move much nearer the college. My new place, on Girard Avenue, was more spacious and a mere two-minute walk to the College gates, and being so close meant that I often stayed late, practicing the organ to my heart's content.

By the time I had arrived, Bob Morrison had left Girard College, having retired the previous summer. Hiring me was virtually the last thing he did. I was one of the two full-time faculty members who made up the music department. My colleague, John Baji, a fine French horn player, handled the instrumental lessons, marching band, and capably headed the department. Part-time instructors were brought in for special instrumental instruction. John's practical good nature and fine organizational skills produced results which were enjoyed by both pupils and administration alike.

Meanwhile, I took care of the chapel duties in addition to classroom work, piano and organ lessons. One organ student I remember well was Chuck Gibson, a promising young man who developed from being a player into a career in organ-building. For a while, he was on the curatorial staff at Wanamaker's, assisting Nelson Buechner to maintain and restore the Grand Court organ. Two of my choristers also developed a special place in my affections. One was Glen Sutphin, a fine singer whose enthusiasm helped to smooth the running of the choir and the other was Richard Smuzinsky, who quickly made himself indispensable. In addition to studying organ, he was passionately devoted to the choir, not only with his strong voice but in his regular assistance with organization and music-library work. He could find humor in anything and seemed addicted to laughter. Even after he had moved on to Temple University and I had started to concertize more steadily, we remained good friends. Richard even joined me on a few concert tours, where we laughed our way across the country and throughout Europe. Almost twenty years later, this dear friend was to return to Girard Chapel to assist in my recording sessions for Decca.

My choir was a large and enthusiastic group. From Bach to the Beatles, we sang it all. On the one hand, we sang selections from *Jesus Christ Superstar*, which was especially popular with the kids. On the other, we attempted the occasional anthem beyond our station, including a few works by Palestrina and Parry. While this proved our undoing on a few occasions, we got through a lot of music and had a fine old time doing it.

Chapel attendance was compulsory every Wednesday. After breakfast, the boys came for the thirty-minute service which included a prelude and postlude, organ solo, lay sermon – either from the president or the executive on duty – full choral anthem and hymns from Girard's own hymnal. On special occasions, such as Founder's Day, the assembled company would belt out 'Hail, Girard!,' a gem in the genre of fiercely proud, if occasionally illogical school songs:

(I)
Hail Girard, acclaim her manhood, Noble, fair and strong;
Cradle meet for civic virtue, Praise her with a song.
First thou art in worth and beauty, First in our regard;
Sing we then our Alma Mater, Mother dear Girard. (*refrain*)
(II)
Sing her shrine of marble wonder, Let the voice be still;
Sing Girard and praise Girard, With a royal will.
Singing as we ever march, with a flag unscarred;
One in voice and heart and will, Brothers of Girard. (*refrain*)
(III)
Harvard loves her crimson banner, Yale her blue divine;
In our pennant, bold and stirring, Steel and Garnet shine.
Brown is busy making scholars, so is valiant Penn;
Our Girard, our Alma Mater, She is making men. (*refrain*)

(refrain)
Children of the Great Republic, Lovers of the flag bestarred,
Mighty masters of the future, Swell the chorus, shout Girard.[9]

The boys always got into the spirit of this song and at the close of the refrain they would indeed *shout* 'Girard!'

The Chapel's acoustics and the Skinner organ's marvelous soft colors provided me with an impetus to learn music of a delicate, pictorial nature, such as the gentler selections from the *Pièces de Fantasie* of Louis Vierne, some of Robert Elmore's delicate cameos and the versets of Marcel Dupré. Not only were these works appropriate in length and mood to the services, they usefully complemented my repertoire, which at that point ran more to big show pieces.

In addition, President Lawrence loved orchestral transcriptions and insisted that I play as many as possible. Difficulty did not occur to him. For example, he once asked me if I would play Beethoven's Ninth Symphony. 'Sure,' I told him – 'on the stereo at home!' But he was my boss and one could only trot out this line so many times. Consequently, I began to oblige him with some selections I knew he liked, such as the Grand March from *Tannhäuser*, Meditation from *Thaïs*, *Peer Gynt* Suite and others of this genre. Learning orchestral transcriptions was an interesting development, since Robert Elmore had kindly paved the way for me to begin sitting in on Philadelphia Orchestra rehearsals at the Academy of Music downtown. Being allowed to observe Eugene Ormandy at such close quarters was a privilege indeed and I carefully noted the diligence with which he shaped detail and form. It was not unlike one of Virgil's practice sessions, but with a hundred people contributing to the final effect. And the sound, velvety smooth and rich, had at its core the legendary Philadelphia string tone. Every time I began thinking of myself as a musician, I would sit and listen to this world-class ensemble and begin to feel insignificant indeed.

Reconditioning the Chapel organ was the major project I undertook during my time at Girard. When I arrived, the instrument was in its thirty-eighth year.

9 Words by Henry Hanby Hay, reprinted courtesy of Joseph T. Devlin, Head of School, Girard College, with kind thanks. Once female students gained admittance to the college, the words of this song were altered to incorporate non-gender-specific references.

Although it had held up remarkably well, given its heavy use, it was clearly in need of an overhaul. Having brought the instrument's condition to the attention of the College authorities, they supported the need to put it in better shape. Once I had received the go-ahead to commission the work, I naturally turned to Virgil for advice. He recommended without reservation the firm of Burger & Schafer. Jack Burger and Ed Schafer had installed organs for Möller and Æolian-Skinner, and for several years had performed service work for Æolian-Skinner's New York office. It was through this connection that Virgil had come to know the two men, since they would occasionally come over to tune or maintain the Riverside organ. At the time, in 1972, Burger & Schafer were one of the few firms with any sympathy for the style of instrument Girard represented.

Most organs require an overhaul every forty years or so to address the passing of time. It is similar to taking care of a home, where the cleaning and lawn work are handled on a weekly basis – like organ tuning and small mechanical problems – but the pointing, roofing and painting are done at larger intervals to keep the house in top shape. At Girard, Burger & Schafer thoroughly cleaned the organ chambers and made repairs to the console – standard procedures for such work. They also addressed a long-standing problem involving the blower, whose rumbling noise had always filtered through to the chapel. By hoisting the blower up and reseating it, the noise was greatly reduced – no easy job, and a task Jack Burger good-naturedly tackled.

In the overhaul, some of the stops in the organ were altered, certain wind pressures were raised, the chorus of Solo Tubas was re-voiced to yield a brighter tone, the Harmonics mixture on the Great was replaced, the Tuba Mirabilis pipes were turned upside down and mounted directly over the ceiling grilles for added emphasis and the lowest twelve notes of the 32' Bombarde were re-voiced on 32" of wind – up from the original 20". All these changes were suggested by Jack Burger, whose aim was to make the organ more brilliant and thrilling. Otherwise, the remaining pipes were simply cleaned and replaced in their respective toe-holes.[10]

Over many years, I have given much thought to that rebuilding work at Girard. Certain people may have difficulty in reconciling my enthusiasm for the original organ with the sanctioning of what were, in some cases, substantial revisions. Certainly there are those who regret that so fine an example of Skinner's work was changed at all – an entirely valid charge, I admit. The explanation lies in the circumstances and the times. In 1972, the organ world was just awakening to the cause of preserving old organs, and most of what little effort existed was directed toward saving 19th century instruments. Organs of the Girard era (the early 1930s) were regarded poorly, when they were regarded at all. And from my

10 I should stress that Virgil had not suggested any changes.

standpoint – and remember I was barely twenty years old – the best I knew was to follow Virgil's advice. In the end, however, I do regret the course of action that followed and, with the benefit of much subsequent experience, would certainly demand a strict restoration were I to commission the project today. However, I do take some consolation when I contemplate what might have been had I entrusted the work to a different firm – for example, the large firm of Möller, or perhaps even Æolian-Skinner – had either company remained in business. Instead of undergoing a few changes, this marvelous instrument would probably have suffered wholesale and unsympathetic revision in the then fashionable neo-baroque style.

To prove just how imperiled such great instruments were in the prevailing mind-set of those times, I recall with no little amazement that a local organ-builder managed, through his friendship with a College board member, to have his name included on the tendering list. Soon after, he visited to survey the instrument and as we climbed the stairs he began what was to become a tirade against big romantic instruments. If given a choice, he said, he would only build tracker organs with bright trebles, no enclosed divisions, no playing aids, and so on. Surprisingly, I managed to hold my tongue but as we toured through the chambers, his already glowing embers of hatred burst into flame. Glancing disdainfully at the towering wooden 32' Diapason, Violone, and Bombarde ranks, he declared that when he was given the contract, 'those useless things will be sawed up and made into book-cases'! There was the briefest of pauses before I exploded and I can assure you that his departure from the Chapel was not a slow affair. I literally chased him downstairs and off the campus, hurling the ripest of invective in his wake.

Some of the Burger & Schafer changes have already been reversed. Most wind pressures have been returned to their original levels, the Tuba Mirabilis has been mounted horizontally and the 32' Bombarde has been softened. But there was one change about which I have no regret whatsoever. The concrete wall behind the console was at last removed and I was delighted to see it go. It had limited leg-room and made pedalling unduly uncomfortable.[11]

11 In 1985 Austin Organs Inc. provided a new console, incorporating the original wooden casework and stop jambs, ivory drawknob heads and coupler tablets. The console now faces forward (with the back of the player to the audience) and sits on an Otis scissors lift. With this modification, the console can now be elevated into a prominent viewing position for recitals – an excellent course of action.

Completed rebuilding projects are usually celebrated with an inaugural concert. Naturally, I invited Virgil to play, but he countered with the suggestion that George Thalben-Ball – the doyen of British organists – should give the recital. It was another terrific Fox idea.

At Virgil's behest, I had already met George Thalben-Ball, having traveled to England to study with him. Virgil reminded me that Thalben-Ball had not concertized in the United States since 1956, when he played for the American Guild of Organists' National Convention in New York City.[12]

Having agreed a date – May 3, 1973 – I exerted every effort to ensure a packed house. We began publicity months before the event, mailing flyers to the Philadelphia and New York organ communities and taking out radio advertisements on classical radio station WFLN. Old friends pitched in to help. Florence underwrote the airtime, Terence Mulligan wrote snappy ads and Bob Eaton, one of my colleagues at Girard, lent his wonderfully resonant voice in the recording studio. Not only was he a Girard housemaster, he had grown up in Erie, Pennsylvania with Jack Burger. The combined result of all our efforts was a capacity audience.

George was elated. But due to the strict stipulations in the founder's will, happiness did not reign universal that evening. A bus-load of nuns who had travelled from Delaware were turned away at the gate. Naturally, even for nuns, they were somewhat indignant and George, hearing about the problem later, suggested that they should have come in disguise.

George played brilliantly, elegantly, fluently and with studied efficiency. He barely moved at the console, knowing how to achieve maximum effect through minimum physical effort.[13] He had no time for histrionics and excessive display. His playing was unquestionably energetic but had a dignified reserve, betraying a love for subtle color. Perhaps his style was not as immediately captivating as Virgil's, for he depended more on an engaging emotional and intellectual subtlety. Comparing him with dear Virgil is well nigh impossible, but I can say that I found the playing of both of these great performers equally electrifying. Virgil's was AC where George's was DC; one a brightly lit Broadway marquee, the other the façade of a sumptuous hotel.

In the masterclass George gave in the days following the recital, his

---

12 For this Convention, Thalben-Ball played twice: on a temporarily installed Allen in Lewissohn Stadium and again at Temple Emanu-El on its Casavant/Austin.

13 Given that there is more than 90 feet between organ and console, a slight delay exists between depressing the key and hearing the tone, since sound (unlike light) travels at only about 1030 feet per second (depending on temperature). I had taken a while to become accustomed to it. George didn't give it a second thought.

technique and acumen came clearly into focus. During the recital, the audience could sit back and bask in his musical intellect. During the masterclass, we could examine his methods through his comments and criticisms. He knew just how to put a student at ease, while at the same time offering valuable suggestions. Again, the turnout was impressive: students and teachers alike attended from Boston, New York, Philadelphia, Baltimore and Washington.[14]

For the remainder of George's stay, I played host as best I could. Florence not only attended his recital, having enjoyed it enormously, but also provided a champagne supper at the city's most elegant French restaurant. Later, at her invitation, we travelled down to Atlanta and after a few happy days with her, returned to Philadelphia, calling on the way at Macungie, home of the Allen Organ Company. Thalben was fascinated by their new digital instruments and the overall efficiency of the operation. For their part, the Allen staff could not fail to be impressed by him in general and by his playing in particular.

While College duties inevitably occupied the majority of my time, I continued my extracurricular activities as much as possible. In this context, the Girard schedule was helpful, since it left weekends free for concertizing, learning new music and practice. Realizing how much I missed the weekly lesson with Bev Howerton, it was suggested that I study with Robert Elmore, who had been a pupil of Pietro Yon. I admired Elmore's playing – he was equally well versed in theatre-organ as well as classical performance – and leapt at the chance. He taught at his home in Wayne, Pennsylvania, a suburb of Philadelphia, where he lived with his sister.

Dr. Elmore was a devout Christian. Lessons began not with music but with prayer, sometimes quite lengthy. Given my upbringing and inclinations, I

---

14 In all these endeavors at Girard, one especially dear colleague always smoothed the bureaucratic path to success; Edith Feld, the faithful and knowledgeable assistant to the president. Edie has devoted her life to Girard and is a fount of 'Girardiana.' She enthusiastically followed my playing and musical work in the Chapel, and we have kept in touch in the years following my Girard tenure. Together with a Girard librarian, Edie came to London in 1977 for the Queen's Silver Jubilee; it was fun to play historian for *her*, and we had a memorable dinner in the Savoy's River Room with George Thalben-Ball. Many years later, Edie returned the favor in spades when she obtained permission for me to make my series of recordings for Decca on the Chapel organ.

thoroughly disliked the notion of having religion forced upon me again. But for once I remained patient. Come Amen-time, I would sit down and play my prepared pieces. Very much a details man, Elmore concentrated on registration, just as he did in his own playing. The music in which he really excelled came from the impressionistic repertoire, such as Sigfrid Karg-Elert's *Seven Pastels from the Lake of Constance*. His own music – he was a prolific composer – owed much to the same late romantic mood, as did his entire style of playing. I remember studying the Bach *Fantasia and Fugue in G minor*, in which he demonstrated how to manipulate the fugal theme so that every entrance was distinct and colorful. He had a fascinating ear, and was adept at demonstrating how the smallest change in color or dynamic control could make or break the subtlety of a melodic line.

Through it all, Elmore exhibited a gorgeous rubato within a steadfast meter, all very subtle and refined. His reflective, introspective playing may have lacked ultimate dynamism, but it was nonetheless a valuable new perspective. He was also a superb service player, and watching him direct and accompany a choir was a lesson in itself. If Elmore shared one objective with my other teachers, it was the attempt to get me to slow my tempi, and in this he was probably the most successful of them all. I was saddened when my increased concert schedule forced us to conclude our sessions together.

During this period, I also became friendly with John Weaver, the head of the organ department at the Curtis Institute and a consummate musician. He flattered me by asking if I would listen to a performance class with him at Curtis – in which students bring pieces to play before their peers and faculty. This was a touching gesture, and I accepted his offer with alacrity. I felt a bit self-conscious at first, but soon got into the spirit, offering comments on nearly every selection. It was quite an eye-opener for me to contrast my marriage of solid piano training and such a broad spectrum of organ instruction against the regular conservatory training the students had received from John.

I have Earl Ness to thank for providing me with my first concert opportunity in Philadelphia. Earl was a highly respected name in church music circles, and a busy man besides. In addition to his duties as director of music at First Baptist Church, he directed the Philadelphia Oratorio Choir, taught organ at Temple University and also directed the music at Temple Knesseth Israel in Elkins Park – one of the area's principal synagogues. I don't recall how we met. Almost immediately he invited me to play a program at First Baptist – more momentous than it may seem, since it afforded a rapid entrée into the local organ community. Earl became a staunch ally and some years later we played a duo-organ concert at First Baptist.

While Earl became a great colleague, Sam Singer turned out to be a most welcome and vociferous supporter. He reviewed classical music for the

Philadelphia Inquirer, the big morning daily in town. Interested in the organ, he came to most of my concerts and sang my praises in many generous reviews. When I came to know him personally, I found the man to be as kind as his pen. To this day he remains active as a music critic and continues to be much involved in Philadelphia organ circles. The city's organ community is indeed fortunate to have such a public personality on its side, many large newspapers having long since abandoned any critiques of organ recitals.

One enduring pleasure about Philadelphia was the obvious pride the city took in romantic organs and organ playing. The strong presence of the Curtis Institute's organ department was largely responsible for this. Beginning with the virtuoso Lynnwood Farnam in the 1920s and continuing with Alexander McCurdy, and more recently, John Weaver, Curtis has perpetuated the late romantic organ-playing tradition. Better still, Philadelphia is a repository of fine 20th century romantic organs, and not just Wanamaker's and Girard College. The fine 1937 Æolian-Skinner in St. Mark's Episcopal Church on Locust Street, the remarkable 1931 Möller in the Convention Hall, the magical small 1931 Skinner organ in Old St. Peter's, Society Hill – these are merely a few in the long list. Superb examples of their respective styles, these instruments have been jealously guarded and well maintained under the aegis of their incumbent organists. It is always encouraging to see a tradition kept alive; better still when a worthy tradition is kept alive intelligently.

After two years in Philadelphia, my concert schedule was once again becoming too hectic, and it began to interfere with my duties at Girard. I was also coming to the conclusion that it was time to follow Virgil's example and acquire a touring organ. So, with much regret, I left Girard College in the summer of 1974, having been on the staff just two years. Since I no longer needed to be in close proximity to the College campus, I moved back to Center City, basing my operations from there until I moved to New York City in 1978. Florence gave me some grand old furniture from Briarcliff, and a friend helped me decorate. As with my first apartment, I regained the advantages of a central location. A five-minute walk brought me to Wanamaker's, with the chicken salad, iced tea, be-hatted dowagers and the Grand Court organ. It was good to be back.

As an afternote, I recently returned to Philadelphia for a visit and what afforded me the greatest joy was to discover that the historic Wanamaker Store, now under the Lord & Taylor banner, was once again being run in the truly grand tradition. To my great relief I learned how the new owners have developed a strong affection for the great pipe organ that has so long distinguished the Grand Court. I was equally thrilled to know that Lord & Taylor and its parent, May Department Stores of St. Louis, are making a substantial and ongoing investment, not only in the instrument's restoration and the music program but also in the fabric of the building itself. Hallelujah!

Sitting at the console, as soon as I began playing I sensed a new and pleasing bloom, the result of some upper floors having been enclosed in glass. It had all the richness and incandescence I remembered, and more. As I explored further, it suddenly dawned on me that, at long last, the great flight-deck now boasted a host of working pistons! I am confident that Virgil would have shared my joy at this long-awaited enhancement and I reveled in watching the myriad stop tabs move obediently to my every command. Finally, Mary Vogt's rolled-up newspaper could now be well and truly consigned to the museum! Bravo, Lord & Taylor!

Philadelphia was certainly still a great city. For me, it was New York minus the hassle and the haughty attitude – provincial in the best sense, in that it combined big-city amenities with a small-town charm. It *is* friendlier, less intimidating and far more relaxing to walk than New York. Not only does it boast one of the world's greatest orchestras, it exhibits a healthy commitment to all the arts. Contrasting architecture defines each neighbourhood and the various ethnic communities seem to mesh in happy diversity. And I cannot forget my Philadelphia audiences. I never played to anything less than a full house – itself a good enough reason for enduring gratitude.

CHAPTER SEVEN

FRIENDS AND FIREWORKS

As must by now be abundantly clear, I owe a great deal to Virgil Fox. Throughout my lengthy association with him, he carefully monitored my development and always knew which musical path I should follow next. He had long been an admirer of the venerable English choral and organ tradition which he had experienced first-hand on many occasions. Although the Christian world is filled with magnificent churches and cathedrals, they are rarely filled with music of sufficient quality to do them justice. However, England is one happy exception. For example, in countless cathedrals, collegiate churches and chapels throughout the land, the office of Choral Evensong is sung daily, to say nothing of a wealth of Sunday services. The music is usually provided by a resident choir of boys and men, the standard of which is undoubtedly among the highest in the world. Virgil knew that I could not fail to benefit from some form of contact with this great tradition and, once again, his connections proved invaluable.

As a result, a few months later, in the fall of 1972, I found myself seated at the organ of London's Temple Church, beginning my first lesson with Dr. George Thalben-Ball. The console of the Harrison & Harrison was immaculately tidy and Rolls-Royce to the touch. To say that I was a bundle of nerves would be an understatement.

'Well, Carlo, shall we begin?' Determined to improve upon my past auditions, I did not draw full organ, instead beginning my first piece on a moderate registration. But in my nervous state, I soon started pouring it on, accelerating and adding stops until I had attained a treacherous speed and absolutely full organ – the Solo Tuba lobbed in for good measure. Meanwhile, standing quietly by, Thalben was letting out enough rope for me to hang myself from the tallest pipe. I did glance at him from time to time, and he seemed to be nodding in approval. How wrong I was, for as soon as I was finished in a torrent of perspiration, he allowed a moment of telling silence. Then, adjusting his stance slightly, he regarded me thoughtfully before pronouncing in dulcet tones, 'Dear Carlo, if you learn nothing else from me during our time together, let it be this: the first and perhaps most important rule of organ playing is not to show everything in the shop window all at once.'

I was shattered. Had I yet again gone too far? Luckily, as it turned out, not irreparably. The experience was symbolic of Thalben as teacher: kind, direct, effective. That first statement was to stay with me forever and, since then, I have begun almost every program with a hushed, melodic selection, designed to encourage an audience to open its ears and focus on delicate, quiet sounds. In our noisy, modern world this technique reorientates the ear to what is loud and what is soft. My second piece, by contrast, is usually quite powerful, but, in my estimation, *appears* louder than it really is – since, by then, the ear has become attuned to a more subtle spectrum. From a wider perspective, Thalben's opening comment was so typical of how, by the economic use of words, he could reduce large musical concepts to comprehensible terms. His message was that by the exercise of restraint, an artist has better control not only in a single piece but also throughout the entire program.

Thalben was unquestionably my favourite teacher, albeit for somewhat contradictory reasons. First of all, he excelled in the role and possessed possibly the keenest pair of ears I had ever known. There seemed no slip he didn't catch. His criticism, however, was always constructive and unfailingly gently offered. I was undoubtedly privileged to study with him for, by this time, he accepted very few private pupils. I worked harder for him than for anyone else. Furthermore, my being an American pupil, and not British, meant that we were answering to no one but ourselves. Yet ours was the most traditionally structured teacher-student association of my experience. Beyond the organ loft, our innumerable common interests – good food, wine, cigars, steamships, trains – only served to strengthen a bond I have valued greatly ever since.

Our regular lessons were always at the Temple Church where Thalben had been Organist and Director of the Choir since 1919. Situated to the west of the City of London, it had been founded by the crusading Order of Knights Templar. The main body of the building – the Round Church – was consecrated in 1185 and the Quire on Ascension Day, 1240, in the presence of Henry III and his court. At the beginning of the 14th century, lawyers settled into the Temple, forming themselves into two of the four Inns of Court.

Closely surrounded by the working chambers of Britain's top legal establishment, I was indeed fortunate to be allowed to practice in this ancient building, but daytime playing during weekdays had to be quiet, especially during summer months, when the lawyers' windows were always open. Embarrassingly, I wasn't immediately made aware of this fact and, one day, while I was going through Franck's *Chorale in E Major*, a work which achieves a colossal climax, a messenger arrived bearing a rolled-up missive tied in red ribbon. Addressed to 'Organist in Temple Church,' it read, 'Dear Sir – Would you kindly moderate the volume of the organ as it is disturbing the working practices of this Inn.' Whoops! Tuba rapidly became Dulciana!

But practice I did, for without saying so, Thalben made it perfectly clear that his expectations were high. Like Virgil, he placed emphasis on the development of vocal quality in my playing and was eminently well placed to do so for, unlike Virgil, he had trained voices almost every day of his working life. Indeed, his Temple Church Choir was world-famous and under his directorship had achieved a gold disc for their recording of Mendelssohn's great verse anthem, *Hear My Prayer*, in which Master Ernest Lough sang his celebrated solo, *O, For the Wings of a Dove*.

Much has been written about George Thalben-Ball and his influence on the English choral tradition. For example, Robert Eddison's retirement tribute to Thalben in the *Observer*, stated:

> he hates abrupt cut-offs in choral singing and aims at 'warm endings' with no sharp edges. He has always maintained that the nearer we approach the edge of silence, the more lovely the sounds become.

Or, as he said to me once, 'when we observe the rests properly, we approach the *soul* of the melody.'[1] The same principle applied to phrasing and over-phrasing. He was a romantic to be sure, but a late romantic who abhorred over-sentimentality – not a Paderewski but a Rachmaninov. 'Don't be *too* respectful of that phrase,' he would say. 'The melody's *got* to move forward. Seek *nobility* instead.' He would use any device to bring out a line and it seemed impossible for him to shape a melody without using the swell box – even when he played on unenclosed stops, his foot would instinctively manipulate an expression pedal. Where

---

1 Other celebrated performers shared Thalben's sentiments about breaths and rests. Artur Schnabel commented, 'The notes I handle no better than many pianists. But the pauses *between* the notes – ah, that is where the art resides!' *Chicago Daily News,* June 11, 1958.

Thalben and Virgil enjoyed the greatest common ground was in their desire to explore and exploit color. Thalben would encourage me to search out novel stop combinations, especially in lighter scherzo-type pieces.

In addition to his post at the Temple Church, he was also not only Birmingham City organist but also organist to Birmingham University. Additionally, he was organist of the Royal Albert Hall and many were the occasions when he and I visited that great arena for a good old play. While these were not formal lessons, I could not fail to learn from his every move and when he invited me to 'have a go,' he guided me gently and wisely through the intricacies of this amazing instrument. Little did I think then, that some years later he would happily come along to my own Royal Albert Hall galas and applaud as loudly as the rest.

There were no consoles in London where George was not welcome. He would often take me to Westminster Cathedral for a late evening play. The Willis III organ was an old and cherished friend of his and, in his inimitable way, he would sit down and play as if he were dancing with his kid sister. Some years later, while I was living in Denmark, I received a call from the Precentor, Fr. Daniel Higgins, whom I had originally met through Thalben. Dan told me that the organ was due to be restored, although at that time, there was no specific plan in place. He suggested that I make a recorded documentary before it became unplayable. This developed into a fascinating project and I have been forever grateful to Fr. Dan for prompting me to do it. We spent three late evenings in the darkened cathedral recording some of my favorite pieces as well as a detailed stop-by-stop demonstration.

During one of these sessions, a priest in a black shirt with open collar approached us in the loft, his shock of silver hair gleaming through the gloom. He smiled, shook my hand, and asked how I was finding the organ. We spent a lovely hour together as I showed him many of the organ's colors, not failing to demonstrate the largest pedal pipes. I also played a few pieces for him, all the while enthusiastically proclaiming my love, and that of Thalben before me, for this great instrument. Finally, with a hearty handshake, he took his leave saying, 'So you think it's worth restoring, then?'

The next evening Dan Higgins came by to see how it was all going. 'Did you enjoy meeting the Cardinal?' he asked. Cardinal? What Cardinal?

'But he told me you had given him the whole tour!' Dumbfounded I suddenly realized that our visitor had been none other than His Eminence, Cardinal Hume, leader of the Roman Catholic Church in England and Wales. Dan intimated that His Eminence had been impressed by the experience, which could only help in the decision to restore the instrument. Yet another marvelous episode for which to thank George Thalben-Ball.

Thalben's organ teaching echoed his choral conducting. The distinctive timbre of his boys was neither the sanitized pure-as-snow straight tone – which came into vogue during the 1960s – nor the highly developed vibrato of the opera chorus, but instead trod a unique middle ground in which the men and boys always delivered a gentle, natural vibrato over a rich, full 'plummy' quality. Accustomed as I was to the tone of many boys' choirs, the Temple sound seemed abnormal at first but I soon grew addicted to its luscious quality. Beneath the inimitable tone lay the boys' maturity of musical expression. They always sang and were expected to sing like adults, perfectly mirroring the fluid quality of Thalben's accompaniment.

Thalben's demeanor with the choir echoed my experience with him in the organ loft. Here, his respect for *his* teacher, Sir Walford Davies, was evident. Thalben never showed anger with his choir but rather would cajole them into producing the effects he sought. During one rehearsal of Davies' moving setting of verses, 'Tarry No Longer,' I remember that the boys were singing just a bit too purely for his liking. 'Good gracious, no!' he said. 'Come on. Sing more like girls! *Sing more like girls!*' Doctor inspired such respect and affection that his choristers would never have taken offense at such an admonition.

Like every great teacher, Thalben's own work was a lesson in itself. When in London, I would attend as many of the boys' practices as I could, always the Friday full practice with the men *and* the Sunday service. For unaccompanied works, Thalben would descend from the loft to direct the choir. But, unlike most churches or cathedrals where the choirmaster conducts and the assistant organist accompanies, Thalben continued to play almost every accompaniment himself. From the console, he communicated via a mirror to the head chorister, who led his colleagues unobtrusively by means of modest head gestures.

His accompaniments were masterfully imaginative, especially in psalm chant. One might have thought that, after a half-century of service playing, he would have grown weary of this particular musical form. On the contrary, Thalben continued to revel in word-painting, reinforcing the timeless poetry of the psalmists. Nor was he afraid to use the organ as a kind of bully-pulpit with the choir, challenging them to a duel in the more dramatic anthems, and I always marvelled at the fluidity of the crescendi and diminuendi. He manipulated the stops and swell boxes so smoothly that there were never any bumps, rather a seamless build-up and reduction. Furthermore, since the establishment of the modern Temple Church Choir in the mid-19th century, the art of hymn-singing and its accompaniment had become something of a tradition, and one which Thalben had done much to foster and enhance. His hymn playing, while always authoritative, was richly colored by almost kaleidoscopic changes of registration. It was rather like dining in the best five-star restaurant, where each course, like each verse, would come and go as if by magic.

I often remarked that because his thumbs were so busy pushing pistons to change the stops, he had the best eight-finger technique in the world. His total mastery can be appreciated from the last recording he made with his choir, *Music from the Temple Church*, produced in 1979 by Paul Vaughan – who later became my manager. At age eighty-three, Thalben was still in perfect control; his choir as distinctive as ever.

During my many regular visits to the organ-loft, it became clear that Thalben never spoke while accompanying. His concentration was absolute. Admittedly, he was fond of chatting quietly during services, but only between musical offerings or when he played the voluntaries. 'Dear Carlo, you see the obvious place about twenty bars ahead, could you possibly just draw the Pedal reeds for a few bars, I'll give you a nod when they should go in' – this during some of the most difficult passages by Bach or Reger.

But it's always the exception which proves the rule. During one final hymn, he glanced with a modicum of surprise at the service sheet. 'Carlo, go downstairs please, quickly, and find me the Reubke Sonata' – incidentally, one of the most challenging pieces in the repertoire, and unthinkable for most mortals to perform without diligent preparation. I flew down the steep stairs to his cupboards, dived straight for the R's, and ran breathlessly back up clutching the score just as the hymn's final chords were rolling through the vaulting. Thalben always dated his music by performance and location as a precaution against duplicating repertoire in certain venues. The last date on the Reubke score indicated that he hadn't played it for nearly two years. Of course, he proceeded to give the most electrifying and note-perfect performance of the work that I have ever heard.

But this was the essence of Thalben. Having been devoted to the piano from an early age, his keyboard technique was legendary. And among his many achievements as a pianist was the fact that, when he was just nineteen years old, he had given the first British performance by anyone other than the composer of the Rachmaninov Third Concerto, from memory and with full cadenza, under the baton of Sir Charles Stanford.

As an organist I never failed to remark on his calmly dignified posture at the console. Rather like a swan swimming upstream, the effect might be one of great serenity while the feet might be double-pedaling furiously throughout some near-impossible passage. He never moved a muscle unnecessarily.

It is said of many musicians that they 'love music.' With Thalben, the passion was still of honeymoon intensity. He maintained the largest repertoire of any organist I have known, before or since. Indeed, upon his death, when I was fortunate enough to acquire his music library, I was amazed to discover that it contained more than 25,000 titles. The undisputed elder statesman of British organ playing, Thalben possessed an eclectic taste, unusual even among younger players. He was especially fond of contemporary English organ compositions and, representing the French school, the music of Jean Langlais and Olivier Messiaen. Neither was this affinity academic; these works made their appearance regularly in his recital programmes.

In fact, it was George who encouraged me to visit Paris and to discover for myself just why so many organists – including Virgil Fox – raved about the sonority and brilliance of French romantic instruments. On one of my visits I finally met up with the great Langlais and his wife Marie-Louise. They were good friends both of Thalben and Virgil. When I visited Ste.-Clotilde one Sunday and told them with whom I had studied, I received the warmest of receptions. They even invited me to play the *sortie* – postlude or closing voluntary – and despite my nerves I was more than happy to oblige. Here I was, performing in the church of César Franck. To make my visit complete, having brought along one of Jean Langlais' recordings to be autographed, Madame Langlais wrote most flatteringly on his behalf, 'In remembrance of a magnificent performance at Ste.-Clotilde, Sunday 18 May 1984.'

My happy association with George began during a faculty strike at Girard College, extending several weeks. From that point on, I visited England whenever I could – a few weeks here, a month or two there. Once again, Florence footed the bill. 'If you're going to accomplish what you've set out to do,' she declared, 'you'd better be well fed and rested' – this, I must add, without a hint of jest. God bless Florence, for what she meant was that I was to stay at her London residence, a suite in the Savoy Hotel overlooking the River Thames. I had wisely learned not to protest, and cannot deny that I preferred the Savoy to, say, the YMCA. Who wouldn't? Besides, the room service menu was almost as thick as the Book of Common Prayer and the bathrooms lavish beyond compare – marble floors, heated towel rack, a monsoon-strength shower head, a bidet whose energy would soak the light fixtures if you weren't careful and the most capacious bath-tub I'd ever seen ...

Since Thalben was adamant about accepting no remuneration for lessons, I tried to compensate in other ways. We dined together at least once a week in the Savoy's splendid River Room restaurant, before retiring to the lounge for a *digestif* and cigar. Indeed, cigars became a shared passion between us. Thalben smoked flavourful Burmese cheroots, a small black cigar of unbelievable pungency, kid brother to the typical 'stogie' perennially clinched between Clint Eastwood's teeth. If cheroots are the table-wine of cigars – my friend Terence Mulligan always refers to them as 'road tar with sugar' – Havanas are the rare ports and *eaux de vie*. As a thank-you present, I bought Thalben a box of Larrañagas – exceptionally fine Havanas – which he reserved for the most special occasions. Later on, I discovered the 'Toscanelli' cheroot at Weingott's, a cigar and wine merchant in the Strand, to which Thalben had introduced me. As tightly rolled as possible, Toscanellis were not cigars for the faint-hearted but provided a full flavour to be savoured but never inhaled. So fond was Thalben of fine tobacco that he would never waste the merest inch. As smoking in church was, of course, *verboten*, he would carefully stub them out before squirreling them away for future use into every nook and cranny of the Temple Church's court yard. If you cared to look carefully, the place was riddled with them.

High up on our list of priorities, after good food and smokes, came exotic locations in which to eat and smoke. Naturally enough, money being no object, this led us to trains and steamships. Like many involved with the organ, trains captivated George. He was fortunate to have the weekly journey to Birmingham, where he had been City organist since 1949, playing a lunchtime recital most Wednesdays on the splendid Hill/Willis III in the Town Hall. I often accompanied him on the early train from Euston, arriving mid-morning. After practice, he would relax until concert time, play the program and catch a return train which got him back to London by late teatime. In his Birmingham post, Thalben's discipline reminded me of Virgil's in its precision and persistence. In all, he gave more than a thousand recitals as City organist, in itself a remarkable feat. In time he invited me to play recitals there, and I undertook my first on November 19, 1975.

After literally hundreds of journeys, the ride to Birmingham was a wellworn path for Thalben. He knew every foot of the way. Since the demise of steam, he became uneasy just north of the small Hertfordshire town of Bushey, where the track beds were built up quite steeply. For his taste, the new trains went too fast, and he would peer nervously out of the window, fretting at the exceptional steepness and height of the banks. The complaint never changed; week in, week out, the train went 'too jolly fast through Bushey – one day, Carlo, we're going to fly off the rails and "turn turtle".'

Steamships, however, were more sedate. Thalben and I had the good fortune to cross the Atlantic twice, the more memorable occasion being during September 1976 on the *Queen Elizabeth II*. I did everything possible to make this An Event. For his eightieth birthday that June, I had made him the present of a dark gray, worsted formal suit from a bespoke Savile Row tailor – complete with black velvet lapels and cuffs – and similar to one I had owned for some time. He was delighted with it and thereafter always referred to it humorously as his 'birthday suit.' Terence Mulligan flew to London to join us and as the weather was unseasonably warm, I arranged an air-conditioned limousine to take us to Southampton. Stepping from the Daimler, Thalben and I were quite a pair, dressed identically save ties: we almost looked related.

Once on board, we strode into the elevator, joining a lady already inside. Evidently, she believed us to be representatives of the Cunard company, owners of the great vessel. Pouring forth in a strong New York accent, she began 'I want to tell you I *love* being on your ocean liner. It is so wonderful. Thank you *so much* for making it available to us.' Stopping only to breathe, she thrust several letters into my hands. 'Please mail these for me.' Too surprised to speak, Thalben shuffled about and motioned to me. I mustered a formal-sounding, 'Certainly, *madame*,' bowing slightly from the waist. The elevator doors opened and she was gone. Thalben grinned mischievously. 'Well, these suits indeed do the job, Carlo. It really feels as if we *do* own the Cunard line. Should've done this *years* ago!'

The captain of the QE2, Peter Jackson, was a great admirer of George, having been a chorister at Lincoln Cathedral. He soon spotted Thalben's name on the passenger list and an invitation to join his table soon followed. We also enjoyed cocktails in his state room, where Thalben and I took turns playing the Estonia grand piano. Unfortunately, this was one of the trip's few genuine bright spots. It rained most of the time, there were few passengers so late in the season, and it was rumored that Victor Borge had failed to make his scheduled appearance. Not helping matters, Terence became utterly bored and not a little annoyed after spending the first afternoon shooting clay pigeons and missing most of them. But no matter – we made the best of it. A group of youngsters adopted me as their unofficial entertainment officer and followed me all over the ship, even waiting despondently outside the casino while I played the slot machines. For his part, George mingled – a favourite pastime. Each evening at dinner we would exchange notes on the day's discoveries. More often than not for George, it was Lord this, Sir that or 'Good gracious, Carlo! That chap over there is a High Court Judge!' And if we ever needed privacy, our little trio merely had to light our cigars, which would clear the grand saloon in minutes.

I should perhaps add here that, the following year, Thalben and I crossed the Atlantic again but in the opposite direction, especially to make the farewell voyage on the *France* – now the *Norway*. Surprisingly, it was somewhat un-eventful but I do remember that, one evening at dinner, Thalben showed a slight concern that my portion of beef Wellington was larger than his. I suggested that the waiter was merely being professionally observant. He remained unusually quiet until dessert, when I was amused to note that he had ordered a double portion of baked Alaska while I was merely nibbling a few offerings from the cheese board. It was lucky that dinner ended in a draw.

Arriving in New York on the *QE2*, Thalben and I settled in for a few days, notably dining in the Windows on the World restaurant on the 107th floor at the very top of the World Trade Center which he considered 'remarkable.' In truth, it is a breath-taking location which provides an unforgettable panorama. Having looked carefully through what was, by any standards, a most comprehensive wine list, Thalben, whose definition of a wine cellar was a cool and musty chamber well below ground level, asked the sommelier 'How on earth do you manage to have a wine cellar in a place like this?'

Eventually, we reached my apartment in Philadelphia where, alas, we were to have the only serious disagreement of our relationship. Sadly, it involved music. I played him a live recording of Vladimir Horowitz's 1965 Carnegie Hall 'return' concert in which the master performed his own transcription of *The Stars and Stripes Forever*. I honestly believed that Doctor would enjoy hearing it. 'I've made a few recordings myself you know,' he said after it was finished, 'and this is obviously very clever *trick* recording. They've recorded it over, at least twice and perhaps even three times.' 'But, Doctor,' I replied, 'I've heard Horowitz play this very arrangement at Carnegie Hall and know this performance to be genuine.' Thalben was not to be budged however and it went a few more rounds before eventually, and perhaps wisely, we let the matter drop. He seemed somewhat out of humor for several hours and it was clear that he was irritated with me. But even then he was too much of a gentleman to show it for long. I had certainly learned yet another lesson.

Just as with Grand Rapids and Girard College, my time in London was another unexpected turn in the road. When I left Girard to develop my concert career, it had taken off with gusto and I was content to pursue its logical course. Following Virgil's lead, I acquired my own touring organ in 1976, and was taking it all over the United States playing concerts. But I hadn't counted on the London detour, nor my developing ardor for the country. The warmth of the people, my relationship with Thalben-Ball and the high regard for the organs all figured in London's many charms. At the time, I didn't know how to put it all together and become a true transatlantic musician. He offered an answer.

Shortly after we had both returned to London, George took me to visit the Alexandra Palace, a vast complex situated high above the metropolis in the northern residential suburb of Muswell Hill. Built in the 1870s, the Palace was a Victorian extravaganza set amidst rolling lawns. Its Palm Court was majestic and the Great Hall could seat in excess of 6,000. More significantly for music, this had been home to one of Britain's most celebrated pipe organs, the 'Father' Willis of 1876. But both organ and Palace had suffered a turbulent history. Although much applauded when first installed, the instrument only began to gain real popularity in 1901 when G. D. Cunningham – Thalben's teacher and his predecessor at Birmingham – was appointed Palace organist. Extensively damaged in World War I, it then languished, unplayable, during the 1920s. After a successful renovation by Henry Willis III in 1929, the instrument was used frequently for a few years. All the great names played there: the young Thalben-Ball, Cunningham, Germani, Goss-Custard and Darke, to name but a few. The French virtuoso Marcel Dupré proclaimed it the finest concert organ in Europe and, even to this day, people still recall with reverence the late-1930s recitals by the blind French organist André Marchal – admission to which, including a reception with tea, cost the princely sum of one shilling. However, despite all of this, audiences dwindled and funding was slashed. By 1933, monthly recitals replaced weekly ones; the organ was last heard in public in 1939.

World War II closed the organ's second chapter. Bombs fell very near the Great Hall, destroying windows and leaving it open to the elements. Shortly thereafter, it was dismantled but sustained further damage while in storage. By the time I arrived in London, the Greater London Council had sold much of it for a mere five hundred pounds to Henry Willis IV. What remained in the hall was just the empty case, with its huge 32' façade pipes – one rank each of metal and wood Diapasons – the building frame, swell boxes and some bellows.

During that initial visit to the Palace, Thalben-Ball wistfully related the instrument's history and its halcyon days. Then, out of the blue, he made an extraordinary suggestion. Why not bring the Allen touring organ here? The remarkable acoustics hadn't changed and there was no reason why the spirit of the old organ concerts couldn't be resurrected. If we got going, we could arrange a series of recitals for the summer of 1977. Thalben even agreed to play one.

Well, why not indeed? Thalben would never suggest the impossible and other acquaintances enthusiastically encouraged the idea. I began a liaison with the Greater London Council, who owned the Ally Pally and its surrounding grounds, and together we worked out a summer season of six programmes, June to September, all on Sunday afternoons at 3.00. The first two would feature me in solo performances, the third with me and Robin Richmond – the well-known theater organist and BBC radio personality – Thalben for the fourth, Arthur

Wills of Ely Cathedral for the fifth, and a grand organ gala on September 18 to close the series.

Soon the touring organ arrived, whereupon we discovered an essential element of the Ally Pally acoustics. I entered the south doors of the Great Hall one morning – just underneath the clock, if you know the place – and the technicians were already arranging the speaker cabinets behind the façade of the Willis organ. I heard clarion-clear voices all around my head, but they were those of my technicians hundreds of feet away. Every word was distinct, despite the great distance. It was the quarter-dome above and behind the organ case which, acting as a reflector in conjunction with the barrel-vaulted roof, shot tone into the great space with uncanny clarity. Thalben had always said that Henry Willis III said the best place to hear the organ was under the clock, since it received the sound reflection perfectly. With this knowledge in mind, we spent the day refining speaker placement and exploiting the quarter-dome to make the touring organ sound as fine as possible.[2]

A week before my opening recital, the Royal Philharmonic Orchestra, performing at the Palace, required an organ for Walton's *Belshazzar's Feast*. Emyr Davies, the UK Allen dealer, was to have rented them an instrument but since mine was already in place, it was used instead. Actually, it was a golden opportunity to judge music and the organ with a large audience present. In fact, the big crowd barely altered the reverberation or the acoustical response; the sound was still clear, and the organ was undeniably impressive, especially with full orchestra and choir.

It was after the RPO concert that I met Barry St John Nevill, who was reviewing the performance for the *Hornsey Journal*, part of the North London News Group. Having introduced himself, he offered me his services as agent and publicist. Since I needed some form of representation, in addition to help with promotion for the Ally Pally series, I readily accepted. The next day I started preparing for my first recital, but amidst my enthusiasm I still harbored a few doubts. Was all of this not a great gamble? Could the tradition be revived? Would the crowds return? We had made an excellent stab at publicity, including a nationwide mailing underwritten by Allen UK who naturally wanted the British public to hear what their *magnum opus* could do. Anyone in the country who had ever had the remotest affiliation with the pipe organ received a brochure on their breakfast-table. Meanwhile, I practiced my programme which included my usual balance of serious and lighter selections; the first half leaning distinctly towards Bach.

2 Sadly, in the rebuild of the hall after the fire, the quarter-dome was not restored, neither was the clock!

Any misgivings I may have had evaporated immediately when I came on stage and saw the audience. While hardly immense, it nevertheless amounted to more than 1,000 – encouraging enough, and a wonderful turnout for any London organ recital. Of course, the hall could seat 6,000 if necessary, but at least it was a start. What's more, the hall crew hadn't put out enough chairs and had had to provide more. I took this as a good omen. After greeting the crowd, I launched into a quiet cameo, followed immediately by my signature piece, Bach's *Sinfonia* from Cantata 29. We might not have reached the greatest heights, but we were at least airborne.

From the crowd's enthusiastic response, I began to have real faith in the potential of the project. The second program, just one week later on July 3, drew an even larger audience than the first, and excellent press notices pulled in yet more for the third. Better still, when we were blessed with good weather, people would make an entire afternoon of it, spreading out picnics on the grass. While petticoats and parasols may have been absent, the atmosphere was almost Victorian. By the third concert on July 17, the crowd exceeded 2,000. Success seemed assured.

Of course, I would like to believe that it was my playing alone that drew the crowds but, in truth, it was the entire package. Looking back on that first Alexandra Palace season, it becomes clear just how many pieces of the puzzle already existed, merely waiting for someone to drop them into place. To begin with, there was the Ally Pally recital tradition, remembered fondly across the generations and, coupled to this, the reputation of the legendary Willis organ, the marvelous acoustics and the gala spirit.

Ripe for the plucking, we also had a direct link to the media. The BBC's Alexandra Palace studios were adjacent to the Great Hall. This was where they produced the television programs for the Open University, whereby students of all ages could obtain home degrees following broadcast courses. An organ devotee named Roger Tucker worked as a producer in this complex. A few years back he had been largely responsible for bringing an Allen to the Palace to accompany the regular Open University graduation ceremonies. Consequently, Roger had the best possible awareness of what was possible with the touring organ.

I met Roger in 1975, not at the Palace but at Westminster Central Hall, where I occasionally practiced on the four-manual Hill, rebuilt by Rushworth & Dreaper, always being most kindly received by the then Director of Music, Dr.

W. S. 'Bill' Lloyd Webber, father of composer Andrew and cellist Julian. Involved on other business, Roger happened to be showing the instrument to the Open University's graduation-ceremony organist and before long, we were all chatting away.

It was inevitable that I should meet up with Roger at the Palace. He was overjoyed to be hearing organ music come from the Great Hall and, as the summer wore on, became eager to help with promotion, even arranging live television spots for us on BBC TV's popular evening magazine show, *Nationwide*. The response from these was phenomenal and the booking office telephones became red hot.

Roger also introduced me to Robin Richmond, the eminent British theater organist and another popularizer. Nicknamed 'The Old Organ Grinder,' Robin had for seven years hosted *The Organist Entertains*, a weekly BBC radio show primarily directed toward theater organ enthusiasts. Ever the bridge-builder, Robin also covered mainstream classical concert repertoire, sometimes interviewing the artists whose recordings he broadcast. My appearance on the show provided yet more publicity for the Ally Pally series. When he joined me on the stage for the third concert in the series, his inimitable playing had the audience on its feet.

As a result of my *Nationwide* appearances and *The Organist Entertains*, the series skyrocketed. For the July concert with Thalben at the console – fourth in our run of six – there were upwards of 3,500 in the audience. Thalben-Ball graced the afternoon by re-enacting his stunning performance of the wonderful Lemare transcriptions of Wagner's works he had recorded on the Willis organ in 1930, along with a first-class line-up of original organ compositions. Dressed in his Savile Row 'birthday' suit, he looked magnificent, and handled the crowd with smiling charisma – ever the class act.

On this occasion, the crowd was not merely more plentiful. People had traveled from as far afield as the Shetland Islands, Belgium and Holland and regional organ societies had even chartered buses. Surely the standard of performance, publicity and good old American hard-sell could take some of the credit. But I still feel that much was due to the, until then, dormant Ally Pally magic. Many still wanted to believe in, and be part of, this curious Victorian underdog – originally billed as the 'people's palace.' The festive, every-person style merely served to reinforce this and it was certainly much helped by the eulogistic previews and reviews which Barry Nevill was writing.

One rather large piece of the puzzle remained. Not content to rest on his laurels, Roger Tucker convinced his television bosses that a full-length broadcast would prove popular. Fortunately they agreed, and a taping session was set for Saturday night, September 17, 1977. Frankly, it wasn't the best time since the next day was our series-closing gala with four organists. But for a 35-minute program on national television, I could catch up on my sleep another time! The format for *Virtuoso Organist: Carlo Curley* was a televised organ recital. Unlike our regular Sunday afternoon programmes, audience members were invited to sit not only in the regular seating area but also in the choir stalls beneath the Willis organ façade and in front of the Allen console. With a crowd surrounding me, I would be seen with an audience in the background no matter what the camera angle.

Although the atmosphere of the television show was deliberately similar to that of our Ally Pally concerts, it was very much a different experience. The BBC's design department transformed the Great Hall with masses of potted trees, shrubbery and cut flowers. Admission was by ticket only, but these were supplied free by writing the BBC.[3] We had a 3,000-plus audience, and they were marvelous, especially given the circumstances. Taping began at 7.30 and went on for four hours – all for a 35-minute broadcast. Recording a recital for television is much harder work than playing one. Just like a sitcom episode, where some scenes have to undergo numerous takes to make the final version acceptable, so too the BBC required seemingly endlessly repeated versions of each piece. In one case, I had to play one movement of a Bach Trio Sonata no fewer than eight times. The audience could not have been more tolerant. By night's end, I was bushed, and still to come, the following afternoon, we had the biggest concert of the season!

To be fair, I only had four pieces to play the next day, so it wasn't that bad. When the series opened, we had purposely left the roster of gala artists unannounced, wanting to wait a while to see how events unfolded. When it became clear that the series was a winner, we went all out for the finale. Robin Richmond, Ronald Perrin – the superb organist of Ripon Cathedral – the young firebrand Jane Parker-Smith and myself. The thing that astonished me most was again seeing so many of those who had sat so patiently through the previous evening's taping session, a delighted George Thalben-Ball among them. Naturally we all had high hopes but such loyalty surpassed everyone's expectations. By this point, Barry Nevill was in high gear, having linked forces with the GLC's press department. Under his direction, the publicity was comprehensive and almost radioactively glowing.

---

3 Such a practice was the easiest way for the BBC to maintain crowds, and also know beforehand how many would show up. I always liked it, because it was precisely the same method used at the John Wanamaker Store in Philadelphia in the heady days of the 1920s, when the Philadelphia Orchestra would perform with the organ in the Grand Court to audiences of 10,000.

My greatest regret was that Florence Candler never attended any of the Ally Pally events, having become by this point too infirm to travel. How she would have loved these events, with their pomp and variety. Indeed, it is right to say that the whole thing had come about largely because of her quiet patronage. She died a month after that first grand gala, and it was as sad a day as I could imagine. But from my first conscious moments I've always tried to emphasize life and not death. I never go to funerals, mainly because I can't bear the thought. And to me, even in death, Florence would have encouraged me to live life to the full. In one sense, she has never stopped knocking on my bedroom door, cane in hand, admonishing me to 'get out of that bed' and get on with living.

All the same, I felt so terribly alone that October day. Florence had played such a unique role in my life. She did more for me than anyone else, and for no reason in the world other than her sheer faith in what I might become. I could not fathom what I had been able to give back to her, save for the proof of the pudding, that I had fulfilled her mandate – and so it is poignant that she never witnessed those thousands of people enjoying organ music on many a fine summer's afternoon. Even though they weren't Southerners, Florence would still have liked them. But the show goes on; death spurs us to life. *Requiescas in pace*, dearest Florence.

The 1978 season benefited greatly from all the lessons we had learned the previous year. By this time, Barry Nevill's proven gift for promoting unusual events, coupled with the confidence that we could achieve an audience of more than 3,000 at every concert, spurred us to still greater things. The multi-performer concept struck a chord with audiences, so at every concert I paired up with at least one other organist. Again, Thalben accepted my invitation, and his July 23 recital included two of his own works and a repeat of Wagner's *Ride of the Valkyries* that had been such a hit the previous summer. And rather than just one gala, we scheduled two, the first in mid-August, the second in September, but this time with *five* artists. When I was asked for my autograph on the London Underground and while walking along Regent Street, I knew the series had reached cruising altitude.

By the second season, I had rented a basement apartment on Dukes Avenue, a ten minute walk from the Great Hall. My witty landlady, Emma Dickinson, was a longtime Muswell Hill resident and a fount of Palace history and local folklore. She took me under her wing, making me comfortable in the neighborhood and, whenever I went on tour, writing me everywhere and forwarding my mail. Many years later, when I acquired Thalben-Ball's vast music library, Emma spent hundreds of hours sorting through the thousands of selections. At about the same time, I was given two delightful kittens, which I named Sebastian and Wagner. They were playful and funny and we all got along famously. I hated the thought of leaving them in the apartment while I practiced, so from time to time I brought them to the Ally Pally in a cat-carrier. Someone suggested that, since they seemed to enjoy the music, why not bring them to a concert? Carrier atop of the console, Sebastian and Wagner attended several programs, brave souls! Given the British affinity for cats, it isn't surprising that they rapidly won their own devoted following. Later, they were comfortably resettled in Brooklyn, New York, with Marilyn Brennan, the President of the Virgil Fox Society.

The 1978 Grand Gala Finale on September 3 was probably the single most outrageous day of my life. Publicity for this concert exceeded anything hitherto attempted. In addition to the normal blitz of announcements, posters graced every other lamp post, not only in Oxford Street but also elsewhere throughout the capital. Our theme was Americana, and together our group devised a novel means of celebrating. As people arrived – 4,000 in all this time – they were handed pocket-sized Union Jack and American flags. Alan Foster, a London car dealer who loved the organ and also played a bit himself, brought a crimson Cadillac convertible to the hall. I armed myself with streamers and bags of glitter.

On the stroke of three, the spectacle began. Barry Nevill launched into the *Star Spangled Banner* on a near-deafening full organ, while at the back of the Hall I perched myself on the folded-back convertible top, glitter at the ready. At a snail's pace, Alan Foster chauffeured me down the center aisle of the Great Hall. The crowd went wild, waving their flags and cheering, while I fired salvo upon salvo of glitter back at them. We kept it up until reaching the stage where I was greeted by my co-performers. Well, after all, I did have to get to the stage somehow!

After the commotion had died down, we settled into the music – Harold Britton, the well-known organist of Walsall Town Hall, William Davies, a brilliant talent who played regularly for the BBC, Roger Fisher, the distinguished organist of Chester Cathedral and the celebrated theatre organist Arnold Loxam. A gentleman of enormous vitality, Arnold had a terrific rapport with the audience, owing not only to his style and musicianship but to his celebrated and oft-imitated 'Loxam Bounce,' whereby he bobbed up and down on the bench in a total rhythmic frenzy. His was indeed a performance to behold – and one which I was wise not to emulate – especially since even his movements could grow sufficiently intense as to un-chock the movable console and dolly, weighing in at more than half a ton, which was held in place with six large wooden wedges. Loosened by Loxam, the console became entirely too movable and exhibited a dangerous tendency to roll right off the stage and into the audience. Needless to say, we were all at the ready during his practice and performance to guard against catastrophe.[4]

The supreme bonus at this gala was the presence of Virgil Fox and David Snyder, who were taking a much-deserved European holiday. Before the encores began, I could not resist introducing Virgil to the audience. From near the back of the hall, he stood up on a chair and without a microphone proclaimed his greetings to the cheering mob. 'GOD BLESS YOU ALL! YOU HEARD *REAL MUSIC* TODAY!' Better than anyone, Virgil knew how to talk in upper-case letters.

Fun as they were, the Alexandra Palace concerts were only one aspect of my emerging career in Great Britain. In a mood for success, I would play any instrument anywhere for virtually any fee. This rather left the door open and I was soon inundated. To give one example from 1978, I was booked for thirty-five concerts between May 27 and October 15 – these in addition to the Ally Pally series. One brilliant stroke in Barry's promotional flyers was to list all the venues I had played in a given season, reinforcing the notion that every recital was part of a crusade. His newspaper connections certainly helped the cause, since he seemed able to arrange advance articles and interviews with the local press wherever I was next headed. I gave almost a hundred interviews that first year, helping to establish my name on the media circuit.

My policy of accepting any engagement sometimes involved rapid response. In 1979 the Master of the Queen's Musick, Malcolm Williamson, was due to play a recital for the St. David's Bach Festival in Wales. Unfortunately, he became indisposed two days before the due date, and a replacement was needed pronto. When the call came through, I repeated to myself 'Anything, anywhere, anytime ...' Organ-builder Matthew Copley collected me and we drove straight away to St. David's Cathedral, which is almost as far west as one can go in Wales without falling into the Irish Sea. In the flurry of the circumstances, I hadn't thought to

4 Arnold's son, Keith Loxam, is a good friend to this day. A producer for BBC radio, he has been responsible for several of my BBC organ galas.

expect anything of the venue, and was overwhelmed to come upon a magnificent building in an idyllic setting, with a Willis organ, responsive audience, and one incredibly relieved cathedral organist, Sir Nicholas Jackson. With precious little preparation, I played my recital, signed autographs, got back in Matthew's Citroën and arrived at his London home bleary-eyed and exhausted – a 24-hour turnaround precisely. There was no race to win here, merely another recital the next evening.

Barry's publicity, press notices from other concerts and the overall Ally Pally success all converged to create sizable audiences everywhere I went. More remarkable and gratifying in the extreme is that many fine individuals came forward to offer their help. For example, Richard Hadingham and George Priestly, two unswervingly loyal supporters who worked for British Rail, drove me around the country to dozens of recitals during and after the Ally Pally years. Their good nature helped pass many long hours. Sophie Yauner, Bert Neale, Mike Crozier, Robert Etherington and Edwin Robinson did much the same later on, tirelessly chauffeuring me to concerts and providing the sort of conversation which makes tedious journeys pass in a flash.

I soon discovered that being an American in England allowed me to get away with antics perhaps not possible for an American in America or a Brit on home turf. When I played in Norwich Cathedral in June 1979, the organ developed a cipher – when the mechanism malfunctions so that a pipe sounds constantly whether it is asked to or not. Sometimes, if the affected pipe is quiet enough, one can actually disregard it. But this one was impossible to ignore and prevented my continuing. I stopped in mid-stream and humorously addressed the crowd. 'This organ is meant to be *subservient*, and I will not be defeated!' Cheers of agreement rose from the crowd. 'Is there a tuner in the house?' The chap came forward, climbed into the organ and located the misbehaving pipe. 'Show it to us!' I cried. After handing it to me, I held it aloft, proclaiming 'This is the *offender*!' Of course, in reality, the pipe had no control over its ciphering. The fault lay with the mechanism that played it. But I didn't think that hauling out the 800-pound windchest would be quite as practical, so I carried on. 'Ladies and gentleman, the tuner has found the culprit – now it must be *disciplined*.' More cheers! 'Pass it around. Accuse it. Reprimand it. Talk to it severely. And then let me have it back in good condition. I can promise you it will *never* misbehave again.' While I resumed playing, the poor pipe began to make the rounds of the entire crowd. As I was signing programs after the concert, a sweet comely-looking gal came over, pipe in hand. 'I was the last one!' she said, innocently. 'Here it is – intact but well punished!'

Most of the time, however, the joke is on the organist. At one memorable performance in Tewkesbury Abbey, I began a major work on the splendid 1885

Michell & Thynne 'Grove' organ. Situated in the north transept, it is invisible from the nave. My good friend, Roy Massey, who has served church and organ music with great distinction for many years, latterly as Organist of Hereford Cathedral, was kindly assisting at the console, reached by a steep, narrow wooden staircase. After I had finished the selection, Roy darted down the steps so that he would not obstruct my journey to take my bow. I wasn't overly careful, however, and hooked my right trouser pocket on the top of the banister. Wood clearly had the advantage over mere cloth, and by the time I reached floor level my trousers had entirely torn apart and had fallen into an undignified heap around my ankles. Having witnessed this ripping event in its entirety, Roy could barely contain his laughter. 'Gosh,' he said dryly, as only an Englishman can, 'that's torn it!' In desperation, I threw on my full-length fur coat and raced out into the nave, feeling particularly vulnerable all the same. After explaining the problem – rather than exhibiting it, thank you – the audience and I enjoyed a good laugh together, and I played the balance of the program decked out like a Russian bear.

In such circumstances, haste makes one chaste but sometimes it sure is necessary. About an hour before one particular touring organ concert at London's Barbican Hall, I discovered that I had left the organ computer cards at home in Hammersmith, quite the opposite side of London. Sadly there is no permanent pipe organ in this splendid place, the very home of the London Symphony Orchestra! These cards supplemented the touring instrument with additional tone colors, some of which were necessary for the afternoon's music. I begged my co-landlord Michael Crozier to leap into his chariot – a fast BMW – retrieve the cards and come back as soon as possible. Owing to heavy traffic, it took him longer than usual to reach Hammersmith, so on the return journey down the Westway he really put his foot down and was duly stopped for speeding by a leather-suited motorcycle patrol officer. When questioned about the need for speed, Mike held up the cards, saying that they were vital to an organ concert to begin in fifteen minutes. The officer replied, 'Oh, I like organ music. Who's playing?' When he heard the response, the policeman said, 'Do you mean *the* Carlo Curley? I must be one of his greatest fans! Follow right behind me and I'll get you there in no time.' Off they sped, blue light flashing and siren wailing, arriving at the Barbican with hardly a couple of minutes to spare. I hesitate to mention the officer's name however, as he may have gone somewhat beyond the call of duty.

Once again, here is an advantage of being an American organist in England. In the States, a cop might break the rules for Isaac Stern or Luciano Pavarotti, but in England, an organist still has a chance to be a king. Organ lovers lurk around every corner, aching to help. I need only look back to the Alexandra Palace years to remember how many friendships were instigated as a result of that series and a genuine desire to pitch in. One longtime pal is Bob Grover, a keen theatre organ aficionado who managed cinemas for the Essoldo, Rank and Independent circuits, taking on the unenviable job of closing the unprofitable ones. My friendship with Bob has flourished over the years and is evidenced by many happy dinners and organ crawls to say nothing of his overseas visits with me. Chris Sprague falls into the same league. I met him in 1979 at my first St. Paul's Cathedral recital. Later we got to know each other better through our mutual friend, Matthew Copley. Although a weekend organist, Chris enjoys a distinguished career in the television industry. He also has a natural talent for lighting and special effects and, for my 1979 Alexandra Palace gala, devised additional theatre lighting and a pyrotechnic display right inside the Great Hall. Such occasions never failed to put a smile on his face. Few fireworks people have the joy of setting them off indoors. More recently, Chris has contributed to some of my concerts with explosive confetti canons. Great fun, and a sure-fire way to surprise an audience. More recently, to celebrate my fortieth birthday, he organized a splendid display in the garden of my London home, the explosions from which managed to set off dozens of car alarms for blocks around. And I'm still apologizing to the neighbors.

CHAPTER EIGHT

'SILENCE! I MUST CREATE!'

Touring, especially with a complex and heavy road organ, is possibly the most exacting and exhausting way to spend one's life. I could not have traveled the countless miles that I have and performed at so many venues without the help and expertise of a number of loyal assistants.

One blessed godsend arrived in the form of Tom Bailey, an organ groupie I'd met in New Orleans. A robust, heavy-set guy with a lovable nature, silky brown hair and a coarse, cackling laugh that could fill the Grand Canyon, Tom was yet another organist and a fan of Virgil's so bad it hurt. He had the makings of a perfect assistant. He was fascinated by popular concerts and enthusiastic crowds, knew the organ well and was itching to see the world. Did I have a job for him! During 1979 he took a year off to act as my assistant, touring around the States and Europe. Supplementing his efficiency and organization was an innate Southern ability to charm. A single sentence in Tom's thick accent – he hailed from Laurel, Mississippi, very much the 'Deep South' – could melt the most hardened cynic. Concert sponsors – particularly the British – lapped it up.

Although Tom and I had many hilarious times together, what sticks fast in my memory is a trip we took together to France, not to concertize but in search of an honest vacation. Addicted to any and all recordings of French organs, Tom came to France with high expectations, so it was something of a relief when they were exceeded. I practically had to drag him out of St.-Sulpice, the organ captivated him so. Equally important was our visit to Notre-Dame, where the ever-gracious *titulaire*, Pierre Cochereau, welcomed us to the tribune on Sunday morning. Tom and I carried on jabbering, but as the Mass was about to begin, Pierre raised his hand and declaimed, '*Silence*! I must *create*!' I had visited before and knew this to be a stock line, but first-timer Tom took it as an edict from the Almighty himself, buttressed by the fact that we were, after all, in Notre-Dame de Paris. Once Cochereau had built up to his trademark 'white heat,' full organ with chamades – it took perhaps thirty seconds – Tommy could not refrain from a fusillade of joyful expletives. 'Gaaaw *Damn*! Isn't this where *Lewis* Vierne played?' Yes, Tommy. 'Didn't he drop dead in th' saddle while playin' a recital on the original Cavaillé-Coll console?' Yes, Tommy. And with Maurice Duruflé acting as console assistant at that very performance. 'Whew! Ain't that the way to die? If *I'm* gonna die, that's the way I wanna go, playing either a recital or a service. *Real* romantic!' I had serious reservations about his assessment of Vierne's tragic passing. Of course, there are some things I wouldn't mind dying in the middle of, but a concert is not one of them. However, I wasn't about to deny Tommy his moment.

After our year together, Tommy returned to the States and eventually moved to Fort Lauderdale, Florida where he worked as office manager for Mike Dunne, the highly successful Allen dealer there. He also became organist at the Church of the Little Flower in Coral Gables, just south of Miami. Just as he had been devoted to my affairs, Tommy threw himself wholeheartedly into his new jobs and, over the telephone, would relate with great pride the satisfaction he took in playing to a responsive congregation in a glorious acoustical setting. It came as a real shock in June 1992 to get a call from Mike, telling me that Tommy had suffered a heart attack and died during Mass, in the heat of playing a free-style re-harmonization during the closing verse of a hymn. This sorely missed treasure wasn't just a Man Friday, but a loyal and charming friend with a huge spirit and loving nature to match. I can only hope for him that the manner of his passing was indeed a wish come true.

In the fall of 1979, it became clear that a fourth Alexandra Palace season would not take place. We had only given one concert that summer, due partly to the Palace schedule, but also to the demand for other concerts which tied up the touring organ elsewhere. It was also rumored that the Greater London Council had plans for undertaking a modicum of renovation before disposing of the Palace altogether. This came as quite a blow not only to me but also to all those who had worked so hard to make our concerts such a success. But I reassured myself that a renovated Palace under fresh ownership might mean the revival of the great Willis organ, and an even more welcoming space for large crowds.

But the situation was to worsen beyond my greatest fears. In August 1980 a major fire broke out. Happening to be in England, I rushed at once to Muswell Hill. In a daze, a group of us huddled on the terrace just outside the Great Hall's south doors and watched in horror as the flames consumed the scene of so many cherished memories. Most unbearable, however, were the agonizing wails which emanated from the old Willis as hot air and flames rushed up the towers. The enormous pipes became unsoldered and then, with an unearthly groaning and screeching, they fell in on themselves like giant fallen warriors, finally evaporating. Eventually, the inferno consumed the entire Great Hall and all the Willis framework and façade pipes. I remembered that the first Palace had also been destroyed by fire more than a century earlier and history had now savagely repeated itself. Once again, the poor old Alexandra Palace seemed inexorably jinxed.

I am grateful that, before the fire, I was able to record on my touring organ in the grand acoustics of the Palace. *Carlo Curley Concert Curios*, an LP for RCA Red Seal, contained popular concert selections from the Ally Pally concerts and now documents the sound of the touring organ the way the crowds heard it in the halcyon summer days of the late seventies.

By this time I was being invited to make a number of recordings. *Virtuoso French Organ Music* at the Royal Albert Hall was again for RCA, and I appeared large on the cover beaming through the console, above the four manuals, in place of the music desk. Long before the days of computer graphics, it was, in fact, quite a production to achieve this shot, since the console sits high above any position inside the organ where one can comfortably stand. The father-and-son tuners, Ken and Hedley James, set up a table inside the unenclosed Choir section, directly behind and somewhat below the console level. Well out of shot, they clasped my legs firmly as I stood teetering for the photographer! My life as a mannequin ... I was elated when the album made *Billboard* magazine's top recommended LPs:

> This is an organ recording that audiophiles will admire, good in dynamic range, true stereo image and fullness of impact. Curley puts across all of the pieces very persuasively, taming the giant Royal Albert Hall instrument and making it responsive to his every command. That's incredible.

Both records came at the behest of Ralph Mace of RCA, best known for having spear-headed James Galway's recording career and a true lover of organ music. Ralph also had a faculty for catchy titles, *Carlo Curley Concert Curios* being one of them. For me, the ultimate compliment came much later, in 1990, when RCA dug back into their archives to create an eleven-piece compilation CD entitled *The Organ's Greatest Hits*, including selections of Virgil Fox at the Royal Albert Hall and Riverside Church, interspersed with several of my own offerings at the Albert Hall and on the Allen touring organ at Alexandra Palace. I had never dreamed I would be so honored as to share a disc with Virgil Fox.

With the Alexandra Palace, alas, no longer available, Alan Foster – of Ally Pally Cadillac fame – decided that the gala concerts must continue. He decided to act as sponsor himself, hiring no less a venue than the Royal Albert Hall. This had certain unquestionable advantages, among which were a notable concert organ, comfortable seating and better sight-lines all around. The trade-off came in the acoustics, which were nothing like as splendid as those at the Alexandra Palace. But the important thing was we were carrying on and, beginning in 1980, we made some magnificent music at the Royal Albert Hall.

Arguably the most notable of our concerts was in April 1982, when I invited the world-renowned organist of Notre-Dame, Pierre Cochereau, to share the stage with myself, Robin Richmond, Sheila Lawrence and Lyn Larsen. Four organs and five organists! We had the Albert Hall's Willis/Harrison, my touring organ, Alan Foster's own digital theatre-style Allen and Sheila's charming portable Peter Collins pipe organ. The variety in sound and repertoire put a unique spin on the event. Sheila's selections were elegant and jewel-like, made all the more interesting when juxtaposed against the offerings of the two theatre organists, each of whom played in his own distinctive style. And against my usual fare, we had the improvisational genius of Cochereau, who hadn't played in England for nearly thirty years!

In common with all great French organists, Cochereau was famed for his ability to improvise – to create music on the spot based on a given theme. I had watched him create individual pieces at Notre-Dame but it was the memory of having heard him improvise a large-scale work in New York's Philharmonic Hall which convinced me that his skills must be shown off. To prepare for the Albert Hall gala, we advertised in the national and music press for submissions of slow and fast themes, each not to exceed four bars in length. I rented two top hats from Moss Bros and all themes received were deposited in the appropriate hat (slow or fast). The event received excellent pre-publicity. *The Times* published a lengthy interview with me on the day of the event and the *Daily Telegraph* ran a short photo-item with Pierre under the headline 'Out of the chapeau.'

On the big night, I put the hats on-stage and, at the appropriate moment, dug down deep and selected one from each – *Liebestod* from *Tristan und Isolde* by Wagner and Scott Joplin's *The Entertainer* – for the improvised symphony, which was to consist of five movements. Pierre gave a dismissive shrug of the shoulders and proceeded to embark on this uncharted once-in-a-lifetime voyage.

Not only did he manipulate both themes to novel ends, but he concluded with a big double fugue, and he even managed to work in *Rule, Britannia* as he approached the conclusion. All agreed it was an amazing feat, even if some had doubts about the actual musical worth. Ralph Mace summed it up afterwards when he said that, although he was very impressed, the symphony 'didn't necessarily bear repeated hearing.' While there is perhaps merit to his assessment, the effect on the audience was spellbinding.

In planning the event, Alan Foster had been somewhat concerned that Pierre might carry on too long. As the Albert Hall was a union house, the duration of our concert was critical and, if we over-ran by so much as a minute, the management would have to impose something like a £1,500 surcharge for staff overtime. Alan nervously approached Pierre just before the concert began and begged that his improvisation not exceed thirty minutes. Fortunately, unlike my visit to Notre-Dame with Tom Bailey, the strains of '*Silence! I must create!*' did not ring through the dressing room. Instead, Pierre replied reverentially, 'Alan, when I improvise, my spirit leaves my body. Please sit near the console and, when you wish, make for me a sign and my spirit will return. This will be not a problem for me.' Thinking this was all very fine and *exceedingly* French, Alan, not entirely convinced, did as instructed and took up his position by the console. After twenty-five minutes, a conclusion did not seem forthcoming although beads of perspiration were certainly evident on Alan's forehead. Not only had Pierre's spirit left his body, it appeared to have floated across the Channel and gone all the way back to Paris. Alan coughed and cleared his throat, but Pierre, his eyes firmly closed, had long since drawn virtually full organ. Alan tried a desperate wave of the hand but this failed too. Finally, the businessman in him overcame all reserve and he moved across and tapped the player's forearm firmly. At once, the master's eyes flew open, he nodded, and true to his word finished triumphantly within a few minutes. Alan breathed an enormous sigh of relief.

I have to confess, on a different matter I was somewhat less subtle. One characteristic of French organ playing is to draw almost every single stop in loud combinations. On French organs this may make sense but in English organs many softer stops not only contribute little or nothing to the full organ ensemble, they also waste precious wind. And while the Albert Hall organ possessed many fine qualities, an ample set of lungs was not among them. If a big chord were held for more than a few seconds, the supply would run short causing the pitch to sag noticeably. It was less than attractive and certainly not musical.

As I listened to Pierre's practice sessions, I realized with growing concern that he was regularly 'pulling out all the stops' and, whenever he did so, the instrument appeared to be fighting for its life. Something had to be done so, once he had finished his final rehearsal, I took it upon myself to edit his combination pistons to remove the dead weight. This is, admittedly, an arrogant thing to do. An artist must be free to choose his stops as he pleases, and I emphasize that I have never done this before or since. As soon as I had begun my modest weeding, I realized that I was in for a surprise. Not only were all the stops set on a couple of the pistons, but also every coupler, the 64' Acoustic Bass, Tubular Bells, Carillons and the Bass Drum! The Bass Drum hadn't worked in years but the bells certainly did. The result in performance was a much steadier and assured sound – and without the ding-dongs and bongos.

Of course, the audience was never aware of these small production adjustments, but it would be wrong to imply that everything always went smoothly. At one of our earlier galas in October 1980, the spotlight operator missed a cue when Noel Rawsthorne – of Liverpool's Anglican Cathedral – took his place at the console. Apart from a wan glow provided by the goose-necked lamps over the stop jambs and music desk, Noel was in darkness. The packed audience remained hushed, waiting to make sense of the scenario. Never slow to miss an opportunity, Noel drew the softest stop – a Dulciana – and began playing the hymn *Lead, Kindly Light.* The crowd exploded with laughter, the spotlight operator sprang to attention and both organ and performer were instantly bathed in light.

Encouraged by the success of our Albert Hall ventures, Alan Foster decided to go one better, focusing his attentions on London's South Bank and the Royal Festival Hall. The Festival Hall's was a famous organ and although there was a regular Wednesday recital series at 5.55, programmes could run no more than an hour, to enable the hall to be cleared before the almost inevitable 7.30 orchestral concert. When Alan Foster put his proposition to the authorities, they practically laughed at him. They hadn't had a full-length evening organ recital since the instrument had been inaugurated in 1954 and they just did not believe that a large crowd would turn out. Undeterred, Alan hired the hall for a Saturday evening and, in typical fashion, we publicized it to the gills. Jane Parker-Smith, Noel Rawsthorne and I would share the programme.

As I mapped out my selections and became better acquainted with the instrument, I devised a method of increasing the organ's sense of presence and vibrancy in this acoustically dry venue. Occupying a shallow area running the entire width of the stage behind the orchestra, the departments of the organ are laid out logically. Thus I discovered that if I wanted a particular color, say a flute tone, it helped immeasurably to couple one flute stop on the left side to another on the right. The resulting stereophonic effect greatly increased the sense of depth and dimension, adding warmth and helping to counteract the acoustics.

I also noticed that the tremulants – the mechanisms that impart a singer's vibrato to organ pipes – were adjusted as to make only the merest flutter, while the celestes – the sets of pipes tuned deliberately sharp to provide an undulating 'wave' – were almost dead in tone, producing a sterile and not a sensuous effect. So I decided to telephone the curator of the organ, Ralph Downes, to ask if anything could be done. At almost any other venue, this would have merely amounted to calling the organ tuner. But here, 'curator' is a loose term, for this was no mere organ tuner. Ralph Downes was a major figure in the history of the 20th century British organ, more responsible than anyone for the neo-classical organ reform movement. Widely traveled, he was also a well-known player and expert musician. His design of and involvement with the Festival Hall's 1954 Harrison & Harrison revolutionized organ-building in England and, since its controversial installation, he had remained curator, overseeing its maintenance and looking after its best interests.

It's hardly surprising then that I was nervous when I called. Having introduced myself and told him about our forthcoming gala, I politely registered my desires regarding the tremulants and celestes. His reply was curt if not downright rude. 'Certainly not. They are adjusted properly and nothing will be changed.' Without allowing me to draw breath, he hung up. I was livid! After all, we were paying to use the hall and organ. I was not to be denied return service and, having called him straight back, threatened in no uncertain terms to cancel the concert – which would involve refunding ticket money to some 2,000 pre-booked ticket holders – citing his intransigence as the sole reason. Even as I said my piece – and say my piece I did – I was shaking. This was Ralph Downes after all, and I hated having been forced to put my foot down.

But as soon as I had finished, his attitude changed completely. 'Well, Carlo,' he said, 'I suppose we could help you out.' The storm clouds had cleared as if they had never existed and, when I next went over to practice, he was waiting for me, friendly as could be. Having reviewed the tremulants and celestes as I had asked, he made a few other adjustments before, to my astonishment, remaining until the very end of my rehearsal. We chatted like old friends afterwards – he knew Virgil and Robert Noehren from their Festival Hall visits – and he made some helpful comments on the program I was playing, particularly Widor's Sixth Symphony. During the concert itself, he stayed in the organ the entire time, having promised to stand by in case of any problem.

The program came off magnificently, and to a full house. Noel was in top form – the organ lights were on this time – and Jane played up her usual storm. I was particularly pleased with my contributions. The Widor went really well, as did the Langlais *Chant heroïque*. And I think I gave my best performance ever of Saint-Saëns' *Marche Militaire*, a favorite encore. It was the ideal piece for the mood of the crowd and I let out my 'whoop' at precisely the right moment. Having been recorded, my portions of the program were subsequently released as a compact disc on the Pro Arte label – in fact, the first CD ever made on the Festival Hall organ.

I am glad to say that Ralph Downes and I later came to know each other far better and in 1982 he invited me to open the Peter Collins instrument he had designed for St. David's Hall in Cardiff. Once again, he was the untiring 'curator,' standing watch inside the organ throughout, in case something went amiss.

At the same time that my UK career was going supersonic, US bookings were increasing with every passing year. Having acquired my touring organ in mid-1976, I used it for a year before having it shipped permanently to England. From that point on, Don Westfield kindly supplied me with instruments for pipeless North American venues while pipe organ dates were handled by Richard Torrence, Virgil Fox's manager. Richard was every bit the go-getter and was quick to capitalize on my English publicity. For example, he made excellent use of the Ally Pally photographs, including a spectacular panorama taken during the BBC TV filming session.

Early in 1978, a friend convinced me that there was no longer any pressing reason to base my life in Philadelphia. Diminutive in stature, with a laser wit and a great gift for having fun, Pete Rich proved the ideal flatmate. After meeting him at Druid Hills Baptist in Atlanta, Pete quickly gained entrance into Mrs. Candler's young set. After I left Atlanta, Pete kept company with Florence and the two grew close. But much as Terence Mulligan had gotten the sudden urge to move to New York to get into advertising, Pete had similar ambitions to write humor. Within weeks of his arrival in the Big Apple, he had landed a job writing material for Bob Hope. When he suggested we secure an apartment together, it sounded like a good idea. My agent was in New York, I had many friends there and it provided a most convenient hub for international travel.

I moved up in mid-February. The apartment on West 95th Street was typical of Manhattan living. Several spacious rooms, each furnished with Candler hand-me-downs, led off a long, narrow hallway. Pete and I did the place up in as much style as we could afford. While the building wasn't quite grand enough for a doorman, we did have a gem of a landlord, large, loquacious and one thousand percent Polish. His method of solving any problem began by sitting down and opening a can of beer. I found this attitude so frustrating that eventually I saw no other choice but to join him. Although I could barely understand a word he said, it didn't much matter; he helped make the new place feel like home.

The move to New York was fortuitous because in early 1980 a significant change took place in my career. I joined the large stable of Columbia Artists Management, Inc. of New York (CAMI), a firm which represented nothing less than the world's finest musicians. This was their fiftieth anniversary and, as part of their celebrations, they took on a number of new artists. In this regard, I must mention Ralph Mace of RCA, who had generously put my name forward.

An offshoot of CAMI was the enormously popular Community Concerts series, in which hundreds of CAMI artists were offered to Community Concert Associations throughout North America. About 600 municipalities would hold several performances each year, presenting orchestras, dance companies and soloists in small towns as well as big cities. CAMI had made a brilliant move, in that they were the only concert management to own their own series. Community Concerts provided ideal venues for the touring organ, each one backed up by their well-oiled publicity machine. As an added bonus, Community Concerts were certainly frequent. By way of a small example, I played twelve dates between February 6 and 28, starting in Malden, Missouri, thence to Salem, Ohio; Dubois, Pennsylvania; five further dates in North Carolina, concluding in my hometown of Monroe; then a five-date swing through Florida, from Homestead to Marathon, down to Key West, back up to Melbourne before Bradenton; and finally closing in Lincolnton, North Carolina. Sometimes this intensity of schedule would continue for weeks on end, resulting in up to forty consecutive dates. I would head home completely exhausted.

As with all the previous touring organ work, I had a succession of drivers/technicians without whom I could never have undertaken the venture. The first was Tom McGee, who drove and installed my first touring organ and then, in turn, Don Faasen from Grand Rapids, Mike Dickinson and Ron DeJonge. Just like the Pony Express, these great guys persevered through any weather and in all sorts of conditions – including my company!

The year 1980 was a wow in all respects, and not merely for the CAMI contract, the RCA recordings, the Festival Hall success and the Community Concerts. During my USA tour that fall, I received a call from my old friend, Bob Maddox, the former assistant pastor at Druid Hills. It was patched through not from Atlanta but from Washington where he was now the President's Liaison to the Religious Community. After the initial pleasantries, he relayed the President's formal request that I play a classical organ recital at the White House on November 25, as part of the commemorations for National Bible Week. The nation's leading clerics would attend the performance. *Now let me just consult my schedule ...*

Actually, the invitation, while the greatest honor, was less surprising than it may have first appeared. Jimmy Carter had been Governor of Georgia before being elected President. He knew Druid Hills Baptist when I was organist there and had offered a lay-sermon one Sunday, remaining afterwards for my unofficial 'postludial' recital. I had also performed at the Governor's Mansion – right around the corner from Florence's house in Buckhead. Since the White House has no organ, I rang the Allen Organ Company and they rapidly agreed to provide a suitable instrument. It was set up in the White House entrance hall – quite an acoustically live space – and the audience was to stand or promenade. As I was rehearsing, First Lady Rosalynn Carter popped up from behind to say hello.

President and First Lady Carter were as gracious and unaffected in private as they appeared in public. The President even stood alongside the console for my entire performance. And I confess to a secret pleasure. It was lovely to have the clergy stand to listen to organ music! At last, the shoe was on the other foot.

But fate did not seem satisfied for me to play for the President of the United States alone, for it was shortly thereafter that I was called to perform in the presence of Her Serene Highness, Princess Grace of Monaco. Truly a red-letter day, the occasion was the Gala Premiere of an Earle Mack Film, *The Children of Theater Street*, which was to take place at the Beacon Theater in New York City and to be narrated by Princess Grace herself. My appearance had been arranged through Richard Torrence and I was thrilled at the chance to play for the Princess.

The Beacon Theater had an excellent and entirely original 'Mighty' Wurlitzer, a wonderful bonus but something that had me worried, since I had never performed publicly on any theater organ. It took many rehearsals to master the console, with its multi-coloured stop keys in place of drawknobs, numerous tremulants and a horse-shoe arrangement in place of the traditional classical console layout. As the premiere was to fall only a few days before Christmas, I labored over a medley of Christmas carols and standard repertoire until I felt more at home at the keys.

Princess Grace was by far the brightest light in the place, every bit the diamond-bedecked royal star. When we spoke together afterwards, I was struck by her legendary aura. Without doubt, with her reassuring presence and down-to-earth personality, she was the most elegant woman I had ever met. I had never been much of a movie fan but, that night, I fell asleep with real stars in my eyes.

The three years leading up to 1980 saw the true blossoming of my career. But careers do not happen, they have to be molded, shaped and, ideally, directed. No artist can accomplish this alone and my success in the UK would not have been possible without considerable help. In this context, Barry Nevill was ideal, for he combined in one person plentiful talents to achieve both publicity and bookings. Unfortunately, his journalistic work was full-time and his connection with me very much a freelance affair. It soon became obvious that, by devoting so much time and energy to my business, he was sacrificing his own career. Coupled with other complications, among them his desire to work solely on UK bookings when my career was becoming increasingly European in scope, it became clear that I needed another agent.

Matthew Copley suggested that an acquaintance of his might fit the bill. Selwyn Jones was an academic but a great fan of the organ and its repertoire. In appearance an impressive combination of the prophet Elijah and George Bernard Shaw, he spoke several languages, was the epitome of organization and continued ably in Barry's footsteps for several years.

In due course, he was succeeded by Audrey Frank, who represented a small stable of internationally renowned artists, but when her husband became ill, they decided to retire to France. It was round about this time that the finger of fate pointed once more. I met Paul Vaughan for the first time as a guest on BBC TV's hugely popular *Wogan* show. He was there representing one of his clients and one of my fellow guests, Lord Montagu of Beaulieu, the then Chairman of English Heritage. Paul and I chatted briefly at the reception where he also met Audrey. Having spotted serendipity in action, she later telephoned him to ask if his company, PVA Management, would be interested in taking me on.

Curiously enough, our paths had nearly crossed – or should I say collided – on a number of previous occasions. An experienced record producer, he had worked as a free-lance for RCA and, while later employed by BBC Television, had been a member of the production team at *Nationwide* during my Ally Pally appearances on that highly successful show. More importantly for me perhaps, he had worked closely with George Thalben-Ball, managing against all the odds to tempt him back to the microphone to record his last ever organ recitals both from Birmingham Town Hall and the Temple Church before producing the final great recording of the Temple Church Choir. Thalben clearly trusted and admired him and that was more than enough for me.

I am indeed lucky to be able to say that all the people who have helped in the nurturing of my career have understood precisely what I am trying to do and each of them has devised effective promotion for my work. Better still, they have all been friends, and have helped through thick and thin. I cherish them all. Less than three years from the first Ally Pally concert, one magazine could write:

'No American organist has ever been so well received in England. No English organist has either.'[1]

When George was eighty-five and had just retired from the Temple, Robert Eddison's *Observer* tribute also included this ultimate compliment:

> Of the new generation of young organists, he [Thalben] says: 'There are a lot of very good young organists around, with the British and the Americans still the world leaders. The organ is a great promoter of discipline and integrity in music, and the best players welcome the challenge. That young American, Carlo Curley, is a first-rate player. I don't think he's gone over the top as a populariser; I'm a populariser myself, remember.'

Amazed, honored, and humbled to have been singled out, I am clear that the beneficent presence of dear Thalben was a most influential and all-important motivating force for my work and music. More than anyone, he led me to the doorstep of his country and introduced me to its people and their ways. It was the saddest of days when he died in 1987. Barry Nevill and John Thalben-Ball, George's son, organized a memorial service which took place in St. Paul's Cathedral on May 26. At John's request, I played a prelude recital of Bach's music, including *Come Sweetest Death, Nun Danket alle Gott*, the *Toccata, Adagio and Fugue*, and my traditional *Sinfonia* from Cantata 29.

The Cathedral was packed to hear the combined choirs of the Temple Church and St. Paul's under the able direction of John Scott. Sir Edward Heath, the former Prime Minister, gave a stirring address touching upon George's individuality and vitality. But there was a ghostly magic when John Thalben-Ball read one of the lessons. Echoing around that vast space, John's voice sounded eerily like his father's. It was as if he was still with us. All who knew George personally were much moved by this, but in a positive way I think – reminding us that people live on through their work and kind deeds and Thalben had certainly left countless of those in his wake.

Seated quietly in the lofty organ gallery, I thought back fifteen years to that first enduring lesson with him at the Temple Church, when I had exploded in all my youthful abandon before he had gently begun the task of curbing my excesses and teaching me a superior approach. After years of study and friendship with this great man, and all my trials and successes in England, I hoped that my shop window was now more modestly arranged.

1 *Ovation*, March 1980, Vol. 1 No. 2, page 6.

CHAPTER NINE

ONCE UPON A TIME

For a number of years, the Danish Tourism Board ran advertisements under the headline, 'So, you don't believe in Fairy Tales ... ?' I should never have doubted them, for in my case at least, they weren't kidding.

On September 1, 1978, I played a recital at St. Augustine's, Kilburn in north-west London. I don't recall much about the program itself, certainly not in the light of what happened afterwards. As audience members lined up to greet me in the church hall after the recital, I sat down at a table to sign autographs. At the other end sat a striking young woman, small in stature with jet-black hair and striking features. She wore no make-up and kept her hair simple. Her natural beauty was stunning.

She chose not to join the queue, but instead sat quietly sipping a cup of tea, observing me steadily. I was so distracted that I could barely pay attention to my autographing, pretending not to look over but staring more fervently all the same. She didn't approach me until the last person had gone.

Introducing herself as Kirsten, it became clear that waiting around for me had been bravely uncharacteristic on her part. Demure, shy and exquisitely softly-spoken, she was a Dane, studying English at Oxford, but would shortly be returning home to Scandinavia. 'Have you ever been there?' she asked. 'No,' I replied, 'but I bet there are some fine organs there?' Wow, this was really shaping up to be one of my more articulate moments. She told me that not only had she attended a program of mine at New College, Oxford the previous June, she had also been present at one of the gala concerts at the Alexandra Palace. Clearly, she greatly enjoyed the organ and its music. Sure, fine, peachy and nice – how could I possibly have missed her?

As we continued to talk, we seemed to trade places, she gaining in confidence while I fell to pieces. I figured I could either look away only to melt anew with each gaze, or stare at her like a Sphinx and hope to avert complete system shutdown. Meanwhile a quiet voice inside me kept insisting that the Danes, however many million there were, were all exclusively golden blondes, and therefore this woman must be fraudulent and would require intensive further questioning.

As you can tell, it was a bit of a moment. The spell broke long enough for me to write out my Muswell Hill address, but even as I did so, I sensed foreboding. What if she forgot? What if she never came to another concert? But a fortnight later – it seemed like six tortuous months – a letter arrived bearing gentle, flowing penmanship and a colorful Danish stamp:

> Dear Carlo, perhaps you don't remember me at all – though I hope you do ... have you ever felt like this about somebody you met for a short time or a face you saw in a crowd, that you would like to find out what sort of person it was, that you wouldn't like the person to disappear? Perhaps you meet too many people to take any interest in individuals, but on the other hand, I can imagine that even if you meet people after your concerts, you don't really get to know them ... No matter how nice and relaxed a person you are, the fact that you're a famous organ player makes it difficult to get to know you. As I said, I liked talking to you, but that was quite difficult since various people wanted to communicate with you at the same time and tell you what a good concert it was ... Organ music is my favourite music, but I'm not writing to you because you're a famous organ player. I would have written to you if you had been some anonymous person I'd met on a train or somewhere. I wish you were, then I wouldn't feel I was intruding on some private and inaccessible person, and you perhaps that I'm just another person writing to you because you're a famous organist. Would you feel like writing to me? I'd be glad. My name and address are as follows. If all this sounds incredibly stupid, have a good laugh! Love, Kirsten.

Alas for me, these things never seemed to happen at all, let alone on the tube or the bus, and had thus far only occurred once at the end of an organ recital. 'So, you don't believe in Fairy Tales ...?' Boy, did I ever feel like writing to her! It was high time for me to experience the land of Hans Christian Andersen for myself.

Trying to schedule that visit took months. I was headed to the States for touring, and my spring dates were already booked solid. The summer and fall

1979 UK concert season alone had twenty-six scheduled appearances, in addition to a by now regular summer engagement at the Interlochen Music Camp in Michigan. But Carlo Curley in love was a force to reckon with, and having searched the diary for the slightest gap, I figured I could just get away for a few days in early July.

But July was ten months away! Woe! Agony! Angst! Suspense! Kirsten and I began corresponding regularly. Her letters followed me around the world – a great feeling, believe me – and every time I saw the Danish stamps, it was a tonic to the stress of touring. In those days, I was still in good shape. I was exercising regularly under Don Faasen's continuing regime and eating well but sensibly. This all seemed to tally with Kirsten, whose letters recounted her devotion to diet, yoga and a healthy environment. She also wrote of those things she loved best, architecture, art, poetry, nature. In her zest for life, she clearly viewed the world around her as something to cherish. In the event, it was probably a good thing that I wasn't able to go to Denmark right away, for our correspondence ensured we became acquainted without starry eyes and candlelight. And by the time our Danish reunion did come to pass, our pent-up suspense was terrific.

That first visit was utter magic, as good as any fairy tale but thankfully lacking in gingerbread houses and boiling cauldrons. Kirsten herself was certainly as divine as any fairy tale heroine, and thankfully she had no evil step-mother and kept her flat as tidy as her person, which tidiness appealed greatly to my Virgo sensibilities. All I had to do was straighten a few picture frames, and her home was nigh unto perfect.

Before long, Kirsten and I discovered the things which correspondence could never reveal. For instance, we found that we shared a love of promenading for hours through the magnificent city of Copenhagen. We also strolled often through the scenic forest surrounding Birkerød in the north of Sjælland. She loved picnics and, basket in hand, we would head off to Sjælsø (Soul Sea), a beautiful nearby lake, staying for dinner at Jægerhytten, a cozy, romantic restaurant in a thatched cottage right at the water's edge. About the fifth day, I began to realize how deeply I was falling 'head over heels.'

I found Denmark as enchanting as Kirsten, perhaps a bit more European than Scandinavian, but with all the famous qualities nonetheless in place: the manicured countryside, the opulent castles, the storybook charm. Most appealing though, were the Danes themselves. They seemed as fresh as their land, their culture geared towards the individual in a way I had never experienced before. With efficient public transportation and services, the government clearly served its people well. Denmark seemed as distinct from England as I found England to be from the United States. And the change was refreshing. To those who believe that Denmark is boringly flat, I suggest a bicycle tour just north of Copenhagen.

Perhaps then they will discover for themselves that they have been talking through their hats.

One day I happened to notice a Danish architectural magazine on Kirsten's coffee table. A new church with a new pipe organ was prominently displayed on its cover. Vangede Kirke had been designed by one of Denmark's premier architects, Johan Otto von Spreckelsen. The organ case was of black-painted steel clad in wood, as opposed to the traditional practice of wood framing. As Kirsten translated the article for me, we learned that Frobenius, the venerable organ-builders from nearby Lyngby, had constructed the instrument. In fact, Kirsten had already attended a recital there and it wasn't difficult to sense my interest, so she called the factory to arrange a visit.

A few days later we met the principals of the firm: Walther and Erik Frobenius, an older and younger brother, respectively, and Mogens (pronounced 'Moans') Pedersen, their voicer at the time. We arrived in mid-afternoon, joining both our hosts and the draftsmen in the Danish mid-afternoon custom of a beer – the equivalent of English tea-time. Touring the works, we saw organs taking shape conceptually in the drafting room and materially in the erecting hall.

That same day we drove to Vangede Kirke itself, its striking exterior reminding me more of a contemporary university library than a church. But inside, it epitomized the clean, tailored sensibility of Danish modern design, sleek, linear, asymmetrical, and everywhere flooded with natural light. Having sat down at the organ, I had to remind myself to be polite, since mechanical-action, neo-classical organs have never really been my thing. But I was in for a surprise. The Frobenius was an unusually engaging and beautifully voiced instrument of a kind I had never come across. The principals were silvery and clean, the flutes liquid and rich and the reeds were uniform and energetic, especially in the pedal. Even the old-style reeds, Krummhorn and Dulcian, which can be most unpleasant in organs of this ilk, had charm, depth and control. Instinctively I began to play Bach. The music came to life at once without any contrived registrations, and sounded beautiful in the process. Every pipe seemed alive and I found it difficult to stop playing.

Perhaps because the organ was such a revelation to me, I quite honestly believe that my playing produced a similar reaction in our hosts. The Danish organ ethos revolved around the music of Bach, Buxtehude and the early composers and was exemplified by a style of playing similar to that which I had instinctively disliked at the North Carolina School of the Arts – aridity of performance, literal and detached. In addition, most Danish organists regarded romantic music – when they regarded it at all – as unquestionably inferior to that of the Golden Age of the Baroque. My manner of playing, and the tradition it represented, was as foreign to Denmark as I was. From the builders' reaction, I knew that my contrasting style of playing had made its mark.

As the day wore on, what was originally intended to have been a brief visit to Vangede Kirke stretched into the evening. Unfailingly courteous throughout, when I had at last finished, the Frobenius brothers invited us to dinner at Skovshoved Hotel, right on the Øresund, the body of water separating Denmark from Sweden. Amidst elegant surroundings, we discussed organs in general and the Vangede instrument in particular. These were people I wanted to know better.

During the next few days, Kirsten and I visited other churches and organs, starting with St. Mariæ Kirke, Helsingør, which housed an essentially new Frobenius but with a few pipes dating from 1636, all housed within older casework. This was where the great composer and organist Dietrich Buxtehude had played from 1660 to 1668.[1] We also visited the unforgettable 1609 Compenius organ in Frederiksborg Castle church. A large chamber organ designed to accompany court dance, the Compenius is justly famous for its distinctive tone, a one-man Glenn Miller orchestra of the early 17th century if you will, but in an unparalleled upscale version. In its lavishly decorated case and keydesk lie perhaps the instrument's true celebrity, for even in a land of ornate organ cases, this outshone them all. I've certainly never come across another organ with stop knobs of *solid silver*. Its façade pipes and pedal natural keys were clad in ivory – just ponder that for a moment – and the case contained richly carved pipe shades, statuary, panel ornament and cornice-work. Every organist has played upon ivory keys – standard in any good organ – but ivory *pedals*? Peerage quality all the way.

But the apotheosis of decorative opulence was to be found in Vor Frelsers Kirke in central Copenhagen. Anyone who believes that the biggest and the best is always to be found in America ought to come visit here. Set atop a large rear gallery, apparently supported by two vast elephants, is a magnificent organ case. At last, a baroque organ for Barnum & Bailey! The organist cordially welcomed us to his loft. He had visited America and was initially delighted to let me play – that is, until he discovered I was a former pupil of Virgil Fox. His demeanour at once grew chilly and in no uncertain Danish tones he told Kirsten that Virgil was a charlatan and that his pupils could be no better. It was but a small foretaste of the Danish organ fraternity which I would come to know.

---

1 Later on, I made a Danish television special there.

The time flew by and, all too soon, I had to return to England to resume my tour. The separation from Kirsten was wrenching, ameliorated only by our pledge to reunite at the earliest opportunity. Where it had hindered before, my schedule now helped since an early September gala had been unexpectedly rescheduled, leaving another week free. My second visit to Denmark would prove to be everything the first had been – well, almost.

When I returned to Copenhagen in September, Kirsten and I took up where we had left off: more cooking and walking, talking and playing, and further exploration of this magnificent city. No magic carpet was necessary. We were already floating on a cloud. But it was a cloud that was to darken.

One afternoon I borrowed Kirsten's typewriter to write to a close friend in the States. In my unbridled enthusiasm, I was bursting with the news of my first great love. Unwisely as it turned out, I did not spare the detail, perhaps going a tad overboard – who, me? In my usual tidy fashion, I made a carbon as I typed and, with the original secure in its envelope and ready for posting, I folded the copy and stuck it in the back pocket of my jeans.

The rest is almost laughably predictable. Keen to send me on my way with clean clothes, Kirsten, checking my pockets before doing the laundry, discovered the letter, read it over with mounting anger, and confronted me with pure rage. How dare I violate the intimacy of our relationship by conveying such intensely personal details to others? I tried to explain, but every word dug me in deeper. In desperation and defense, I ended up cursing everything from letters to women and love itself – in retrospect, probably not the most prudent tactic. But Perry Mason wasn't around and I just couldn't find the words to argue my innocence. It brought to mind the adage 'Do right and fear no man. Don't write and fear no woman.' Too true.

Indubitably our relationship had been terribly scarred, but I clung to hope and tried to console myself in the belief that 'Time heals.' Flying back to London, I continued to tell myself that joy and heartbreak were as much a part of life's rich tapestry as success and romance itself – which really masked the desperation I felt.

Kirsten simply disappeared. As a future landlady would caution me, 'You can go off people, and stay off 'em.' As she had no phone, I couldn't contact her that way. I knew that she was about to move but all my letters were returned unforwarded while directory assistance provided no new listings under her name. I hadn't expected the reconciliation to be easy but I was totally unprepared for her to disappear into thin air.

Nonetheless, I was not prepared to accept defeat. My dander well up, I resolved that if Kirsten was going to play Lois Lane, I would just have to become Superman. Although, luckily for the Danish population, I didn't dash into a phone box to change, I did call the Frobenius brothers. Having heard me pour out my story, they pledged to help, Erik even going so far as to offer me his guest house as a base of operations from which to carry out 'Mission Kirsten.'

'Lille Lundehøj' was situated in the grounds of Erik Frobenius' main house Lundehøj – meaning 'high-lying forest.' But it was rather more than a typical guest house and the two were widely separated – neither visible from the other, with entrances on different roads. Set into a hill overlooking paddocks and rolling countryside, Lille Lundehøj was a snug frame cottage of two bedrooms, living room, kitchen and bath. A fireplace and giant picture window completed the intimate setting. The view from the window was the very image of tranquillity and the sheer silence of the place was deafening. I settled into my temporary headquarters resolute but comfortable.

Although I was determined to find Kirsten, it was also vital that I maintained my busy practice schedule. In order to stay in good technical shape, I had to spend at least a few hours at the console every day. Confronted with a quandary, practice has always been my salvation. From an afternoon of learning notes and perfecting a performance, solutions to other problems often reveal themselves. I don't know why this is so, but it has been true all my life. Additionally, I simply had to divert my fixation with Kirsten.

At first I thought it logical to practice at Vangede Kirke, but without a car it was hardly convenient. Coming to the rescue yet again, Erik introduced me to another Frobenius organ in Gammel Holte Kirke (Old Holte Church). This was a two-manual of novel architectural design where the large bass (Bourdon) pipes, flanking the console on either side, were suspended upside-down (!) underneath the organ case. Although considerably smaller than the Vangede instrument, Gammel Holte possessed the same fine tonal qualities, and if anything was more versatile for its small size – just seventeen speaking stops. The church was only a ten-minute bicycle ride from Lille Lundehøj and I would pedal over for many a productive afternoon.[2]

Despite my best efforts and the help of the Frobenius brothers, I still could not locate Kirsten. Her apartment provided no clues. I talked to neighbours, even her relatives, but to no avail. The post office turned up nothing either. Ultimately, I had to accept defeat. It was the profoundest disappointment, and for quite some time thereafter, I found it hard to see the way forward.

All things in life happen for a reason, I am convinced. This whole experience caused something significant to take shape in my affections; Denmark itself. I had fallen in love with the country. Spending time with the Danes was a joy; the Frobenius brothers and Mogens were already good chums, and their organs were

2 See Chapter 12 for the design of the Frobenius in Lake Wales, Florida, which I based upon the Gammel Holte instrument.

delightful practice instruments. Furthermore, the little cottage was a dream come true – a dream I had not been able to identify up until this moment.

It only dawned on me slowly just how tired I was. Aged only twenty-eight, my life was akin to an uncontrollable whirlwind. I was playing fifty, sixty, sometimes seventy concerts a year to large and appreciative crowds. My touring organ dates were a growing success and I also did well in the United States. Additionally, thanks to all my supporters there, the United Kingdom had welcomed me with open arms. This was, after all, precisely the career I had wanted so badly. But it had come at a price I could never have anticipated. So little time was left over that I had no chance of a private life. My romance with Kirsten had reminded me just how much I craved a life companion. The ten-month wait for the first date had only served to underscore how little time was my own.

But I was living in Denmark, a place of tranquillity and repose, with three kind organ-builders as friends, two fine instruments at my disposal, and a beautiful hillside retreat. Was there not a lesson here? Even after the debacle with Kirsten, I felt more refreshed than I had in years. Why not settle in peaceful Denmark?

Having broached the subject with the Frobenius brothers, they encouraged me warmly. Erik made Lille Lundehøj available for my visits and by early 1980, I had transferred a few belongings to the cottage, secured a phone line and had new stationery printed. My life had berthed at its next port of call.

Shortly after I was settled into the cottage, it became clear that I needed a housekeeper. Once more, Erik Frobenius had the answer: Julie (pronounced 'Yulia' in Danish) had been acquainted with Erik's and Walther's sister Rita since 1921. She would soon become *min danske mor* – my Danish mother. Born in England of Danish parents, Julie was like some fairy godmother from central casting: broad of beam, quintessentially lovable, and speaking impeccable English with a divine accent. Retired from a catering business she had run in Copenhagen, Julie now decided to watch over me.

At first, I don't think she quite knew what to make of my eccentricities: the Dickensian clutter, the frantic schedule, the rampant *telephonitis* – or black-cord disease, one of my life-long afflictions. But in time there was nothing she would not do for me, from filling the freezer with homemade foods to keeping the house spotless. When I had small dinner parties, she would fuss in the kitchen, serve hors d'oeuvres, fix drinks and follow all that up with a multi-course dinner.

Happily a cook of the old school, Julie produced real heart-attack food – every dish a vegetarian's nightmare and the antithesis of nouvelle cuisine. Butter and cream were lifelong neighbours, and she salted her food with abandon. Her oxtail soup was a speciality, and her roasts never failed to be tender and succulent. I fondly recall her unique, flavorful brown sauce (exquisite over roast potatoes). And when she made fun of my eccentricities, I would remind her of some of hers. For instance, she never used a meat thermometer to check if the roast was done. She would simply throw open the oven door, stick her finger directly onto the meat, and pronounce: 'Fifteen minutes more!' I envied her culinary prowess and resolved to savor every bite.

Julie also looked after me in more maternal ways, and became something of a confidante. Her razor-sharp mind could slice through the thickest emotional fog and I soon came to depend upon her sage advice and loving ear. Often after working all day, she and I would chat over a drink and perhaps it was her favourite *solbær* (black currant) rum that helped her to counsel me so wisely. In time she came to personify the unique serenity of Lille Lundehøj. She and it come to mind as one.

Having waxed eloquent about my time in Denmark, I must confess that I wish I had been able to spend more of my time there. But international professional commitments continued to involve long absences. However, Denmark's relaxing effect on me strengthened my resolve to make the most of my time there. I decided to make new friends and attempt to establish myself on the Danish concert circuit. It seemed only natural to begin at Vangede Kirke.

My first Vangede recital was presented on January 23, 1980. Its success was largely due to the first-class publicity generated by Walther and Erik Frobenius. The venue was dear to their hearts, as this was their showcase instrument. Given that the Vangede organ had already been publicly exhibited several times, I think the brothers wanted to have the instrument demonstrated in a fresh way. Other publicity included a lengthy interview with Robert Naur, a prominent theatre critic, in the prominent Copenhagen daily *Politiken*. The headline read, '*Orgeltornado i Vangede*' or 'Organ Tornado in Vangede Church.'[3] There were also numerous articles in the local press, radio spots, with posters and leaflets spread

3 Appeared in *Politiken*, section 2, January 23, 1980.

far and wide. I was delighted to co-operate, as the blaze of publicity created an auspicious launch for me in this new home away from home.

Ole Kofoed-Nielsen, the organist of Vangede, supported our efforts from the outset. He was to become a great friend and I always valued his input. In addition to playing the organ and training the choir, his primary profession was playing the French horn in several Copenhagen orchestras. Perhaps this fact shaped his approach to organ performance and led him to appreciate my particular and somewhat symphonic style more than the majority of his colleagues. He was a bit concerned about my program however, particularly the group of Scott Joplin rags with which I planned to open the second half. He actually had to obtain the Bishop's permission for me to perform these. Luckily, the response was in the affirmative and, to my delight, they proved to be among the most popular numbers on the programme, and were enjoyed greatly by Vangede's genial priest, Pastor Poul Knudsen.

The church was packed. Even the architect Johan Spreckelsen and his family were there. I was delighted and not a little honored to see that also in attendance was one of Copenhagen's long-established organists, who had brought along some of his pupils. As I played my transcription of Bach's *Air on the G string*, he suddenly rose to his feet, motioned his pupils to do likewise, and together they trooped straight down the aisle and out of the church. Observing this extraordinary exodus in the organ console mirror, I was flummoxed. Were transcriptions so heretical in Danish organ culture?

This aside, the recital was a great success and, I'm glad to say, the first of many. My continuing love affair with the Vangede instrument led to two world-release recordings for RCA Red Seal in 1981. The first, *Carlo Curley – J. S. Bach Organ Music*, highlighted some of the master's most formal compositions. In keeping with the program, the cover pictures me in front of the Vangede organ, arms folded and wearing an unusually serious expression. The recording contains some of my most unaffected playing which, at the time, surprised some of my friends. A few thought I had been seduced into the 'academic' style of organ playing and its dry literalism. Several welcomed the restraint while others were simply mystified. Although I received some wonderful press notices, I was far more interested in the criticisms of my peers, eagerly anticipating the comments of American master organist Robert Noehren, which I knew would follow. He had his doubts:

> ... your Bach playing [on this occasion] I cannot appreciate. I think I understand, but I am not sure. Like a large number of artists, you are another player when you play Bach. I listened first to the Toccata, Adagio and Fugue, and all I can say is that I cannot understand what you are trying to do with that piece. I don't understand the phrasing, at times so fussy, the way you handle the

rhythm, and, in general, your conception. Nevertheless, you are in good company. I have a recording by the Russian pianist Emil Gilels playing the Busoni transcription of the Bach D Major. It's even less attractive than your playing ... let's talk about your other playing, because there I can praise you ...[4]

I was crestfallen and listened to the record afresh, trying to hear it from Robert's perspective. More perplexing still, I dug out Emil Gilels' recording, played it through, and decided I rather *liked* Gilels' Bach! Oh well. But I was mindful indeed of Bob's words.

Where should I go from here? Of course! I would make another album. The second one, *Carlo Curley Plays the Popular J. S. Bach*, was in a lighter vein and included not only original organ works but also transcriptions, the latter by way of tribute to the teacher who had so rudely led his flock of pupils out of my recital. For this, I managed a wan smile on the back cover, alongside my producer Brian Culverhouse. Common to both albums were my usual rhapsodic liner notes, the style having by then reached a full and noxious blossom. To witness from *Popular J. S. Bach*:

> So these selections – originals and arrangements – are for sheer rapturous listening. I'm mad about them; I've wanted to record them for a long time. When I play them – among the most often-requested Bach pieces from my live concerts – I let my mind roam widely thinking of levels on which I enjoy them. Not least of which, recording them here at last, is the gleeful *frisson* – common to recording performers – that I have beaten fate [!!]. I have fulfilled for my generous audiences and myself the 'What if' yearning for things sometimes sadly left undone by a performer – things left unrecorded that are most happily characteristic. By way of exalted example: *If* only Nijinsky had been filmed *en grand jeté* by a movie camera; had only James Dean lived to bring his dream of Hamlet to Cinemascope ... had Chaliapin recorded his complete *Boris*. But play these grand instrumental pieces on the organ? Yes. My dream is fulfilled.[5]

I'm surprised that the editor at RCA ever allowed this to go to print. At least *Gramophone* magazine was bold enough to say as much. After an unadulterated rave about the music-making, the critic went on:

---

4 Letter from Robert Noehren, December 5, 1981.

5 From the liner notes to *Carlo Curley Plays the Popular J. S. Bach*, RCA Red Seal 1981.

I'm sure it is no longer necessary for Carlo Curley to write us letters on the sleeve. They are warm and friendly letters, because he is an exceedingly nice man. But good wine needs no bush.[6]

I took the point, although, in one sense, my literary outpourings were a gesture towards the Danish organ community which, at that time, appeared to be lagging behind others in embracing perspectives with which it was not in accord. Granted, organ building and playing in the late seventies and early eighties were in a narrower frame of mind worldwide. However, while the playing of Bach transcriptions in America or England may not have been all the rage either, it is hard to imagine any serious listener being so outraged as to march out in the middle of a recital. In light of that and other later experiences, my determination to justify my playing, interpretations and style to the Danes was absolute. And perhaps, the flowery prose had something to do with my *affair de coeur*?

If some organists were against me, the public was unquestionably on my side, a fact I always found encouraging, since there were more of the latter. The good reviews and packed crowds kept on coming. More significant though was the staunch loyalty of the Frobenius family, especially given that many of my detractors could have been prospective Frobenius clients. With Walther and Erik, I include Mogens Pedersen. A brilliant voicer, he worked at Frobenius from 1967 to 1996, learning his demanding craft from master-voicer Erik Frobenius. Mogens was a patient man with a big heart and an ear that respected many traditions of organ-building. He played a critical role in producing the tonal patina of literally hundreds of Frobenius organs. While innately fond of the Danish classical style, he was equally interested in romantic instruments, particularly those of France, England and America. He often spoke of the 'mystery' of English organs, in which all was not immediately obvious, regularly confiding to me his yearnings to work on full-length 32' Bombardes which were quite out of fashion at that time. Later on, in 1985, we would happily get to know each other even better, when he voiced – no less than superbly – a Frobenius for Lake Wales, Florida, which I designed.

---

6 *Gramophone,* 'G.R.,' October 1981, review of *Carlo Curley: J. S. Bach Organ Music,* RCA Red Seal 1981.

Vangede Kirke was a magnet for organ-lovers, and I made many new friends through my association there. One who was to become close was Tokugoro Ohbayashi. As you might infer, Toku is not Danish by descent but Japanese. His soul, however, is utterly European. As a teenager in Japan he came to organ-building through the neo-classical tradition, having been drawn to the recordings of Karl Richter and Marie-Claire Alain. After university he came to Denmark to serve his organ-builder's apprenticeship with P. G. Andersen – another highly respected Danish organ-builder. Thereafter, he established himself as a consultant. In addition to masterminding unusual organ projects, Toku also produced recordings of Japanese, French and Danish organists under the label *Ars Organica*.

It was the Frobenius brothers who introduced me to Toku. At that time, he was involved with a fascinating instrument for the 7,500-seat Mahikari Shrine in Takayama, Japan. Although Frobenius were building this, it was entirely to Toku's design – both visual and tonal – and he eventually took charge of the on-site voicing.[7] He lived in Charlottenlund, on the outskirts of Copenhagen, roughly fifteen minutes away from my place by car.

Highly introspective and of a poetic nature, Toku's sensibilities are almost of another time and place. While his central love is the organ, his aesthetic appreciation includes art, photography, typography, wine, fine food and antiquarian books. He is one of those renaissance men who values and seeks out creativity. Anything he chooses to do, he does well. More recently he has established himself in Japan as an organ-builder and at an interesting time for the development of the organ in that country. Since Christians comprise no more than one percent of the Japanese population, churches do not sustain the role of the King of Instruments as they do in most Western countries. While a few American organs were imported around the turn of the century, serious native Japanese organ-building dates only from 1966 and has been based mostly upon northern European baroque models. Toku's aim is to build large-scale concert hall organs in a new romantically-based style, a particularly fertile field just now. He perceives his role as expanding the vision of the modern Japanese organ to include other traditions of historical organ-building, and eventually the contribution of a style uniquely Japanese.

Since his earliest interests in the organ involved mostly tracker action organs suitable for early music, I saw fit to introduce Toku, through recordings at first, to some of the great romantic organs of England and America. At Lille Lundehøj we had numerous sessions with the stereo, anticipating the time a decade later when we would hear and play these organs for real. Toku and I much

---

7 See Chapter 12. I would become well acquainted with this organ, and played its tenth anniversary concert in 1994.

enjoyed these times together. They formed the foundations of a strong bond between us. Given his quiet nature and my all-embracing exuberance, it just goes to show that opposites do indeed attract.

By acting as liaison for my premiere concert tour of Japan, Toku introduced me to that fascinating country. It was a tour on the grand scale, and I made my Japanese debut in February 1983 on NHK national television, playing the five-manual 92-stop Schuke organ in Tokyo's NHK hall.

It may appear as if all my friends in Denmark were organ-builders, but it was hardly so. However, to some extent, all my friends loved music. One of my early champions was Hansgeorg Lenz, the trenchant and outspoken doyen of Danish music critics. As well as being a respected radio presenter, he reviewed for the newspaper *Information*. Married to an organist, he needed no conversion to the instrument or its music and during my time in Denmark, Inger Marie Lenz was the organist at Marmorkirken (The Marble Church), which stands just opposite Amalienborg Castle in downtown Copenhagen.

From the first recital at Vangede, Hansgeorg took a shine to my playing, and became almost crusading in his enthusiasm. In one review, he went so far as to suggest that I be appointed to the organ faculty at the Royal Danish Conservatory of Music, so as to 'put the cat among the pigeons'! How could we not become fast friends? Our musical philosophies were even similar. The source of his musical pleasure stemmed from a lifelong passion for Wagner, both the man and his music. Indeed, during the time I knew them, Hansgeorg and Inger Marie made a night-time pilgrimage to Wagner's tomb at Bayreuth. While Inger Marie stood guard, Hansgeorg having crawled over the mausoleum wall, approaching as near as he dared to the master's final resting place, clipped a sprig of ivy from the sarcophagus. He smuggled this back to Denmark and having planted and nurtured it, was overjoyed when it spread all over his house. Later, he was to transplant the contraband foliage to his new residence. Hansgeorg swears that because he plays so much Wagner on the stereo, the ivy has grown more vigorously as a result. And people call *me* a romantic!

Another supporter-turned-friend was Johan Spreckelsen, the architect of Vangede Kirke whom I had met immediately before my first recital there. I showed him the organ, and he in turn showed off his church, elaborating on its most distinctive features. He lived one town beyond mine and kindly drove me back to Lille Lundehøj when we were finished. As I alighted, he looked me in the eye and said, 'We will definitely see each other again.' True to his word, a few days later Johan phoned to ask if he could bring some of his architecture students to hear me play in Vangede. Gladly!

From these beginnings, Johan's family and I developed a warm and ulti-mately intense friendship. He differed from most Danish men, not so much by

virtue of his quiet demeanor, but by the way in which he allowed his solidly ana-
lytical faculties to serve his exuberant imagination. He was a mature visionary,
with bold concepts of open space, beauty and light. In his home and in the
churches he designed in Denmark, he was able to put much of his ideology into
practice. Yet all of this seriousness was infused with a dry, sparkling humor, like a
crisp white wine. He took life and art most seriously, but always smiled in the
process.

The Spreckelsens were the sweetest family, and they came to call me *lille
Bamse* or *store Bamse* ('little teddy bear' or 'big teddy bear'), being taken from a
term of endearment of Kirsten's: *'Jeg elsker dig, lille Bamse'* ('I love you, little
teddy-bear man!'). Johan also visited me frequently. Over drinks and a winter
fire, or in summer on my front porch, we would gaze over the panorama and
conjure images of a future Curley villa. In charcoal pencil, he sketched out this
fantasy, built directly into the hillside and with every room exposed to the glorious view. Space would of course be provided for a pipe organ – dreams being
the most affordable luxury – as well as agreeable gathering spots, conversation
corners, guest quarters for friends and, of course, a state-of-the-art kitchen.

During the mid-winter of 1982 Johan came over to discuss a design he was
submitting for an architectural competition in Paris. Unrolling the plans over the
piano, he explained that the proposed building at la Défense was envisioned as a
world communications headquarters which would also house several French
government ministries. Most importantly, the structure was to crown the historic axis of Paris, a symbolic line of monuments beginning at the Cour Carrée of
the Louvre, continuing to the Carrousel Arch, the Concorde Obelisk and the Arc
de Triomphe, and arriving at the new structure at la Défense. While startlingly
simple, Johan's design was brilliant. Rather than create a building that completed
the historic axis absolutely, Johan conceived of a massive open cube, a gateway to
a possible future rather than a certain conclusion – a building not just for the
French, but for all people. Both architecturally and symbolically, his proposal
addressed the competition brief in inspired terms.

While Johan was celebrated in Denmark, he had yet to achieve international
prominence. Having entered several competitions unsuccessfully, he harbored no
illusions about this one. Still, he had enormous faith in his concept, and treated
his submission with great seriousness. His visit to my house stemmed from a
concern for language. The entry could be submitted in either French or English,
and having chosen English, he asked if I could review his proposal for wording,
especially the philosophical and conceptual sections. Delighted to help, I correct-
ed a few things and together we devised and improved a few key slogans such as
'a window upon the world,' 'like a brief pause on the road with a glance towards
the future,' and 'a meeting place for all peoples.' I also suggested that he employ

the most vivid and imaginative language possible. Knowing how the French infuse simple phrases with fantasy, romance and mystery, I knew it would be important to do the same in English. While the wording was hardly original, I felt it was essential to articulate the ideas behind the concept, and thus give the project a marketable identity. Perhaps my experience writing flowery sleeve-notes had not gone to waste, after all.

Several months later, as summer was approaching, unusually for me I was mowing the lawn when a sleek black Mercedes crunched slowly up the gravel drive. Leaving the mower, I prepared to give directions to an obviously lost soul but lost soul it certainly was not for there was Johan, Karen at his side with a chilled magnum of champagne in his hand. *'Lille bamse,'* he cried, 'we've won!' I was not only taken aback but also somewhat embarrassed since I hadn't been keeping up with the news. From hundreds of entries, Johan's design had made the short list of four submitted to President François Mitterrand. Mitterrand had selected Johan's.

La Grande Arche – la Défense transformed Johan's life and career. As it would later be described:

> The result is an almost perfect cube, 108 meters wide, 110 meters high, 112 meters deep, ground space covers, along with the roof terrace, 3 acres. And there is the central empty space in which Notre-Dame de Paris could stand easily. ... Spreckelsen's work at la Défense is without doubt the ultimate monument of the '80s, the most well-publicized large Presidential project ...

At once he had to establish a Paris residence and office, while maintaining his operations in Denmark. Overnight, his face and his plans were splashed throughout the world's press, including *Time, Newsweek, International Herald Tribune,* and the like. Unfortunately for our friendship, he grew busier than ever, but we did manage to fit in a rare evening here and there. On one of those get-togethers, I voiced my regret, half-jokingly, that an edifice as monumental as La Grande Arche would contain no organ. 'But why not?' he asked, grinning. 'There might just be a place for one.' Johan's imagination was predictably busy and he was serious.

In this connection, in 1985 he asked me to arrange a visit to Paris, somewhat along the lines of our initial introduction at Vangede. This time round, he wanted to show me the progress on la Défense and, in turn, I wanted to introduce him to Paris organ culture. We would meet Jean Guillou, the famous Parisian virtuoso, teacher and *titulaire* at St.-Eustache, who would arrange for Johan to experience a great organ.

Guillou has galvanized an entire generation of Parisian audiences through his performances at St.-Eustache. Furthermore, he has asserted himself as a force to be reckoned with in modern organ thought, notably through his treatises and the organs he has designed. An iconoclastic composer, his works are in constant demand. A slender figure crowned with a Lisztian mane of white hair, it is extraordinary to observe him at the console. Kindly and with a soft speaking voice he is, by contrast, both powerful and exciting and his forceful and unorthodox interpretations never fail to excite controversy. He is a consummate technician and his pedal technique is surely the best in the world – of this there can be no discussion.

Shortly after my arrival, Johan was handing me a hard-hat and leading me on a tour of the site. The huge excavation was already well advanced and the sides of the cube were just beginning to emerge. Equally remarkable as the building's formidable scale was the ingenuity of its construction. I had never fully appreciated the high level of coordination demanded by architecture and building. He remarked that the project was becoming like the Tower of Babel with a host of nationalities speaking numerous languages. This was causing not a few problems. Organ-building may be complicated, but it is nothing compared to this. The project's scope was staggering. The enormous excavation allowed for motorways and inter-city rail links, not to mention the Paris Metro. Johan commented wryly, 'This is probably the most expensive hole in the history of France!'

After the tour, we proceeded with my half of the bargain. Jean Guillou, by this time a much valued friend, was eager to meet the famous Johan. Both were in the midst of prestigious projects, Johan with La Grande Arche, Jean the new five-manual Van Den Heuvel organ at St.-Eustache, the enormous Renaissance church at Les Halles. A visit had been arranged by Jean to the famous church of St.-Sulpice, well known to organ lovers for its 102-stop 1862 Cavaillé-Coll organ – the largest instrument of this master French builder. Here, organists Charles-Marie Widor and Marcel Dupré had successively reigned supreme for more than a century. Johan was so excited that he asked if a group of his architect colleagues could tag along with the party which also included some highly influential players in the la Défense project as well as the distinguished Organ Expert to the City of Paris, Jean-Louis Coignet. In recent years he has become another of my most treasured friends.

That evening was matchless. Locked inside St.-Sulpice without any interruption, we listened to Jean Guillou bring this incredible instrument to life; its sonorities flooding out into the all-enveloping acoustic. I then took my place at the console to play Wagner's *Liebestod*, Jean kindly helping with the stops. Almost precisely as Cavaillé-Coll had left it in 1862, this was an instrument truly steeped in tradition. To step into the organ loft was like entering a shrine. To sit down on the organ bench and play was an emotional experience second to none.

The console is *en amphithéâtre* in style with drawknobs placed in terraced stop jambs of 90-degree curves, much like a small Greek theatre. Of the 500 or so organs for which this builder was responsible, only three were made this way. Beautifully constructed yet easy to maneuver, the console exudes elegance and practicality. And the sound! While this is not a loud organ, the blend, beauty and harmonic depth are incomparable. For example, all the unison flute stops when combined create a transcendental, mystical beauty.

Afterward, we took in a breathtaking French supper at a nouvelle cuisine restaurant nearby. Here it became clear that Johan had more than just *fraternité* in mind. By acquainting his guests with the majesty of organ sound, he hoped to pave the way for a unique, 21st century pipe organ at la Défense. Johan and I had already discussed the matter in preliminary terms, but a radical notion was to grow from that evening at St.-Sulpice.

Beneath the structure of La Grande Arche was a cavernous undercroft, its floor steeply raked. Jean Guillou and I put our heads together to devise an instrument of entirely novel design inspired by the concept of the building itself – drawing together and uniting all peoples and cultures(!). The organ would consist of some dozen sections, each with its own console, projecting organ tone from the front, back, sides and even above – pure surround-sound. Solo performance would be executed from a grand console, but as many as ten organists could play or even improvise together. We were so fired up with enthusiasm that we immediately began setting out the specification. Dreams soon overtook practicality, and our stop list quickly grew to 268 ranks, including trumpets on 50" of wind, an unusually complete chorus of harmonic flutes and a 32′ Bombarde – all mounted horizontally! Ultimately Jean suggested the term *Métaphone* (Music Evolution in Technical Arts, or META) to summarize the multi-organ, multi-performer concept.[8]

Unfortunately, it was to be no more than a spectacular idea for, tragically, Johan would only work on La Grande Arche for approximately one more year before developing cancer. His infirmity increasingly confined him to his home in Denmark and he was never able to make the concept of the big organ a reality. In January 1987, I was amazed when he showed up at a Danish television recording of one of my Vangede Kirke recitals. Honored that he would spend so much of

---

8 Speaking of names, the Arche project engaged, through Terence Mulligan, a New York think tank (The First National Brain Trust of New York, Inc.) to come up with a name for the organ space and concept, some of which were hilarious: 'Notre Dane' (in respect to Johan), 'Mitti Gritti' (in respect to President Mitterrand); 'The Nose of God,' 'Skymother,' 'Place de Resistance,' 'Vivacube,' 'Napoleon's Hatbox.'

his precious energy in this way, I was nonetheless dismayed to see the state of his decline.

Johan died two months later, on March 16, 1987, at the lamentably early age of fifty-seven. Moreover, it is tragic that he did not live to see his great creation completed. La Grande Arche opened to universal acclaim in a two-day festival, July 14 and 15, 1989, and soon earned its rightful place among the monuments of the world.

Johan's death was a great blow to me, as significant in every way as the passing of Virgil Fox or Florence Candler. It had as much to do with timing as with Johan's nature. He was perhaps more serious than the other influential figures in my life: more of a philosopher and traditional artist. When I first met him, I was entering my thirties and my life was taking on a more serious note. To have a friend with such a wonderfully artistic and complex mind and, what's more, to have a friend who was *not* an organist, provided an all-important contrast for me. From time to time I still visit his buildings to remember the man and to mourn his passing.

above: Carl, Carlo, Gladys and Ella on the front porch of the family home in Monroe, North Carolina.

right: Carlo's father

Florence Candler

Right: Carlo on his appointment s Organist at Druid Hills Baptist Church, Atlanta, Georgia.

Above: With Virgil Fox, Tommy Teaver and Charles Walker following Virgil's reinaugural recital on the newly rebuilt organ at Druid Hills.

Above: With the first Allen touring organ.

Right: With Jerome Markowitz, founder of the Allen Organ Company, in the firm's Octave Hall prior to a recital.

Above: The interior of Fountain Street Church, Grand Rapids, Michigan, during Carlo's tenure.

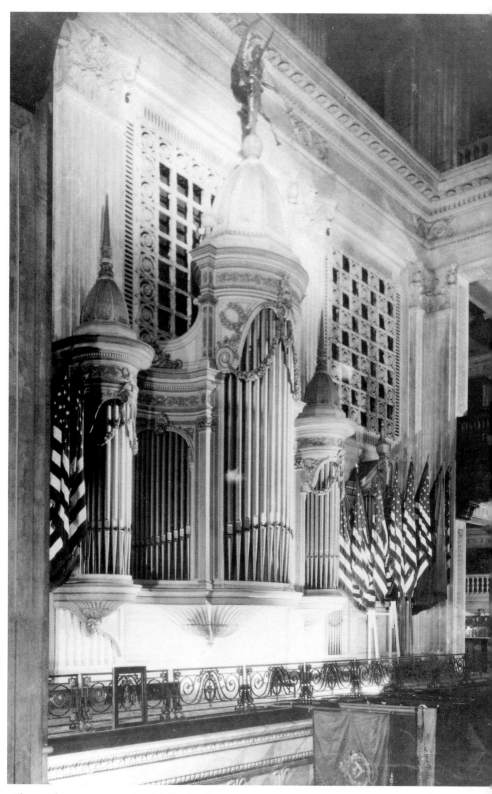

Above: The organ in the Lord & Taylor department store (formerly the John Wanamaker Store) in Philadelphia.

bove: Carlo and pupils with George Thalben-Ball at the reinaugural recital of the Skinner organ at
irard College Chapel.

bove: Carlo at the organ of Westminster Central Hall during rehearsal sessions shortly after his
rival in London.

Above: Carlo with Sebastian and Wagner at the Great Hall, Alexandra Palace, London.

Above: A typical Gala Concert audience, the Great Hall, Alexandra Palace.

Above: At the White House with President Jimmy Carter and his wife Rosalynn.

Above: With the Archbishop of Canterbury, Robert Runcie and his wife Rosalind, after a recital at Peter's, Vauxhall, near Lambeth Palace.

Above: With Roy Plomley and producer Derek Drescher at the recording of 'Desert Island Discs' BBC Radio.

ove: With Richard Baker at the Ulster Hall, Belfast, following the BBC television recording of 'The
o Z of the King of Instruments'.

Right: 'In action' at St Eustache, Paris.

Below: With the Copenhagen Boys' Choir at the Silver Wedding Royal Command Performance, Copenhagen.

ove: With H.R.H. Prince Henrik at the chapel organ of Fredensborg Castle, the Summer Palace of Danish Royal Family.

Above: With Dame Thora Hird, Father Paul Andrew and his mother, Edna, at St John's Chu[r]
Hammersmith, following a Gala Christmas Concert.

Above: With Japanese school-children in Tokyo.

ove: With H. I. H. Prince Tomohito of Mikasa, Tokyo.

ove: With Chris McDonald, Managing Director of Rolex (Japan) and the King's Singers.

Right: Carlo at the console of his touring organ.

Below: With the Duke of Marlborough and Lord and Lady Wilson at Blenheim Palace following the Winston Churchill Memorial Recital.

CHAPTER TEN

AND IT ALL CAME TRUE ...

Freshness and inspiration were the touchstones of someone who would prove to be my most unforgettable soul-mate. Mette was a clear-eyed young organist, diminutive in stature (opposites again!), blessed with the customary Danish features of blonde hair, blue eyes, and radiant skin, all crowned with a thousand-watt smile. Her laugh was elixir and so infectious it was hard not to join in. We met at Vangede – who didn't I meet there? – since Mette also practiced on the Frobenius. Initially, we would exchange pleasantries but eventually she invited me to dinner – she lived only a five-minute walk from the church, via a small moor of considerable beauty. Eventually we were to enjoy a full-fledged relationship.

It is said that first true love is but an instructive prelude to the second, the latter stronger and more vibrant. Mette proved this beyond a shadow of a doubt. While our immediate acquaintance lacked the spectacularly drawn-out anticipation of a ten-month correspondence, those details of storybook romance were replaced by a more practical love and ultimately a far deeper and richer bond. While Kirsten was a dream that did not come true, Mette was life for the living, and she proved herself to be both a steadfast friend and caring sweetheart. It was with this young woman that I would enjoy the most significant relationship of my life.

Traveling was something Mette and I did well together. We made a sweeping tour of the United States – her first visit there – in conjunction with my programs for Community Concerts. Setting out from Grand Rapids, we drove to the

California coast, pausing to pay our respects at Virgil's grave in Princeton, Illinois before continuing to Salt Lake City and a marvellous audition of the great Mormon Tabernacle organ. We had a merry stopover in Las Vegas for my recital at the University of Nevada before heading on to Los Angeles and then through the Southwest into New Mexico before ending up in Kansas.

Non-stop travel of this kind requires will, determination and a kindly disposition to the unpredictable. Mette had all of this and, what's more, a light-hearted sense of how to roll with the punches. Wherever we were, she imbibed the experience with infectious enthusiasm. Nightly hotel stays introduced her to the wonders and horrors of American television. I remember her shock the first Sunday morning she watched American televangelism. Normally an energetic talker, she was speechless. Such bible-thumping was unthinkable in her culture. She was also speechless when we shopped at Neiman-Marcus – a reaction which isn't confined to the Danes, of course. The panoply of richness and excess perhaps left her more bemused than impressed.

Our experiences in the States proved that we could travel well anywhere together. Among our other memorable excursions was a holiday to Alpe d'Huez in the French Alps. The Church of Notre-Dame des Neiges – Our Lady of the Snows – is well known to organists because of the organ case shaped like an open hand. Designed by the architect Jean Marol, tonally conceived by Jean Guillou and built by Detlef Kleuker of Germany, the instrument sounds stunning, despite having only 23 stops. Jaap Reuten, the priest in charge, extended us a warm welcome, as did Jean Guillou and his engaging wife Suzanne, who took a special liking to Mette.

In fact, everyone took to Mette. When I played the Winston Churchill Memorial Concert at Blenheim Palace on March 2, 1985, she stole the show in a stunning black dress and pearls. Afterward, she confessed to having been a little uneasy about her English. She was amazed that a lady had begun speaking to her in Swedish and they ended up having a good old chat in a combination of Swedish, Danish and English. It turned out to be no less than the Duchess of Marlborough, herself a native of Sweden.

Mette had an abundance of what the Danes call *pli*: good manners, polish, miles of common sense and a practical ability to see herself through any situation. My friends all told me to waste no time in proposing marriage. I considered it strongly. Foolishly and to my eternal loss, I failed to pluck up the courage. At that stage of my life, still in my early thirties and with more, not less work on the horizon, I lacked the foresight to appreciate the value of a life-long commitment. Various disagreements coupled with my frequent and lengthy absences abroad caused us to grow apart, and I naïvely thought that if this relationship didn't work out, there would be others. But it's not always true that there will always be

another bus along in a minute (as it were) and sadly, we eventually went our separate ways.

Among all the friends I have been fortunate enough to make in Denmark, the
Royal Family naturally holds the place of honor. To have known them at all
would have been a blessing; to have become their friends was my extraordinary
good fortune.

As royal families go, the Danish are unusually down to earth, living as
much like normal people as royals can. While formalities exist of course, the
Danish royals exert every effort to make themselves accessible to their people. To
give one example, security issues are downplayed. Whereas Buckingham Palace
is protected by multiple layers of high level security, one can walk right up to
Amalienborg, or any of the other Danish palaces, and ring the doorbell. Such
openness and warmth shows itself in the enormous affection the Danes hold for
their royals. The more usual distance between subject and monarch is replaced by
a closeness that, at first, seems hard to believe.

French by birth but born in Vietnam, Prince Henrik was educated in Hanoï,
and for a time served as a diplomat to the French Embassy in London. He is also a
vintner with a château in France. While never appearing for an instant to be a
highbrow, he maintains the highest ideals and pursues art with vigor. He is one of
the most refined people I know.

To my delight, several people had already told me that Prince Henrik played
the piano rather well and adored the organ. Thanks to the great press I received
over the first Vangede concert, perhaps it was not to be entirely unexpected that
the Prince came to hear of me. One day when I was practicing at Vangede Kirke,
Elly, the church secretary, came rushing out of the office. 'It's Amalienborg calling!' she exclaimed breathlessly, referring to the royal family's downtown
Copenhagen palace. Prince Henrik's secretary was on the line, quite literally
requesting an audience for him at one of my practice sessions. I was not slow to
suggest that he come over that very evening.

Presently His Royal Highness arrived in the company of his two sons, Crown
Prince Frederik and his brother, Prince Joachim. Prince Henrik strode in and greeted me warmly. Polite to perfection, his sons joined me at either side on the bench. I
proceeded first to demonstrate the organ, after which it was request time. The
prince became animated and asked whether I played the music of Louis Vierne. I
said, 'Mais oui, Your Royal Highness.' 'Prince Henrik will do, Carlo,' he replied.

So, you don't believe in fairy tales ... ? I was certainly beginning to.

As it happened, Prince Henrik and I shared a mutual friend in Pierre Cochereau, organist at Notre-Dame de Paris and an acknowledged exponent of the works of Vierne. Having chatted briefly, I happily played his request, then more music, then still more. Our 'audience' had been scheduled to last thirty minutes, but the Prince and his sons stayed for hours. Midway through, he asked the church caretaker to phone Amalienborg and let the Queen know that they would be late for dinner.

I was able to cultivate an incredible friendship with the Prince, simply because of the normality with which it developed. To give one example, he began attending my Copenhagen concerts and at one of them, in his honor, I played Vierne's Second Symphony. Having not played the work since Atlanta days, I had to rely on the music and therefore needed a page-turner. I decided to have a bit of fun. 'This piece,' I told the audience, 'written by a *Frenchman*, is *so* complex that only *another* Frenchman could possibly follow all these accidentals. Perhaps there is a *Frenchman* in the audience who plays the organ and who reads music?' His Royal Highness proudly raised his hand. 'Fine!' I said, 'you'll do!' A chair was placed beside the console, and the recital continued. I cannot conceive of this scenario taking place in any monarchy other than Denmark's. Whatever Prince Philip may think of me (if anything at all), and I think very highly of him, I still can't quite imagine asking him to turn pages for the Elgar Sonata.

As our friendship developed, Prince Henrik extended several invitations to Amalienborg. But when he learned that I lived in the village of Høsterkøb, he declared, 'You must come and try the organ in our summer home at Fredensborg, not far from where you live.' The words 'summer' and 'home' are not the two I would have combined to describe this immense castle. The guide book is predictably less modest in stating that the main building alone is 'an almost square block in modified Italian baroque.' The chapel, itself a glorious essay in the late baroque, became a familiar place to me with its marvelous acoustics and two-manual 1848 Marcussen organ, which I tried and found enchanting. With characteristic generosity, the Prince arranged for me to have a key to the *Slotskirke* – castle church – so that I could make use of this opulent 'practice room' whenever I pleased.[1]

I was honored to be invited to give two Royal Command Performances in Denmark. The first was on October 21, 1987 as part of Queen Margrethe and Prince Henrik's ongoing 'Musikaften på Fredensborg' (Musical Evenings at Fredensborg Castle) series. Held in the Slotskirke, it was decided that, as my

---

1 The Chapel serves not only the royal family but a small parish.

Allen touring organ was by chance on its way to Sweden, it should be diverted for this performance.

With the touring organ in Denmark for the first time, I could offer an altogether different kind of program than I had originally conceived for the Marcussen. First of all, the audience could see me perform – a first for any organist in this particular edifice – and secondly, my repertoire could now include music other than baroque and early romantic. Consequently, I performed works by Saint-Saëns, Widor, Franck, Dupré, Pierné and Wagner as well as Handel, Bach, Buxtehude and Stanley, climbing the steps to the ancient Marcussen for a couple of works by the earlier composers in the second half. At the Prince's special request, the chapel was lit only by candle-light – with the exception of discreet spot-lights on the touring organ console. All of this produced a delightfully *hyggelig* (cozy) ambiance. The Chapel was filled to capacity and both instruments sounded very fine.

I was pleasantly surprised when the esteemed critic of *Fredriksborg Amts Avis*, Hr. Børge Friis, wrote not only about my efforts but how much he was taken with the touring organ. I had to stifle a laugh because his impressions would undoubtedly unsettle the Danish *Orgel Mafia*:

> ... incredibly enough he had brought along his own instrument. Of course because the small pipe-organ of the Chapel has not so much to offer one of the world's finest musicians. And truly incredible because it is difficult to transport an organ in a suitcase. But there – in front of the altar – was the big 'chest of drawers' on its own platform. A Digital Computer Organ from the Allen Organ Company in America. With its thousands of electronic pipes it can do ANYTHING – except perhaps making up a bed. But for me it's pure magic. Of course you may frown or turn up your nose or whatever you wish [at such an instrument]. It is always the easiest but also the most stupid thing to do. However, it is not only magic; you could also try to set aside your traditional way of thinking and take the magic seriously. We are in fact witnessing a revolution in the organ field – in the new way, a revolution which demands everything of its man and its instrument. And in which I am sure a Buxtehude or Bach would have rejoiced ... this was an evening where everybody let themselves get carried away. Carlo Curley also, who declared his love for us: 'I love you, little Denmark' were his last words of the evening as he left the platform.

Of course the Danish audience was not accustomed to hearing an organ such as the Allen, which was not only conceived as a creator of moods to whisper almost inaudibly but also to crown a performance when battling against the full power of a 100-piece symphony orchestra. In my usual manner, I opened the evening on the softest celestes and vox humana, supported by soft 32' stops. As low D played, I remember that the room purred in sympathy, not loudly but in a sensuous way, much like the candle-light.

Afterwards, a few of us adjourned to a truly royal feast hosted by the Queen and Prince Henrik. I felt that certain euphoria which only a fine audience and such an exceptional venue can produce. Furthermore, this warm glow was perfectly enhanced by the unforgettable viands and *vino* of dinner. Like the 'bottomless' coffee cup of American diners, my champagne flute remained magically brimming all evening.

It was far from magical however when, having returned to my palace guest suite, I dove into bed and shot like a rocket straight through to the other side, landing on the floor with a thunderous bang. And I was meant to *like* silk sheets! What a painful climax to this magical evening.

My second Command Performance in Denmark was to celebrate the royal Silver Wedding which was held on June 3, 1992 at one of Copenhagen's more unusual venues, the Østre Gasværk Teater (Eastern Gasworks Theater). Originally a gas processing plant, the building had been beautifully converted into a theater and performing arts center, regrettably without a pipe organ. My housekeeper Julie recalled that as a child she had lived opposite the Gasværk and used to play in its surrounding grounds. I knew the place from having ridden by it regularly on the public rail network, and to me its circular structure and large dome all looked vaguely extra-terrestrial.

On holiday in January 1992, I visited Denmark and, together with the Queen and Prince, we decided that this Silver Wedding concert would be based on my successful gala UK performances, involving the new touring Allen, a large choir and other instrumentalists. I was joined by the sixty-strong Københavns Drenge Kor (Copenhagen Boys Choir, Patron: Prince Henrik) conducted by the talented Ebbe Munk. They contributed works by Mozart and Gade. A gifted young Danish violinist, Bodil Rørbech, performed the Vitali *Chaconne* and, last but hardly least, the Trumpeters of Den Kongelige Livgardes Musikkorps (The Queen's Life Guard Music Corps) rendered – what else? – *The Prince of Denmark's March* by Jeremiah Clarke, with bold organ accompaniment. All of this in addition to my own organ solos.

However, the logistics were somewhat complicated, seven of Denmark's best-known foundations and companies underwriting the event. To supervise the theatrical presentation and lighting, my manager Paul Vaughan traveled from England. Don Westfield flew in from Michigan and, in collaboration with Paul Arkwright, my UK touring organ engineer, coaxed the maximum effect from the instrument. At my request, Steve Markowitz, president of the Allen Organ Company, generously supplied additional audio equipment which entailed more than seventy-five speaker cabinets, non-directionally installed, including eight special bass cabinets – the touring organ normally travels with two – sonically moving the theater down to the 16Hz range. It took two days to set up with some two miles of audio cable linking everything together, and a full day to disassemble. This was Paul Arkwright's most complicated touring-organ installation.

We received overwhelming advance press, extraordinary for any organ event and unprecedented for me in Denmark. In addition to the normal notices, a full-page cover ran in the culture section of *Jyllands Posten* (a prominent Danish daily), including a color picture of Prince Henrik and me at the Marcussen console at Fredensborg Slotskirke. Another full-page piece appeared in *Information* on May 25, 1992, this time an exhaustive interview with Hansgeorg Lenz exploring pipe organs, the computer organ, Danish musicianship, my philosophies and life in general. For this effort, Hansgeorg and I spent an afternoon with the tape recorder which was akin to being put through a wringer. But it was certainly worth it, for Hansgeorg captured better than anyone else the essence of what I have set out to do. Coupled with superb promotion from the theater's managing director Morten Grunwald, we had a standing-room-only crowd.

The majority of the royal court attended – even the crew of the royal yacht *Dannebrog*. For me, the event brought about a wonderful reunion in which I saw, among other friends, Julie, Walther Frobenius, Mogens Pedersen, Mette's parents and many other friends. Even Father Paul Andrew, my parish priest in London, made his first trip to Denmark in order to attend.

Father Paul's presence, in all his ecclesiastical finery, was not lost on the Queen and Prince. My guests, together with the sponsors and organizers, were presented to the Queen and Prince Henrik at a champagne reception. After introducing everyone else, I presented Father Paul. The Prince shook him firmly by the hand and, turning to the Queen, remarked with a glint in his eye, 'This Carlo is remarkable! We really should worry – his court is almost as extensive as ours! And like the King of the Belgians, he travels with his own chaplain.'

Her Majesty replied: 'He probably *needs* to!'

In the years between my two Danish Royal Command performances, I was honored to dedicate my first Decca recording, *The Emperor's Fanfare*, to Prince Henrik. The powers-that-be at Decca resisted at first, citing their policy against record dedications of any kind. But persuasive campaigning won me the opportunity to include my expression of devotion and respect for a wonderful friend.

Like all of the best people I met in Denmark, the Prince was not afraid to dream about enhancing his country's already splendid cultural assets. Being French and a keen organ aficionado, he often lamented the lack of any organs, other than those of the baroque school. Significant romantic instruments barely exist in Danish organ culture, and there are certainly none of the orchestral or late-symphonic style so dear to my heart. Even though the beautiful sound created by Frobenius inspired me greatly, the majority of organs in Denmark still had all the characteristics that married them irrevocably to Danish anachronistic traditions: the cumbersome touch of tracker action – especially with manuals coupled together, the necessity of placing the console so close to the organ – making balance judgment difficult, short compasses and flat pedal-boards and only one or two stops included as a token gesture to the needs of choral accompaniment or romantic repertoire. Together, the Prince and I would dream of introducing a significant non-baroque instrument to the Danish people. Perhaps someday, under the patronage of the visionary Prince, such a world-class romantic instrument may yet be built, leading Danish organ building, kicking and screaming, into the 21st century – by way of the 19th and 20th, that is.

Such an organ would not find its way to Denmark during my years in that country. But on a recent return trip, I was delighted to discover the work of Karsten Lund, introduced to me by my old friend Mogens Pedersen. In 1996 Mogens had left Frobenius, both brothers having by then retired, to work for Hr. Lund. Lund's instruments employ beautifully engineered tracker actions that are light, responsive and easy to play, even with manuals coupled together. And the sound! Both in an historic organ he had restored and enhanced, and a brand-new three-manual instrument, I finally heard the rich and robust tone I have always sought. I trust the Danes will now take note of other developments in the global organ-building culture and admit an even greater variety into their future instruments.

Perhaps you sense some frustration on my part at trying to be a part of the Danish organ scene. I confess it was difficult during my eight years there. From my perspective, there was little to savor: the same essential repertoire, played mostly in a stifled manner, to small audiences, on wonderful instruments but all of one basic type. I could not fathom how organists derived satisfaction from involving themselves in such a small slice of the organ's rich spectrum. And clearly, they were horrified by my popular programs and concert presentation, the big-label recordings and high-profile publicity.

To be sure, such feelings also exist in Great Britain, France and America and I can hardly fail to be aware of the fury I often arouse among the purists. But many organists, particularly in England, are increasingly ready to do their bit alongside me. During my time there, the Danes' rigid mind-set was not ripe for change. This syndrome was all the more amazing when contrasted to the progressive spirit of other Danish artistic pursuits. Danish design, such as their marvelous furniture, is amongst the world's most innovative. Consider also the iconoclasm of Danish architecture. Moreover, mainstream Danish music-making – and the country's love of jazz – is no less progressive and often far more so than that of other cultures. My most recent visit gave me great hope. Clearly their organ world is now on the verge of a breakthrough, and in that I rejoice.

More than anything, my years in Denmark made me feel not so much an organist *per se* but a mainstream musician whose instrument happened to be the organ. The distinction is important, because it places me in a curious niche somewhere between the organists, few of whom enjoy full-time concert careers, and high-profile musicians, most of whom perform regularly but without the logistical complications and stigma of being an organist. If I have learnt nothing else, it is that that particular niche lies between a rock and a hard place. Sadly, it became increasingly clear that Denmark was not for me after all. Beautiful, relaxing and something I cherished, my out-of-the-way hillside retreat was, I realized, an indulgence my career could increasingly ill afford. London, so clearly a centre of world musical activity and the scene of my greatest triumphs, would once more, in late 1988, resume its place not only as my professional base but also my home.

In a sense, I have left Denmark twice; my separation from Kirsten, and subsequently from Mette and the country itself. Those years were probably the happiest of my life, certainly the most stress-free, productive and enjoyable. A very large part of my heart and soul still pines for little Denmark and her people. Perhaps someday, it will be right to return.

> The trouble with music appreciation in general is that people are taught to have too much respect for music: they should be taught to love it instead.
>
> – Igor Stravinsky
> *New York Times* Magazine, September 27, 1964

CHAPTER ELEVEN

CANDLES AND CONFETTI

Although it was a wrench to leave Denmark, I could have hardly foreseen the many exciting career developments which awaited me in Britain. Shortly after I arrived, I signed a contract with Decca, which soon led to a series of five recordings at Girard College, an all-Bach recording at St.-Eustache in Paris, and *Organ Imperial*, an all-English programme from St. Mary Redcliffe in Bristol, the latter being released on CD and also video. That same year I played in Australia and Hong Kong for the first time, and in 1990 the Carlo Curley Concert Circle got underway. There was hardly time to brood.

The Carlo Curley Concert Circle, curiously enough, has its origins in the City of London's smallest church, St. Ethelburga's in Bishopsgate. Sadly, this beautiful little gem was later to attract world-wide attention through its near devastation by an IRA bomb. One of the churchwardens was a lady called Cherry Stevens who, unbeknown to me, had followed my career avidly for a number of years.

Cherry was delightful, smart and with reserves of energy she seemed determined to expend on my behalf. Shortly after we met for the first time at St. Ethelburga's, we had a try at the church's small Harrison (a honey) followed by dinner, all the while talking non-stop. We soon discovered a mutual passion for words and, before the main course arrived, had already begun writing our first newsletter.

During the happy period when Audrey Frank was my agent, she had written excellent newsletters for an ever-expanding mailing list. Eventually however, the task proved too difficult for her to administer and the token charge she made hardly began to cover the costs involved. When Paul Vaughan took over my management, he made a point of meeting Cherry as soon as possible and subsequently suggested that she might like to establish an 'appreciation society.' While the title 'Carlo Curley Concert Circle' was Paul's idea, he insisted that the new organization should be totally independent, though enjoying our enthusiastic endorsement. Cherry designed the logo and, right from its inception in the spring of 1990, the CCCC has thrived. It has grown into an enthusiastic band of several hundred supporters with members on every continent. Cherry writes several newsletters each year and, while they include details of concerts, recording projects, radio and television broadcasts and so on, she always relays other interesting snippets.

Among the other manifestations of her seemingly limitless energy – one would never know she had a demanding and highly responsible full-time job – Cherry comes to almost every concert I give where she greets audience members and is generally indispensable. She also organizes an annual party so that Circle members – 'Circlets,' as we affectionately call them – can become better acquainted. To reflect and accommodate the wide geographical base of the membership, she holds these happy functions in different areas of the country, and always in conjunction with a particular concert date. What's more, Cherry is an inveterate and skillful baker and I never seem to leave a concert venue without some of her marvelous flapjack or a fresh fruitcake in hand. The woman is a marvel. So is her fruitcake! Here's the recipe:

The Carlo Curley Concert Circle's
Currant, Cognac and Cinnamon Christmas Cake

4 oz. margarine/butter
5 oz. granulated sugar
12 oz. mixed fruit
8 fl. oz. water
1 tsp. bicarbonate of soda
1 tsp. mixed spice
1 tsp. cinnamon

Put above ingredients into a saucepan.
Heat, then simmer for 1 minute. Cool.

Then add:
2 beaten free-range eggs
1–2 tbsps. brandy or cognac (to taste)

4 oz. plain flour
4 oz. self-rising (self-raising) flour

Pour into lined 7" square or 8" round tin. Bake in centre of oven.
350°F (or Gas Mark 4) or 180°C (150–160°C if fan oven) for 75 minutes.

But cake is not the only occasional bonus for our contented band. Some while ago I received a letter from the wife of Henry Peat, one of our members, who revealed, in the strictest confidence, that she was eager to fulfill her husband's lifelong ambition – to play the organ of Westminster Abbey. She told me that he played regularly at their village church and, having attended my own Abbey concert, inquired if there were any chance that I might help to make this dream come true. His birthday was imminent and she could think of no gift he would appreciate more.

Martin Neary, the distinguished Organist and Master of the Choristers at Westminster Abbey, immediately and most kindly agreed to allow us an evening on the organ, provided that I would be in the loft throughout. Allow me to say that not every custodian of such an instrument would have been so generous.

On the big day, the birthday boy was carefully led to believe that his wife and her parents were taking him to tea at Fortnum's, followed perhaps by a theater visit, with the celebrations being concluded over a festive dinner. Curley mischief however was afoot and, following Fortnum's, they all bundled into a taxi which mysteriously trundled its way to Parliament Square. Leading him towards the Abbey, which towered above them in the late afternoon sun, it is hardly surprising that he was, by now, growing more than a little curious. It must have been something of a surprise for him as they approached the Great West Door – almost to the minute on our carefully prearranged schedule – to be greeted by Martin Neary and myself. We could hardly believe his expression when, with the massive doors closing behind us, we wished him many happy returns of the day. As we led the bewildered Henry to the organ gallery, it was clear that the poor fellow was bordering on shock. He had never expected this and it was some minutes before he realized what had been secretly and so successfully planned. He played away to his heart's content, later assuring me that this was the most marvelous of birthday treats.

My own debut concert at Westminster Abbey was, for me, no less exciting. Broadcast live on Classic FM and also involving the Abbey choristers, under Martin Neary's direction, this was organized to raise funds, in equal measure, for the Abbey choir school and the remarkable, world-wide work of The Royal School of Church Music. Sponsored by the Hospital Saving Association (HSA), this was the closing event of a 'Fun Day,' held in the Abbey cloisters and the adjoining Dean's Yard. Attractions included, besides the many stalls, an RAF helicopter simulator, bouncy castle, balloon race, tombola, and both maypole and Scottish country dancing. Being broad of beam, it is, alas, hardly surprising that I was refused entry to the helicopter simulator and when one photo-journalist suggested that the Dean and I be photographed 'bouncing around' in the bouncy castle, the horrified attendant immediately barred our way, my career as a jolly giant thus never even reaching the launching pad! Well, *we* had been game. Thousands attended merrily throughout the day but just before half past four, the squeals of the fun-fair were silenced as the age-old tradition of the ancient Abbey wove its magic. Choral Evensong provided a calming focus in the midst of that busy day. Sung as always to the highest possible standards, the glorious and particularly English sound of boys and men soared unerringly around that vast hallowed space and, for a while, time stood still.

In order to give even more edge to my concert's pre-publicity, Paul Vaughan had suggested that an on-air auction be held; the successful bidder or bidders being invited to broadcast a short selection during the concert. Firstly, the Abbey's Precentor, sponsored by the choristers and some of their generous parents, played superbly for three and a half minutes, leaving us time to accommodate another generous aspirant, who climbed the stairs bursting with pride. 'I only wish to play one chord on the full organ,' he announced, subsequently giving us five seconds of E major at full throttle. Having bid £500 for the privilege, this must surely have been the most expensive single chord in history.

Originally built by Hill in 1848 and latterly restored and enhanced by the august firm of Harrison & Harrison, the Abbey instrument surely ranks as one of the treasures of the organ world. Recently extended by Harrisons to five manuals, it exemplifies the considerable care which this dignified company takes with every instrument bearing its builder's-plate. Glancing briefly through the souvenir program before we went on air, I was startled to see the text of their full-page advertisement (see over page) in which they had caught the spirit of the occasion perfectly, allowing themselves, possibly for the first time ever, to lift the hem of their full-length skirts a few inches to reveal a fleeting glance of a humorous and perfectly formed ankle!

My association with the Hospital Saving Association of Andover in Hampshire has been more than happy and, I hope, successful on all sides. Their generosity has enabled my management to promote 'spectaculars' and raise considerable charitable funds in a wide variety of splendid venues. Furthermore, the majority of these have been broadcast nationally by BBC Radio. Winchester, Ely, Lichfield, Guildford, Gloucester, Norwich, Belfast, Birmingham, Portsmouth and Salisbury Cathedrals and the imposing Lancing College Chapel feature among a growing list which have been packed to the doors.

AN ORGANIST'S ABECEDARIUM

ACOUSTICS amplify the

BELLOWS of frustration made by an organless organist whom the organ-builder can only

CCCCONSOLE by providing a large number of manuals, pedals and

DRAWSTOPS (131 here) suitably

ENGRAVED with fanciful names.

FLU(E) stops organist changing their combinations.

GLUE is one of the things that have made

HARRISON & HARRISON stick to organ-building for 130 years.

IVORY got too many elephants into

JAMBS – so now we use bone for

KNOBS and KEYBOARDS on which organists play

LOUDLY more often than *piano*. Not all organists are

MEGASTARS, with size 12s on their feet and 132 memories at their finger-tips; and some approve of

NICKING PIPES (but not all 6871). Did you know that the Abbey

ORGANIST is also a Bombardier?

PEARSON'S graceful organ cases once more adorn the

QUIRE, thanks to Stephen Dykes Bower and Cuthbert Harrison.

ROCKING TABLETS will not be found in Poets' Corner.

SWELL BOXES are Positively Great for Solo or Choir accompaniment.

TUNER David Chapman keeps the Abbey organ well-tempered, leaving the Vergers Tremulant.

UNSTEADY WIND? Take the appropriate Mixture, or try a

VIOLA DA GAMBA, with or without Viole Céleste, to accompany the

WALD FLUTE. There's plenty that's

XENOPHONIC in the Cornopean of languages on the stop knobs. Are

YOU languid or are your tubes exhausted after reading this? In that case

ZZZZZ – but *not* during Carlo Curley's recital!

The majority of my sponsored galas feature not only the *in situ* instrument but also my Allen touring organ, which enables me to join forces in duet selections with some of Britain's foremost organists and also with their choirs. For example, my 1996 Norwich Cathedral gala included the cathedral choir and also oboist Melinda Maxwell. After the performance, still attired in crimson cassock and pristine white ruff, the smallest chorister I had ever seen came up to me and, in a pure, clear voice, asked, 'Please, sir. May I have your autograph?' Such displays of good manners in this day and age must surely not go unrewarded, so, having dutifully signed my name with a even greater flourish than usual, I shook him by his tiny outstretched hand, and asked, 'Which was your favourite piece?' Without a second's pause he replied, 'The Stanford *Magnificat in C*, sir' – the only piece in the entire program in which I had played no part whatsoever! Out of the mouths of babes and sucklings ...

Guildford Cathedral, a modern building which stands high on a hill at the heart of rural Surrey, has provided the background for a number of my concerts. It is always a pleasure to visit, not only on account of the warmth of the welcome which is always extended, but also because it provides the opportunity to renew old friendships. Andrew Millington, the Cathedral's Organist and Master of the Choristers, is always ready to involve all the musical forces at his disposal. Additionally, he is an arranger of considerable experience and, at the drop of the proverbial hat, produces manuscript paper and pen in order to provide something contemporary and exciting. The Cathedral's sub-organist, Geoffrey Morgan, formerly assistant organist at Westminster Abbey, could conquer organ stages world-wide, should he so choose. He began an organ-building apprenticeship with J. W. Walker and also spent some time with Peter Collins. Thus, he is far better versed in the mechanics of his instrument than most players. His accompaniments are as colorful as the finest stained glass while he always *interprets* music, thus illuminating his own ideas and not anyone else's. I make every effort to attend his recitals whenever I can and was particularly rewarded on one occasion at St. Paul's Cathedral. He calmly exploited the full range of that huge instrument as if it were a direct extension of his imagination, moving me and the large audience with his phrasing and dynamic control. My joint performances with him, both at Guildford and at the Fairfield Halls, Croydon have proved salutary experiences. Just by listening to him, one can learn much.

In the lofty and often wind-swept Lancing College Chapel on England's south coast are two fine instruments which, at the invitation of Director of Music, Neil Cox, I was honored to inaugurate in the mid-1980s – a Walker on the west gallery and a Frobenius in the choir. At a more recent 'summer spectacular,' for which my Allen organ had also been installed, I was delighted to be joined in selections for *three* organs by Adrian Partington and David Briggs, both of whom are former organ scholars of King's College, Cambridge. Additionally, the 'gala' format included contributions by the baritone soloist Peter McGregor and the English Symphony Orchestra Choir which, among other items, gave us Verdi's 'March of the Hebrew Slaves' from *Nabucco*. As I greeted the audience at the chapel doors, as is often my custom, a large lady sailed up, a veritable beacon of joy on legs, and declared, 'Mr. Curley, I am simply thrilled that you've programmed a selection from *Nabisco*.' Almost unable to contain my mirth – and recalling not only that firm's famous Shredded Wheat cereal but also the vanilla-wafer cookies of my youth – I thanked her kindly and away she went to her seat. And, let me tell you, this tale doesn't improve. Just before I went out to back-announce the chorus, Paul Vaughan, tongue-in-cheek, suggested that as this was indeed being broadcast by the BBC, I might make a slight political correction to the title. 'Ladies and gentlemen,' I announced. 'That was the "March of the Hebrew Home-Helps" from Verdi's *Nabisco*.' Well, the place erupted and I've never eaten Shredded Wheat since without a wry smile.

Although the English are not usually thought of as being improvisers in the same way as the French, anyone with half an ear would think differently after hearing David Briggs, currently the celebrated Organist of Gloucester Cathedral. A disciple of Pierre Cochereau, he has developed a similarly dazzling method of improvisation within his own style. When I first heard and indeed performed with him at Truro Cathedral, where he was Organist before his Gloucester appointment, it was a spine-tingling experience. Unlike a few incumbents of some organ lofts, David is never pompous and has always been great fun in our 'Battle of the Organs' concerts. For our most recent collaboration, a Christmas broadcast from Gloucester in the presence of HRH the Princess Royal, David – the master of instant music, complicated polyphony and diabolically difficult double-pedaling – had readily agreed to play a light-hearted two-organ arrangement with me of Waldteufel's *Skater's Waltz*. Having determined that he would play a particular bar bridging one section to another, I knew, when his first note failed to appear bang on cue, that he had forgotten. I covered as best I could. Whew! So busy were we afterwards that no mention of this slight hiccup was made. But, a few days later, in addition to his usual cheery seasonal card, I received a fax with the offending line neatly written out in his own fair hand. He had circled the missing measure and added 'I think I owe you this bar! Happy Christmas.'

While it would be impossible to undertake a program with David Briggs without also inviting him to improvise, his talent and enthusiasm is reflected on the other side of the Atlantic by someone else I am proud to call a treasured friend. The ebullient Dorothy Papadakos is Organist and Composer-in-Residence of the Cathedral of St. John the Divine in New York City, where I have been honored to perform. When visiting the Big Apple, do not fail to attend a service or one of her thrilling Vespers Organ Improvisation Series performances. Her playing and improvisations bring a breath of fresh air to the traditionally staid organ world and owe much not only to classical thinking but also to the disciplines of jazz, soul and rock. A graduate of the Julliard School and pupil of several international players, Dorothy and her sparkling approach to music sets her well apart from those organists whose only wish is to play to each other. As a composer, her second ballet was premiered in no less than Carnegie Hall. Since 1984 she's been a member of the Paul Winter Consort. Hers is a wide view and it's no wonder that she's fast becoming a media figure. Working with and accompanying such luminaries as Jessye Norman, Judy Collins, high-wire artist Philippe Petit, the Klezmatics and Sherrill Milnes in this glorious space is clear evidence of splendid possibilities.

The Cathedral of St. John the Divine, despite the fact that it remains unfinished, is a vast and impressive space. Visiting it one late Christmas afternoon with Paul Vaughan – we had just driven up through the snow from Philadelphia and our marathon recording sessions for Decca at Girard – we found ourselves in the midst of a children's carol service. Alas, the organ was silent, the singing being accompanied by guitars, tambourines and a somewhat underwhelming little wind ensemble. In the gathering gloom of that awesome place it seemed sadly inadequate. After a moment or two Paul, clearly frustrated, turned to me and whispered, 'What this really needs now is Harold Darke's *In the Bleak Mid-Winter*.' 'Ha!' I retorted. 'You'll be lucky.' It can't have been twenty seconds later that the great organ, as if by celestial instruction, began the plangent G major introduction to that most moving carol. We listened in grateful silence, and as soon as the last chord had died away, I collared Paul and rushed him into to the Cathedral gift shop, wide open for business in spite of the divine service. 'Listen, you!' I hissed. 'While you're in this mood, give me next week's Lottery numbers NOW!' While I don't have time for mumbo-jumbo, I have to confess that there is something a wee bit odd about my manager from time to time.

Back on this side of the Atlantic, I was proud to be invited to perform the Winston Churchill Memorial Recital at Blenheim Palace, not only the magnificent Oxfordshire stately home of the Duke of Marlborough but also Churchill's birthplace. The 'Father' Willis instrument, with its gleaming Cornish tin façade, stands at one end of the Long Library and the recital took place before a capacity audience and in the presence of a number of distinguished guests, including not only the Duke and Duchess but also former Prime Minister Harold Wilson, who gave a most impressive address. Later, I was fortunate enough to have a long chat with him over dinner in the Duke's apartments. The most astute of men, he had been the first Prime Minister to realize and exploit the full power of the media in general and television in particular. A former Oxford don, who clearly knew more about fine claret and cigars than most, it was amazing how he had cultivated the image of a raincoat-wearing pipe-smoker in order to endear himself and his policies to the British working-class public. He, and his wife Mary, made the most fascinating and entertaining dinner companions it had been my privilege to meet for many a year.

It certainly surprised a number of English organists when I was invited to make the first compact-disc recording on the Blenheim Willis. Entitled *The Finest Hour*, the cover of the insert-booklet – in the design of which I hasten to say I had no hand at all – featured two prominent color photographs; Sir Winston himself, in typically bulldog pose and, quite rightly below him, me trying my best to look suitably serious. Sometime later at one of my recitals in Texas, a lady sidled up to the table, saw *The Finest Hour*, and exclaimed, 'Mr Curley, I jus' think it is so *naaaiiccee* that you would allow *this reco'd comp'n*y to put a picture of *yo' father* on the cover with you. The Bible says to *respect yo' pa'ents*, and I am *so* pleased to know that you abide by that good rule! *Gawd bles' yo' '* ... Likewise, madam, likewise.

The rigors of touring are perhaps difficult to understand but allow me to assure you that life on the road is, to say the least, exacting. All of this has been made so much easier by the loyalty of a number of supporters, three of whom have their own special place in this small volume.

Robert Etherington, Edwin Robinson and Ewan Lewis are affectionately known as my three musketeers. A medical photographer from Sunderland, Robert thinks nothing of driving hundreds of miles to a concert. No matter what the distance, he always seems to arrive early and I never dare ask how fast he has travelled. Edwin works for organ-builder Peter Collins in Melton Mowbray where he serves as a fine pipe-maker and restorer. He is also a first-class theater organist, but that's supposed to be a secret. Like Robert, he also travels far and wide for my concerts. Ewan plays keyboards in a pop band, an unusual line of work for an organ enthusiast perhaps, but his ardor for the King of Instruments remains strong.

Together, they help with everything from ferrying me to concert venues and lugging things to and from the car, to putting up posters and distributing leaflets. When I am fretting half an hour before concert time, perhaps because something isn't up to my seemingly impossible Virgoan standards, my musketeers always manage to create harmony. So attuned are they to my pace that they seem to know instinctively just when to help and when to make themselves scarce. I couldn't think of performing a big program these days without them.

Compared to my frenetic schedule in the late seventies, when I was playing upwards of ninety concerts a year, the last few years have certainly been calmer. Although I sometimes play three or four concerts a week, such pressure is now less frequent due to more considerate scheduling. Given good management,

ncreased personal experience and the support of Cherry and the three muske-
eers, big concerts no longer daunt me. The passage of time has certainly mel-
owed the landscape.

I continue to base myself happily in London, with extended tours around
he world, in particular in North America, Europe and, more recently, Australia,
South Africa and the Far East. My limited spare time is carefully allotted to prac-
ice or special projects, such as recordings, videos, this book(!) and the activity I
njoy most, consulting on unusual organ projects.

I have been lucky in many respects but – and this is the greatest boon – it
ears repeating that I have never wanted for good friends. Mysteriously, they
ften seem to make their appearance in just the right place and at just the right
ime. Perhaps I do have a fairy godmother.

During the late 1980s, whenever the touring organ and I were not on the
oad, I was allowed to store it in a London church. Designed by the distinguished
rchitect Butterfield and blessed with excellent acoustics, it provided me with a
lace to practice, despite the damp winter cold and Chinese water torture which
vas an inevitable result of rainy days and a leaking roof. In course of time, the
lderly incumbent retired and was succeeded by a younger man who came to the
arish with energy and enthusiasm.

If I had been a little concerned at the arrival of this new broom, I need not
ave worried. Fr. Paul Andrew adored music and, so it turned out, even owned
everal of my recordings to boot. I breathed a sigh of relief. The status quo
eemed assured. Accompanied and supported by his redoubtable mother, Edna,
e soon set about bringing new life to the parish and to the church. Before long,
unds were found to fix the roof and much more.

If the Andrews and I started out as friends, we have ended up as family and
hey now offer their home as mine whenever I am in England. Interestingly, Fr.
aul shares many of the qualities of my good friend, Toku Ohbayashi, whom I
riginally met in Denmark. Outwardly quiet and retiring, the glint in Fr. Paul's
yes belies a generous soul and the sharpest of minds. Again, as with my friend-
hip with Toku, it is our opposite qualities which draw us together. Paul's mother,
dna, is proudly Cornish, more Cornish even than clotted cream. She barely tol-
rates London, since the capital city has the temerity not to be located in
Cornwall. A short, well-preserved woman with a disarming smile and china blue
yes, she is one of those resilient and naturally funny women without whom
elevision comedy would be bereft. Deftly and without pause, she skips from one
visecrack to the next, regularly dousing my sweet talk with an extinguisher of
ayenne. Her years defy her incessant smoking and occasionally she will even
ight up a second cigarette before the first is concluded. 'Well, it kills the germs,'
he says. Perhaps her longevity results instead from a strict adherence to the

many superstitious edicts with which she punctuates our daily exchanges.

'Don't stay in bed all day, Carlo. People *die* in bed.' True enough.

'Don't pass anyone on the stairs, 'tis unlucky. No reason, just *'tis.'*

'Never cut your nails on Friday, 'cause 'tis unlucky.' While this must surely be patent nonsense, she keeps the tradition anyway.

'Put a silver coin on the doorstep on the last day of the year, then bring it in New Year's morning. It'll keep money coming in all year' – where we live, it probably wouldn't survive the night.

'Say "White rabbits" and "black cats" three times each on the first day of the month. This makes a lucky month.'

'Under no circumstances are you allowed to wash clothes on the 28th of December or New Year's Day, else you will wash one of the family away' – Edna is no mean poet. It's unclear whether washing machines fall within the scope of this decree.

Whenever I've been away a long while, she always greets me with, 'I thought you were dead, buried and your clothes washed.' Hmmm, that washing thing again ...

But my favourite for sheer nonsense value is '*No* cleaning brushes are to be bought in March.' Even Edna doesn't know the reason for this one!

Superstitious sayings aside, Edna makes a smart surrogate mother, chiding and lambasting me as only a parent could – especially when I am foolish enough to attempt passing her on the stairs. But, without a doubt, mother and son share a heart of gold.

One of the ways in which I attempt – poorly perhaps – to repay the Andrews' many kindnesses is by serving as honorary artist-in-residence at their church, a haven of Anglo-Catholicism which stands at the heart of a busy West London parish. Holy days and high days provide occasions for particular celebration, when a special choir, the Peter Beaven Singers, joins us for a full choral mass. Pete Beaven and I have been great chums for some time and we have also organized several Christmas concerts in an attempt to raise money to rebuild the old Lewis/Willis III three-manual instrument which has fallen on sad times. Incidentally, Marcel Dupré played his first UK recitals here in 1920. In addition to Pete's choir, these Yuletide efforts have often been enhanced by guest appearances of such stars as Dame Thora Hird; much-loved theater organist Ena Baga ('The Queen of the Keyboards'); Barry Rose and the St. Albans Cathedral Choir; veteran broadcaster Richard Baker; the enchanting Angel Voices led by BBC Music Adviser Robert Prizeman; the choristers of Trinity Boys' School; Classic FM presenter Michael Mappin and Richard Ingrams, founder and original editor of *Private Eye*. The 75-strong Ashford Choral Society, also directed by Peter Beaven, even came along one year and Chris Sprague brushed off his old magic and provided theater lighting, together with his favourite confetti cannons. The crowd loves these seasonal events with the familiar carols, Christmas trees and candle-light later complemented by mulled wine and mince pies. And when he was alive, our beloved Bishop, Dr. John Hughes, would be there to send us on our way with a stirring Christmas blessing.

No reminiscences of mine could ever be complete without due reference to this dear man, who passed away peacefully in August 1994 while I was touring in South Africa. Bishop John and his wife Maureen became good friends of our church, priest and household. He was perhaps the most genuinely Christian man I have ever met and truly exemplified through his own life all that he preached and held dear. Though certainly not poor in spirit, ours is hardly a wealthy church. The congregation is primarily of West Indian origin and includes some of the most devoted and highly entertaining people I know. But Bishop John was not slow to realize that the Spirit was being well served in this historic building and it was a visionary move on his part to appoint Paul Andrew, bringing him from a challenging parish in inner-city Salford, at the end of the Manchester Ship Canal. Most of the other powers-that-be in the Diocese of London wanted to see the church closed and the congregation dispersed, with vicarage, church and spacious grounds sold to the highest bidder. And make no mistake, property speculators were already sniffing around a slice of highly valuable real estate. But, in direct conflict with his advisers, the bishop remained steadfast.

It could be no secret that Bishop John was a high churchman. Bells, incense, stations and vestments of velvet and lace were much to his liking, given the proper context. With tears in his eyes, he once confided quietly to me, as he gazed around the church which he had saved with a stroke of his pen, 'Carlo, I will go to my grave happy in the knowledge that this precious place is open, even if the accountants and bottom-liners despise me for it.' He and his wife visited us many times, not only for our Christmas concerts, and a professional relationship soon turned to genuine friendship. I will never forget his blessing of the vicarage soon after Paul and Edna arrived. His generosity with the aspergillum – holy water dispenser – managed not only to 'bless' but nearly to beatify the interior workings of a newly restored Bechstein piano. If he had witnessed the panic he'd caused, as a bevy of friends rushed round mopping up the puddles and drying off the strings, he would have smiled, if not laughed out loud. He is much missed and I commend his life and memory to anyone who wishes to be inspired to higher things.

Church, friends, concerts and good support – now that I can no longer claim to be in the first, or even second flush of youth, some of this can become repetitive. But just when I think the routine is getting a bit stale, something else comes up to revitalize my excitement. Thanks to Cherry Stevens' friendship with Chris McDonald (managing director of Rolex Japan), I joined the King's Singers for a concert tour of Japan to coincide with the celebration of Time Memorial Day. This uniquely Japanese act of remembrance was established in 1920, to 'educate people in the importance of keeping good time.' With no little irony, Rolex Japan has sponsored these concerts since 1989. It was a thrill not only to appear with the King's Singers but also to follow in such illustrious footsteps as those of Dame Kiri te Kanawa, Isaac Stern, James Galway and Yo Yo Ma.

I much looked forward to working with the King's Singers, but I could never have anticipated how much fun it would be. We hit it off on the plane ride to Japan, and rehearsals were instantly harmonious. At one concert, the boys gave the first encore, 'All You Need is Love.' Their bass – speaking in passable Japanese, I might add – implored the audience to assist them by joining in the chorus, 'because Carlo plays so loudly.' Naturally, I tried my best to drown them out, but I had been outsmarted – for now. On their third encore, 'Crocodile Rock,' the King's Singers stood at the lip of the stage and the audience was in a great mood. On an impulse, I sidled up behind them, just out of their line of sight, and started twisting and jive-dancing to their infectious rhythm, to the absolute delight of the audience.

Upon learning that I no longer spend the majority of my time in the United States, many people express surprise. 'Why don't you live in your own country,' they inquire, perhaps somewhat indelicately. Were I a more sensitive soul I might misread this question as an invitation to pack my bags and go!

I love the United States. Its freedom, candor and opportunity are unmatched anywhere, and I would not relinquish my citizenship for an instant. I am especially thankful for my Southern upbringing. It gave to me the naturally gregarious quality that allows Southerners to make friends with almost anyone – to walk with kings yet keep the common touch, as Kipling so ably put it. The facility to strike an on-the-spot rapport has helped to open practically every door in my career.

However, more than being a citizen of one country, I see myself as a musician trying to spread a message far and wide. Anyone attempting to do that today faces an unprecedented degree of competition. In our information- and entertainment-saturated age, people increasingly spend their leisure time in front of a computer, video or audio appliance, rather than getting out into the world to become part of their communities or neighbourhoods. This phenomenon takes its toll on music, since it becomes less of a spontaneous activity for an audience and more of a carefully choreographed musical exposition for a microphone.

People continue to attend concerts, of course, but just as frequently they are heading to Tower Records, where they can obtain a century of music-making right off the racks.

Recordings have produced more knowledgeable audiences. Not surprisingly, they are more jaded as well. In previous days, one could justifiably take issue with audiences that behaved as if they had 'heard it all.' These days, many *have* heard it all, or a great deal of it, and in crystalline digital sound besides. Whereas before, people either learned the music at home on the piano or attended concerts, in today's world of miraculous fidelity, why bother with crowds, parking and an uncomfortable seat?

Musical events, therefore, have to be doubly spectacular to draw a large audience, otherwise listeners are indeed better off at home with their CD players and remote controls. Musical events suffer another indignity as they become submerged beneath a frenzy of news bites and sensationalist media rubbish. Bold, daring harmonies, exquisite interpretations or dramatic rapport with an audience no longer galvanize public attention – it is mostly murderers, lottery winners and the like. It takes a happening of extraordinary nature to turn someone's ear. Even the impact of a Rachmaninov or a Horowitz might seem remote and unimpressive to some in our modern age, but no more awe-inspiring than the wonder of an automobile. The joy, beauty and poetry that can come of a fine musical performance is viewed almost with suspicion against the reality of modern life, in which all that captures our eye is so often negative and inflammatory. In this modern climate, music is certainly not the only artistic discipline to suffer. All art seems in jeopardy, especially as the touch-of-a-button style of entertainment continues to proliferate.

What does this have to do with Europe, the reader will patiently ask. I feel that in the United States, the sin of availability is at its most widespread. Too much is at one's fingertips: 24-hour stores, fast food, hundreds of television channels, e-mail, internet, fax machines, characterless 'strip' and shopping malls erected overnight without any ideological underpinnings. All of it brings us vital information and contact, and we are probably more informed about our world than ever before. But the act of becoming informed now requires precious little intellectual or emotional investment. This passivity has tended to eradicate substance and meaning from our lives.

Many of us seem to be losing our sense of wonder. These days, very little is sacred or hallowed. When I was young, a long-distance telephone call was a special occasion, to be used sparingly. Today, we are bothered when we talk from Los Angeles to London and the line suffers even slightly from static or time-delay. The easy life has eroded standards, weakened the imagination and turned an entire generation to cynicism.

Of course, the same syndrome is spreading the globe, and Europe is hardly immune. But in general, I find that Europeans of most classes are still sufficiently grounded in – and proud of – their culture, their art, their architecture, even their cuisine, and this fact makes them less likely to be overtaken by commercialism, at least to the degree that Americans have been. Artistic entities here are more a part of everyday life, not because they are easily available, but because the culture has always valued them as an integral part of daily life, not some disposable aesthetic attachment.

Some Americans will scoff at this thought. They might say that all this culture may continue to prevail in such places as Paris, Vienna or London, but not elsewhere; furthermore does not an equal level of culture exist in our great American cities? The point is valid. Certainly the citizens of New York, Boston or San Francisco could fill every waking hour with concerts and plays, dance and opera, all performed to high artistic standards. But I'm describing something more fundamentally personal than the mere accessibility of fine artistic endeavor. Artistic curiosity is fostered in the European mind in an essential, fundamental way. Interests in art, literature and music are not looked down upon as being esoteric or *highfalutin'*. They take their place in the development of a fine character, not as special, extracurricular interests to be regarded as unusual. It is always dangerous to generalize but, after crossing back and forth from America to Europe for more than twenty-five years, I have found this to be true. Europe is still in love with art and, even in our disposable age, art shows no signs that it will easily relinquish its grasp on the Europeans. If art is the conscience of society, then the conscience of the Europeans is still raised high, drawing me to them and their continuing quest for beauty.

For me, London remains the capital of many artistic disciplines of which music is just one. Opera is superbly performed and magnificently staged. There are many orchestras ranking among the world's finest. The choral art enjoys its highest expression here, from the men-and-boy choirs of the cathedral and university traditions to the great metropolitan choral societies. Lots of good choral music requires the organ and, in turn, the organ benefits from the security of this tradition.

And most importantly, there is no question that the organ thrives here. More than in any other place in my experience, the organ is viewed as a legitimate instrument for the concert stage. For instance, can you imagine any American broadcast network, ABC, NBC, CBS, even PBS having an organ society? Never!

The BBC has had one for many years, and it still flourishes alongside the large Compton pipe organs in Broadcasting House, Langham Place, and the BBC Maida Vale studios in London. Perhaps I'll suggest to Ted Turner that he start a new American trend and commission a grand organ for CNN Center in Atlanta.

Furthermore, while the town hall organ tradition has palpably dwindled, its embers can and must be fanned. The important fact is that the instruments are still there. Major and minor municipalities alike can still boast some fabulous instruments, although only some of them, alas, remain well-maintained and cherished as objects of civic pride.

In spite of this, the English still harbor a secret love affair with the organ, which can be drawn out if done properly. Of course, long gone are the days when such municipal instruments represented the sole avenue for a provincial audience to hear fine music, either organ or, in arrangements, orchestral. The radio and recordings have changed that forever, and these new forms of musical enjoyment have made audiences far more sophisticated than they were a hundred years ago. But the reason an audience comes to music has not changed at all: the necessity for emotional excitement is part of human nature, and if a performer delivers that excitement, success can be assured for all.

The British town hall organ tradition makes such a program more achievable than practically anywhere else. The thread is still there, and so is the foundation while the influence lingers on. Effectively done, the tradition of town hall organ playing can still work. I was hardly the only player at the Ally Pally to make a success of the summer concerts in the late 1970s. The real success came from effective publicity; a certain amount of 'hype' (in the best sense of the word); careful programming of repertoire which welcomed, not alienated, the audience; and ensuring that the crowd knew they were at an *event*. Furthermore, the programs were designed around an almost 'ecumenical' concept, binding the different denominations of the organ fraternity together on a weekly basis. A concert would marry the swing and jazz of a great theater organist to the dignity and grandeur of an eminent cathedral organist. And, within programs, the musical content centered around contrast. In this way, every selection represented a new fork in the road.

So ... these are some of the reasons why I choose to be based in London. The choices that have led me to this point in life were not all conscious, but looking back at how events have unfolded, I fail to see how it could have happened in any other way.

CHAPTER TWELVE

COPIOUS NOTES

I am often asked to name my favorite organ – an innocent-seeming but really rather impossible question, like asking you to choose your favorite piece of music. The world is blessed with hundreds, even thousands of fine and distinguished pipe organs. Some are centuries old, others are modern, and they come in all sizes, shapes, styles and colors.

With so much variety, it is difficult to define what makes for a 'good' organ. An organ can sound beautiful in many different ways, the tones which would make one instrument sound beautiful in its style being totally alien in the context of another. Besides, musical tastes change with the passage of time. Doubtless I knew instruments in my youth that may have thrilled me then but which I might not enjoy now. Similarly, I find that, these days, I might warm to instruments that did nothing for me twenty-five years ago. Although my taste has not changed radically over the years, it has certainly shifted.

Another factor considerably colors my assessment of an instrument. Amateur organ enthusiasts can enjoy the luxury of being able to appreciate an instrument on tonal merit alone. As a concert organist, I usually have to fight to make a program communicate with an audience. Indeed, on some occasions I only get half a day to prepare a concert. Therefore, if the organ proves difficult to play, or hard to hear from the console, or if the action is slow, or if the tuning and pipe regulation has been allowed to slip, or if the console controls malfunction or are inadequate, the glory of the instrument will surely be obscured by the reality of playing it.

As you look through the list that follows, I am sure you will spot my preference for romantic organs, built between about 1850 and 1950, and especially those with electric action. Mechanical action, far from being displaced by electric action, has staged a remarkable comeback since World War II. This kind of key action certainly has its devotees, and in recent years has been elevated to cult status in some quarters. Its adherents claim that the mechanical linkage between the keys and valves offers a subtle control over pipe speech. For me, this is science fiction. At best, if you are playing slowly on a single stop on a very sensitive mechanical action (such as a small continuo instrument) such intimate control may perhaps be possible. But is it desirable? Not to me. Pipes are voiced for the onset of wind as it is provided normally. Any variation in its supply or release simply exaggerates all kinds of non-musical sounds within the pipe speech, detracting from beauty rather than creating it. The differences are utterly unlike those that the pianist can effect through the control of his instrument. Furthermore, the idea that a player can exercise such subtle control while playing at any reasonable tempo is simply unrealistic. Clearly, to some organists, a good tracker organ can be most gratifying to play, much like a fine harpsichord. But, in the final analysis, there is no difference for the audience to hear and I trust that they prefer to pay for things which they *can* hear!

Robert Noehren was not only an organ-builder, but Professor of Music and chairman of the Organ Department at the University of Michigan at Ann Arbor from 1949 to 1960, continuing as university organist until 1976. In this position he helped to educate a generation of young organists. He puts the case most eloquently:

> The mechanical restrictions of the action dictate the placement of its divisions, requiring them to remain as close to the keyboards as possible, with the key-desk in a location where it is impossible for the organist to hear the instrument as it is heard by the listener. No musical instrument can be played artistically unless the player is able to hear and judge exactly how his instrument will sound in performance …
>
> … The key action of an organ cannot affect dynamics, like that of a clavichord or piano. It can only open and close a valve to admit wind to the pipes. With mechanical action it is claimed that some control of the speed of the opening and closing of the valves is possible and to some extent may affect the speech of flue pipes providing expression in playing. However, if carefully observed, even in the playing of a slow movement, a reasonably fast action of the finger is required to overcome the wind pressure against the pallet [valve] or the key will not go down. Thus the subtle differences of touch which may seem possible are always compromised. In order for the key to be depressed, it

is obviously impossible to control the speed in the descent of the key when it is necessary to play in rhythm even in the slowest movement. However, expression is achieved rhythmically, and any subtlety of attack is camouflaged by slight alterations of the rhythm (rubato), and it is this that deceives the player into believing he is controlling the speech of the pipes.[1]

There is an additional difficulty in controlling the 'speed of descent' and it's the organ's equivalent of the 'pluck' in a harpsichord – once the seal around the pallet has been broken, the resistance to the player's finger drops markedly and the key 'plops' down. So exercising control in this motion is akin to attempting to break a piece of glass in slow motion. In real music and with manuals coupled, it is more like trying to break several pieces of glass at the same time.

Instead of opening up new horizons, tracker action for me imposes a number of distressing limitations. I need a prompt attack and release, as one gets on a Steinway or Bechstein piano. And most tracker/mechanical actions simply cannot offer this. They all seem to suffer from an uneasy compromise. To achieve acceptable return speed, strong springing is indicated. But that makes the action heavier to play. However light (or otherwise) the builders contrive to make the forces needed to move the keys when playing slowly, tracker actions can be hopeless for really fast (e.g. toccata) playing, simply because there is such a mass of inert wood- or metal-work flailing around. Coupling manuals together means that each key then must open several pallets at once, and things get harder still. Obviously there is no way in which the touch can remain the same over independent and coupled keyboards. Even playing legato, the accumulated weight of coupled manuals can be unendurably burdensome. Furthermore, tenor and bass notes, needing bigger pallets for extra wind, are harder still to press down.

Electric action offers the artistic solution. It involves an electric switch of some kind on each key and usually an electro-pneumatic gadget inside the organ to admit wind to the pipes. Its most important attribute is a uniform touch from the bottom note to the top on every manual, regardless of how many stops are drawn or manuals coupled. No surprises, no variations. A quick electric action allows repeated notes to be executed in a clean and exciting fashion, whether on one stop or full organ. And since there is little if any physical strain required to depress the keys, one can launch into the Widor *Toccata* with the same ease-of-touch as Franck's *Cantabile*.

1 Robert Noehren, 'Notes on the Design and Construction of a Modern Organ,' *The Diapason*, May 1993, pp. 10–13.

I abhor the fact that the consoles of mechanical-action organs have to be so close to the pipes themselves. To me, rapport with the audience means we need to see one another and rapport with the music means I need to sit where I can balance and control the same sound picture that the audience is paying to enjoy. After all, what captain of a ship would wish to slave away down in the engine room amidst all the sweat and heat? I can assure you that Captain Curley much prefers to be vigilantly serving on the bridge.

Electric action is the only scheme which enables the console to be moved around to best advantage. For church services, it can be sited close to the choir. In orchestral contexts, it can be placed where best for cooperation with fellow instrumentalists. And, for recital work, it can occupy a prominent, central position.

However, in the end, one can only generalize so much when discussing action types, and I think organists have wasted a lot of time pondering which action is best. If you want to argue against tracker action, you can find numerous poor examples to support your case. The same holds true for too many organs with electric action, in which sluggish response and poor repetition militate against clean, well-organized playing. If an organ sounds good and has a responsive action, then it is well worth playing, and a good musician will know how to make music on it. Furthermore, it is clear that both types of action are going to be around for a long time.

Far more troublesome than mechanical or tracker action itself is all the polemic that accompanied its revival after World War II. The rebirth of tracker action stemmed from a reaction against the excesses of romantic organs and electric or pneumatic action. Tracker action, for many, was just one part of a larger back-to-basics movement in organ-building, a trend that has roughly paralleled the 'early music' movement. Browse through any record store, and you are likely to find conventional performances of Bach and Mozart alongside offerings which feature 'period instruments' (of the kind believed to be in use when the works were composed) and an attempt to recreate the sort of performance the composer might have heard in his own day. In a complex world, the early music movement represented a haven of simplicity and purity, one in which the disciplines of scholarship and musicology might provide new answers. In the organ world, a kind of crusading political correctness railed against what it saw as the monstrous excesses of previous generations. In its zeal, it was responsible for sweeping away far too many of the really magnificent and unrepeatable monuments to Victorian and Edwardian craftsmanship – a cultural vandalism that began to be identified only during the last decade.

In organ-building, this same kind of philosophy took hold in the tone of new organs. The first wave of tracker organs became synonymous with a particular style of sound: extreme amounts of transient noise in the speech of pipes (commonly known as *chiff*); small-scaled, unison-thin ensembles; insufficient fundamental tone, both at the unison and sub-unison level; screeching mixture stops that not only sounded like breaking glass, but shattered the clarity of the music they were supposed to enhance; and reed stops which no longer played their part in solid or full-blooded choruses or climactic solo effects, but rather sounded like small anguished animals, or even worse, buzzing insects. This 'neo-classical' style permeated the industry, and, soon enough, most organ-builders, regardless of the action they chose to employ, were producing essentially objectionable organs in the pursuit of an ignorant and false 'classical' ideology. Let's face it: when there are no elegant sounds to savor, the argument between mechanical or electrical action hardly matters. The truly beautiful-sounding organ from this period is all too often the exception. And having played a number of grand old Dutch, Scandinavian and German organs, I know that the baroque masterpieces of the 17th and 18th centuries bear little relationship to their neo-classical counterparts. The Schnitger and particularly the Silbermann organs, with their rich and shimmering ensembles, weighty grandeur and majestic pedal reeds, are nothing like the imitators.

In the 1960s, the polemic was not merely in the tonal design, but in the arrogant attitude of its proponents, who argued that the classically-based tracker organ represented the only 'true' organ. Unfortunately, their attitudes were often as limited as the organs – which might have been worth enduring had their arguments translated into compelling musical performances. At the same time, it was easier than ever to enjoy music in the home, through recordings and radio. The average music-lover could now pick and choose a musical menu right from his armchair. The vast audiences at organ recitals in the first third of this century dwindled after World War II, to be reduced to a trickle in the 1970s. (Virgil Fox used to say that the majority of New York organ recitals were so dull that 'the fugue subjects entered one by one as the audience left two by two.')

More recently, the organ world has had to come to terms with the consequences of its recent legacy: the unappealing instruments produced by the neo-classical era, the negative effect on audiences, and the reality of the shrinking place of the organ as a serious musical instrument. As classical music becomes more accessible than ever before, the organ world has been busily infighting, failing to realize that its core audience has been slipping away. Therefore, it has been something of a relief to see a new trend emerge in the 1980s. First of all, distinguished old organs (of all kinds) began to be appreciated and retained, not drastically rebuilt or discarded. Builders of new organs, realizing the short-sightedness of their zealous neo-classical ways, developed a new interest in romantic organ sounds and the music of the era, and with them have slowly come a renewed pursuit of strong unison tone, rich reeds and grand ensembles. It is perhaps ironic that this trend started with the mechanical-action organ-builders but, since they were the first to go awry, it is perhaps understandable that they would be the first to return to their senses. A few American electric-action organ-builders who never had a great investment in the neo-classical organ have more readily focused their attention on a new direction for the romantic organ, roughly taking up where developments left off in the late 1920s and early 1930s. One recalls Saint-Saëns' telling aphorism, 'In Art, a difficulty overcome is a thing of beauty.' Would that all organ-builders could take these wise words to heart.

It is impossible to respond to an organ's sound without responding to the space in which it is placed. The organ is unique in that it depends on its acoustical environment for its resonance and ultimate development of tone. Every other musical instrument is a self-resonating entity; stringed instruments develop their rich sonority from their bodies, the piano from its soundboard, and woodwinds from their long cavities. While organ cases have certain resonating properties (in some ways good, in others bad), ultimately organ tone must rely on the room in which it is placed to develop sonority and warmth. In fact, it is an oft-repeated maxim that the best stop in any organ is the room. Just as no two organs are identical, so no two buildings offer the same acoustics. Some buildings, such as St. Paul's Cathedral in London, have tremendous periods of reverberation; other edifices, such as the Royal Festival Hall and most carpeted churches, have virtually none. Some buildings will reinforce certain sound frequencies (such as bass) more effectively than other areas of the tonal spectrum.

As a rule, organists prefer buildings with plentiful resonance and strong reinforcement of tone. Such acoustical conditions impart a gorgeous warmth to organ sound, as well as the mystery and drama of reverberation. Perhaps the general exception to this rule is the building so large and reverberant that music loses its intelligibility. This might be said of the enormous cathedrals such as Liverpool Anglican, St. John the Divine in New York or St. Paul's in London. On the other hand, these buildings sound as overwhelming as they look, and thus have a beauty all their own. Hearing a chord on full organ die away in these vast spaces can be such a powerfully emotional experience that I will happily sacrifice some clarity for the added thrill. And with some practice, you can learn to 'play' such a space with dramatic effect, while keeping every note of the music clear.

I much prefer an organ that collects many small ensembles into a grand one, where every stop relates to every other stop in a logical fashion. Some organs are so well scaled, voiced and balanced, so harmonized with themselves, that they are like an intelligent family, every voice performing its duty exactly. A glorious ensemble is first of all a well-organized sound, one in which the melody constantly soars (from the softest combination to the loudest), the pedal supports nobly, and yet the inner voices are not left confused. More exciting still is when the organ's minor ensembles perform in the same musical fashion, yet at the same time combining into the large ensemble just as effectively. Of course, beautiful solo color is a must; but the ensemble comes first and last.

A substantial ensemble need not necessarily imply either tremendous power or extremes of tonality. Of course, powerful organs have their place, especially in large churches whose congregations sing heartily. And power is essential in relationship with a symphony orchestra, lest the organ be lost underneath the brass and percussion. However, loudness is not synonymous with *energy*, a quality I find more exciting. By this, I mean the wide spread of a chorus sound across the aural spectrum, creating a clean, transparent effect which, whilst still majestic and impressive, manages to avoid being cloying, shrieking or just plain loud. For example, when listening to a fine old organ of 'Father' Henry Willis, England's most noted builder in the second half of the 19th century, one cannot fail to observe tremendous excitement and energy, while noting an absence of anything blatant, coarse, or downright loud. Unless there is a genuine need for sheer decibel strength, such an instrument is often much more beautiful. And in my experience, audiences prefer such a sound as well. After all, who wants to have their ears bombarded for the duration of a full recital?

It is my great good fortune to have played and to continue to play upon many of the world's distinguished organs. But my enthusiasm for visiting organs has hardly diminished over the years. I still derive pleasure in discovering previously unseen and unheard treasures. And, please believe me, not all the good organs are the famous ones.

A few of the instruments in the list that follows have been detailed elsewhere. Nevertheless, in a compilation of favorite organs, they merit mention yet again.

AUSTRALIA

- St. Paul's Cathedral, Melbourne, Victoria
  Lewis & Co 1890
  Restored with three additions, Harrison & Harrison, 1990
  53 stops, 58 ranks

In the history of 19th century British organ-building, the name of Father Henry Willis has stood out. To the cognoscenti, however, the work of Thomas Christopher Lewis has always equaled Willis, but working towards a different ideal in ensemble tone. Both firms were typical of 19th century British organ-builders in that they exported many instruments to Australia. Among Lewis's best work is the now-restored organ in Melbourne. The Melbourne Cathedral is high Victorian to a phantasmagoric degree, with its decorative polychroming, stencils and tiles, hallmarks of its architect, the Englishman William Butterfield (1814–1900). Its hard surfaces and lengthy nave produce a satisfying but dry reverberation. Although the organ does not saturate the building with sound, owing to a side chancel placement, it is nonetheless a masterpiece for its beautiful flutes and strings (French in influence), its brilliant choruses, clear reeds, and arresting gravity in bass registers. The organist, June Nixon, deserves high praise for spearheading the restoration.

- Sydney Town Hall
  William Hill & Sons, Ltd., 1890
  5 manuals, 126 stops, 160 ranks, 64' Contra Trombone

One of the world's most extraordinary ensembles, based upon a 40-rank Great with 16 ranks of mixture-work, and the whole crowned by superb tubas of a chorus-enhancing nature and magnificent pedal reeds. The fascinating historic console is nonetheless awkward; many of the organ's color possibilities are virtually impossible to use in concert because the combination pistons are limited in number, non-adjustable and none is 'general' (acting on the entire organ). The organ's novelty stop, the 64' reed, doesn't produce much of an effect (Thalben-Ball used to refer to this stop cheekily as 'that antipodean, expensive slow-beating 32' reed').

FRANCE

- Basilica of St.-Sernin, Toulouse
  Aristide Cavaillé-Coll 1889
  Tracker action with Barker Machine (pneumatic assist)
  3 manuals, 54 stops, 71 ranks

- Church of Ste.-Clotilde, Paris
  Aristide Cavaillé-Coll (since rebuilt)
  Electric action
  3 manuals, 60 stops, 73 ranks

It is impossible to think of French organs without invoking the name of Aristide Cavaillé-Coll, who worked in Paris from 1832 until his death in 1900. More than any other French organ-builder, Cavaillé-Coll transformed the 18th century organ of the classical period into a rich, vibrant, suave yet energetic instrument, one that paralleled contemporary developments in composition, orchestration and pianism (Chopin, Berlioz and Liszt). Cavaillé-Coll soon eclipsed his contemporaries, and furnished organs for many of the famous Parisian churches, including Notre-Dame, St.-Sulpice, St.-Augustin, La Trinité and La Madeleine.

Late in his career, Cavaillé-Coll built two organs that set his scene with future admirers. One was the 1889 three-manual instrument at the Basilica of St.-Sernin in Toulouse, the other built a year later for the Abbey Church of St.-Ouen in Rouen. St.-Sernin is without a doubt one of the most thrilling organs in the world. Its rich, fiery ensemble, its exquisite softer stops, the sonorous foundations which fill every crevice of the basilica with a buttery yet transparent tone – all of this approaches the magical. St.-Sernin is a prime example of an *energetic* organ which is not necessarily loud. The texture and character of the ensemble is so charged, so harmonically complex, rich, yet well-balanced, that it offers complete satisfaction.

Of the many spectacular Parisian organs, that in the Church of Ste.-Clotilde stands out fondly in my recollection. This is the historic church where César Franck, Gabriel Pierné, Charles Tournemire and Jean Langlais have been organists – four giant names of organ composition and playing. Ste.-Clotilde breaks with the customary musical arrangement for a French Catholic church. Normally, one finds the large organ in the nave gallery and a smaller instrument (choir organ) in the chancel to accompany the singers. The two instruments alternate, but are rarely used together. But at Ste.-Clotilde the nave has a double gallery; at the first level are the choir organ and choristers, at the second level the grand organ.

Although the original assisted tracker action has been converted to electric and several stops added, the core of the original 1859 Cavaillé-Coll organ is still very much intact. This is the instrument where César Franck played and improvised sublimely, Sunday after Sunday. Here also his distinguished successors contributed so much to French organ culture.

GERMANY

- Weingarten Abbey
  Joseph Gabler, 1737–50
  Restored Orgelbau Kuhn, Switzerland, 1980–83
  Mechanical action
  4 manuals, 66 stops, 6,666 pipes

Weingarten Abbey is the closest ecclesiastical approximation of heaven I know. This baroque 'fantasy' is all-out madness, mostly white, of opulent soft textures throughout, married to resplendent decoration. Set into an elaborate gallery with six large apertures for windows, the organ cases are of a deep golden hue, all the more striking for how they stand out in relief to the white interior. You would think it part of Mungo, a distant city from Flash Gordon.

The organ is programatically derived from the Abbey's dedication, *dem Heiligen Blut Christi*, or the sacred blood of Christ. In keeping with the story of Jesus' 666 whiplashes at his Passion, the organ contains 66 stops and 6,666 pipes. Certainly the builder sweated blood in the construction of this instrument. Since the various cases are linked by decorative bridges, each span contains a functioning section of the organ, and the whole instrument works entirely by tracker action: here is a mechanical nightmare fully worthy of the baroque era. No wonder it took thirteen years to build!

First and last, the ensemble has an arresting sound; chunky, cheerful and complex, it rings through the building to stunning effect. The softer foundations and flutes are exquisite, the color reeds squawky and rich. But the organ is perhaps best known as an apotheosis of late baroque novelty effects. In addition to all the marvelous organ colors are the percussion stops: Zimbelstern (called Cymbala), cuckoo (Cuculus), nightingale (Rossignol) and drum simulation (Tympanum, four 16' wooden pipes tuned to rumble like timpani), as well as two sets of bells. One is a delicate carillon or glockenspiel right in the organ console, the others are larger, hanging beneath the centre of the case and arranged as immense bunches of grapes (echoing the region, which is wine country). Because of their proximity to the console, these large bells handily succeed in shocking unwary visiting organists.

Not only are these effects novel, but they sound marvelous, especially the little glockenspiel played with smaller flutes. Yet one can scarcely imagine how organists were supposed to exploit such effects in divine service.[2]

2 You can hear this organ beautifully demonstrated on a recording by Piet Kee, Chandos CHAN0520, released 1991, with music of Pachelbel, J. S. Bach, Walther, J. M. Bach, Lebegue, and Murschhauser.

GREAT BRITAIN

- Westminster Cathedral, London
  Nave Organ: Henry Willis & Sons 1922 & 1932
  Electro-pneumatic action
  4 manuals, 69 stops, 75 ranks

I have many, many fond memories of this building and instrument, which is one of my favorite organs in all of Europe. It is one of the few English organs that truly fills a large building with sound and it has a certain abandon that never exceeds the boundaries of good taste. Building up to full organ and crashing down on large chords, you can just feel the organ explode out of the gallery. The Cathedral has magnificent acoustics, not only with plentiful reverberation, but in its clarity and in the way it reinforces bass tone. The trumpet reeds of the organ possess an entirely distinctive snap and fire, its diapason choruses are brilliant and clear, and the softer voices are exquisite, especially the strings and the uncommonly ethereal Cor de Nuit celeste. One would never mistake Westminster Cathedral's for a French instrument, but it is like an Englishman who speaks French fluently. The voicing makes the melody sing out nobly over the rest, and when the pedal reeds are drawn (as in a big French organ), the effect is devastating.

In 1984 the organ received a thorough restoration at the hands of Harrison & Harrison. In all respects the job was exemplary. The stoplist was not changed, and the style of voicing was preserved.

- St. Paul's Cathedral, London
  Henry Willis & Sons 1872, 1900, 1925, 1930, 1952, 1960, 1966
  N. P. Mander 1977
  Electro-pneumatic action
  5 manuals, 105 stops, 135 ranks: chancel, dome and nave sections

I have said previously that one cannot appreciate an organ without responding to its environment. St. Paul's, London is perhaps the ultimate example of this axiom. Here is a space that not only dazzles the eye, but sounds even more impressive than it looks. Playing the organ there, hearing the sound swirl across mosaic, marble and stone – feeling the room slowly fill up with tone – is like sensing the true presence of the divine. While I find the grandeur of the full organ entirely magnificent, I single out the chancel Tubas for special mention: they perhaps tie with those in Salisbury Cathedral for the finest Willis Tubas in the realm.

Having said that, St. Paul's is no easy organ to play. Given its multiple locations and the regrettable position of the console high above the south choir stalls,

it is difficult to judge balances between the various sections of the instrument –
granted, a minor inconvenience when one hears the sheer wonder of the effect.
(Here, certainly, is one place where a movable console would be a godsend.)

- St. Mary Redcliffe, Bristol
  Harrison & Harrison 1912 (restored 1974/1990)
  Electro-pneumatic action
  4 manuals, 57 stops, 74 ranks

I consider the Redcliffe organ to be Arthur Harrison's finest and most characteristic work and this is why I chose it above all others to record my all-English CD
and video for Decca. It has always been considered typical of work of its period,
and yet it contains many distinctive features not found in other Harrison &
Harrison organs. From a relatively small number of stops, it contains all the
essential ensemble stops, a full complement of orchestrally imitative sounds
(woodwinds, keen strings and flutes), and staggering bass registers, including *two*
full-length 32' reed stops. Another astounding aspect is the swell box, with two
sets of shutters, one facing the choir and the other the nave, each front available
from its own swell pedal. Opening the chancel shutters gives all of the normal
dynamic range one expects from a good swell box; then opening the nave shutters extends the dynamic range yet further and to an astonishing degree.

- Royal Festival Hall, London
  Harrison & Harrison, 1954, Ralph Downes, designer
  Electro-pneumatic action
  4 manuals, 98 stops, 143 ranks

A path-breaking instrument in the history of British neo-classical organ-building,
and vastly under-appreciated in my opinion. As the hall is lamentably dry of acoustic, one can only wonder how this organ would shine in a great, reverberant space.

- Royal Albert Hall, London
  Henry Willis 1871–72; Harrison & Harrison, 1924, 1934, 1973
  Electro-pneumatic action
  4 manuals, 131 stops, 174 ranks

- Temple Church, London
  Harrison & Harrison, 1927, 1934, 1973
  Electro-pneumatic action
  4 manuals, 49 stops, 58 ranks

- Westminster Abbey
  Harrison & Harrison, 1937, 1982, 1987
  Electro-pneumatic action
  4 manuals, 90 stops, 122 ranks

Favorite Harrison & Harrison organs and fine specimens, these three are ideally suited to the needs of their respective environments. At the time of writing, the Albert Hall instrument is in need of an overhaul and is therefore somewhat treacherous to play. The recent additions to the Abbey organ, particularly the new Bombarde department, make that instrument one of the capital's most thrilling.

- Hereford Cathedral
  Henry Willis 1892–93, 1908, 1920, 1932–33
  Restored with some additions by Harrison & Harrison, 1984
  Electro-pneumatic action
  4 manuals, 59 stops, 69 ranks

Sumptuous, magnificent, splendid, brilliant, wonderful, a real jewel. And yes, I like it. Perfectly restored under the aegis of its curator for many years, Cathedral Organist Dr. Roy Massey.

- Oakham School Chapel
  Peter Collins, 1992
  Mechanical action, electric stop action
  3 manuals, 29 stops, 37 ranks

A tall spacious building with decent acoustics houses this elegant instrument. Visually spectacular with its carvings of the Gospel writers, horseshoes and herons, the organ ably leads congregational song (in the best English public school tradition). Beautiful voicing can be found throughout, especially in the pedal division in which the pipes of every stop are made of pine. Individually clear and prompt-speaking, these stops combine in an uncommonly sonorous bass.

JAPAN

- Sukyo Mahikari Great Hall of Worship, Takayama
  Th. Frobenius & Sons, Lyngby (Copenhagen), Denmark.
  Architectural and tonal design by Tokugoro Ohbayashi
  Attached tracker console; two electric-action mobile consoles
  3 manuals, 45 stops, 67 ranks

- Matsuzakaya Department Store, Nagoya
  Casavant Frères, Ltée, St.-Hyacinthe, Quebec, Canada.
  Electro-pneumatic action
  3 manuals, 40 stops, 54 ranks

Japan is proving to be one of the most interesting places for the development of modern organ culture. Japanese religion was never introduced to, nor developed a need for, pipe organs. But in the late 19th and early 20th centuries, as missionaries began spreading Western religions into Eastern culture and churches began sprouting, a few instruments inevitably began to appear.[3] Since World War II, organ culture in Japan has developed considerably, almost all of it imported from Europe and America. While most of the emphasis has been on mechanical-action instruments based upon historic Germanic or Dutch models, nonetheless an incredible range of styles and builders has been explored.

In general, the imported organs by Beckerath, Klais, Schuke and Rieger to be found in Japan do not differ materially from other instruments by these firms throughout Europe and America. The two organs I have listed strike me as being truly distinctive and unusual instruments, both in their designs and as examples of their respective builders' work. The Frobenius in the Mahikari Grand Shrine in Takayama is primarily the work of its designer, Tokugoro Ohbayashi, my friend from Denmark who had apprenticed with P. G. Andersen. More recently he has built his own factory in Japan for new organs and restorations, but when the Takayama organ was built, he was engaged as an organ architect and designer. In close collaboration with Frobenius, Toku designed the case, devised the pipe scales, and oversaw the final voicing of the instrument.

3 E. M. Skinner sent a small organ over in 1906 for Tokyo Cathedral; no record of it remains, and it is assumed to have been destroyed by enemy action in World War II. Interestingly, at a time when Skinner was perfecting his electric actions, the Tokyo organ had tracker action – probably because this would be simpler to repair by non-organ technicians.

Headquarters of the Mahikari sect, the 7,500-seat shrine is an immense space to fill with organ tone. As one ascends to higher levels within the building, one must undertake additional preparation. Since the organ is two stories above the platform where the Golden Shrine is placed, anyone ascending above that level must be 'purified,' as is common to traditional Japanese Shinto custom. The ritual entailed my first being draped in a special smock of white linen; then our guide requested purification, hand-clapping (to attract the audience of the gods) and much bowing. Being a large lad, I needed two smocks tied together!

The organ possesses the same fine Frobenius craftsmanship I knew from their instruments in Denmark, but with an entirely different sound. Rather than pursuing a silvery, clean 'Bach' effect of the north German baroque, Toku instead looked to the rich, reedy sonorities of 18th and 19th century French organs. The bright reeds and bold mutations lend themselves to the swashbuckling early French music, while the foundation stops and beautiful diapason celeste (called 'Vox luminis') drench the room in rich organ tone.

As we have seen from Wanamaker's in Philadelphia, an organ in a department store is not exactly novel. But leave it to the Japanese to revive in the late 20th century an extreme example of bygone American elegance. The Matsuzakaya Department Store in Nagoya is similar to Wanamaker's in that a multi-story shopping boutique faces out to an atrium. But at Matsuzakaya, the Casavant organ is situated at one end of a much longer corridor, one side of which is entirely of glass alongside the sidewalk. Thus the organ is visible from outside. At the far end of the atrium are balconies with sales counters and eateries. A circular, unique fan-shaped display of trumpet pipes crowns an open pipe display, flanked on one end by a cluster of large 32' metal flue pipes. Superbly designed, scaled and tonally finished by Casavant tonal director Jean-Louis Coignet, the organ adapts French and American classic elements into a fiery, thrilling ensemble. Jean-Louis has recalled his crusade with the authorities to insert a 32' Bombarde into the organ. After protests such as, 'But we can't have this stop! 32' Bombardes give Japanese people headaches!', Jean-Louis was finally able to persevere, and this vital rank was included.

SOUTH AFRICA

- City Hall, Cape Town, South Africa
  Norman & Beard 1905
  Pneumatic action
  4 manuals, 49 stops, 55 ranks

A glance at the specification gives the impression that this instrument is perfectly typical of its era and when I arrived I was expecting a serviceable and enjoyable English civic organ, but I encountered conviction itself. It was like a gold-plated presidential Pullman car gliding inexorably down the floor of the Grand Canyon. The ensemble has a chesty brawn that steamrolls down the hall, but is nonetheless quite bright and thrilling. The powerful bass registers deliciously ravage every seat in the place. In fact, the mouth of bottom C of the 32′ Open Diapason could easily accommodate my girth. It looked like part of a suspension bridge. Its larger sister, in Wellington Town Hall, New Zealand, on which I have also performed, is proof positive – were any needed – that the great Norwich firm of Norman & Beard were indeed master-builders of distinction.

UNITED STATES

- Castro Theater, San Francisco, California
  Wurlitzer, 1921; rebuilt and installed in San Francisco by
  Richard Taylor & Edward Millington Stout III, January 1982
  Electro-pneumatic unit action
  4 manuals, 21 ranks

An aristocrat among theater organs, a superb restoration and re-finishing of a vintage and slightly enlarged Wurlitzer has set the standard for elegance and refinement in theater organ tone. Equally noteworthy is the curatorship of the organ by Ed Stout and Dick Taylor, who keep the instrument in virtually Smithsonian condition week after week.

- Grace Cathedral, San Francisco, California
  Æolian-Skinner, 1934; changes 1952; addition of Bombarde and Gallery
  divisions by Casavant, 1974; console by Ruffatti, 1968; new console provided by Schoenstein & Co. in 1998
  Electro-pneumatic action
  4 manuals, 92 stops, 123 ranks

An aristocrat among cathedral instruments (San Francisco must be filled with aristocrats), the Grace organ creates absolute magic for choral accompaniment and liturgical atmospherics.

- The Church of Sts. Peter & Paul (San Francisco)
  Schoenstein & Co., 1989, designed and finished by Jack Bethards
  Electro-pneumatic action
  2 manuals, 25 stops, 30 ranks

For its size, I know no finer organ than the Sts. Peter & Paul's Schoenstein in San Francisco. It is a marvel of efficient design which produces maximum result from minimum resources. While quite large, this hybrid Victorian-Romanesque-style edifice possesses only marginal reverberation. From its perch in the rear gallery, however, the organ sounds immense, but is so skillfully designed as to have much better manners than the usual caged giant. Enclosing both Great and Swell is one secret to the organ's success; another is the careful balancing of stops so that the various colors blend both in traditional combinations and unorthodox juxtapositions. It deserves a much wider following. (The Schoenstein firm has also been justly feted for their tonal restoration of and additions to the famous Æolian-Skinner organ in the Mormon Tabernacle. In Washington D.C. their 63-rank instrument built for St. Paul's Parish Church on K Street has also been justifiably acclaimed.)

- First Presbyterian Church, Oakland, California
  Rosales Organ Builders, 1993–95
  Tracker action (electric-action: 32's, Antiphonal and Chamade)
  3 manuals, 59 stops, 76 ranks

Unquestionably, this is the most astounding new tracker organ I have played. An eclectic instrument, taking its inspiration from classical and romantic French organs as well as the North German style, the Oakland organ stops short of being overwhelming, and succeeds in delivering the thrill of the decade. In many details Oakland reminds me of Toulouse without the acoustics: a big foundation sound, delightful flutes, good strings, an effective swell box, rip-roaring reeds (with the sort of pungent and quick-speaking lower octaves I adore) and exceptional cornet stops. The organ's real signature, however, is its *devastating* pedal (Toulouse again), fully capable of stimulating its nearby neighbor, the Hayward fault. For all its elegant and elaborate design, the console remains a model of simplicity and logic; everything is where it should be.

- First Methodist Church, Van Wert, Ohio
  Robert Noehren, 1977
  Electro-mechanical action, entirely enclosed in two divisions
  4 manuals, 32 independent stops, 39 ranks

The Van Wert instrument is a tour de force of unit-organ design, in which the same stop is made to play at several pitches, and sometimes on more than one manual. (By comparison, an organ such as that at Sts. Peter & Paul is a relatively 'straight' organ, with stops generally being available only at one pitch.) The triumph of the scheme is that the multiplication of voices does not interfere with the texture of complicated music such as fugues. During my visit, I registered a lot of music and was hard pressed to uncover any tonal deficiencies, a testament to the ingenuity of the concept. Like Sts. Peter & Paul, Van Wert benefits from being entirely enclosed, for absolute flexibility and expressive potential.

- The Victorian Palace, Place de la Musique
  (Sanfilippo residence), Barrington Hills, Illinois
  David L. Junchen and successors
  Electro-pneumatic unit action
  5 manuals, 80 ranks

Walk in the front door of the Victorian Palace and you will find a grand staircase (patterned after the one on the Titanic). Grasp the stair rail (which used to be in St. Louis' Ambassador Theater) and ascend to the landing (home to one of the world's rarest barrel-operated organs). Turning left would lead you to a portion of one of the world's most sizable collections of phonographs; turning around allows you to gaze down on the main floor (where all available wall space is hugged by incomparable and wondrous automatic musical instruments) or casting a glance upward at the chandelier (one of a pair from Chicago's United Artists Theater), or still higher up at the 400-square-foot domed skylight (patterned after early Tiffany work and constructed anew by American stained-glass masters Mark and Jeannie Bogenrief). If you continue up the right-hand stair, a 100-seat balcony beckons, part of an intimate theater. From this perspective, the stage is now apparent. Here at last is the organ.

You can be nowhere else than at the Sanfilippo residence. Home to the world's largest collection of automatic musical instruments, the Victorian Palace's largest treasure is its pipe organ. In its design, the instrument attempts to solve a musical dilemma: how can one instrument be made equally effective for classical and popular music? In the 1920s and early '30s, a few American builders and John Compton in England tried to respond to this dilemma, designing special organs and providing a proper draw-knob console for classical use, but also a horseshoe cinema keydesk for theatrical playing. In America, such instruments were usually marvelous in their classical guise but pretty miserable for popular music; the Compton successes are better balanced.

The late David L. Junchen spent a lifetime involved in the American theater organ scene, relocating and rebuilding instruments for pizza parlours nation-wide just as the 'pizza and pipes' trend was cresting. In the 1980s, his attention migrated to sophisticated musical instrument collectors who desired home theater organs. He also spent the decade compiling the first two volumes (more than 1,250 pages) of his monumental *Encyclopedia of the American Theater Organ*, the most significant treatise of its kind to date. I first got to know him at the Pasadena Civic Auditorium, where he had re-installed the famous Reginald Foort Touring Organ built by Möller. Lyn Larsen and I were collaborating on a 'dueling organs' concert, with myself at an Allen touring organ and Lyn at the stupendous Möller (I also played a few pieces on the Möller). The concert afforded the perfect opportunity to get to know David better, since he lived in Pasadena. Easy to befriend, talented, articulate and engagingly opinionated, he became a good chum, and one whose opinion I trusted because his ears and musical sense were so acute.

When he died, David was working on his *magnum opus* for Jasper and Marian Sanfilippo. Not surprisingly, the couple already had a Junchen-Wurlitzer of 28 ranks. But the new organ was not to be just another theater organ but an 80-rank instrument designed to do justice equally to concert and theatre music. As with Dave Junchen's other instruments, the guiding philosophy was to use as much vintage material as possible in creating the new organ – just as the Victorian Palace itself was made 'new from old' in most respects.

The theater and organ took almost five years to complete, with teams of restorers working in concert: Joseph R. DuciBella took charge of all interior decoration while Dave Junchen labored away on the organ with his staff. Dave's death in January 1992 was a tragic interruption. Eventually, the restoration team was reorganized under the direction of Lyn Larsen, who took over as music coordinator of the Palace, overseeing the organ's completion and attending to its final finishing. Robert Ridgeway (a recording engineer who, incidentally, captured the Girard organ for my Decca CDs), is now curator of the entire Sanfilippo collection, assisted by L. Curt Mangel III, a mechanical restorer of considerable talent.

I visited the Sanfilippos shortly after the original Junchen-Wurlitzer had been installed in the old music room, where Jasper and Marian welcomed me warmly. In recent years, I would learn of the new organ from Dave Junchen, and then later from Lyn Larsen and Tom Hazleton. Finally in July of 1995 I had the honor of performing on the new behemoth, in concert with Lyn and the British theater organ prodigy Simon Gledhill. We had a ball, taking turns playing what we each do best.

Of course, such an instrument and setting are so overwhelming that they cannot be fully appreciated in a single visit. But some indication of the impact it makes can be found in the words of Jean-Louis Coignet,[4] who visited there in autumn of 1995 and told me, 'The Sanfilippo organ is a unique masterpiece. It goes beyond any established tradition and is as close to organ-building perfection as is humanly possible.'

- The John R. Silber Symphonic Organ at Boston University
  Skinner and Æolian (1930) with additions; restored, installed by
  Nelson Barden Associates, Inc. 1980–94
  Electro-pneumatic action

Nelson Barden has the distinction of being highly regarded among organ-builders without ever having built an organ. Concerned instead with the preservation of older 20th century instruments, he has secured respect through exemplary, high-quality restoration work and innovative use of vintage instruments.

I originally met Nelson by accident at Blenheim Palace during the summer of 1987. I had recorded there in May, and the Duke of Marlborough asked me to demonstrate the organ for a study-group visiting 'from abroad.' Nelson was one of the 'foreigners,' and he didn't recognize me sitting at the console. As I commenced the Dupré *Prélude in G minor*, Nelson blurted out in his flat Boston accent, 'My *Gawd*, who *ahhh* you?' We both burst into laughter, quickly became acquainted, and an invitation to Boston followed shortly.

Like the Sanfilippos' instrument, the Boston University organ is unique in many ways. Originally, it combined two 1930 player organs which had formerly been installed in millionaires' mansions. These were restored to perfection and arranged as a walk-through display, complete with brass handrails and a parquet floor. During the 1980s, many additions were made, and the studio always had a work-in-progress aura about it. In fact, the project took fourteen years to complete.

The instrument became widely known while still in the studio. Much discussed in organ circles, it began to draw visitors – first locally, then from all over the world. Constantly besieged for demonstrations, Nelson had written a dramatic narrative about the discovery and restoration of the instruments. His delivery of this was no less than a virtuoso performance, repeated so many hundreds of times that he could recite the tale in his sleep. From time to time I would bring new groups of friends and marvel at the consistency of his script, which included such details as how the organ had been terribly damaged by a broken

---

4 During the past twenty years, M. Coignet has designed some of the finest organs of our time for churches and concert halls. In addition to serving as tonal director of Casavant, he is the organ expert of the City of Paris, where he assumes a critical role in directing the restoration, renovation and preservation of 150 organs.

sewer pipe, how rats had eaten all the electric wiring, how the player mechanisms were so complex that no one believed it could ever work ... As the story unfolded, one small section of the organ would begin to play, followed by another, then still more, until finally the whole instrument had come to life.

It was great theater, and I happily provided music used for every demonstration. The organ was equipped with one of the first computer recorders, and during one of my early visits Nelson asked if I would record a favorite piece, the *Scherzando* of Gabriel Pierné. Unfortunately, I had a miserable case of flu and perhaps wasn't at my best. It was a pleasant surprise to return later and find the piece entirely reworked on the computer into a perfect performance with all manner of registrational flourishes – the musical equivalent of taking cotton shirts to the cleaners and getting them back in silk.

In its original configuration, the Boston University instrument curled around the audience like a huge question mark – unintentional but ironic nonetheless, its permanent location was uncertain for many years. In 1993, it was moved to a permanent home in the student union building across the street, where it could be heard regularly in historical performances, live programmes and accompanying silent films.[5] I was honored to play at the inaugural festivities, a private gathering for the University Board of Trustees. After a mini-recital and a few requests, I loosened my collar enough to trot out a splashy rendition of Leroy Anderson's 'Fiddle Faddle,' perhaps a curious selection for an academic institution, but a sure-fire hit nevertheless.

The instrument contains more than 7,500 pipes and incorporates many unusual features, including a library of more than 2,000 paper roll recordings, some of which date back to 1890. These, as well as live performances of virtually any length, can be stored on a custom-built computer. The significance here is the degree of control available to the performer. All facets of one's playing can be altered at will on the computer, and music of great complexity can be built up on-screen. Imagine the possibilities! Live performances will always entertain and thrill audiences, but in the long history of the pipe organ, every substantial advance in control has eventually become standard. Before long, I venture to predict that computers such as this will extend organ playing into a new realm, freeing the artist from every limitation save that of imagination. It is the shape of things to come.

---

5 In the fall of 1995, I attended a showing of the original silent film *Phantom of the Opera* starring Lon Chaney with a splendid accompaniment by Walt Strony.

- Girard College Chapel, Philadelphia
  Æolian-Skinner Organ Company, 1932–33
  Electro-pneumatic action
  82 stops, 107 ranks

- The Grand Court, Lord & Taylor, Philadelphia
  (formerly the John Wanamaker Store)
  Los Angeles Art Organ Co; Wanamaker Staff, 1904, 1911–28
  Electro-pneumatic action
  396 speaking stops, 461 ranks, 28,579 pipes (!)

- First United Methodist Church, Lake Wales, Florida
  Th. Frobenius & Sons, Lyngby, Denmark, 1986
  Tracker action with electric stop action
  25 stops, 30 ranks

Heavens – that *must* be more than enough favorite organs!

CHAPTER THIRTEEN

DISSENSION IN THE RANKS

On December 6th, 1931 in the town of Villemomble one of the great French
organists and composers, Charles Tournemire, dedicated the first electronic
organ. Tournemire had been a pupil of César Franck and had succeeded him as
organist at the Parish Church of Sainte-Clotilde. The instrument built by the
Lille workshops of the firm Coupleux had been devised under the supervision
of Tournemire himself and he considered that 'this extraordinary instrument
opens new horizons for the organ and for sacred music ... Here is an overwhelming discovery called to a secure and sensational future!'[1]

One of the more controversial aspects of my career, and one which is calculated
to send the purists rushing for their smelling-salts, has been my unashamed
involvement with, and my championing of, the Allen digital organ. Many
assume, quite wrongly, that I am employed by Allen, or that they pay me to promote their instruments.

1 Joël-Marie Fauquet, in the liner notes from *Orgues et Organistes Français en 1930*, EMI 2C 153-
   16411/5 (five-record set, released September 15, 1981).

My initial introduction to the Allen came early, when I had become organist at the Baptist Church in my North Carolina hometown. Downstairs in the Fellowship Hall was a small early example, a model TC-4. This was not a pipe organ, but a keyboard instrument that generated sound via oscillators and loud-speakers. All of the mid-range speakers were placed on the equivalent of a small Ferris wheel inside specially constructed cabinets. In an effort to avoid sterility, these revolved behind the grille cloth thus providing a certain life and movement to the tone; hence the name Gyrophonic Projector. Allen's competitors used to claim – I thought somewhat desperately – that the Gyro Cabinets created too much airflow and therefore, choir-members would be susceptible to catch colds from mysterious draughts – somewhat improbable, but funny nonetheless.

Whenever another organist was practicing on the Möller upstairs, I would use the tiny Allen. It had some memorably odd controls. One was called 'Diapasons become Dulcianas,' which, at a stroke, altered the Diapason-toned stops to Dulciana strength. A similar control was labelled 'Trumpets become Oboes,' similarly thinning out the Trumpets until they more closely resembled Oboes. These transforming controls got my mind thinking to all kinds of others: Organist becomes Bored, Console becomes Nativity Scene, or Bench becomes Wrapped-Around-Choir-Director's-Head!

At that time, the Allen appealed to me far more than the Hammond, primarily on account of its suitability for classical music. By contrast, the Hammond was undoubtedly more at home in popular music and jazz. In all other respects, I placed both instruments in the same category: useful for practice. I was always eager, though, to head back upstairs to the Möller for the serious work.

The first change in my perspective came when I heard Virgil play with the Atlanta Symphony on his Rodgers Black Beauty. While the sound of that particular electronic did not do a great deal for me, I had to admit that by the end of the concert, it had fulfilled its basic role, if only by virtue of sheer power and the tremendous impact of its bass registers. Furthermore, as I grew to know Virgil better, I saw how he was able to extend his own mission through the use of his electronic organ. Wherever there was no pipe organ, it came into its own. Audiences at Community Concerts for example, often held in high-school gymnasiums, assembly halls and the like, might never have heard or seen Virgil without Black Beauty. Thus, he spread organ music further and wider throughout the North American continent than anyone else. The Atlanta experience taught me the valuable lesson that *any* organ could serve as a vehicle for his virtuosity and music-making.

Later, when I had moved to Atlanta and was living in Mrs. Candler's house, she decided that it would be delightful to have an electronic organ for her sun porch. I could use it for practice and play to her on pleasant Southern summer afternoons. Typically however, she could not simply go out and buy an organ. As with her

Cadillacs and the Capitol Automobile Company, she demanded service, attention and a background study before she would sign the check. So she summoned the local Allen dealer, George MacKenzie, before deciding that he and I should embark on a fact-finding mission to the Allen factory in Macungie, Pennsylvania.

The vast Allen plant was undeniably remarkable. The sweet aromas of different wood and the unmistakable sounds of the manufacturing process conspired together to create a lasting impression. There was also an engaging Pennsylvania Dutch ethos evident in the outgoing and friendly manner of all the employees, many of whom, of their own volition, stopped to describe to us proudly what they were doing. Three people in particular made that first Macungie visit memorable: James Feller, the president's assistant, Bob Pearce, the vice-president and, of course, the president himself, Jerome Markowitz, whom we later met unexpectedly in the showroom once we had completed the factory tour. He was a man of few words and many disciplines: inventor, theorist, businessman. He was also a great theater organ aficionado, an enthusiasm which for him sat in perfect comfort alongside his professional interest in the classical instrument. He greeted us with a hearty handshake, and asked the purpose of our visit. After outlining our mission, he invited me to play. While I can't recall precisely, I must, typically, have chosen a flashy *fortissimo* selection, for as soon as I had finished I gesticulated exuberantly. 'What I love about this pedal, Mr. Markowitz, is that it has *real guts!*' He laughed right out loud, and we were friends from that moment on.

Bob Pearce, the vice-president in charge of sales, played more the role of the traditional gentleman. He could not have been more hospitable, especially in the circumstances. After all, here was this wild kid, dressed as if from another planet, acting as proxy to some rich lady. Generously overlooking this entirely, Bob seemed to be impressed by my playing – or its zest anyway – and made me feel like the most valued customer in the world on the verge of purchasing the company's *magnum opus*. He was, and is, a salesman's salesman.

Jim Feller, Jerome's assistant, had fallen into his profession almost by accident. Early in life, he had developed an interest in automatic musical devices such as music boxes, singing bird cages and the like. His formal training was as an engineer, and he had worked at the Bureau of Standards in Washington D.C. between 1949 and 1953. When he was moved from hands-on engineering work to a desk job, he became restless and having just happened to call into the local Allen dealer, he became so interested that he made a trip to Macungie to learn more about the company where he met Jerome, who offered him a job.[2]

2 Jerome passed away in 1991, to be succeeded as president by his youngest son Steve Markowitz. Jim and Bob are now retired.

Initially, Jim was appointed head of the key-making department, but soon became indispensable as Jerome's right-hand man and assistant. Having become a licensed pilot, he was also the in-house aviator, flying the company's planes. Furthermore, his interest in automatic musical instruments led him to establish his own home business, in which he soon became renowned for his restoration of Swiss musical movements.[3] Like Bob Pearce, Jim was another gracious diplomat who welcomed me kindly.

Fascinated by what I had seen, I returned to Atlanta to report back to Florence. Unfortunately, her interior decorator advised that an organ console, speakers and cables would consume too much space in the sun porch, preventing the use of the room for large gatherings. I was more than a little disappointed and had to content myself with the value of the trip to Macungie.

My next involvement with Allen came with Don Westfield, the dealer in Grand Rapids, with whom I attended the Allen Seminar in mid-1972; this resulting in a number of bookings around the country. More than any other factor, the Allen bookings essentially launched my career in the States. Furthermore, I took Virgil's advice to heart and always did my best whenever in a city for an Allen booking to visit the prominent pipe organs and strike up acquaintances with the organists. As more bookings followed, I was able to build a career on both sides of the pipe/electronic fence but, as the early 1970s wore on, it became clear that the next stage of my career should involve a touring organ.

The concept of touring organs had not begun with Virgil Fox, but in Britain during World War I. In 1916, cinema organist G. T. Pattman decided that, in order to bring music to the people, he would commission from Harrison & Harrison of Durham a three-manual portable pipe organ of seventeen stops enclosed in two swell boxes. Historian Laurence Elvin writes:

> The instrument was built in sections and was transported from place to place in
> six railway trucks, a special lorry being used to move each unit to the theater.
> Pattman's brother was in charge of a staff of six and the general running
> expenses amounted to an average of £200 a week.[4]

3 For many years Jim was involved in the Musical Box Society International, America's most prestigious organization devoted to this specialized branch of instrument-making. He was president for two years (1977–78) and a trustee for twelve years afterwards.

4 Laurence Elvin, *The Harrison Story* (Lincoln: Laurence Elvin, 1973), p. 126 (plus other information pp. 126–129).

Designing a pipe organ to be movable, like some overgrown piece of stage scenery, had been done before in the realm of small chamber organs, such as a baroque orchestra might employ. But a self-respecting concert organ? It was an unprecedented endeavour, and in light of all the difficulties, amazing that it was such a success.

However, the nightmarish difficulty in dismantling, shipping and re-erecting the organ against a busy schedule eventually took its toll and Pattman stopped touring in 1923. Recently in the UK, I played a recital at Durham School Chapel, and was delighted to discover that Pattman's organ had eventually found its way here, reconfigured by the builders for its new home.

Another eminent British theater organist, Reginald Foort, who was an FRCO,[5] also concluded that a touring cinema organ would serve his purpose well and accordingly, in 1938, commissioned the American firm of M. P. Möller to build him a transportable theater instrument of twenty-seven individual stops, divided into nine separate units. Foort's instrument was somewhat more audacious than Pattman's, requiring no fewer than five trucks and a permanent staff of twelve. But Foort's was such a big talent and his popularity so well established, both in classical and cinema organ venues, that he was bound to make a considerable success of the venture had it not been for the untimely intervention of World War II. The Möller was subsequently acquired by the BBC and ultimately returned to the States. Several decades later, having been restored, it was installed in the Pasadena Civic Auditorium, remaining there to this day. Indeed, in the auspicious company of theater-organ supremo Lyn Larsen, I performed a concert there in the late 1980s.

Given the considerable distances between major towns and cities in North America, there was no need for such elaborate touring instruments. Furthermore, at the time that Pattman and Foort were trying to bring organ music to the masses, most American theaters already had pipe organs of their own, as did many municipal auditoriums. Nevertheless, a few touring organs did come into being, the Wanamaker Organ Shop in particular creating a small touring instrument with six sets of pipes called the 'Cappella'. Originally designed to accompany an ensemble of ancient stringed instruments owned by Rodman Wanamaker, its most famous appearance took place at no less a venue than the White House, with the Belgian-American organist Charles M. Courboin at the console. In fact, it may be the only pipe organ ever to have been inside the White House.

5 Fellow of the Royal College of Organists.

When Virgil came on the touring scene in the 1960s with Black Beauty, times had changed considerably. But his basic motivation was essentially the same as that of Pattman and Foort. In common with them, he was determined to bring organ music to the masses. And with a far more easily transportable electronic touring organ at his disposal, he could indeed appear in any pipeless venue. By the time I came to know him, he had already enjoyed several years' increasing success in this vein. Performing on Black Beauty was a most significant and vital part of his work.

As someone who had always wanted a full-time concert career, I looked to Virgil's example as a model. And as my relationship with Don Westfield and Allen developed, it became inevitable that I would tour with one of their fine instruments. At first, I travelled with rented stock models but these instruments, while sturdily crafted, were not designed to cope with the widely varying acoustics that one meets on the road. I needed something as powerful as Black Beauty but, taking every advantage of the rapidly developing technology, more elegant-sounding.

By 1975, it was clear from my bookings that the time had finally arrived. I petitioned Florence Candler and asked her what I should do (or, as a good fundraiser might say, 'We would not wish to offend you by denying an opportunity for your generosity'). While she knew exactly what I was after, she also had Virgil's successful example as a reference. Generously, she agreed to buy the touring organ on the strict condition that I take full responsibility for its upkeep and transportation. I got right on the phone to Allen to begin design discussions.

By any standards, this first touring organ was an unprecedented project for Allen. 'Large' described every aspect: four manuals, seven computers, 5,000 watts of audio power, some fifty cabinets enclosing literally hundreds of individual loudspeakers, 98 stops, the equivalent of 120 ranks of pipes, 12 alterable voices (stops that could be programmed immediately through the use of computer cards), and the largest Allen console to date. The amplifiers were specially built by RMI (Rocky Mount Instruments), Allen's subsidiary for electronic keyboard instruments used by popular musicians. My concern for power stemmed from my experience on tour. The organ had to be delicate in small rooms and powerful in larger ones, while filling vast cathedrals and responding ably to all the forces of a full symphony orchestra.

Throughout the design and building process, two Allen employees were particularly invaluable, always ready to stretch the available technology to the limit in a desire to create as innovative an instrument as possible. Since Jim Feller was now handling all custom organs, this project fell under his domain. He was adroit at sifting my practical needs from my excesses, and did me the honour of listening attentively and patiently to my every wish. Clark Ferguson took charge of the audio design. He knew that a certain element of brute power would be required, which led him to use the RMI equipment. With that came the notion of incorporating some of the RMI's special synthesizer-like effects. Right at the console, I could alter speech characteristics (both attack and release) as well as obtaining certain percussive effects. We also included sostenuto devices to facilitate the playing of transcriptions and improvisations. The final accessory – a godsend, as it turned out – came in the form of sophisticated graphic equalizer attachments on the amplifiers, allowing us to adjust the frequency ranges to suit the acoustics of any building.

Together, Jim and Clark determined that the organ should be constructed with all the reinforcements necessary to withstand the rigors of touring. After all, the console together with its permanently attached dolly weighed in at more than a thousand pounds, and that took no account of the driver 'in the saddle'!

My long-awaited touring organ finally made its debut on May 16, 1976 at 4.00 p.m. to a packed house at the Church of the Advocate in north Philadelphia, a vast neo-Gothic church, the marvelously reverberant acoustics of which were in no way diminished by the attendance of a capacity audience. Even Mrs. Candler flew up, curious to hear for herself the result of her largesse. The press reports were wholly positive. The *Evening Bulletin* headline read 'Keyboard Wizard Carlo Curley Unveils Organ.' And there was more. They went on to say that 'if the Phantom of the Opera had owned this organ, it might have been an end to silent movies.' The *Philadelphia Inquirer* wrote, 'Move over Virgil Fox. America's popular concert virtuoso and his three-manual Rodgers electronic touring organ have a rival ... Curley demonstrated not only the capabilities of this versatile instrument but also his own innate musicianship and his amazing memory.'

I was much relieved that Virgil didn't see the *Inquirer* review, for obvious reasons. As I've said, it would have been impossible for me not to adopt some of Virgil's ways, but I had no desire to ape Virgil Fox – which he respected.

He certainly heard about the program however, and paid me a supreme compliment: 'Honey, that concert must have been a great success. I didn't hear *one* negative thing.' Curious to hear the touring organ for himself, we made a date at – where else? – the Center City Stouffer's, where we had an enjoyable meal and another predictably harrowing altercation with one of the waitresses. The preliminaries happily out of the way, we headed north to the church.

The Allen console stood impressively under the crossing. Virgil circled it several times saying nothing. Then, inviting me to play, he proceeded to listen from every pillar and post, nook and cranny. In all, I must have played for about half an hour before it was time for his verdict. 'You have made a wise decision, Carlo. With this, you can go anywhere and make an *impact*.' He also pointed out that, in his experience, this was the first electronic organ where he could delineate the inner voices in addition to bass and soprano parts while the instrument was either playing very softly or on full organ. 'That is a *very important* element of any organ, and you've *got it right.*'

Virgil knew his subject only too well, having been acquainted with electronic organs for many years. When he first considered having a touring instrument, he had approached Allen and asked whether they would provide one. But Allen, being nothing if not strictly business orientated, would only agree to sell him an organ, not to supply one *gratis.* Consequently, he approached Rodgers, who proved delighted not merely to provide Black Beauty but, in the early years, to transport and set it up at their expense too. This was not only a dream come true for Virgil, but also a bold stroke of advertising savvy on Rodgers' part. In light of this considerable investment, it is all the more surprising that he did not ally himself entirely with the Rodgers product. In the final analysis, his primary objective was making music.

By the mid-1970s, Virgil had moved beyond Black Beauty to Royal V, another Rodgers so named on account of its five manuals. But where Black Beauty had been generally reliable, Royal V was having more than its fair share of gremlins. These problems, and a desire to keep pace with ever-improving technology, were clearly leading him toward the purchase of his own touring instrument. That evening, at the Church of the Advocate, he had been clearly impressed with my Allen and having outlined his aspirations and plans, I was delighted to give him the names of Bob Pearce and Jim Feller. Consequently, it was no surprise to me that he soon commissioned his own large four-manual Allen.

My touring organ held up admirably under the strain. It was hauled and heaved across the breadth and width of the North American continent, before crossing the Atlantic to continue its faithful service throughout Britain and Europe. It required a twenty-foot truck for transport and a crew of four for set-up. At the Alexandra Palace we developed a pre-concert ritual. Once all was ready for the performance, we would all gather in the dressing room underneath the organ gallery for a light tea.

One Sunday afternoon, our little gathering was joined by Ronald Perrin, the organist of Ripon Cathedral who was to perform on the afternoon's program. Having just finished a little last-minute practice, he came into the dressing room and in his retiring, groomed English voice said, 'Pardon me, but I fear something is wrong with the organ.' His demeanor was so apologetic that he almost seemed embarrassed to disturb us – how quintessentially English. Every pastry fork dropped in unison, and a joint gaze fixed itself upon Peter Hanlon, my technician at the time. Without a word, he bolted onto the stage to discover that a low-voltage power supply had failed. While stops were working, the manuals could not be coupled together and the combination pistons were defunct – a grim prospect indeed.

Realizing that if he could not fix the power supply in the fifteen minutes remaining, it might be possible to save the day by rigging up a car battery, Alan Foster, who was on hand, dashed to his Alfa Romeo and came staggering back up the steps, salvation in his arms. Peter walked off the stage just as I made my entrance and it was with considerable relief that I launched into my first piece.

The organ was fixed, but the excitement wasn't over. I began with Bach's chorale *Liebster Jesu*, using the mellifluous celeste effects, most ethereal in that hall's milky acoustic. In fact, the cooing and chirping of the birds that flew freely about the hall was often louder than the music. Perhaps I should have been play-ing Delius. About a minute or so in, a piercing shriek rang out. I didn't stop but, glancing behind me, observed a middle-aged lady, her head crowned in a monu-ment to the hairdressing techniques of a former age. Struggling from her seat, she fled down the aisle clasping her coiffure in horror. Being careful not to miss a note, I was nonetheless concerned that she was either in the midst of a serious medical episode or was yet another purist distressed at my romanticizing Bach. However, the audience in her immediate vicinity was doing its valiant best to stifle titters if not guffaws. But, at the intermission, I discovered that her lamen-tations had been entirely justified. One of the pigeons had delivered a generous personal air-mail packet from a height of eighty feet and, to her at least, it had not been funny.

Soon enough, however, I was to arrive at the same conclusion about my big Allen that G. T. Pattman had reached with his Harrison pipe organ. Regularly moving such an instrument is neither a happy nor an inexpensive chore. I remember asking myself why I hadn't taken up an easier instrument, like the flute? Performers such as James Galway and Isaac Stern were lucky enough to be able to transport their instruments by hand, while mine needed not only a twenty-foot truck but also a crew of burly men to haul it into position. I was lucky in that it could live on the stage at the Alexandra Palace for some extended periods, but it was rapidly becoming clear that, on account of its bulk and weight, I had to investigate more up-to-date options.

Since those early touring days, technology has continued to gallop ahead and it is amazing how miniaturization has made touring much less of a chore. I have had a number of instruments at my disposal, some provided through the kindness of my good friends Julia and Alan Foster, the successful automobile dealer who had become such a fan at the Alexandra Palace.

George Thalben-Ball also shared something of my enthusiasm for the Allen organ. He had one installed during the rebuild of the Temple Church's Harrison & Harrison, and also recorded a wonderful LP on a large model temporarily in use at Chichester Cathedral.

Some people in the pipe organ community abhor electronic organs with a vengeance I find extraordinary. Additionally, they dislike my playing and endorsement of the Allen. It has been easier for me to have faith in the development of the Allen than in many of the recent trends in pipe organ building. While pipe builders have been dabbling in attempts to rediscover the past – often interesting but rarely satisfying either from a musical or sonic standpoint – digital technology has led the Allen to sound increasingly faithful to the kind of pipe organ sound I like best.

Therefore, I have chosen to accept the Allen for exactly what it is, and consequently have never felt any need to defend the instrument or my use of it. Furthermore, I resent the attitude that equates an interest in the Allen with a rejection of pipe organs or the corruption of an ability to appreciate the subtleties of pipe organs. Such an attitude has reached an especially ridiculous trend with MIDI (Musical Instrument Digital Interface), where many modern pipe organs are being equipped with this capability so that digital voices can be added to the pipe complement. Is this not the electronic organ wearing the emperor's new clothes? It is precisely the same Allen-pioneered technology, introduced into the pipe organ under a seemingly legitimate concept.

Too often, the question of electronics and pipes is reduced to such simplistic either/or questions. For me, it is not a question of weighing options but of applying them intelligently, the bottom line being the musical effect upon the listener. I want to go to a concert and bring music to an audience – be it Couperin, Bach, Widor, Wagner or Scott Joplin. As much as I love the organ, it must be remembered that it is only a means to an end. I will use whatever instrument is at hand to make the music – and the musical excitement – come alive for that audience at that moment.

Few people would contest that a well-built pipe organ represents the ideal for which we all strive. Certainly I concur. But the electronic organ has made indisputable inroads into several sectors of the organ-buying market. Before the days of the electronic organ, those with limited funds and space opted for a diminutive pipe organ. Such instruments were frankly quite dismal, and often very limiting. Today, that class of purchaser is increasingly heading toward the electronic organ. Several factors are at work here: much greater tonal variety, low purchase price, ease of installation, limited space requirements, reduced maintenance costs; besides which, it's always in good tune and regulation.

When a church selects an electronic, under these circumstances, pipe organ people look upon it as a 'compromise.' But as digital technology improves by leaps and bounds, the 'compromise' unquestionably diminishes. The Allen is becoming so good, in fact, that in a few cases I would prefer to play the Allen than the pipe organ. Again, I don't view such a situation as a pipes-versus-electronics debate, but a preference for the sound, the excitement, the delicious soft effects, and the musical clarity of the Allen when I am otherwise confronted with a small, lifeless and difficult-to-play pipe organ. However, where space, funds, knowledge and finances permit, a well-designed, well-built pipe organ of integrity must always be the goal.

One other thing: I should stress that the Allen is the only digital organ I believe in. I have often listened to the work of other manufacturers, and to my ears, they simply don't measure up. Over the years, and especially from the time of the big touring organ, the Allen people have welcomed my input on their work, both laudatory and critical, and in doing so they have given freely of their time and energy. I owe an enormous debt of gratitude to the Allen dealer 'family' who have done so much to promote my efforts – indeed the late Jerome Markowitz was always extremely kind and patient with me and to this day I enjoy a sincere and warm friendship with his wife, Martha and their son, Steve, currently president of the company. And, thanks to the extreme generosity of Florence Candler, Don Westfield, Alan Foster, Emyr Davies – the UK Allen dealer – and many others, I have always had a touring organ at my disposal.

In the final analysis, I look upon the Allen as one element of my larger mission to spread organ music far and wide and I can assure you that my regard for this instrument does not hamper my love for the pipe organ. I can and do play both, admire both and criticize both. As with love, human nature does not mete out artistic interest in limited quantities. I can become passionately involved in both kinds of instruments and still have plenty of passion left over.

CHAPTER FOURTEEN

RIDDLES AND ENIGMAS

In June 1979, Herbert von Karajan brought the Berlin Philharmonic to London's Royal Festival Hall. Featured in the program was Richard Strauss' *Also Sprach Zarathustra*, which includes a considerable role for organ. At the time, the Festival Hall Harrison & Harrison was being overhauled, so the Philharmonic hired my large Allen and I went over for a listen.

Truth be told, I went hoping to meet the Maestro, who had been a musical idol of long standing. I had many of his recordings and listened to them with unbridled ardor. I managed to hook up with one of the orchestra staff, who advised me where to stand at rehearsal's end. When the time came, I introduced myself as a fellow musician and the owner of the rented organ, and then proceeded to swear allegiance to his artistry. He grinned, and replied: 'What a contradiction. Hasn't anyone ever told you that it's not possible for an organist to be a musician? Quite impossible! What gives you the right to consider yourself a musician? I have known only one organist I would hail as a musician.'

The Maestro was known for his provocative personality and he certainly had me fishing for a response, but 'nice weather we're having' is about all that came to mind. And maddeningly, he gave me no clue as to the identity of his chosen organist, although having turned the matter over in my mind numerous times I have come to think he must have meant either Richter or Cochereau. However, I had as much respect for von Karajan as any living musician, so I chose flattery, replying in essence that what helped me to become a better musician was listening to great orchestras such as his. 'Ah! That's fine, then!' he said with a twinkle before taking his leave.

I've often said that the organ needs more marketing and promoting than any other instrument mainly on account of its centuries-old accompanimental role in church in which the organist is expected to be heard and not seen. A few of my colleagues have scoffed at my self-appointed 'missionary' work and I think the following proves why I've devoted my life to spreading the word about the most glorious of instruments.

After one of my Royal Albert Hall performances, I was introduced to a fine violinist who had played in several of London's top orchestras for decades. I consider him to be a consummate musician and very much at the top of his profession. He enthused about the concert and went on to ask a question I would never forget. 'Mr. Curley,' he questioned, pointing upwards at the instrument, 'how on earth are you able to draw such an enchanting variety of color and such an enormous *tutti* from those fifty or sixty gray old tubes up there?' I almost didn't have the heart to reveal that the towering 32' 'tubes' were called 'pipes,' behind which were hidden 10,000 of their relatives ranging in a gamut of sizes and shapes. His question seemed so unbelievable that I felt sure he was jesting. But no, he was deadly serious and, having arranged to take him on a tour of the chambers, was suitably gratified to witness at first hand his amazement at everything he saw.

If a fully trained musician has no idea how the organ works, how can the lay public, however fascinated, be expected to have even the slightest clue? This is why I seize every opportunity to outline what I'm doing, which stops I'm highlighting and, in simple terms, how the most complex of all musical instruments achieves its powerful effect.

The mission continues.

It is worth bearing in mind that you can't give concerts by yourself. In almost every instance, I have been blessed with thoughtful, energetic and generous concert sponsors, people so ready to go the extra mile that I have come to depend on them. There have also been some fantastic exceptions. Ten minutes before a recent inaugural recital, the organist pulled me aside so that I might give him the utmost assurance that 'God would come first, and Carlo Curley second on this special evening.' Now, in the first place, I do not discuss such personal topics as politics and religion with people I don't know, and in the second place, I found it offensive that the issue should ever be raised. After all, there isn't the slightest question in my mind as to who comes first.

But such scenarios are thankfully rare, and most sponsors stop at nothing to ensure that concerts run smoothly. I think of Michael Chamberlain and Geoffrey Palmer in Leicestershire, who organized no fewer than three appearances for me in a single day. At 2.30 pm I played a ninety-minute recital at Leicester Cathedral and, after meeting the audience, we had a white-knuckle car ride over to St. Mary the Virgin, Burrough-on-the-Hill where, at 5.00 pm precisely, I presented an hour-long 'tea-time' recital on a small two-manual tracker organ. Having met my audience once again, we hastened down the path and across the road to the Manor House, my sponsor's gorgeous Georgian home, for the third full-length recital of the day which, beginning at 7.00 pm, I played on the 1989 Harrison & Harrison of 34 ranks. To conclude this exhausting schedule, there was a splendid feast and I was accommodated in great style.

I mention all this merely to reinforce the fact that with such wonderful sponsors, good publicity and well-organized logistics, it is quite possible to play three concerts in one day. And, to prove what a resilient fellow I am (!), the following morning, I was back in the Cathedral to play for hundreds of local students.

Publicity is also a major part of concert-giving. No one can give programs single-handedly. As studiously as one practices the notes, one must also learn how to play the media. I well remember the days when I was establishing my career in Great Britain; not only did I agree to play in any building on any organ for virtually any fee, but, just as importantly, we stirred up a whirlwind of publicity. At the same time, I was not only learning to adapt to unfamiliar organs in a flash, I was also developing an ability to talk effectively into a microphone, to speak in quotable phrases, and to sustain the pulse of an interview. One reporter said that interviewing me was like conversing with a machine gun – set to automatic fire. Whether this is good or not, the media now know that I give 'a good interview,' which in turn opens more doors.

Publicity rarely falls into anyone's lap. Very few musicians are so famous that they need none at all. It requires being constantly available to the press, and being vigilant about following through with appointments and leads. Recently, I was visiting Russia when the BBC wanted an interview before a concert at the Albert Hall in Nottingham. No problem: I did the interview down the line from Moscow. Certainly this helped to fill every seat.

Equally important are non-traditional methods of publicity. Early on in my time in England, I came to know Richard Baker, the hugely popular BBC broadcaster. My friend Michael Crozier made his acquaintance working on a television special, and suggested that Richard and I put together a musical entertainment called *The A to Z of the King of Instruments*. Chris Sprague and Matthew Copley provided information on the organ's history and helped to write an entertaining script that the lay listener would understand immediately. In performance, Richard narrated the organ's development while I demonstrated and chatted with him from the console. I offered several solos, we played duets (including an infamous arrangement of the Widor *Toccata* for piano and organ), and Richard even sang songs to my accompaniment.

After its premiere at the Speech Room of Harrow School, we toured our little production around the country, including Salisbury and Exeter Cathedrals, Plymouth's Theatre Royal and Tewkesbury Abbey, our Ulster Hall, Belfast performance being broadcast on BBC television.

Special programs need to have a 'peg.' It certainly attracts the public's attention. For example, when I was once in urgent need of a snappy concert title, I called Ralph Mace, the marketing mastermind at RCA. In conjunction with the appeal for a new organ at St. James's, Piccadilly, London, I was planning a concert around works either composed or arranged by the many famous musicians associated with this Wren church, among whom are Purcell, Handel, Haydn, Mendelssohn and Stokowski. Although he was just about to go into a meeting, Ralph heard me out, paused briefly before declaring, ' "In Praise of Famous Men." How's that? Bye!' *Here* was my hook. Equally entrancing was an amusing incident recounted in the *Daily Telegraph*'s Peterborough column just before the St James's concert. The piece mentioned that I had returned to my 'fighting weight of 20 stone' (280 pounds), and continued, 'When he arrived at the church for a reconnaissance the other day, he was accosted by two earnest-looking ladies who asked him, breathlessly: "Are you in charge of the Fasting for Peace programme?" '[1]

Sometimes the press provides the best marketing idea. In 1981 a certain newspaper dubbed me 'the Luciano Pavarotti of the organ.'[2] This title is both flattering and in certain ways appropriate and, believe me, it has stuck. All these years later it is still fresh. It also represents a lesson learned. Some years before, the Houston *Post* labeled me the 'Babe Ruth of the organ,' to which one might have added 'every piece a home run?' A much niftier analogy in my opinion, but at the time I didn't think to take it on board. So when the Pavarotti line came along, I grabbed it.

1 'Fortissimo,' *Daily Telegraph*, Thursday September 15, 1983, a diary piece in the 'London day-by-day' column.

2 The comment appeared in the San Jose (California) *Mercury*, November 23, 1981, after an appearance with George Cleve and the San Jose Symphony.

Although, by virtue of luck and hard work, you may achieve full and eagerly expectant audiences, waiting for you to set them metaphorically on fire, you will throw everything away if you fail to realize the importance of projection, the true touchstone of any good performer. Interacting with a full house requires a far different dynamic from everyday talking or playing. The pianist Josef Hoffman put it perfectly:

> If someone entered this room and you spoke to him in a normal conversational tone, he would hear you easily. If you used the same tone from the stage of a theater, the people in the fourth row would ask: 'What's that? What's he saying?' Public communication necessitates heightened projection; otherwise we are talking or playing to ourselves. And it is a far larger problem than one of amplified volume. It embraces our choice of tempi, textures and architectures; the degree and kinds of accentuation and pedaling we can use; the variety and proportions of agogic and dynamic effects we make, and much more. Remember, we are playing to express ourselves through the music we play, but we are expressing ourselves to *others*.[3]

In this regard, I have always looked, once again, to Virgil Fox. Through his vocal inflection, dialogue and humor, Virgil brought to the recital experience a unique charismatic aura, and it left audiences spellbound. While I appear to have taken on many of his techniques, I have been careful to put my own spin on them. I think I would have arrived there independently, being the kind of extrovert Southerner I am. But seeing Virgil's success certainly confirmed that such methods could work famously.

But there is a fundamental difference in my approach. Most artists perceive their communication as coming solely from the stage. I am careful to enter into a start-to-finish communicative process with my audiences, beginning as they walk in and not ending until the moment they leave. The critical first step is being prepared to greet audience members as they arrive. Nevertheless, I confess that, in general, I have to confine this to venues with fewer than 1,000 attendees, otherwise my hand can become so shaken out that playing becomes difficult! But patrons really enjoy meeting the performer. It takes any pomposity out of the proceedings and I believe it helps to embrace them into the gala feeling of the event.

---

3 *Speaking of Pianists*, Abram Chasins (New York: Knopf, 1958), p. 13. Chasins is quoting Hoffman.

From that point on, everything revolves around de-mystifying the instrument and making the experience fun and moving. After the handshake, talking personably to the audience is my second line of communication, because it helps them to understand the instrument. If I played the piano this might not be so necessary because people have pianos in their homes, they take lessons, and there is no mystery there. But few people have organs in their homes, instead knowing them only as large, imposing instruments from Sunday morning, the music 'churchy' in feel. Furthermore, the organist is often hidden away, sometimes shielded by a silken modesty curtain. Thus, to the uninitiated, the instrument appears to play itself. By addressing the audience, I open a line of communication, not so much between them and myself, but between them and the instrument.

In tonal terms, it would be futile to try to pinpoint precisely what sounds audiences like to hear. But I can name two tonal qualities to which they almost always respond. The first is *substantial bass*. The large 16' and 32' registers, which shake a building to its foundations, inspire awe in almost every listener. Such effects are larger than life, and I believe a music-lover attends a performance to be reminded of that fact. The other qualities are *brilliance, power* and *contrast*. An audience may not be able to articulate what they don't like. In general, however, I find that they usually react negatively to any sounds that are shrieking and piercing, whereas they seem to enjoy a sweet, silvery kind of brilliance which the best organs enjoy. I have spoken before about powerful organs being different from those that give the *sensation* of power. As a famous organ-builder has observed, 'organs become loud just at the point at which they cease to be beautiful.'[4] Here again, balance in the program and reserve on the part of the player will extend the enjoyment of the audience over two hours. So too will contrast, with each piece introducing some new color or stop combination, once again drawing the listener's attention to something fresh. Pinning them back in their seats once or twice doesn't hurt either.

Most important, however, is the program's architecture, which must have regard to balance, reserve and the thread of melodic content from start to finish. The musical selections must subscribe to an underlying logic. By first playing familiar, communicable music, I can build a sense of trust with the listener. They are not alienated and, with luck, begin to enjoy the concert from the outset. This lays the groundwork of receptivity to an original organ work of Bach, Reger or Franck. My feeling is that, even if their interests lie elsewhere, they are now willing to hear me through a big piece because I have won their attention and because I have first sold them the music in words.

4 Manuel Rosales of Rosales Organ Builders, Los Angeles.

In this respect, it is interesting to walk through the planning of a recital. Here is how I would currently organize a typical inaugural concert for a new organ:

FIRST HALF

1 *Hushed introduction*: Bearing in mind my first lesson with Thalben-Ball and his metaphorical shop window, I like my opening number to be quiet, melodic and introspective, focusing the listener's ear to the quietest sound possible and thus defining a threshold of *pianissimo*. In the last few years, I have tended to use the Welsh folk-tune 'All Through the Night,' but many pieces fill the bill here, such as the Largo from Dvorak's *New World Symphony* or Mascagni's Intermezzo from *Cavalleria Rusticana*.

2 *Jolly, toe-tapping piece*: Here we identify the limit of *forte* playing, which I will exceed only once or twice elsewhere in the programme. Something such as Bach's *Sinfonia* from Cantata 29 works ideally here. It is of moderate length and is good, digestible music.

3 *Melodious, sonorous number, with a build*: Here we return to melody, something familiar and memorable. Rather than merely returning to soft colors, this piece has more direction, allowing several solo colors to be exhibited on the road to a moderate climax. The Largo from *Xerxes* goes perfectly here.

4 *Charming piece with birds*: I travel with a small mechanical bird cage since it has proven to be a universal hit. (In Japan, they give the cage its own microphone and sometimes even its own tiny camera.) Moving to a lighter vein, this selection permits an exploration of the charming flute colors, and the introduction of the birds. Options abound here, favorites being the *Largo, Allegro, Aria and Two Variations* of Michael Festing (arranged by Thalben-Ball) or any of the Stanley concerti.

5 *Major Bach work*: By this time, the audience is ready for a serious work: any of the Preludes and Fugues, or the *Passacaglia*, or the *Toccata, Adagio and Fugue*. With this piece, we have a definite sense that the first half has come to its midway point, and the audience and I can take something of a collective breath.

6 *Melodic interlude*: After a large Bach offering, I find that a 'song without words' offers the right kind of mood change. An unforgettable melody relaxes the ear from the mounting tension of the Bach work, but gradually gives way to its own climax, almost but not entirely reaching full organ, then fading away. Here I try to show the quiet percussions, if any, such as Chimes and Celesta.

7 *Prestidigitation*: Here we have a finger display, taking us into a slightly humorous direction and perhaps discovering some of the more charming

flute combinations. Pieces such as Joseph Bonnet's *Elves* or Seth Bingham's *Roulade* function well in this role. I want this piece to avoid getting too loud, because all too soon we have arrived at:

8 *Barn burner:* It makes obvious good sense to close the first half with a bang, so that people smile to themselves over the intermission. Such a selection can take many forms, perhaps a big transcription, one of the Handel concerti (capped by a big cadenza), or a frenzied toccata.

INTERMISSION

Unlike most artists, I like to mingle during the intermission, for two reasons: firstly, it allows me to meet anyone whom I didn't greet at the door and secondly, I can begin signing programs and recordings, reducing lines at the concert's conclusion – a sure way to please the hall staff, who will remember your thoughtfulness next time.

SECOND HALF

1 *A surprise:* An idea taken from Virgil Fox, in which an unannounced selection opens the second half. If the organ has some remarkable stop that I didn't expect to find (like a magnificent Tuba, or a Zimbelstern), I'll play a trumpet tune or one of the d'Aquin *Noëls.* Perhaps I'll lighten the mood with a Joplin rag, 'The Entertainer' or 'Maple Leaf.' Or if the crowd is boisterous, I might choose to restore calm by playing the *Londonderry Air* arranged by J. Stuart Archer. (In a non-inaugural concert where I have the touring organ, I will occasionally play this from the performance recorder, introducing the device allowing organists to assess their own playing, and thus to become their own best teachers. As the organ plays itself, I have taken to walking amongst the audience.)

2 *Big selection:* Since the second half is usually shorter than the first, we dive into a big piece right away. Here is the place for a Mozart Fantasia (K608 or K594) or a Franck Chorale, depending on the audience, organ and venue.

3 *An ear-rest, a plangent melody:* My last chance to show the organ's luscious, captivating qualities (if any), and to provide a simple, plaintive melody. Time for Sullivan's 'The Lost Chord,' the Meditation from *Thaïs* by Massenet, or Vierne's *Clair de Lune.*

4 *Building to the finale:* A piece of moderate intensity works well here, re-establishing tension and seeing the program towards a conclusion; perhaps one of Dupré's Preludes and Fugues (equally good music and ear-tickling), or perhaps a mad scherzo such as Pierné's *Scherzando.*

5 *The grand finale:* Here again, the venue, crowd and organ determine the piece's length and style, but dexterous fireworks are in order. It can be short

and splashy, such as Saint-Saëns' *Marche militaire française*, or a French toccata of moderate length, such as Mulet's *Tu es Petra*, or something of major proportions, such as one of the Reger Chorale Fantasies or the Liszt *Weinen klagen* variations.

ENCORES

Provided an audience isn't thoroughly sated, an encore or even two may just be appropriate. The last programed selection plays a big part in choosing what to play, as well as a sense of what the crowd might like to hear. A fairly heavy conclusion may merit something light and sassy, such as the *Washington Post* or *Liberty Bell* marches of Sousa (in the latter I insist the audience clap in strict rhythm during the reprise). Or perhaps something more delicate: another melodic number or a movement from one of the Bach Trio Sonatas. Another variation is to sing a hymn, especially where hymnals are at the ready and the crowd could benefit from burning off some energy through their lungs and vocal cords. Besides, with a big instrument at my disposal, there are few greater personal thrills than leading a huge crowd in congregational song. It is especially appropriate for a church organ inauguration, where the parishioners who purchased the instrument can hear it in its most traditional role.

Admittedly, there is a fine line between educating audiences in an entertaining fashion and patronizing them. Obviously, I hope to err on the educational and entertaining side, and trust that my zealousness is not misconstrued. Whilst some organists shudder at the notion of such chestnuts as 'The Lost Chord' or the Largo from *Xerxes*, it doesn't bother me in the slightest, rather the reverse, that these pieces bring many average listeners through the door, where they can become acquainted with great organ works and be exposed, perhaps for the first time, to the grandest of all instruments. *A performer must not forget his audience.* If organists continue to play exclusively for each other and for themselves, they will soon be playing to no one. Many already are.[5]

5 In a letter of February 1, 1940 to *The Diapason*, E. M. Skinner told the story of a recitalist who refused the request of the donor of a $50,000 organ to play Schumann's *Träumerei* at the dedication recital. Said Skinner, 'There may be some things I wouldn't play for $50,000, but they do not occur to me at the moment.'

As any organist will acknowledge, there's hardly a shred of originality in any of this. Turn back the clock a hundred years, and you will find countless Victorian and Edwardian organ recitals with different music but similar principles in the planning. Organists of that era agonized over the choice and order of the music, in a great effort to make the programs as appealing as possible. It paid off in large, recurring audiences.

Although this approach is fairly flexible, it hardly applies to *every* concert I give. For large-scale events, I return to the Victorian idea of combining several artists together in a big variety format. Drawing together a local choir, a first-rate instrumentalist or larger ensemble (brass or strings) with solo organ performance makes for an impressive evening. For example, my 1992 Danish Royal Command Performance was exactly such a program: brass, choir and solo violinist in addition to the organ. My presentation with Richard Baker constituted a different spin on the same approach.

A two-organ concert logically extends the multi-performer concept, where the touring organ wages 'friendly' battle with the resident instrument. Since the local organist joins in the festivities (often with the choir), we have the added draw of local and known musical personalities in addition to my appearance. Elevating the event still further is to be fortunate enough to have it broadcast. At Ely Cathedral in October 1994 we went for broke, exploiting all of these possibilities in the program, before adjourning to the deanery meadows for a big fireworks display.

A fascinating twist on the double-organ idea is to pair up both classical and theater organs. Lyn Larsen and I have given many successful programs along these lines, as well as making a recording entitled *Dueling Organs*. In addition to the unusual variety of music that can be presented, the juxtaposition of pure classical organ power against the theater organ's throbbing thrill creates a most interesting, dynamic massed ensemble.

So how in blazes is it possible to make music on the organ? Churchill's words, 'A riddle wrapped in a mystery inside an enigma' ... could well be the answer! But for me, in practical terms, the essentials of exciting music-making boil down to four aspects: voice leading, technique, registration, and dynamic phrasing (swell box manipulation). The following suggestions may seem simple enough, but the more disciplines a musician practices, the better his music will be.

- Assuming you have developed a respectable grasp of the piano, the best way to attain a natural sense of rhythmic playing is to discard your metronome and either arrange to accompany ballet classes or play duets with a colleague. Metronomes are unfortunately addictive and performers can soon get to sound like one! If you want your rhythm to communicate and be supple, the best way to learn is to supply someone else's heartbeat.
- Join the best choral ensemble you can – all the better if in the course of the year two or more large-scale oratorios are sung. Better sight-reading and musical understanding are bound to result.
- Attend orchestral rehearsals (hopefully under the baton of a competent conductor) and listen to the group's concentration, integration and balance. Taking stock of how individual instruments blend into an ensemble will assist your ear in guiding you to combinations of organ stops that are pleasing and *clear.*
- As I learned as a teenager from Rose Bampton at NCSA, singers are the true musicians, since they create everything from within (or *biodynamically*, as they say in the health-food store). Accompanying them gives you a ringside seat into how a good vocalist will shape and color musical lines.

Once you have returned to the console, explore your instrument to the fullest. Get to know every stop from top to bottom. Find ways of using the colors, of switching between them, of combining them engagingly. Even if you are a firm believer in the *Urtext* and strictest rigors of performance practice, such investigation can only help you serve the composer's intentions better. If the 4' Spitzflöte sounds better in its range than the dull-as-gray-formica 8' Rohrflöte the composer seems to be requesting, isn't the Spitzflöte the obvious choice? Go ahead, let yourself go. Don't be afraid to play down the octave. Unless you are seated at the very instrument for which the piece is conceived, chances are you know the organ far better than the composer.

In my experience, an important way for an organist to develop a musical personality is to spend time with art other than music. Many threads run in common through all artistic disciplines, and exposure to other kinds of art may illuminate previously hidden aspects of your own. Touring the galleries as a young man in New York, London, Paris, Madrid and Milan, especially the paintings of the Impressionists, revealed to me a new level of imagination and fantasy, which are, for me, two vital building blocks in musical interpretation. The score is our canvas; the stops, pistons and expressive devices our palette. Arthur Friedheim, a pupil of Liszt, sums it up masterfully:

I recall one of my later lessons with Liszt in the Villa d'Este, in Tivoli, not far from Rome. Late one afternoon, I sat down at the piano to play his *Harmonies du Soir*. Before I had time to begin he called me to the window. With a wide sweep of his arm he pointed out the slanting rays of the declining sun which were mellowing the landscape with the delicate glamour of approaching twilight. 'Play that,' he said. 'There are your evening harmonies.'[6]

The above is, in my opinion, every bit as important as anything learned in traditional organ pedagogy, because it demonstrates the bottom line, musically speaking. Despite the medium, all good musicians strive for intelligent phrasing, elegant rhythm, a luxurious tone and exalted expression. And, as a musician knows, words are ultimately inadequate to describe good music-making. The New York music critic Roger Evans put it perfectly when he said, 'Writing about music is like dancing about architecture.' Better, I think, to direct the ear to music than the eye to still more words. If I were addressing a performance class of technically competent organ students who were yet to attain their maturity in musicianship and the development of a vocal line, I would know no better way to start than to introduce them to recorded performances that were pivotal in shaping my own playing.

- Horowitz
  Vladimir Horowitz, piano
  Deutsche Grammophon, 419-045-1, 1985
  Track 1: Bach/Busoni, *Nun komm' der Heiden Heiland*

Perhaps the most moving Bach playing I know, transparently expressive. It succeeds in demonstrating how Bach's writing transcends its era and style into something universal, timeless and ultimately poetic. To Horowitz, of course, all music was romantic. (It's also refreshing to hear organ music played on the piano.)

- Music of Franck, Prokofiev, Ysaÿe, Paganini and Bach
  Ruggiero Ricci and Martha Argerich
  Etcetera Records, KTC 1038, 1985
  Track 9: Ysaÿe, *Sonata No. 3 in D Minor for Solo Violin (no. 3)*

6 Excerpted from *Life and Liszt* (Taplinger, 1961). Friedheim studied with Franz Liszt at Weimar and later enjoyed a successful concert career in the United States.

This performance exemplifies the sort of controlled abandon that defines a virtuoso. And as a model of accompaniment, listen to Argerich's rich yet always respectful piano role.

- O Clap Your Hands: Music of Ralph Vaughan Williams and William Walton
  David Hill conducting the Choir of Winchester Cathedral,
  Waynflete Singers and the Bournemouth Symphony Orchestra,
  Timothy Byram-Wigfield, organ
  Decca/London Argo 436 120-2, 1992
  Entire disc

One of the most dramatic discs of the decade recorded in a venue in which I'm honored to have performed twice. *Gramophone* sums it up:

> Vaughan Williams' majestic setting of the Old Hundredth can rarely have sounded so splendid. The Winchester organ thunders, the brass and percussions give it their all and the recording has impressive depth and spaciousness. There's no lack of fervour ... with the chorus, orchestra and organ pealing in dazzling streams of antiphony ... an immensely enjoyable disc.[7]

- Richard Wagner: *Siegfried-Idyll, Tannhäuser* (Overture), *Tristan und Isolde* (Prelude, Isolde's *Liebestod*)
  Jessye Norman, Herbert von Karajan, Vienna Philharmonic
  Deutsche Grammophon, 432 613-2

I owe a debt of gratitude to Colin Johnson of Melbourne, Australia who introduced this recording to me in his enviable cathedral-ceilinged music room during one of my many recent trips to that fair city. Simply put, the *Liebestod* is the pinnacle of musical experience for these ears. I cannot think of another performance that has moved me more. Oh, that the organ could do this!

- *Oedipus Rex*, Igor Stravinsky
  Jessye Norman, Thomas Moser, Alexandru Ionita, Michel Piccoli
  Colin Davis conducting Bavarian Radio Symphony Orchestra and Chorus
  Orfeo C 071-831 A, 1983
  Entire disc

7 *Gramophone*, May 1993, 'M.R.'

What can I say? Jessye strikes gold again.

* Mozart Piano Concertos KV 482, KV 488
  Mitsuko Uchida, piano
  English Chamber Orchestra, conducted by Jeffrey Tate
  Philips 420 187-2, 1986
  Entire disc

These timeless performances are both stylish and fresh, a seamless interplay between conductor and soloist. Here is a sensible Mozart, not precious, not precocious, not emasculated, but sylvan, fleet and gloriously honest. It is the music itself and nothing less. The performances only improve with repeated listening.

* Liszt Piano Works, Vol. 3 (from a set of complete piano works)
  Jorge Bolet, piano
  London (Decca) 410 115-2, 1982
  Entire disc, especially track 7

In much music criticism, Bolet is characterized as an enormous virtuoso afraid of exploiting his abilities for fear of being branded a 'technician.' So be it: whatever the origin of his reserve, I cherish it in this music, the complexity of which invites precisely the kind of clarity Bolet furnishes. The *Grand galop chromatique* is particularly attractive and inspiring.

* The Best of Bach
  Jacques Loussier, piano
  Music Club MCCD 113, 1993
  Entire disc, especially track 10

Here, in the best sense, is thrilling abandon, and once more the marvelous adaptability of Bach. Augmenting his piano with drums and string bass, Loussier spins out Bach as pure jazz, showing his cultural affinity to the organ improvisation tradition in France. Perhaps this is liberty taking, but surely to a worthy musical end.

* Brahms: Symphonie 1, Tragic Overture, Academic Festival Overture
  Otto Klemperer conducts the Philharmonia Orchestra
  EMI Studio CDM 7 69651 2
  Entire disc, especially tracks 1–4

The Brahms Symphony on this disc is virtually without peer, demonstrating throughout a sweep, power and drama that epitomize Brahms's conservative yet inherently lyrical romanticism.

- Scarlatti Sonatas
  Alexis Weissenberg
  Deutsche Grammophon 415 511-2, 1985
  Entire disc

Some of the most sophisticated piano playing can be found here, etched into high relief by a sharp technique and a beautifully pliable rhythmic control. My affection for Scarlatti was immeasurably enhanced after hearing this disc.

- Over the Rainbow: Music from three USA tours
  Barry Rose conducts the Boys and Men of the Choir of the Cathedral and Abbey Church of St. Alban
  Lammas Records LAMM 085 D
  Entire disc

I can attest that working with Barry Rose is a singular honor. He draws an affection from his singers I have not witnessed since the days of George Thalben-Ball, and it translates into a richness of tone and a level of blend also unachieved since Thalben. Barry is capable of coaxing one perfect tone from some three dozen voices. It is not merely a sonic thrill but a deeply musical one, as he shapes phrases and elicits from his choir an expressive quality fully equal to great operatic singers.

- *Messi di Gloria*, Rossini
  José Carreras, tenor; Hermann Prey, baritone
  the Ambrosian Singers and Philharmonia Orchestra
  conducted by Claudio Scimone
  Erato ECD 88022

A great love of my life is choral accompaniment, a busman's holiday from standard organ repertoire. Rossini was trained as an organist, and this Mass (begun when he was only eighteen) elegantly melds secular and religious ideas into a moving masterwork. Here is a model of tasteful and elegant accompaniment, unfolding naturally out of the vocal material.

What comes after planning and giving the concerts? More fresh ideas and more promotion! Bless their hearts, but concert-goers have the shortest memories of anyone. Even after the crowds have gone home, you must be ever vigilant in the business of keeping your name in lights. In my early years Barry Nevill's talents worked wonders in spreading my name. He knew how to exploit his contacts to make an event appear larger than life, and it succeeded.

However, sometimes the best publicity is completely out of one's own hands. And, just like it takes money to make money, so too you have to stir up a lot of recognition to ascend to a higher level. When I received an invitation to appear on BBC Radio's *Desert Island Discs* with Roy Plomley, I felt that I really had arrived. The show features prominent guests who are asked which eight musical recordings, book and luxury item they would want if stranded on the proverbial desert island. It is amusing to recount my choices of those many years ago:

1 Variations on 'America,' Charles Ives
  (played by E. Power Biggs)
2 'How Lovely is Thy Dwelling Place' from Brahms' *German Requiem*
  (Otto Klemperer conducting the Philharmonic Orchestra and Chorus)
3 'Whispering Hope' from *Songs my father taught me*
  (Robert White, tenor; Ralph Mace, conductor)
4 Symphony No. 4 (beginning of third movement), Brahms
  (James Levine conducting the Chicago Symphony Orchestra)
5 March from *Love of Three Oranges*, Prokofiev
  (Artur Rubinstein, piano)
6 Double Violin Concerto in D minor (slow movement), J. S. Bach
  (Jascha Heifetz playing both parts; Franz Wachsmann conducting the RCA Chamber Orchestra)
7 *Noël polonais*, Alexandre Guilmant
  (Odile Pierre playing the Cavaillé-Coll organ of St. Michel de Castelnaudary, Languedoc)
8 *Ride of the Valkyries*, Richard Wagner
  (George Thalben-Ball playing the 1876/1929 Willis organ of the Alexandra Palace, London)
9 LUXURY ITEM: 'A small portatif organ, built by my Danish friends, Frobenius'
10 BOOK: a Julia Child cookbook

Yes, I am aware that not a single item from my earlier recommended recordings is listed above. Like the concert-going public, perhaps I too have a shorter memory than I realize. Alas …

CHAPTER FIFTEEN

PULLING OUT ALL THE STOPS

My life to date has been rich in memorable incidents. I have almost come to expect the unexpected, or certainly to be struck by it. As a child growing up in North Carolina, I could not have dreamed that I should one day live in Europe or perform at the White House or St.-Eustache. And as a teenager in school, I could not have imagined that I would one day have Fox, Elmore or Thalben-Ball as teachers, let alone appear at New York's Carnegie Hall, St. Paul's Cathedral, London or Tokyo's Suntory Hall.

Many organ folk are raconteurs to the core and Virgil Fox surely led them all. Among the numerous stories, I remember his tale of being involved with the Huntington Hartford Gallery of Modern Art in New York (right on Columbus Circle). The museum had an Æolian-Skinner organ, which he had been invited to open. Furthermore, the concert was to be televised as a benefit for saving the Egyptian temples of Abu Simbel. Heir to the A&P supermarket fortune and culturally astute, Hartford asked Virgil if he might play something 'Egyptian.' Virgil replied disparagingly that there really wasn't any Egyptian music. 'Well, what about *Aïda*?' came the immediate response. For once, Virgil was silent.

It was in London during September 1979 that I saw Virgil for the last time. Our most recent visit had been a year before, when he attended the Alexandra Palace gala with the grand Cadillac entrance. Later that month I played for the Windsor Festival at St. George's Chapel, Windsor Castle. Having enjoyed my program, the committee asked if I could suggest other artists whose style was similar. Go to the source, I told them. Happily, they accepted my advice and Virgil came over to play the following year.

During that visit, my friend Chris Sprague and a good friend of his, who was a master chef, decided to throw a festive dinner party for Virgil and David Snyder. The evening was to begin with music-making at the church where Chris played, St. James, Norlands in Holland Park with its noble old Binns organ.[1] Hors d'oeuvres and champagne would be served in the church (!), after which we would return to the flat for dinner.

While David looked as fit and healthy as ever, it was impossible to ignore the decline in Virgil's health. He had lost weight and energy, his pace was slow, and his ankles were terribly swollen from water retention. His fingers were in fine shape, though. He needed a helping hand while climbing out of the taxi and up the organ loft stairs, but he sat down and gave a brilliant rendition of my old comrade, Bach's *Fugue à la Gigue*: the same, sensational Virgil. Downstairs again, he naturally declined the champagne, but dived straight into the canapés.

Seated later at the table, Virgil was his old self again. However the illness might ravage his body, it clearly could not extinguish his spirit. Ever the good sport, he insisted on playing the dreary old Compton Melotone Chris used for practice. The sight of Virgil Fox playing this wheezy electronic instrument in a cold hallway – it was *so* Virgil. He was unstoppable.

As we parted that night, I think we both sensed that we would never see each other again. He grew reflective, and in a private moment, congratulated me on my success and thanked me for becoming my own man and not a clone of himself. He reiterated what a triumph he thought I had made of the Alexandra Palace concerts, the touring organ, my RCA contract, and my relationship with Thalben-Ball. What could I say? So much of it had been at his direct behest; everything about Virgil had been a constant inspiration. We gave each other an intense, long hug, and bade farewell.

A little more than a year later, I was in my house in Denmark enjoying a rare day off and a bit of lazy time. It was one of those brilliant autumn days with a resplendent sky, crisp air, just cold enough for a log fire. The phone trilled; it was Don Westfield ringing from Michigan to say that Virgil had gone on. I was

---

1 Barry Nevill and virtuoso Jane Parker-Smith had previously been organists of St. James.

stunned. I could do nothing else but walk about, listen to his ever-inspiring recordings, and weep. Just as Florence had been, Virgil had been an anchor in my life, and she had been gone now three years to the month. I felt very much at sea.

After Virgil died, I was honored to assume some of his engagements, including, of all places, Ambassador College in Pasadena on March 15, 1981. To think, all that time spent lying awake in my childhood bed in North Carolina listening to Garner Ted Armstrong's radio posturing from that very campus, and here I was playing right in the man's front garden. Even if fortune-tellers could have actually forecast the future, would I ever have believed it?

One of my favorite Virgil recordings is *The Christmas Album* recorded in New York's Church of St. Paul the Apostle on the 1965 Möller organ. The church's reverberation (about seven seconds), the organ, and some of Virgil's most reserved yet powerful playing all combine to make this a thrilling disc. I came to know the organ when I lived in New York, for it was less than a five minute walk from Richard Torrence's office and I was allowed to practice there.

The organ had two unusual stop names. One was the 'Paulistenposaune,' a commanding horizontal trumpet stop named in honor of the Paulist Fathers. The second involved the Vox humana, which had not been originally included in the organ. As Virgil told the story, the Möller people were so keen on his recording and the resulting publicity that they added the Vox humana especially for him, since Virgil couldn't conceive of making a Christmas recording (or any recording) without one. (The Vox humana is a soft, sweet reed stop, meant to be used with the tremolo to emulate the human voice.) Since the console had not been prepared for any additions, Möller affixed a little box to the left of the keyboards with an additional control. Evidently trying to outdo themselves with 'Paulistenposaune,' the Möller people labelled it '*Fox* Humana.'

Virgil's fixation with Vox humanas was legend. If the Vox wasn't right, the organ was well nigh useless. Since Virgil's definition of a good Vox meant softer rather than louder, I was often sent to the Candler Cadillac for a couple of car blankets (a holdover from the days before automobiles had heaters). Once the technician had tuned, he and I would carefully drape the blankets over the pipes, muffling and refining the tone to the master's liking.[2]

While I studiously tried to avoid copying Virgil's mannerisms, I eventually concluded that a full-length cloak (or cape) was in order, particularly in drafty European churches during winter. Not finding anything in the usual clothing stores, I went in desperation to a recommended ecclesiastical outfitters. They could create exactly what I wanted: a full-length black cloak with red silk lining. When they asked for my name, I merely said (quite fraudulently), 'Father Curley.' I was greeted thus at the first fitting, when the tailor, short in stature, had to use a small stepladder to measure my shoulders. A week later I would have the final fitting and delivery.

In the interim, I made a guest appearance on BBC television's *Wogan* show (the UK equivalent of Johnny Carson), which meant tremendous exposure for me – perhaps too much. When I returned to collect the garment, the tailor cried, 'Father! We *so* enjoyed your appearance on the telly! Now which church did you say you served?' Panic-stricken I answered, 'Actually, mine is a *world-wide* congregation.' Quickly flashing my best sheepish smile, I gave them the check and managed to flee the shop, perhaps without much dignity but with the cloak swinging over my arm. Clearly in London, you can't pull the ecclesiastical wool over the eyes of the ecclesiastical tailor.

For my Decca recording at St.-Eustache in Paris, I was allowed to practice in situ for a solid week before Decca balance engineer Simon Eadon came over to set up the mikes. By the evening of the first day we were ready to lay down Bach's great C minor *Passacaglia*. During one of the quiet variations, there was an enormous *boom!!* which echoed and re-echoed throughout the entire length of that great

---

2 I still have a few of these, 'The Brackendale Rug' made in Scotland of a cashmere and wool blend. Although I now drape it over a chair, it has been over more Vox humanas than anything else.

church. Then there came another, and still more until eventually the sound as of a rioting crowd. Perhaps the French Revolution had started up again in earnest. The truth, thankfully, was slightly different, for we had all overlooked one slight detail: it was the eve of Bastille Day. As Cherry later pointed out in the Circle newsletter:

> Although this was only 13 July about 6 pm, the French like to get in the mood for 'Le Quatorze' during the previous evening ... I have heard a first tape, unedited, of the recording, and can vouch for the unmistakable audibility of the fireworks, and there's Carlo's laughing shouts to the engineers, too. One of the assistants went up on to the ramparts, and had a spectacular aerial view of the festivities. Thanks to modern technology, in the form of a sequencer, and to the skills of the Decca engineers, it has not been necessary to re-name this recording *Music for the Republican Fireworks*.

On another occasion, the plans and organ were both ideal, but other things got in the way. I was filming for a BBC television children's program called *What's That Noise?* We began shooting at St. Paul's Cathedral, London early one morning before the doors were opened to the public. Moving from the chancel Tubas and the fiery dome ensemble to the powerful Royal Trumpets over the great west doors, I demonstrated the various locations of the pipes. The camera crew asked me to repeat the entire sequence several times, since they wanted to film from several angles. By this time, it was nearing opening time and just as the director called 'It's a wrap,' a uniformed gentleman appeared in the organ loft. 'I'm the chief of security, sir. Could I beg you to refrain from blasting out on those lorry horns at the rear of the cathedral? You are distressing the book-stall staff.' He seemed so relieved when I told him we were finished.

From St. Paul's, we moved on to the Odeon Leicester Square, home to a large Compton theater organ. Typical of its genre, the console lives in the orchestra pit and, complete with performer in full flow, rises up on a lift to public view during the opening number, a traditional theatrical device known as 'playing up the house.' Determined to do the same for the camera, I began playing and pushed the *up* button. The lift got about one foot in the air, suddenly lurched violently and stopped altogether with a shudder which said 'Enough.' My future did *not* seem assured. Was this my fault or was the lift suffering from old age? Not necessarily wanting to know the answer, we carried on to a third venue while the elevator repairmen were called.

It has been my privilege to play three recitals at St. Paul's Cathedral. The first was unallayed joy; it was impossible to escape the thrill of thinking, 'I am *actually playing* the organ in *St. Paul's Cathedral*!' There was a memorable footnote to my St. Paul's debut. The evening before, attending a drinks party given by one of the Cathedral clergy, I was discussing the program with one of the canons. After the pleasantries, he asked that should I be asked to play an 'extra item' – I'm sure he couldn't bring himself to use the word *encore* – perhaps I could offer 'something ... *American.*' I promised to give it every good consideration. The next night, having stormed through a meaty formal program, for which I received a standing ovation, I knew precisely that I was going to give him 'something American' he would never forget. And so, having announced the opening theme of John Philip Sousa's *Liberty Bell March* on the Royal Trumpets over the west door – a city block away from the console – there was no stopping me. Believe me when I say that there weren't enough stretchers in the City of London to haul the stunned clergy from their stalls. If they wanted American, I was happy to give it to them from sea to shining sea.

My second recital, which could not have been more different, was given as part of the memorial for my former friend and teacher, Sir George Thalben-Ball. I do not like to think of people in death but, all the same, I was terribly conscious of the surroundings. And I kept on thinking of the constructive comments he might make: 'A little more slowly here, dear Carlo,' 'try this color,' 'how about this, Carlo?' One could hardly bear to contemplate London without him.

However, I consider my third St. Paul's recital to have been particularly successful. I spent many evenings preparing, relying on Fr. Paul to judge the effect down the nave and make valuable registrational suggestions. Especially in the *Grand Pièce Symphonique* of Franck and Bach's *Passacaglia*, the outcome was one of great personal satisfaction.

I have written earlier of my great affection for the Harrison & Harrison instrument at St. Mary Redcliffe, Bristol. Thus it was a great delight, in 1991, for me to be allowed to choose it to record, again for Decca, my all-English album, *Organ Imperial*. The performances were among my best, I feel, and the recorded sound is wondrously faithful to what one hears in the church. Back in London, I was taking a refreshing shower – I get some of my best ideas in the shower – when it suddenly struck me that a video recording would be an excellent idea. In any event, I was due to perform the same program there again, this time in public, to mark the release of the new CD. I telephoned Paul Vaughan to discuss the idea. Having spent a number of years as a producer at the BBC, Paul knew precisely the man to ring, a distinguished former colleague named Herbert Chappell, who was now head of film, TV and audio-visual projects at ... Decca. Now didn't I record for them???

As soon as we made contact, it was clear that the video project could not fail to fall into place. He told me that he was a great lover of organ music, had recently been listening to *Organ Imperial* and knew the church well, having been born and lived much of his early life just up the road. Sometimes it seems that there are only 200 people in the world.

Bert Chappell ensured that Decca made an outstanding program. After all, it was to be the first commercially available classical organ video. I had contacted Bert on Paul's recommendation, not realizing then just how impeccable his credentials were. He had been closely involved in the barnstorming Three Tenors video and he knew just how to exploit a fine venue to the full. The church was beautifully lit, not only inside but outside, thus ensuring that the gorgeous stained-glass could be captured in all its glory. There were no fewer than eight cameras – and no shot was left unturned. Every movement of my feet and hands was recorded for posterity. Particularly impressive was a special miniaturized camera positioned carefully below the bottom manual and just above the swell-shoes.

Preparation for filming night was five times more hectic than any other concert I'd ever played. While primarily consisting of solo selections, the program also featured two pieces with the St. Mary's choir, under the direction of my longtime friend, John Marsh. The pressure for all of us was enormous. Between the packed house, the sound and vision crews, the riggers, and the complicated program – to say nothing of my responsibility to ensure that literally every note was as spot-on as possible – I felt nervous as never before. Thank goodness there were no major mishaps, and the results amply justified Bert Chappell's confidence in me.[3]

After the concert, I surely must have shaken hands and greeted far in excess of a thousand people. I can hardly remember a warmer and more giving audience. Talk about writer's cramp! My signing arm ached for weeks after.

It never ceases to amaze me what people will say and do when they approach the table with a program at the ready. Usually they are keen to shake me by the hand and request my sprawling 'curl(e)y' signature and I am always happy to oblige. But I remember on one occasion when the person opposite wanted considerably more than a signature!

A few years back, a strikingly elegant, tall woman in her late twenties asked if she could have a private word with me once I'd finished signing. In a businesslike yet friendly manner she confided that my interpretations had much moved her and that she had heard several Curley concerts during the previous eighteen months. She told me that she was a professional academic, was divorced into the bargain and had undertaken never to marry again. She also assured me

---

3 A special surprise for me was the appearance of Iris Lemare, an orchestral conductor and daughter of Edwin Lemare (1865–1934), the celebrated English organist. Before playing Lemare's *Rondo Capriccio: A Study in Accents*, I was proud to introduce Iris to the audience.

that she was of comfortable means and was in no way seeking any form of finan-cial support. All of this was very well, if not a trifle perplexing, but nothing could have prepared me for the proposition which followed next. She stated quite clear-ly that the time had come for her to have a child and that she yearned not only for this but also for the opportunity to raise and care for the little mite quite independently. Fixing me with a beady eye, she asked, 'Are you quite clear on that point?' 'Why, yes,' I stammered, not knowing whether to giggle or weep. 'I have heard you perform on a number of occasions,' she continued, 'and clearly we are genetically compatible. I have little doubt that the result of our union would be nothing short of a genius!'

Struck dumb, I wrapped my cape around me and ran.

After a span of years, I was pleased to meet up with a sculptor pal at a London supper-party, who relayed the astonishing news that he had met and married his other half through an ad in the 'Eye Love' section of *Private Eye*, a satirical mag-azine to which I've subscribed for ages. I had always felt that he was an 'eternal bachelor' so this came as quite a surprise. Not one for personal ads, I was nonetheless on the road so much that meeting members of the fairer sex was difficult. If it could work for him, why not throw my own bread on the water? I ran the following:

> ONE-OFF, good humoured, single, handsomely statuesque Yank teddy-bear classical male musician (39) seeks a prospective Mrs. Bach to experience fugues with forever. You are 25–40, European (possibly Scandinavian), without issue, well read, sensitive, sensual and exquisite in every way. Letter/'phone/ASAP. Reply to ...

I didn't expect much, did I? But 'handsomely statuesque'? At any rate, my friend's luck sadly did not visit its magic upon me, though the ad was much dis-cussed by my friends and in the press. That isn't to say there were no replies. As *Private Eye* has excellent circulation (probably better than mine), there were actually hundreds of responses, which I found genuinely interesting to read – yes, I did read them all! And it was a salutary lesson for me to discover there are so many lonely people out there looking for someone to be with; it's just that none of them was my 'prospective Mrs. Bach.'

At least in the classified ad there were no typos. When I signed with Decca, I was surprised to learn that it was company policy that artists played no part whatsoever in the production, or even checking, of their insert booklets. Despite repeated assurances that, with Decca, additional proofreading was unnecessary, Paul and I persevered, being finally permitted to see the proofs of my first Girard CD. Imagine my surprise when, even at first glance, a small number of typos stuck out: 'French Trumpet' had become 'French Strumpet' and 'Diapason' appeared as 'Dyinpason.' We have been supplied with proofs ever since.

Of course, everyone makes mistakes. I can hardly sit in the Crystal Palace and throw stones and, to be fair, Decca's were minor and would probably have been picked up at a later stage. A favourite blooper appeared in one Pro Arte CD booklet: the words 'insert Carlo Curley signature here' appeared on thousands of copies in place of the obvious. And in one of Decca's Japanese releases, my signature got in just fine – merely upside down. As a Japanese friend pointed out, it probably didn't make a whit of difference.

On my first trip to Russia, I had the good fortune to meet Natalia Malina, who is professor of organ at the Moscow Conservatory and curator of the splendid Mutin–Cavaillé-Coll organ in the Great Hall, imported from France in 1901. (If you have *Horowitz in Moscow*, look for the organ at the rear of the stage.) After playing the organ, walking backstage Natalia offered me a drink. I accepted, assuming she meant a cup of coffee. Hardly! Deeper into the organ case we went, where, secreted into part of the mechanism, was a hidden bar, with liquor, beers and mixers.

Natalia jealously guards this instrument, which had a peculiar threat some years ago. It appears that the Russian military were so captivated by the deep sonic force of the 32' Flûte stop (Open Wood) that they wanted to remove the big pipes and use them as a prototype for subsonic artillery on the battlefield. Can't you just picture it? Strapped atop a tank, a 35-foot-long wooden pipe emitting rumbling tones, toppling troops left and right and perhaps even setting forests alight? The organ-builders could now have a chance at those much coveted defense contracts! Fortunately, Natalia stood her ground, and the pipes remain safely inside the organ.

CHAPTER SIXTEEN

POSTLUDE AND FLOURISH

One facet of any performer's career is the receiving of notices, critiques, reviews, etc., some favorable, others less so. Curiously, some are non-committal although, mercifully, there are very few of these. However, sometimes, a muse contributes a jewel, transcending the usual hackneyed and limited critical conventions of musical impressions, description of the neighborhood, the setting, the audience, the venue and the instrument.

One of the finest word-smiths I've ever come across is Stephen Bicknell, whose impressions of my re-inaugural recital on a London suburban church organ follow.

While composing is a favorite pastime, he is an eminent organ historian, designer and builder, academic but never dry, as his new book, *The History of the English Organ* (Cambridge University Press – ISBN 0-521-55026-2) attests. Indeed, this is rapidly becoming a cornerstone on the subject.

The man himself? Tall and narrow, almost too fragile for high winds – sharply sculpted features – a modest sprinkling of hair (as Florence Candler put it: 'Grass doesn't grow on a busy street!') – eyes which are as articulate as his mouth and continue the dialogue when the latter is tightly closed – an abrupt, brusque style upon first meeting – a steely façade which protects a kind and generous human being. His knowledge of the organ and every imaginable sideshow (architecture, furnishings, glass, plumbing, hydraulic power, transport ...) is truly catholic and virtually unrivalled – he holds great affection for many styles of art and music other than the organ.

In his following piece, contributed to the PIPORG-L Internet organ chat-list, allow me to include a guide to some of the more arcane references. When I suggested that he submitted these outpourings to the local rag, the *Kensington Vox Humana Dispatch*, his modesty got the better of him and he graciously and gently declined. Surely he will be thrilled to discover it here!

Count Paulo Pauloni – Carlo Curley

Abbey of the Mauve Thought – My lodgings when in London

St. Frideswide's Notting Hill – St. James, Norlands, London, W11

Messrs. Arbuthnot & Pew – Bishop & Sons (who restored the instrument)

Mr. Josiah Greatorex – Mr. Christopher Sprague, Organist of the church and a long-time friend from my earliest days in England. Chris is a master at organizing and running firework displays and indeed there was a most impressive manifestation of his pyrotechnical skills in the church garden following this recital ...

(Rector) Sharpe-Hatchett or Sanders-Porcelain – The Vicar of St. James

Holland Park – A fashionable London district, where the church is located

BIOS – British Institute of Organ Studies

Choir Posaune – In this particular instrument, a brightly voiced Trumpet-style register, playable in the Choir (and Great) divisions

Brock's patent Niagara Falls – a brand of firework

THE GREAT PAULONI
by Stephen Bicknell

I have had such an interesting evening ...

First, I must say that I am not in the habit of attending organ recitals. The usual prospect is of sitting for a couple of hours on a hard bench in a cold and sad church, listening to music of indeterminate quality written by composers of still less determinate reputation. It will be played on an instrument of crudely mechanical and prosaic effect by a third-rate performer, who is (mercifully) hidden from view by a dusty maroon velvet curtain. An occasion of this sort does not fill one with anticipation and excitement – in fact it has all the appeal of the funeral of a dearly loved relative.

Luckily the normally undistinguished world of organs and organ playing is occasionally enlivened by the appearance of an artist of real merit: one who is able to transcend the mere mechanics of this most intractable medium, and who is able to bring organ music vividly to life. Such a man is the great Pauloni, and having just had the good fortune to attend a concert given by him, I must relate to you the sequence of events.

It all started yesterday when I received a note through the letterbox of my quaint eighteenth-century East London dwelling. From the scrolled decoration on the edges of the envelope, and from the gilded crest on the back, I immediately knew that this missive hailed from none other than our great friend Nobilissime The Count Paulo Pauloni, the greatest organ virtuoso of our age, at present (as you know) resident in West London where he has been studying for many years at the Abbey of the Mauve Thought in the Goldhawk Road.

I snatched the intriguing post from the doormat ('GO AWAY' written in large letters thereon), laughingly tossed aside a handful of bills and letters from gentlemen in chambers, and took the important remaining mail into the conservatory to devour it under a good light. Oh joy! Hastily written, but from the great man himself: 'Come! I play, tomorrow, it will be SUPERBO!' – and an address.

Aha! I thought. The maestro is indeed to make one of his rare appearances!

I immediately rang my publishers and cancelled lunch the following day (these things do drag on so), put aside the hundred-and-one little tasks that occupy the day, and reached for the A-Z map of London; for, as you may already have guessed, I was not going to turn down an opportunity to hear Pauloni on an occasion of his own recommending – indeed I would have been an idiot to do so. Close examination of the pages with a strong glass revealed that St. Frideswide's Notting Hill was at the end of a grand crescent on the smart side of Ladbroke Grove. I immediately set about making preparations for the journey.

Thus it was that early this evening I found myself in what Count Pauloni engagingly describes as my barouche – a motor-car of considerable age and beauty left to me by my Auntie Ellen and used as my main conveyance when I am in town. Bowling along the Western Avenue Extension at seventy-five miles per hour I eagerly anticipated the concert. Paulo Pauloni, as you know, is the only man on this planet who – no, let me start again – well, how does one describe the great Pauloni?

Appointed as organist at Siena Cathedral at the age of five, kissed by His Holiness at six, engaged to Princess Lucia of Liechtenstein at seven (how tragic that her untimely death has led him to a life of devotion and celibacy...) ... the list of his triumphs is beyond recall and in any case the Pauloni phenomenon has been reported widely in the press. And to find him playing, on a warm breezy evening in late summer, in, of all places, W11! – well, this was a great event, not on any account to be missed! And to be advised of it in person by the artist – what an honour!

There was naturally a considerable hubbub round the building when I got there, but I found that I was able to park right in front of the porch, after moving a few plastic cones that someone had foolishly left in the road. A gloomy little church from the end of the first wave of the ecclesiastical boom in the nineteenth century – about 1845, and ordered from a catalogue. I went in, waved aside the requests for alms from impoverished local residents, and looked around. Ah yes – those prefabricated triangular roof trusses – I have seen them a dozen times before: in those days you could order them from Wipple's Ecclesiastical Supply Company along with the cassocks and surplices and the 'Empire' brand communion wine. And, on the west gallery, stood an equally gloomy little organ.

I racked my brains to see if I could recognize the builder. Thanks to the work I have recently done on the subject (cf. Bicknell S. – 'Certain Patterns of Stencilled Decoration on Organs by Provincial Builders', BIOS Journal Vol. 146 pp. 76–144), I at once realized that I was standing in front of an early work of James Jepson Binns of Leeds. My loud exclamation of his name seemed to surprise some people standing near (one of them fell awkwardly onto a card-table stacked with programmes) but all was soon put to rights and I took my seat at a vantage point where I could see both the audience and the performer, several other people kindly moving back a row so that I could do so.

I had just enough time to scan the notes before the appointed time for the start, and was able at last to understand why we were all assembled. The church, standing slap-bang in the middle of desirable Holland Park, was a miracle of modern fund-raising effort. The organ had just emerged with all its Yorkshire bluff restored at the hands of Messrs. Arbuthnot & Pew, the well known organ-builders established at Tottenham Court in 1794 and now in premises off the Addison Road. The organist of the church was a wealthy local resident, philanthropist and connoisseur, Mr. Josiah Greatorex, who had had the good fortune to study with Pauloni at Siena. All the links were explained – the great Pauloni was leaving the Hermitage to play informally before friends. He would come, he would play for pleasure and for the art, he would mingle with the people. Mr. Greatorex, his former pupil, would graciously stand aside for the evening, allowing the bench at which he presided to be sat on by ...

My reverie was interrupted by a few words of welcome from the Rector (a double-barrelled name – something like Sharpe-Hatchett or Sanders-Porcelain), who made us feel quite at home, pointed out the deputy Mayor of the Royal Borough of Kensington and Chelsea (I had noticed him, in fact, on account of the fact that he was wearing a heavy chain of office which tinkled when he laughed), and encouraged us to enjoy hospitality offered by the church during the interval and afterwards, but to pay for any second or subsequent glass of wine and not to leave canapés in our pew on leaving. After this humdrum interlude we began.

I need not describe to you something which you all know so well – the astonishing experience of being in the same auditorium as a master of the art. They once spoke of Sarasate, of the reclusive Alkan, of Busoni; but today – you need only glance at *Hello!* magazine – they talk of Pauloni. And of course there are those who are outraged – there was the famous occasion when the entire *Académie Française* walked out of his concert at Notre Dame, and of course Pauloni's crippling lawsuit against the German Society of Musicologists is famous, and there are many more similar incidents. However, the Count's calling is to a much wider audience – that Latin blood! – his is a culture where every street-urchin whistles *Aïda* and every laundry-woman is in love with Caruso! This is classical music as it is enjoyed by the greatest number of people; serious art open to all comers, for their delight and wonder, and it is also the most noble gesture imaginable by a man of such talent.

The music unfolded like a double damask napkin. The first half was no mere warming-up exercise, indeed it was already apparent in the Bach fugue that the organ was not quite able to match the maestro in health and efficiency – though in truth it could hardly be expected that an instrument built in 1890 could have been made to accommodate such a devastating technique. I listened entranced, scarcely believing that an instrument of such an ordinary (though sturdy) kind could be made to utter such bewitching sounds. I cannot begin to recall the myriad details of his renderings, but I can tell you that I saw Elgar afresh, I met Antonin Dvorak as a close friend (and wondered whether he really did write that unresolved final chord so long ago), discovered yet another aspect of the mastery of Bach, delighted in the gentle whimsy of John Stanley (accompanied by a nightingale which happened to be singing in the crescent outside), and reminded myself again never to go to an opera by Wagner (I know I may have enemies in this respect but I really do think *Tannhäuser* is the most dreadful rubbish). I hasten to add – in respect of this last item – that whatever the calibre of the music it is of course notoriously difficult in arrangement for the organ, and Pauloni's breathtaking despatch of his own arrangement of the Overture left the audience roaring for more and dealt some serious damage to my sustained prejudice against German Romantic Art.

After a most intense and exhausting first half we were more than grateful for the wine offered by the church (not 'Empire' brand, I was pleased to note). I overheard many enthusiastic remarks, one gentleman saying to a friend: 'Well, it certainly beats my manual dexterity at the cottage upright!' Twenty minutes later it was a somewhat more talkative and excitable audience that pressed back into the pews and occasional seating.

We enjoyed more Elgar. In Vierne's *Claire de Lune* I gazed at the taste-fully dimmed electroliers in the chancel and imagined they were so many little moons – though in practice in this part of London the heavens are rarely visible through the fog. Oh! – and I should say that the organ acquitted itself excellently – no untoward creaks or clatters, only one duff note on the Clarionet, though naturally no voice of great distinction beyond a well charac-terized Harmonic Flute.

The last advertised piece was the Boëllman *Suite Gothique* – a personal favorite of the organist at St. Frideswide's, Mr. Greatorex – and a work in which we were left in no doubt as to the powers Pauloni has at his disposal. Indeed, at about the recapitulation in the final Toccata, a wine glass shattered quite spontaneously – though I hardly imagine that anyone noticed it do so, as the maestro was elevating a near-cliché of the repertoire into a monument of Parnassian scope.

We stood and cheered – well, we were certainly in the mood to, though the very British gentlefolk of Holland Park would scarcely consider it decorous to show too much enthusiasm in church, and their acclamations were quite dignified, though nevertheless completely heartfelt (during the Vierne I noticed two old ladies staring contentedly at Pauloni's photograph in the programme).

Well, the next few minutes are something of a jumble in my memory. Pauloni, with the most commendable condescension, returned to the organ to play an encore. Indeed it had been so clear, from his playing, that he was enjoying himself that I felt sure this 'extra' reflected reciprocal pleasure more than a sense of mere duty to his admirers. He launched himself with electrifying despatch into a piece of which I have never heard the like – a display of prestidigitation at the keyboard of a kind that few would dare to imitate, and a whirlwind of sound rising to an extraordinary crescendo.

Perhaps more extraordinary than it should have been. What I think must have happened is this: Mr. Greatorex had arranged for a celebratory display of fireworks to be held in the gardens after the concert; the men charged with their firing must have followed the published programme to the letter, and commenced their incendiary task shortly after the conclusion of the Boëllmann (imagining that the hullabaloo thus caused would draw their audience out of the church). Of course in fact they timed the first major barrage of three- and four-inch mortars to coincide precisely with the encore. Within, I was so totally immersed in the power of the performance that I briefly believed that this giant of the organ bench had found yet another miraculous sound that I had never heard before from an organ built north of Camden Town, and I did not notice the explosions and rifle-like crackling as separate from the crashing final chords (at which point I observed that every stop-knob on the organ was drawn, including the freshly rejuvenated Choir Posaune).

I did, however, notice the violent entry of a shell through the roof above the organ, and the rather charming peach-colored explosion which lit up the nave and caused the audience to lose all sense of discretion, and then to panic. In the ensuing barrage it was difficult to tell what happened. I found myself borne along on a tide of well-heeled yuppies, deafened by the most terrifying bangs and reports, dimly aware of a layer of elderly and disabled people over whom we were trampling, and clutching a handkerchief to my nose against the dense cloud of sulphurous smoke. Amidst the yelling and confusion (and the dying echoes of the music) we surged towards the doors; pews were overturned, clothing was ripped against kneeler-hooks, many injuries (some serious) were sustained and (I noticed to my distress) an especially fine window by Clayton & Bell was blown to atoms by an errant Roman Candle.

As I tried desperately to make my way to the west door (I found myself unaccountably clutching the curate's hair at one point) I looked up to see the hapless Pauloni waving frantically from the console above. His situation was dreadful – by now surrounded by flames, he was in peril of his life. The fire had reached the organ, and with so much well-seasoned timber now in its grasp there would only be moments before all was consumed. The stencilled front-pipes began to totter as smoke billowed from the swell-boxes, and I understood at once that there was not a moment to lose.

Reaching up with my cane, I was able to give one of the electroliers a hearty push in the direction of the west gallery. Luckily, Pauloni seized his chance, leaping onto the swinging lamp just as the Open Diapason basses plummeted into the nave (impaling a group of girl-guides in the process). I lost my balance at this point, and while recovering by jabbing out sharply with my cane (it seemed to bed itself firmly in something soft) I briefly saw the extraordinary spectacle of Nobilissime the Count Paulo Pauloni swinging into the centre of the nave, and then, wailing in an uncharacteristically apprehensive manner, back towards the organ again.

For a moment I thought he would be propelled directly into the flames from which he had just escaped! Thankfully, at the moment of crisis, the chain holding the light-fitting to the ceiling broke, and he landed quite safely on an advertising executive and his wife and daughters. I made a last effort to move forward, was carried along again on the tide of people, grabbed the maestro by the hand where he lay, and dragged him out of the west door just as the burning Great soundboard crashed through the floor of the gallery above.

It was indeed a most fortunate escape. Outside in the crescent a crowd had gathered: partly a mob of gawking onlookers, partly the shocked and wounded from the recital, and also a number of sidesmen trying to complete the retiring collection. The fire engines were on their way – we could see the flashing lights where they were trying to reach the church along the crowded street. Without a moment to lose I bundled Paulo into the barouche, pulled the starter, and, horns blaring, drove away as fast as I could between the deftly-parting masses. As I looked back through the mirror I could see, past the Brock's patent Niagara Falls and a very fine group of catherine wheels and lancework tableaux, the burning steeple sink gracefully onto the smoking ruins of St. Frideswide, Notting Hill, London W11 and onto the charred remains of a fine organ by James Jepson Binns, of Leeds, Yorkshire.

I drove Paulo back to the Abbey in silence. When we arrived I let him out of the passenger door and we said good evening to one another.

'Tell me,' he said; 'was I on good form?'

'Paulo,' I replied; 'you brought the house down.'

I wish I could bring this book to a close as if it were one of my recitals – I play the *Liberty Bell March*, you clap along (in strict tempo, please) right through and out of the back cover. Alas, this will have to remain a pleasure deferred and so, by way of compensation, here's a different kind of *sortie*, another small postlude perhaps.

In June 1994 I played at St. George's Hall, Liverpool. Joe Reilly, music critic of the *Liverpool Echo*, ran the kind of piece a publicist prays for:

American organ wizard promises his Mersey audiences:

Big-talking king of the keyboards Carlo Curley jetted into Liverpool today boasting: 'I'm better value than Madonna.'

American Carlo, billed as the Pavarotti of the Organ, takes Liverpool's St. George's Hall by storm on Saturday as part of his international crusade to turn yesterday's classics into tomorrow's pops.

The 6ft 4in maestro reckons he's more than capable of playing the world's top pop stars at their own game.

He's just made the first commercial classical organ video for top company Decca.

'You can see a Madonna video any day – but you ain't seen nothing like this,' says the giant from North Carolina ... 'and I promise you it'll frighten the neighbours!'

I'M MORE FUN THAN MADONNA!

Around the same time, I became something of a pop star myself when *The World of Carlo Curley* appeared in the Decca 'World of' series. When I got the CD, I thumbed through the booklet and noticed the other 'World of' titles: *The World of Mozart, The World of Kathleen Ferrier, The World of Gershwin, The World of Gilbert & Sullivan*, and so forth. Pardon me, I thought, but I'm the only living person on this list. With some concern, I put the question to my friend, John Parry, Decca's product manager. He replied:

The 'World of' series offers popular programmes based on composers, types of music or star performers with popular appeal and you come under the third category, not being a type of music or composer. You're quite right in saying that you are the only living 'World of' and this is intended to be a compliment![1]

---

1 Letter from John Parry, January 11, 1996.

Compliments aside, it is always a relief to learn that one is still above ground. But I do think that I'm at least as much fun as Madonna, and I remain determined in my mission to make the King of Instruments both popular and *alive*. I see no reason why music-making on the organ should not be, at one and the same time, serious, popular *and* fun.

Hopefully, you will have enjoyed at least a few of these outpourings and reminiscences as much as I have taken pleasure in setting them out for you.

Until we meet again,

I remain,

Sincerely,

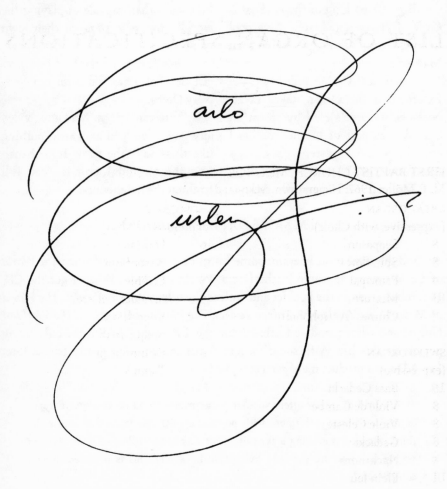

LIST OF ORGAN SPECIFICATIONS

FIRST BAPTIST CHURCH, MONROE, NORTH CAROLINA
M. P. Möller 1962: Hagerstown, Maryland

GREAT ORGAN	
(expressive, with Choir)	
8	Diapason
8	Spitzflöte
4	Principal
III	Mixture
	Chimes (Antiphonal)

SWELL ORGAN	
(expressive)	
16	Bass Gedackt
8	Viole de Gambe
8	Viole Celeste
8	Gedackt
4	Nachthorn
III	Plein Jeu
8	Trompette
4	Schalmei
	Tremolo

CHOIR ORGAN	
(expressive)	
16	Dulciana
8	Nasonflöte
8	Erzähler
8	Erzähler Celeste
4	Koppelflöte
II	Sesquialtera
8	Krummhorn
	Tremolo

ANTIPHONAL ORGAN
(expressive)

8	Flauto Dolce
8	Flute Celeste
4	Principal
II	Grave Mixture
	Tremolo
	Chimes

PEDAL ORGAN

16	Subbass
16	Bass Gedackt (Swell)
8	Violone
8	Subbass (ext.)
8	Gedackt (Swell)
4	Violone (ext.)
4	Subbass (ext.)
2	Subbass (ext.)

PRACTICE ORGAN 'MARTINI':
NORTH CAROLINA SCHOOL OF THE ARTS, WINSTON-SALEM,
NORTH CAROLINA
Holtkamp Organ Company 1966–67: Cleveland, Ohio

LOWER MANUAL			UPPER MANUAL	
8	Gedackt		8	Quintadena
4	Principal		4	Gedackt
4	Quintadena		2	Principal
III	Mixture		2	Flute
8	Schalmey		4	Schalmey

PEDAL		ANALYSIS		
16	Quintadena	16	Quintadena	85 pipes
8	Gedackt	8	Gedackt	85 pipes
4	Principal	4	Principal	73 pipes
4	Quintadena	III	Mixture 26.29.33	183 pipes
8	Schalmey	8	Schalmey	73 pipes
4	Schalmey			

VIRGIL FOX RESIDENCE, ENGLEWOOD, NEW JERSEY
Skinner Organ Co. c.1915: Boston, Massachusetts
Reconfigured, augmented and altered by numerous others.

GREAT		SWELL	
16	Diapason	16	Contra Geigen
16	Violone	16	Gedackt
8	Diapason	8	Salicional
8	Principal	8	Voix Celeste
8	Flûte harmonique	8	Claribel Flute
8	Stopped Diapason	8	Flûte à Cheminée
8	Erzähler	8	Æoline
8	Quintadena	8	Unda Maris
4	Octave	8	Flute Celeste II
4	Principal	5⅓	Quint
4	Flûte couverte	4	Octave
2⅔	Quinte	4	Viola
2	Super Octave	4	Flute
2	Fifteenth	V-VI	Plein Jeu
V	Mixture	16	Bombarde
VI	Harmonic	16	Hautbois
8	English Trumpet	8	Bombarde
8	French Trumpet	8	Oboe
4	Trumpet-Clarion	8	Vox Humana
4	Trompette	4	Clarion

CHOIR ORGAN			
16	Viola Pomposa	2⅔	Nazard
16	Dulciana	1⅗	Tierce
8	Viola	1⅓	Larigot
8	Flûte harmonique	1	Piccolo
8	Dulcette II	V	Cymbal
8	Erzähler	8	Trumpet
8	Erzähler Celeste	8	Corno d'Amore
8	Spitzflöte	8	English Horn
8	Spitzflöte Celeste	8	Clarinet
4	Octave	4	Trompette
4	Viola		Harp

SOLO ORGAN		PEDAL ORGAN	
8	Diapason	32	Wood Open (electronic)
8	Gamba	32	Bourdon (electronic)
8	Gamba Celeste	16	Open Wood
8	Major Flute	16	Metal Open (Great)
8	Orchestral Flute	16	Contra Bass
8	Tuba Major	16	Violone (Great)
8	Trumpet Military	16	Geigen (Swell)
8	French Horn	16	Bourdon
8	Oboe d'Amore	16	Dulciana (Choir)
8	Flügel Horn	16	Lieblich Bourdon (Sw.)
8	Vox Humana	10⅔	Pedal Quint
4	Tuba	8	Diapason
4	Bombarde	8	Octave Geigen (Swell)
		8	Open Flute
ECHO		8	Violone (Great)
8	String II	4	Choral Bass
8	Clear Flute	4	Gross Flute
8	Fagotto	4	Lieblich Flute (Swell)
8	Heckelphone	32	Bombarde (electronic)
8	Vox Humana	16	Bombarde
	Chimes	16	Posaune
		16	Fagotto
		8	Trumpet
		8	Wald Horn
		4	Clarion
		2	Zinc

FOUNTAIN STREET CHURCH, GRAND RAPIDS, MICHIGAN
Skinner Organ Co. 1924; Casavant Frères 1959; Tellers 1970
(new Console and Bombarde)

GREAT ORGAN
(unexpressive)

16	Quintaton
8	Principal
8	Bourdon
8	Erzähler
4	Octave
4	Rohrflöte
2⅔	Twelfth
2	Fifteenth
2	Spitzflöte
IV	Fourniture
III	Scharff
8	Trompette

CHOIR ORGAN
(expressive)

8	Dulciana
8	Cor de Nuit
4	Prestant
4	Koppelflöte
2⅔	Nazard
2	Blockflöte
1⅗	Tierce
1	Sifflöte
8	Orchestral Oboe
	Tremolo
	Harp
	Celesta

SWELL ORGAN
(expressive)

16	Bourdon
8	Geigen Principal
8	Salicional
8	Voix Celeste
8	Gedeckt
8	Flute Celeste II
4	Geigen Octave
4	Flute Harmonique
4	Unda Maris II
2⅔	Twelfth
2	Fifteenth
III	Plein Jeu
III	Petite Fourniture
16	Fagotto
8	Trompette
8	Flügel Horn
8	Vox Humana
4	Clarion
	Tremolo

SOLO ORGAN
(expressive)

8	Cello
8	Gamba Celeste
8	Flûte harmonique
8	French Horn
8	Clarinet
	Tremolo
8	Tuba Mirabilis

BOMBARDE ORGAN
(unexpressive)

8	Major Diapason
4	Major Octave
V	Grand Fourniture
16	Bombarde
8	Harmonic Bombarde
4	Bombarde Clarion

GALLERY ORGAN
(unexpressive)

8	Principal
4	Principal
II	Grave Mixture
8	Trompette

ANTIPHONAL ORGAN
(expressive)

8	Erzähler
8	Erzähler Celeste
8	Concert Flute
4	Concert Flute
	Chimes

ANTIPHONAL PEDAL

16	Rohrbourdon
8	Rohrflöte (ext.)
	Chimes (Antiphonal)

PEDAL ORGAN

32	Erzähler (Great)
16	Principal
16	Violone
16	Erzähler (Great)
16	Bourdon
16	Echo Lieblich (Swell)
8	Octave
8	Violin (ext.)
8	Gedeckt (ext.)
8	Still Gedeckt (Swell)
4	Choral Bass (Violone ext.)
4	Nachthorn
IV	Fourniture
32	Contre-Bombarde (ext.)
16	Bombarde
16	Fagotto (Swell)
8	Trompette (ext.)
4	Clarion (ext.)

GIRARD COLLEGE CHAPEL, PHILADELPHIA, PENNSYLVANIA
Æolian-Skinner 1932–33: Boston, Massachusetts
(finished by Ernest Skinner)

GREAT ORGAN (unexpressive)		SWELL ORGAN (expressive)	
32	Violone	16	Bourdon
16	Diapason	8	Open Diapason
8	First Diapason	8	Geigen Diapason
8	Second Diapason	8	Salicional
8	Principal Flute	8	Voix Celeste
5⅓	Quint	8	Viole d'Orchestre
4	Octave	8	Viole Celeste
4	Principal	8	Gedeckt
2⅔	Twelfth	8	Flauto Dolce
2	Fifteenth	8	Flute Celeste
IV	Chorus Mixture	4	Octave
IV	Harmonics	4	Flute Triangulaire
16	Trumpet	2⅔	Nazard
8	Tromba	2	Flautino
4	Clarion	IV	Cornet
	(expressive, in Choir)	V	Chorus Mixture
8	Third Diapason	16	Posaune
8	'Cello	8	French Trumpet
8	Stopped Diapason	8	Cornopean
8	Erzähler	8	Oboe d'Amore
8	Erzähler Celeste	8	Vox Humana
8	Trumpet	4	Clarion
	Harp (Choir)		Tremolo
	Celesta (Choir)		Harp (Choir)
	Chimes		Celesta (Choir)

SOLO ORGAN
(expressive)

8	Gamba
8	Gamba Celeste
8	Flauto Mirabilis
4	Flute
VII	Grand Fourniture
16	Corno di Bassetto (ext.)
8	Corno di Bassetto
8	English Horn
	Tremolo
	Chimes
16	Contra Tuba
8	Harmonic Tuba
8	French Horn
4	Clarion
	(unexpressive)
8	Tuba Mirabilis

CHOIR ORGAN
(expressive)

16	Dulciana
8	Geigen Diapason
8	Viol d'Orchestre
8	Viol Celeste
8	Concert Flute
8	Spitz Flute
8	Dulciana
8	Unda Maris
4	Dulciana
4	Flute d'Amore
2⅔	Dulciana Twelfth (ext.)
2	Dulciana Fifteenth (ext.)
2	Piccolo
16	Bassoon
8	Clarinet
8	Orchestral Oboe
	Tremolo
	Harp
	Celesta

ECHO ORGAN
(expressive)

8	Diapason
8	Waldflute
8	Echo Gamba
8	Dulcet
4	Flute Triangulaire
8	Vox Humana
	Tremolo

PEDAL ORGAN

32	Resultant
32	Diapason (ext.)
32	Violone (Great)
16	Diapason
16	Contra Bass (Great)
16	Metal Diapason (Great)
16	Dulciana (Choir)
16	Bourdon
16	Echo Lieblich (Swell)
8	Octave Diapason (ext.)
8	Principal (Great)
8	Gedeckt (ext.)
8	Still Gedeckt (Swell)
4	Flute (ext.)
V	Mixture
32	Bombarde (ext.)
32	Fagotto (ext.)
16	Trombone
16	Fagotto
16	Bassoon (Choir)
8	Tromba (ext.)
	Chimes

JOHN WANAMAKER STORE, PHILADELPHIA, PENNSYLVANIA
Los Angeles Art Organ Co. 1904: Los Angeles, California
Augmentations by the organ-building staff, John Wanamaker Store 1911–31
(expressive unless otherwise indicated)

GREAT ORGAN
(unexpressive)

32	Sub Principal
16	Double Diapason
16	Contra Gamba
10⅔	Sub Quint
8	Diapason Major
8	Diapason Phonon
8	Diapason I
8	Diapason II
8	Diapason III
8	Diapason IV
8	Gamba (2 rks.)
8	Major Tibia
8	Mezzo Tibia
8	Minor Tibia
8	Double Flute
8	Nazard Flute (2 rks.)
4	Octave
VIII	Mutation (32′ series)
8	Harmonic Trumpet (expressive with Choir)
8	Covered Tibia
8	Harmonic Flute
5⅓	Quint
4	Principal
4	Harmonic Flute
3⅕	Tierce
2⅔	Octave Quint
2	Super Octave
VII	Mixture
16	Double Trumpet
8	Tuba
8	Trumpet
4	Harmonic Clarion
	Great Tremolo I and II

GREAT CHORUS DIVISION
(unexpressive)

8	Diapason Magna
8	Stentorphone
8	Open Diapason I
8	Open Diapason II
8	Open Diapason III
8	Gamba
8	Major Flute
8	Double Flute
4	Octave
4	Flute
2⅔	Nazard
	Tremolo

SWELL ORGAN
(original String division)

16	Contra Bass
8	Violoncello
8	Viol
8	Viol (sharp)
8	Viola
5⅓	Quint Viol
4	Violina
4	Octave Viol
3⅕′	Tierce
IV	String Mixture
V	Corroborating Mixture
	Swell Tremolo I and II

SWELL ORGAN		CHOIR ORGAN	
16	Double Diapason	16	Double Dulciana
16	Soft Bourdon	8	Open Diapason
8	Stentorphone	8	Violin Diapason
8	Horn Diapason	8	Stopped Diapason
8	Violin Diapason	8	Concert Flute
8	Bell Flute	8	Quintadena
8	Tibia Dura	8	Salicional
8	Grand Flute (2 rks.)	8	Vox Celeste
8	Double Flute	8	Vox Angelica
8	Clarabella	8	Keraulophone
8	Orchestral Flute	8	Dulciana
8	Harmonic Flute	4	Salicet
8	Melodia	4	Forest Flute
8	Soft Dulciana	2	Piccolo
8	Gamba	VI	Soft Cornet
8	Gamba Celeste (2 rks.)	16	Saxophone
5⅓	Quint Bourdon	8	Saxophone
4	Octave I	8	English Horn
4	Octave II	8	Clarinet
4	Harmonic Flute		Choir Tremolo I and II
2⅔	Nazard		
2	Harmonic Piccolo		
IV	Viol Cornet		
VI	Mixture		
16	Double Open Horn		
16	Contra Fagotto		
16	Bassoon		
8	Trumpet		
8	Trombone		
4	Harmonic Clarion		
8	Horn		
8	Fagotto		
8	First Oboe		
8	Oboe		
8	Bassoon		
8	Basset Horn		
8	Clarinet		
8	Clarinet (2 rks.)		
8	Vox Humana (2 rks.)		
4	Musette		

SOLO ORGAN		ORCHESTRAL ORGAN	
16	Double Open Diapason	16	Contra Quintadena
16	Grand Viol	8	Duophone
8	Open Diapason I	8	Tibia
8	Open Diapason II	8	Covered Tibia
8	Open Diapason III	8	Concert Flute
8	Violin Diapason	8	Harmonic Flute
8	Clarabella	8	Mellow Flute
8	Tierce Flute (2 rks.)	8	String Flute
8	Harmonic Flute	8	Double Flute
8	Chimney Flute	8	Hollow Flute
8	Grand Gamba	4	Octave
8	Grand Gamba (sharp)	4	Harmonic Flute
8	Nazard Gamba (2 rks.)	4	Covered Flute
8	Viol	2	Harmonic Piccolo
8	Viol (sharp)	16	English Horn
8	Gemshorn	16	Bass Clarinet
8	Quintaphone	16	Bass Saxophone
$5\frac{1}{3}$	Quint Diapason	16	Bassoon
4	Octave	8	Orchestral Bassoon
4	Harmonic Flute	8	Orchestral Clarinet
$3\frac{1}{5}$	Harmonic Tierce	8	Orchestral Oboe
$2\frac{2}{3}$	12th Harmonic	8	Bassett Horn
2	Piccolo	8	Saxophone
V	Mixture	8	French Horn I
VI	Mixture	8	French Horn II
VI	Grand Mixture	8	French Horn III
16	Tuba	8	Muted Cornet
16	Double Trumpet	8	Kinura
8	Ophicleide	16	Vox Humana
8	Cornopean	8	Vox Humana I
8	Soft Tuba	8	Vox Humana II
8	Trumpet	8	Vox Humana III
8	Musette	8	Vox Humana IV
4	Ophicleide	8	Vox Humana V
4	Tuba	8	Vox Humana VI
	Solo Tremolo I and II		Orchestral Tremolo I and II

ETHEREAL ORGAN		ECHO ORGAN	
16	Bourdon	16	Bourdon
8	Open Diapason I	8	Open Diapason
8	Open Diapason II	8	Violin Diapason
8	Clear Flute	8	Stopped Diapason
8	Harmonic Flute	8	Night Horn
8	Double Flute	8	Clarabella
8	Grand Gamba	8	Melodia
8	Gamba (sharp)	8	Orchestral Viol
5⅓	Quint Flute	8	Soft Viol
4	Octave	8	Soft Viol (sharp)
4	Harmonic Flute	8	Unda Maris (2 rks.)
2⅔	12th Harmonic	5⅓	Open Quint
2	Harmonic Piccolo	4	Octave
IV	Mixture	4	Harmonic Flute
16	Tuba Profunda	4	Mellow Flute
8	Tuba Mirabilis	VI	Mixture
8	French Trumpet	V	Cornet Mixture
8	Grand Clarinet	16	Double Trumpet
8	Post Horn	8	Trumpet
8	English Horn	8	Capped Oboe
4	Tuba Clarion	8	Euphone
	Ethereal Tremolo I and II	8	Vox Humana (2 rks.)
			Echo Tremolo I and II

STENTOR ORGAN and
STENTOR PEDAL ORGAN
(These divisions have not been installed.
The Stentor scheme of 1926 was compiled by Charles Courboin and George W. Till while the 1927 proposal was drawn up by G. Donald Harrison. Both plans called for approximately 40 stops on wind pressures ranging from 15" to 100", including a full-length 64′ Bombarde. Harrison's submission was believed to be the one that came within one week of being approved before Rodman Wanamaker's death precluded its construction. The Stentor manual – the sixth, or top keyboard – is presently in operation so that any of the ancillary divisions may be played from it.)

STRING ORGAN

u:unison - s:sharp - f:flat

16	Violone
16	Contra Gamba I
16	Contra Gamba II
16	Contra Viol I
16	Contra Viol II
16	Viol I
16	Viol II
8	Violin Diapason
8	Gamba
8	Cello I (unison)
8	Cello I (sharp)
8	Cello I (flat)
8	Cello II (u)
8	Cello II (s)
8	Cello II (f)
8	Nazard Gamba (2 rks.) (u)
8	Nazard Gamba (2 rks.) (s)
8	Orchestral Violin I (u)
8	Orchestral Violin I (s)
8	Orchestral Violin I (f)
8	Orchestral Violin II (u)
8	Orchestral Violin II (s)
8	Orchestral Violin II (f)
8	Orchestral Violin III (u)
8	Orchestral Violin III (s)
8	Orchestral Violin III (f)
8	Orchestral Violin IV (u)
8	Orchestral Violin IV (s)
8	Orchestral Violin IV (f)
8	Orchestral Violin V (u)
8	Orchestral Violin V (s)
8	Orchestral Violin V (f)
8	Orchestral Violin VI (u)
8	Orchestral Violin VI (s)
8	Orchestral Violin VI (f)
8	Muted Violin I (u)
8	Muted Violin I (s)
8	Muted Violin I (f)
8	Muted Violin II (u)
8	Muted Violin II (s)
8	Muted Violin II (f)
8	Muted Violin III (u)
8	Muted Violin III (s)
8	Muted Violin III (f)
8	Muted Violin IV (u)
8	Muted Violin IV (s)
8	Muted Violin IV (f)
8	Muted Violin V (u)
8	Muted Violin V (s)
8	Muted Violin V (f)
8	Muted Violin VI (u)
8	Muted Violin VI (s)
8	Muted Violin VI (f)
$5\frac{1}{3}$	Quint Violina (u)
$5\frac{1}{3}$	Quint Violina (s)
4	Orchestral Violina I (u)
4	Orchestral Violina I (s)
4	Orchestral Violina II (u)
4	Orchestral Violina II (s)
$3\frac{1}{5}$	Tierce Violina (u)
$3\frac{1}{5}$	Tierce Violina (s)
$2\frac{2}{3}$	Nazard Violina (u)
$2\frac{2}{3}$	Nazard Violina (s)
2	Super Violina (u)
2	Super Violina (s)
8	Dulciana I (u)
8	Dulciana I (s)
8	Dulciana II (u)
8	Dulciana II (s)
8	Dulciana III (u)
8	Dulciana III (s)
8	Dulciana IV (u)
8	Dulciana IV (s)
8	Dulciana V (u)
8	Dulciana V (s)
8	Dulciana VI (u)
8	Dulciana VI (s)
4	Octave Dulciana I (u)

4	Octave Dulciana I (s)	ECHO PEDAL	
4	Octave Dulciana II (u)	16	Open Diapason
4	Octave Dulciana II (s)	16	Stopped Diapason
V	Dulciana Mixture		
	Mutation 12th		
	Mutation 15th		
	Mutation 19th		
	Mutation 22nd		
	Mutation 26th		
	String Tremolo I and II		

MAIN PEDAL ORGAN
(unexpressive)

64	Gravissima	8	Soft Octave Bourdon
32	Contra Diaphone	8	Cello I
32	Contra Open Diapason I	8	Cello II
32	Contra Open Diapason II	8	Soft Dulciana
32	Contra Bourdon	4	Octave
16	Diaphone	4	Principal
16	Open Diapason I	4	Tibia I
16	Open Diapason II	4	Tibia II
16	Open Diapason III	4	Soft Flute
16	Open Flute	VIII	Mixture (32') (Gt.)
16	Bourdon	VI	Mixture (16') (Gt.)
16	Soft Bourdon (Sw.)	VII	Mixture
16	Violone	X	Grand Mutation
16	Gamba	32	Contra Bombarde
16	Dulciana (Ch.)	16	Bombarde
10⅔	Open Quint	16	Tuba
10⅔	Stopped Quint	16	Trombone
8	Octave	16	Euphonium
8	Open Diapason	16	Contra Fagotto
8	Stentorphone	8	Bombarde
8	Tibia I	8	Tromba
8	Tibia II	8	Octave Fagotto
8	Soft Flute	4	Clarion

ORCHESTRAL/STRING		ETHEREAL PEDAL	
PEDAL		32	Acoustic Bass
32	Contra Diaphone	16	Open Diapason
32	Contra Gamba	16	Bombarde
16	Diaphone	8	Bombarde
16	Gamba		
16	Violone I	PERCUSSIONS	
16	Violone II		Major Chimes
16	Viol		Minor Chimes
16	Viol (sharp)		Metalophone
8	Diaphone		Celesta (Mustel)
8	Gamba		Gongs
8	Violone I		Piano I (prepared for)
8	Violone II		Piano II
8	Viol		Harp I (prepared for)
8	Viol (sharp)		Harp II (prepared for)
4	Violone		
XII	Mixture (32′ Contra		
	Diaphone and following		
	mutations):		
16	Mutation Diaphone		
16	Mutation Violone		
10⅔	Mutation Viol		
8	Mutation Viol		
5⅓	Mutation Viol		
4	Mutation Viol		
2⅔	Mutation Viol		
2	Mutation Viol		
1⅗	Mutation Viol		
1⅓	Mutation Viol		
⅗	Mutation Viol		
16	Vox Humana I		
16	Vox Humana II		
	Pedal Tremolo		

TEMPLE CHURCH, LONDON, ENGLAND
Harrison & Harrison 1924: Durham, England
Originally at Glen Tanar, Aberdeenshire
Installed at Temple Church 1954

GREAT ORGAN

16	Double Open Diapason
16	Bourdon
8	Large Open Diapason
8	Small Open Diapason
8	Geigen
8	Hohl Flute
8	Stopped Diapason
4	Octave
4	Wald Flute
2⅔	Octave Quint
2	Super Octave
IV	Harmonics
	(expressive in Solo box)
8	Tromba
4	Octave Tromba

CHOIR ORGAN
(expressive)

16	Contra Dulciana
8	Claribel Flute
8	Lieblich Gedeckt
8	Dulciana
4	Salicet
4	Flauto Traverso
2	Harmonic Piccolo
III	Dulciana Mixture
16	Cor Anglais
8	Clarinet

SWELL ORGAN
(expressive)

16	Quintaton
8	Open Diapason
8	Rohr Flute
8	Echo Salicional
8	Vox Angelica (FF)
4	Principal
2	Fifteenth
V	Mixture
8	Oboe
	Tremulant
16	Double Trumpet
8	Trumpet
4	Clarion

SOLO ORGAN
(expressive)

16	Contra Viola
8	Viole d'Orchestre
8	Viole Céleste
8	Harmonic Flute
4	Concert Flute
8	Orchestral Hautboy
	Tremulant
16	Double Orchestral Trumpet
8	Horn
8	Tuba Mirabilis *

PEDAL ORGAN

32	Double Open Wood (ext.)
32	Sub Bourdon (ext.)
16	Open Wood
16	Open Diapason (ext. Great Large Diapason)
16	Geigen (Great)
16	Bourdon (Great)
16	Violone (Solo)
16	Dulciana (Choir)
8	Octave Wood (ext.)
8	Flute (ext.)
4	Octave Flute (ext.)
32	Double Ophicleide (ext.) *
16	Ophicleide *
16	Orchestral Trumpet (Solo)
16	Bassoon (Choir)
8	Posaune (ext.) *

* The Tuba Mirabilis and Pedal reed unit are enclosed in an independent swell box.

VANGEDE KIRKE, VANGEDE, COPENHAGEN, DENMARK
Th. Frobenius & Sons 1979: Lyngby, Denmark

HOVEDVÆRK

16	Principal
8	Principal
8	Fløjte
4	Oktav
4	Gemshorn
2⅔	Quint
2	Oktav
1⅗	Terts
VI	Mixtur
16	Dulcian
8	Trompet

POSITIV (expressive)

8	Gedakt
8	Quintaton
4	Principal
4	Rørfløjte
2	Waldfløjte
1⅓	Quint
1	Oktav
IV	Scharf
8	Krumhorn
	Tremulant

SVELLEVÆRK (expressive)

16	Gedakt
8	Rørfløjte
8	Viola di Gamba
8	Celeste
4	Principal
4	Kobbelfløjte
2⅔	Quint
2	Tværfløjte
1⅗	Terts
IV	Mixtur
8	Trompet
8	Oboe
4	Clairon
	Tremulant

PEDAL

16	Principal (Hovedværk)
16	Subbas
8	Oktav
8	Gedakt
4	Oktav (Hovedværk)
4	Gemshorn (Hovedværk)
IV	Mixtur
16	Basun
8	Trompet
4	Trompet

GAMMEL HOLTE KIRKE, GAMMEL HOLTE, DENMARK
Th. Frobenius & Sons 1978: Lyngby, Denmark

MANUAL I (expressive)		MANUAL II (expressive)	
8	Principal	8	Viola de Gamba
8	Rørfløjte	8	Gedakt
4	Oktav	4	Spidsfløjte
4	Kobbelfløjte	2⅔	Quint
2	Nathorn	2	Principal
1⅓	Quint	1⅗	Terts
	Mixtur	1	Oktav
16	Fagot	8	Trompet
	Tremulant		Tremolo

PEDAL
16	Subbas
8	Rørfløjte (Manual I)
4	Oktav (Manual I)
2	Nathorn (Manual I)
16	Fagot (Manual I)

FREDENSBORG SLOTSKIRKE (FREDENSBORG CASTLE CHURCH), FREDENSBORG, DENMARK
Marcussen & Reuter 1846
Restored by Marcussen, 1960s

MANUAL I

16	Bordun
8	Principal
4	Oktav
2⅔	Quint
2	Oktav
1⅗	Terts
II-IV	Mixture
8	Trompet

MANUAL II

8	Gedakt
4	Fløjte
2	Gemshorn
1	Oktav

PEDAL

16	Subbas
8	Gedakt
4	Fløjte
16	Fagot

LA GRANDE ARCHE, LA DÉFENSE, PARIS
Proposed specification 1985: Jean Guillou and Carlo Curley (never constructed)

CLASSICAL DIVISIONS		RÉCIT (expressive)	
GRAND-ORGUE		16	Bourdon
16	Montre	8	Principal
8	Montre	8	Gamba
8	Gemshorn	8	Voix Céleste
8	Flûte traversière	8	Flûte harmonique
4	Prestant	4	Prestant
4	Flûte octaviante	4	Flûte harmonique
2⅔	Quint	V	Plein-jeu harmonique
2	Doublette	III	Carillon
V	Plein-jeu	16	Bombarde
IV	Cymbale	8	Trompette
V	Cornet	8	Hautbois
16	Bombarde	8	Voix humaine
8	Première Trompette	4	Clairon
8	Deuxième Trompette		Tremulant
4	Clairon		Voix humaine Tremulant
	Tremulant		

POSITIF		PÉDALE	
16	Quintaton	16	Principal
8	Principal	16	Soubasse
8	Bourdon	8	Principal
4	Prestant	8	Flûte
4	Quintaton	4	Flûte
2	Flûte	2	Nachthorn
1⅓	Larigot	IV	Mixture
½	Flûte	32	Basson
II	Sesquialtera	16	Bombarde
IV	Scharff	8	Trompette
16	Basson	4	Chalumeau
8	Trompette		Tremulant
8	Cromorne		(8′ and above)
	Tremulant		

GRAND DIVISIONS
GRAND-ORGUE

32	Violoncelle
16	Principal harmonique
8	Grand Diapason I
8	Grand Diapason II
4	Grand Octave I
4	Grand Octave II
2	Grand Doublette (2 rks.)
X	Grand Mixture
VII	Grand Tierce Mixture
16	Bombarde harmonique
8	Trompette harmonique
5⅓	Clairon Quint harmon.
4	Clairon harmonique

GRAND-CHOEUR/SOLO
(expressive)

16	Violoncelle
16	Violoncelle Céleste
8	Triple Principal (3 rks.)
8	Flûte
8	Grand Gambe
8	Grand Gambe Céleste
4	Double Principal (2 rks.)
VIII	Grand Mixture
V	Grand Cornet
16	Cor de Basset
8	Clarinette
8	Cor anglais
8	Cor
8	Hautbois
8	Petite Trompette
4	Chalumeau
	Tremulant
	(very heavy wind)
VI	Grand Principal Mixture
VII	Aliquot
16	Tuba harmonique
8	Tuba harmonique
4	Clairon harmonique

GRAND RÉCIT
(expressive)

16	Gambe
16	Gambe Céleste
8	Principal
8	Flûte harmonique
8	Viola di Gambe
8	Viola Céleste
8	Bourdon
8	Flûte Céleste (2 rks.)
4	Principal
4	Flûte harmonique
4	Unda Maris (2 rks.)
2	Nachthorn
VI	Rauschpfeife Mixture
IV-IX	Plein-jeu harmonique
IV	Cymbale
V	Cornet
32	Bombarde
16	Bombarde
8	Trompette
8	Voix humaine *(mf)*
8	Clairon
4	Clairon
2	Clairon
	Tremulant

GRAND PAN
(all en chamade except for mixture)

8	Grand Bourdon
8	Flûte majeur
8	Flûte harmonique
4	Flûte harmonique
2⅔	Flûte harmonique
2	Flûte harmonique
1⅗	Flûte harmonique
1	Flûte harmonique
VI	Grand Mixture de flûtes
	Tremulant

KRONWERK		GRAND PÉDALE	
(expressive)		32	Principal
16	Dulciana	32	Violoncelle
8	Bourdon	32	Soubasse
8	Cor de nuit	16	Diapason
8	Cor de nuit Céleste	16	Flûte
4	Holz Principal	16	Contre-Basse
2⅔	Nazard	16	Violoncelle
2	Nachthorn	16	Contre-Gambe
III	Acuta	16	Soubasse
IV	Aliquot	16	Dulciana
16	Ranquette *(en chamade)*	10⅔	Quinte
16	Clarinette *(en chamade)*	8	Principal
8	Hautbois *(en chamade)*	8	Flûte
8	Dulzaina *(en chamade)*	4	Prestant
	Tremulant	4	Flûte
	Cloches	2	Nachthorn
	Harpe et Vibraphone	III	Théorbe
	Zimbelstern	VIII	Grand Mixture
		32	Grand Bombarde
BOMBARDE		16	Bombarde (30″)
(all en chamade*)*		16	Trombone
32	Bombarde	8	Trompette
16	Bombarde	4	Clairon
16	Trompette		Tremulant
8	Trompette		(8′ and above)
4	Trompette		

STRING ORGAN and
STRING PEDAL ORGAN
(158 additional ranks situated in
ceiling space)

FESTIVA
(en chamade – *50′ wind*)
16   Grand Trompette
8   Cor de Défense

FIRST METHODIST CHURCH, LAKE WALES, FLORIDA
Th. Frobenius & Sons 1986: Lyngby, Denmark; Carlo Curley, Consultant

GREAT (expressive)

8	Principal
8	Open Fløjte
4	Oktav
4	Gemshorn
2	Nathorn
1⅓	Quint
IV	Mixtur
16	Fagot
8	Krumhorn
	Tremulant

SWELL (expressive)

8	Viola da Gamba
8	Viola Celeste (CC)
8	Gedakt
4	Oktav
4	Kobbelfløjte
2⅔	Quint
2	Principal
1⅗	Terts
1	Oktav
III	Mixtur
8	Trompet
	Tremolo

PEDAL

32	Bourdon (electronic)
16	Subbas
8	Principal
8	Fløjte (Manual I)
4	Oktav (Manual I)
2	Nathorn (Manual I)
II	Mixtur
16	Fagot (Manual I)
8	Skalmej

CHIMES

ZIMBELSTERN

THE MANOR HOUSE, BURROUGH-ON-THE-HILL
MELTON MOWBRAY, LEICESTERSHIRE, ENGLAND
Harrison & Harrison 1989: Durham, England

GREAT ORGAN			PEDAL	
16	Bourdon		16	Sub Bass
8	Open Diapason		8	Principal
8	Stopped Diapason		8	Bass Flute (ext.)
4	Principal		4	Fifteenth
4	Wald Flute		4	Octave Flute
3⅕	Double Tierce		II	Mixture
2⅔	Twelfth		16	Fagotto (Swell)
2	Fifteenth		8	Trumpet (Great)
1⅗	Seventeenth		8	Hautboy (Swell)
IV	Mixture		4	Hautboy (Swell)
8	Trumpet			
8	Cremona			
	Tremulant			

SWELL ORGAN (expressive)

8	Spitzflute
8	Céleste
4	Principal
4	Chimney Flute
2⅔	Nazard
2	Recorder
1⅗	Tierce
1⅓	Larigot
III	Mixture
16	Fagotto
8	Cornopean
8	Hautboy (ext. Fagotto)
	Tremulant
8	Trumpet (Great)

CITY HALL, CAPE TOWN, SOUTH AFRICA
Norman & Beard 1905: London and Norwich, England

GREAT ORGAN
(unexpressive)

16	Double Open Diapason
8	Open Diapason I (heavy wind)
8	Open Diapason II
8	Open Diapason III
8	Claribel
4	Principal
4	Harmonic Flute
2⅔	Twelfth
2	Fifteenth
III	Sesquialtera
16	Contra Posaune (heavy wind)
8	Tromba (heavy wind)
4	Clarion (heavy wind)

SWELL ORGAN
(expressive)

8	Open Diapason (heavy wind)
8	Geigen Diapason
8	Gamba
8	Lieblich Gedact
8	Salicional
8	Vox Angelica
4	Principal
4	Lieblich Flute
2	Fifteenth
V	Echo Cornet
	Tremulant
16	Contra Posaune (heavy wind)
8	Cornopean (heavy wind)
8	Oboe (heavy wind)
4	Clarion (heavy wind)

CHOIR ORGAN
(expressive)

8	Violoncello
8	Viole d'Orchestre
8	Hohl Flute
8	Lieblich Gedact
8	Dulciana
4	Flauto Traverso
2	Flageolet
16	Clarinet
8	Cor Anglais
	Tremulant

SOLO ORGAN
(expressive)

8	Clarinet
8	Orchestral Oboe
8	Vox Humana
8	Trumpet
	Tremulant

(unexpressive)

8	Harmonic Flute
4	Concert Flute
8	Tuba

PEDAL ORGAN

32	Double Open Diapason (metal, ext.)
16	Open Diapason Wood
16	Open Diapason Metal
16	Contra Gamba
16	Bourdon
16	Lieblich Bourdon
10⅔	Quint (ext. Lieblich)
8	Octave (wood, ext.)
8	Principal (metal, ext.)
8	Viola (ext.)
8	Bass Flute (ext. Lieblich)
4	Fifteenth
32	Contra Posaune (ext.)
16	Trombone
8	Clarion (ext.)

GRAND ORGAN (REAR GALLERY): WESTMINSTER CATHEDRAL R.C. LONDON, ENGLAND
Henry Willis & Sons 1922–32: London, England

GREAT ORGAN		SOLO ORGAN	
		(expressive)	
16	Double Open Diapason	16	Quintaten
16	Bourdon	8	Violoncello
8	Open Diapason I	8	'Cello Célestes
8	Open Diapason II	8	Salicional
8	Open Diapason III	8	Unda Maris
8	Flûte harmonique	8	Tibia
5⅓	Quint	4	Concert Flute
4	Octave	2	Piccolo harmonique
4	Principal	16	Cor Anglais
4	Flûte couverte	8	Corno-di-Bassetto
3⅕	Tenth	8	Orchestral Oboe
2⅔	Octave Quint		Tremulant
2	Super Octave	8	French Horn
V	Grand Chorus	8	Orchestral Trumpet
16	Double Trumpet		(unexpressive)
8	Trumpet	8	Tuba Magna
4	Clarion		

CHOIR ORGAN (expressive)		SWELL ORGAN (expressive)	
16	Contra Dulciana	16	Violon
8	Open Diapason	8	Geigen Diapason
8	Viola	8	Rohr Flute
8	Sylvestrina	8	Echo Viole
8	Cor-de-Nuit	8	Violes Célestes
8	Cor-de-Nuit Célestes	4	Octave Geigen
4	Gemshorn	4	Suabe Flute
4	Nason Flute	2⅔	Twelfth
2⅔	Nazard	2	Fifteenth
2	Octavin	III	Harmonics
1⅗	Tierce	8	Oboe
8	Trumpet	8	Vox Humana
	Tremulant		Tremulant
		16	Waldhorn
		8	Trompette
		4	Clarion

PEDAL ORGAN

32	Double Open Bass (ext.)	8	Flute (ext.)
16	Open Bass	4	Super Octave (ext. Principal)
16	Open Diapason	3⅕	Seventeenth
16	Contra Bass	2⅔	Nineteenth
16	Violon (Swell)	2	Twenty-second
16	Dulciana (Choir)	32	Contra Bombarde (ext.)
16	Sub Bass	16	Bombarde
8	Octave (wood, ext.)	16	Trombone
8	Principal (metal, ext.)	8	Octave Trombone (ext.)

ST. PAUL'S CATHEDRAL, MELBOURNE, VICTORIA, AUSTRALIA
Lewis & Co 1890: London, England
Harrison & Harrison 1990: Durham, England, restoration and additions (*)

GREAT ORGAN
(unexpressive)

16	Bourdon
8	Open Diapason I
8	Open Diapason II
8	Gamba
8	Flûte harmonique
8	Stopped Diapason
4	Octave
4	Gemshorn
2⅔	Octave Quint
2	Super Octave
IV	Mixture
16	Trumpet
8	Trumpet
4	Clarion

SWELL ORGAN
(expressive)

16	Bourdon
8	Geigen Principal
8	Rohrflöte
8	Viole de gambe
8	Voix Célestes
8	Vox Angelica
4	Octave
4	Rohrflöte
2	Flautina
III	Mixture
	Tremulant
16	Contra Fagotto
8	Horn
8	Oboe
4	Clarion

CHOIR ORGAN
(unexpressive)

16	Lieblich Gedact
8	Salicional
8	Lieblich Gedact
8	Dulciana
4	Flauto Traverso
4	Lieblichflöte
2	Piccolo harmonique
8	Corno-di-Bassetto

SOLO ORGAN
(expressive)

8	Flûte harmonique
4	Flûte harmonique
8	Clarionet
8	Orchestral Oboe
8	Vox Humana
	Tremulant
8	Tuba

(unexpressive)

8	Tuba Magna*
8	Trompette harmonqiue*

PEDAL ORGAN

32	Open Diapason
16	Great Bass
16	Violone
16	Sub Bass
10⅔	Quint
8	Violoncello
8	Flute Bass
32	Contra Posaune*
16	Posaune

BASILIQUE DE ST.-SERNIN, TOULOUSE, FRANCE
Aristide Cavaillé-Coll 1889: Paris, France
Restored 1993–96

GRAND-ORGUE

16	Montre
16	Bourdon
8	Montre
8	Salicional
8	Gambe
8	Flûte harmonique
8	Bourdon
4	Prestant
4	Flûte octaviante
2⅔	Quinte
2	Doublette
V	Fourniture
IV	Cymbale
V	Grand Cornet
16	Bombarde
8	Trompette
4	Clairon
2	Clairon-doublette
8	Trompette-harmonique (*en chamade*)
4	Clairon-harmonique (*en chamade*)

RÉCIT ÉXPRESSIF
(expressive)

16	Quintaton
8	Diapason
8	Viole de Gambe
8	Voix Céleste
8	Flûte harmonique
4	Flûte octaviante
2	Octavin-harmonique
V	Cornet
16	Bombarde
8	Trompette
8	Clarinette
8	Basson-hautbois
8	Voix humaine
4	Clairon harmonique

POSITIF

8	Montre
8	Salicional
8	Unda Maris
8	Cor de nuit
4	Prestant
4	Flûte douce
III	Carillon
8	Trompette
8	Basson-hautbois
4	Clairon

PÉDALE

32	Principal-basse (draws Contrebasse + 10⅔')
16	Contrebasse
16	Soubasse
8	Violoncelle
8	Grosse flûte
4	Flûte
32	Contre-Bombarde
16	Bombarde
8	Trompette
4	Clairon

THE CHURCH OF STS. PETER & PAUL R.C., SAN FRANCISCO, CALIFORNIA
Schoenstein & Co. 1989: San Francisco, California

GREAT ORGAN
(expressive)

16	Spire Flute (T.C. ext.)
8	Principal
8	Harmonic Flute
8	Stopped Diapason (Sw.)
8	Spire Flute
8	Unda Maris (T.C.)
4	Octave
4	Chimney Flute
2	Fifteenth
IV	Mixture
8	Trumpet
8	Cremone (prep.)
	Tremulant
	(Flutes, Reeds)

SWELL ORGAN
(expressive)

8	Gamba
8	Celeste (T.C.)
8	Stopped Diapason
4	Principal
4	Harmonic Flute
2⅔	Nazard
2	Flageolet
1⅗	Tierce (T.C.)
III	Mixture
16	Bassoon
8	Trumpet
8	Bassoon & Oboe (ext.)
8	Vox Humana (prep.)
4	Clarion
	Tremulant

PEDAL ORGAN

32	Resultant
16	Contra Bass (wood)
16	Bourdon
16	Spire Flute (prepared)
8	Bass (Great)
8	Flute (Great)
8	Stopped Diapason (Sw.)
4	Octave Bass (Great)
4	Octave Flute (Swell)
2	Super Octave (Great)
1	Fife (Swell)
III	Mixture III (prepared)
32	Bassoon (electronic, Sw. ext.)
16	Trombone (Great ext.)
16	Bassoon (Swell)
8	Trumpet (Swell)
8	Bassoon (Swell)
4	Oboe (Swell)

SUKYO MAHIKARI SHRINE, TAKAYAMA, JAPAN
Th. Frobenius & Sons 1984: Lyngby, Denmark
Designed, scaled and voiced by Tokugoro Ohbayashi

GRAND-ORGUE			RÉCIT	
16	Bourdon		8	Salicional
8	Montre I-II		8	Flûte conique
8	Flûte harmonique		8	Bourdon
8	Bourdon		4	Flûte octaviante
4	Prestant		4	Quintadine
2⅔	Nasard		2	Flageolet
2	Doublette		V	Cornet
1⅗	Tierce		II	Cymbale
1	Sifflet		8	Hautbois
V	Grand Cornet		8	Vox humana
V	Fourniture			Tremblant
IV	Cymbale			
8	Trompette			
8	Chamade			
4	Clairon			

POSITIF			PÉDALE	
8	Montre		32	Soubasse
8	Vox luminis		16	Flûte
8	Bourdon		16	Soubasse
4	Prestant		8	Flûte
4	Flûte douce		4	Flûte
2⅔	Nasard		16	Bombarde
2	Doublette		8	Trompette
1⅗	Tierce		4	Clairon
1⅓	Larigot			
VI	Plein jeu			
8	Trompette			
8	Cromorne			
	Tremblant			

MATSUZAKAYA DEPARTMENT STORE, NAGOYA, JAPAN
Casavant Frères Ltée. 1990: Ste. Hyacinthe, Québec, Canada

GREAT ORGAN (manual II)		SWELL ORGAN (manual III)	
16	Sub principal	(expressive)	
8	Open Diapason	16	Bourdon (ext.)
8	Principal	8	Principal
8	Chimney Flute*	8	Stopped diapason
4	Octave	8	Viole de gambe
4	Open Flute*	8	Voix Céleste (T.C.)
2	Super Octave	4	Octave
III	Cornet*	4	Spindle Flute
II-III	Full Mixture	2⅔	Nazard
V	Mixture	2	Quarte de nazard
8	Trumpet*	1⅗	Tierce
16	Spanish Trumpet (T.C., ext.)	1	Piccolo
8	Spanish Trumpet	IV	Mixture
	Chimes	III	Sharp Mixture
	Tremulant	16	Double Trumpet
	(affecting stops marked *)	8	Harmonic Trumpet
		8	Oboe
		8	Vox Humana
		4	Clarion
			Tremulant
		8	Spanish Trumpet (Great)
		8	Tromba (Solo)

SOLO ORGAN (manual I)
(expressive)

8	Double Flute
8	Viola Pomposa
8	Voix Céleste (GG)
8	Harmonic Flute
4	Concert Flute
2	Octavin
II	Clochettes
8	Clarinet
	Tremulant

(unexpressive)

16	Tromba (T.C., ext.)
8	Tromba
4	Tromba (ext.)
16	Spanish Trumpet (Great)
8	Spanish Trumpet (Great)

PEDAL ORGAN

32	Open diapason (ext.)
16	Open diapason
16	Sub principal (Great)
16	Subbass
16	Bourdon (Swell)
8	Octave
8	Bass Flute (ext.)
8	Stopped diapason (Sw.)
4	Super octave
4	Flute
32	Contre Trombone (ext.)
16	Trombone
16	Double trumpet (Swell)
8	Spanish trumpet (Great)
8	Tromba (Solo)
8	Trumpet
8	Oboe (Swell)
4	Clarion
4	Oboe (Swell)
	Chimes (Great)

FIRST METHODIST CHURCH, VAN WERT, OHIO
Robert Noehren 1977: Ann Arbor, Michigan

GREAT ORGAN
(expressive in box I)

16	Quintaton
8	Principal
8	Rohrflöte
4	Octave
4	Spitzflöte
2	Octave
2	Waldflöte
II	Rauschquint
V	Mixture
16	Bombarde
8	Trompette

SWELL ORGAN
(expressive in box II)

8	Montre
8	Bourdon
8	Gambe
8	Voix Céleste (T.C.)
4	Prestant
4	Flûte octaviante
2	Doublette
2	Octavin
	Plein-jeu
16	Dulcian
8	Trompette
8	Hautbois
4	Clairon
	Tremulant

POSITIV ORGAN
(expressive in box II)

8	Principal
8	Gedeckt
8	Flûte
4	Octave
4	Rohrflöte
2	Octave
IV	Mixture
III	Scharf
II	Sesquialtera
8	Cromhorne

SOLO ORGAN
(expressive in box I)

8	Gemshorn
8	Bourdon
8	Quintadena
8	Dulciana
8	Unda Maris (T.C.)
4	Prestant
4	Flute
2⅔	Nasard
2	Doublette
2	Piccolo
1⅗	Tierce
1⅓	Larigot
1	Flageolet
III	Cymbel
8	Trompette
4	Clairon
	Tremulant

PEDAL ORGAN		
(expressive in both boxes)		
16	Subbass	
16	Quintaton	
8	Principal	
8	Gedecktbass	
4	Octave	
4	Flute	
2	Octave	
II	Rauschquint	
VI	Mixture	
IV	Harmonics (32')	
16	Bombarde	
16	Dulcian	
8	Trompette	
4	Trompette	

ANALYSIS		
16-8	Quintaton	68 pipes
8	Principal	56 pipes
8	Rohrfloete	56 pipes
4	Octave	44 pipes
2	Octave	44 pipes
III	Mixture	168 pipes
16	Bombarde	56 pipes
8	Trompette	44 pipes
4	Clairon	32 pipes
8-4-2-1	Gemshorn	80 pipes
8	Flûte harmonique	44 pipes
8	Erzähler	44 pipes
8	Erzähler Celeste	44 pipes
2⅔-1⅓	Nasard	56 pipes
1⅗	Tierce	44 pipes
1	Octave	44 pipes
1	Octave	56 pipes
1⅓	Quint	56 pipes
8-4-2	Montre	85 pipes
8	Bourdon	56 pipes
8	Gambe	56 pipes
8	Voix Céleste (T.C.)	44 pipes
4-2	Flute octaviante	68 pipes
VI	Mixture	324 pipes
16	Dulcian	56 pipes
8	Trompette	44 pipes
4	Clairon	32 pipes
8	Gedeckt	44 pipes
4	Principal	44 pipes
4	Rohrfloete	32 pipes
8	Cromhorne	56 pipes
16	Subbass	12 pipes
1⅗	Quinta Terz	44 pipes

BLENHEIM PALACE (THE LONG LIBRARY), WOODSTOCK, OXFORDSHIRE, ENGLAND
Henry Willis 1891: London, England
A twenty year plan of full restoration is being presently carried out by Peter Wood & Son, curators of the instrument since 1974.

GREAT ORGAN

16	Double Diapason
8	Open Diapason I
8	Open Diapason II
8	Claribel Flute
6	Quint
4	Principal
4	Flute
3	Quinte Octaviante
2	Super Octave
2	Piccolo
III	Mixture
16	Trombone (heavy wind)
8	Tromba (heavy wind)
4	Clarion (heavy wind)

SWELL ORGAN
(expressive)

16	Contra Gamba
8	Geigen Principal
8	Lieblich Gedackt
8	Salicional
8	Vox Angelica
4	Gemshorn
4	Lieblich Flöte
2	Flageolet
III	Mixture
16	Contra Hautboy
8	Cornopean (heavy wind)
8	Hautboy
8	Vox Humana
4	Clarion (heavy wind)
	Tremulant

CHOIR ORGAN
(unexpressive)

8	Gamba
8	Hohlflöte
8	Dulciana
4	Flûte harmonique
2	Piccolo
16	Cor Anglais
8	Cor Anglais
8	Corno-di-Bassetto

SOLO ORGAN
(expressive)

8	Claribel Flute
4	Wald Flute
8	Clarinet
8	Orchestral Oboe

(unexpressive)

8	Gamba
8	Tuba (heavy wind)
	Tremulant
	(except Tuba)

PEDAL ORGAN

32	Contra Violone
16	Open Diapason
16	Violone
16	Bourdon
8	Octave
8	Violoncello
8	Flute Bass
III	Mixture
16	Ophicleide
8	Clarion

GLOSSARY OF TERMS

Action
The mechanism linking the keys of an organ to the valves under the pipes, and also linking the stops at the console to the respective ranks within the instrument.

Antiphonal
A section or division of an organ placed opposite or away from the main organ, where it can be used in dialogue with the remainder of the instrument.

Barker lever
A device invented by Charles Spackman Barker and first used by the French organ-builder Cavaillé-Coll in the organ for the Abbey of St. Denis near Paris, and built in the 1840s. Interrupting the traditional

mechanical key action with a set of pneumatic motors or 'assists,' it harnesses the power of the wind already available in the organ.

Barrel organ
An organ that plays tunes automatically from a rotating pinned barrel, without the need for a player to be present.

Bellows
Until modern times the wind for the organ was supplied by paid helpers pumping at a large bellows. Their work is now done by an electric rotary fan, but bellows survive inside the organ as a means of regulating and storing the wind.

Bombarde
A loud and commanding pedal bass stop of the Trumpet family; also sometimes an independent division of the organ ('Bombarde organ') where the loudest reeds and mixtures may be available.

Case
The enclosure containing the organ itself, with its façade of large bass pipes, often treated architecturally to harmonize with the room and traditionally an opportunity for elaborate decoration and visual display mirroring the musical contents.

Celeste
An organ stop tuned slightly sharp (or sometimes flat) throughout, so that the sound undulates when used with normally tuned ranks.

Cipher
A note sounding unbidden through some fault in the mechanism.

Chamber
Some organs are installed within the confines of internal walls in the building where they stand: these walls form an organ chamber, usually with the side facing the audience (or congregation) open for the sound to get out.

Chiff
An onomatopoeic word describing the aggressive attack commonly heard in neo-classical or 'neo-baroque' organs of the period 1950–80.

Choir organ
In traditional English and American organs, the third manual division consisting of a small chorus of soft and accompanimental stops and some delicate solo reeds.

Classical
Used to describe organs of the period before about 1850, in contrast to the 'romantic' organs that evolved around that date and in the later 19th century.

Clavier
A keyboard.

Combination
A group of stops selected by the organist according to musical rules and personal taste.

Combination pistons
Horizontal rows of buttons placed between the keyboards, where they can be reached with the thumbs while playing, that make changes to the combinations of stops in use.

Compass
The word used to indicate how many notes there are in a particular keyboard: some very early organs have 'short-compass' keyboards missing some low and high notes found on later instruments.

Compound stop
A stop which plays two or more pipes at once for every key pressed by the player; these pipes usually sound

harmonics of the note played (see Mixture).

Console

The organist sits at the console, consisting of two or more keyboards for the hands, a pedal keyboard for the feet, and the various stop controls. A console may be attached to an organ or, with non-mechanical key action, detached some way from it, even on wheels and therefore mobile.

Continuo

The organ accompanimental part in certain music scored essentially for choir and instrumentalists; a 'continuo organ' is a small portable pipe organ with one keyboard designed specifically for this purpose.

Coupler

A device that allows the stops on one keyboard to be played on another, or the stops of the manual keyboards to be played on the pedals.

Crescendo pedal

A pedal that brings on the stops of the organ one by one in a pre-programmed order, to allow a global crescendo and decrescendo through the entire resources of the instrument.

Department

One division or section of an organ, usually consisting of a self-contained group of stops in a specific location in the instrument and playable from one specific keyboard at the console.

Departmental pistons

Thumb pistons that control the stops of one section of the organ (as opposed to 'general pistons' that affect the stops of all divisions simultaneously).

Diapason

A term used in traditional North American and English organs to describe the main stop of the organ, consisting of open cylindrical metal pipes sounding unison pitch at 'normal' power and tone.

Digital organ

An electronic organ in which the sound is created by digital sampling rather than by analogue methods.

Division

One department or section of an organ, usually consisting of a self-contained group of stops in a specific location in the instrument and playable from one specific keyboard at the console.

Drawbar

On the early Hammond electronic organ the stops are controlled by drawbars: sliding controls that allow each stop to be set at a specific volume between soft and loud.

Drawknob

The familiar round knob at the organ console that controls each stop; when it is pulled out, the rank of pipes it controls is ready to be played, or 'on'; when it is pushed in it goes 'off'.

Dulciana
A very soft organ stop.

Dynamics
Gradations of power during the course of a piece of music.

Echo
An Echo organ is a section of a large organ placed remotely so that its delicate sounds are heard from a great distance.

Electric action
A key action in which the link between the console and pipes is made through electric contacts at the keys and a cable running from there to the organ. The term is often used to describe all such organs, although many are strictly speaking electro-pneumatic in operation.

Electro-pneumatic action
A key action in which the link between the console and pipes is made through electric contacts at the keys and a cable running from there to the organ. The final actuation of the valves under the pipes is performed by a pneumatic relay harnessing the power of the wind already available in the organ.

Electronic organ
An organ in which there are no pipes and the tone is generated by electronic sound-producing apparatus of various types.

Ensemble
The term used to describe the collective sound of organ stops of various types used at once, these being rich foundation stops, brilliant high-pitched upperwork, sparkling mixtures, and fiery trumpet-toned reeds.

Expression pedal
A pedal at the console controlling swell shutters in the organ, allowing gradations of power and expressive nuance.

Extension
A technique used especially in theater organs where each rank of pipes is made available at several pitches, each with its own stop control, by means of electric switchgear.

Fanfare trumpet
A loud trumpet stop used for fanfares, sometimes mounted horizontally in the façade of the organ, or placed remotely elsewhere in the building for vivid effect.

Flue
The term used generically to describe all those organ pipes which are constructed on the principle of a flute or whistle, that is with no vibrating reed or other moving parts; also the windway in such a flue pipe.

Flute
A wide-scaled stop of fluty tone, sometimes in deliberate imitation of an orchestral flute.

Full-length
A reed stop with a resonator whose length corresponds to that of an open flue pipe playing the same note, often of full-toned trumpet class (lesser reeds often have half-length or fractional-length resonators; in some instruments this is also done for reasons of space or economy).

Fundamental
The unison tone of an organ is its foundation or fundamental, in contrast to the many higher-pitched stops that sound upper harmonics of the note played.

General pistons
Thumb pistons that control the stops of all sections of the organ simultaneously (as opposed to 'departmental pistons' that affect the stops of only one department at a time).

Great organ
In North American and British organs, the main manual department (see also Swell organ, Choir organ).

Hammond
An early form of electronic organ in which the tone was produced by rotating wheels or 'tone-generators'.

Horseshoe console or keydesk
Theater organs are usually equipped with a console in which the stop controls are in the form of tabs arranged in a wide horseshoe-like sweep up, around and over the manual keyboards.

Key action
The mechanism linking the keys of an organ to the valves under the pipes.

Keydesk
The organist sits at the console or keydesk, consisting of two or more keyboards for the hands, a pedal keyboard for the feet, and the various stop controls. A console may be attached to an organ or, with non-mechanical key action, detached some way from it, even on wheels and therefore mobile.

Manual
A keyboard.

Mechanical action
A key action of traditional type, used in organ-building from ancient Roman times right up to the present day, in which the linkage between the keys and the valves under the pipes is by simple mechanical rods and levers. The longer wooden connections are often called trackers, and mechanical action is sometimes called tracker action.

Mixture
A stop which plays two or more pipes at once for every key pressed by the player; these pipes usually sound harmonics of the note played.

Mutation
A stop which plays a note other than the one played, usually a harmonic of that note such as a fifth or a third.

Neo-classical

The style of organ-building practiced between about 1950 and 1980, in which all romantic effects and much beauty of tone were sacrificed to an ill-conceived musical dogma based on certain inaccurate assumptions about the organs of the true classical period. Compared to fine organs from the baroque and classical periods, many of these unhappy 'reproduction' instruments are too thin in tone, too bright and harsh, have far too much articulation or 'chiff' at the beginning of each note, and lack the many beautiful and evocative tone colors that have characterized the finest organs from the earliest times.

Nick, nicking

A technique developed at least as early as the 17th century for controlling the speech of the flue pipes by making tiny knife-nicks round the edge of the flue, abandoned during the neo-classical period with sometimes unfortunate results.

Pallet

The valve under a pipe that admits wind and allows it to sound.

Pedal

Any device operated by the feet, but specifically a note on the pedal keyboard or pedal-board.

Pedal-board

A regular keyboard of thirty or more notes arranged to be played by the feet, and usually controlling the bass line in organ music.

Piston

Horizontal rows of buttons placed between the keyboards, where they can be reached with the thumbs while playing, that make changes to the combinations of stops in use.

Player mechanism

A mechanism that allows an organ to be played automatically without an organist being present, usually functioning from a perforated paper roll as in a player piano.

Pneumatic

A mechanism in the organ actuated by harnessing the pressure of the wind already available in the instrument.

Principal

A term used to describe the main stops of the organ, consisting of open cylindrical metal pipes sounding at 'normal' power and tone. These may be at unison pitch, or may sound octaves, sub-octaves, or high harmonics such as fifths and thirds (see Mutation, Mixture, Compound stop).

Rank

One row of pipes inside the organ. Usually each rank is controlled by one drawknob or stop control at the console, except in the case of mixtures or compound stops where each knob may control two or more ranks. Each rank has its distinct tone, pitch and placement within the overall scheme of the organ.

Reed
A pipe in which the sound is created by a vibrating brass tongue or reed fitted into the base, and amplified and controlled by a tuned resonator. Familiar reed stops are the trumpets, tuba, oboe, clarinet and so on.

Register
An alternative term for stop.

Registration
The art of choosing combinations of stops according to musical requirements and the taste of the performer.

Roll-player
A mechanism that allows an organ to be played automatically without an organist being present, functioning from a perforated paper roll as in a player piano.

Romantic
Used to describe organs of the period before after 1850 and up to about 1950, in contrast to the 'classical' organs that existed before 1850 and the 'neo-classical' organs of modern times.

Scale
The diameter of an organ pipe relative to its length. A small scale tends to give a soft and/or keen sound; a large scale tends to give a bolder, louder and/or flutier sound.

Solo organ
In the traditional North American and British organ the fourth manual division of a large organ, controlling a number of solo stops (some of them imitating orchestral instruments) and the triumphant Tuba, a powerful stop of broad trumpet tone.

Solo stop
A stop of distinctive power and tone suitable for use in soloing out melody against a softer or milder combination.

Specification
The list of stops and accessories that an organ provides, providing the basic information an organist needs to know before he sits down to try a new or unfamiliar instrument.

Stop
The controls at the organist's command, bringing each rank of pipes into readiness for playing, hence also the individual ranks of pipes themselves.

Stop action
The mechanism linking the stop controls at the console with the ranks of pipes in the organ, bringing each rank into readiness for playing.

Stop control
The controls, in the form of familiar round knobs or tilting 'tablets', which greet the performer at the console and allow him to select the various sounds

available from the ranks of pipes within the instrument.

Stop jamb
The panel at the console on which the stop controls are mounted.

Stop list
The list of stops and accessories that an organ provides, providing the basic information an organist needs to know before he sits down to try a new or unfamiliar instrument.

Stop tab
Stop controls in the form of tilting teeth-like 'tablets,' found especially on consoles of theater type.

String
An organ stop of narrow scale and keen intonation, designed to imitate the effect of orchestral stringed instruments, and often named after instruments of the violin or gamba families.

Swell box
A large enclosure fitted with shutters like a giant venetian blind, enclosing one whole division of the organ and its pipes. The shutters will be connected to a swell pedal or shoe at the console, allowing the sound of that division to be made louder or softer.

Swell organ
In the traditional North American and British organ the second manual division of a large organ, controlling an ensemble contained in a swell box.

Swell pedals
The pedal or pedals controlling the shutters of any division or divisions enclosed in swell boxes.

Swell shutter
The venetian-blind-like shutters of any division enclosed in a swell box.

Theater organ
The type of pipe organ made famous by the Wurlitzer company and destined primarily for entertainment in movie houses and theaters, always with electro-pneumatic unit action and built on the extension principle.

32' stop
A stop of sub-sub-unison tone, whose lowest note (four octaves below middle C) is produced by an open pipe about thirty-two feet long, and (coincidentally) at a frequency of about 16 cycles per second.

Toe stud
A piston for changing the combination of stops, operated by the toe.

Touch
The 'feel' of the keyboards during playing.

Tracker, tracker action
The longer wooden connections in a traditional mechanical action are often called trackers, and mechanical action is sometimes called tracker action.

Tremulant
A device that causes the wind supply to undulate, and the pipes to sound with a gentle pulsing or vibrato.

Trunking
The ducting in an organ, leading air under pressure from the bellows to the various windchests and ultimately to the pipes.

Tuba
A commanding solo reed stop of broad trumpet-like tone, usually the loudest stop on an organ.

Unenclosed
A division of pipes not enclosed in a swell box.

Upperwork
The stops in an organ sounding a note higher than the one played, including all the mutations and mixtures.

Voice
Voicing is the art of making the pipes in an organ sound with the precise musical effect intended by the maker and called for in performance. This hallowed branch of the great craft of organ-building, revered through the centuries, was sadly neglected in the recent neo-classical period, though hopes of a real revival are now running high!

Windchest
The wooden 'box of bits' on which each group of pipes stands inside the organ. Fed with wind, and containing the final stages of the key action and stop action, together with the individual pallets under the pipes, the windchest is at the heart of the organ's function. There is usually at least one distinct windchest for each division or department of the organ.

Stephen Bicknell, 1998

INDEX